REBELS AGAINST WAR

The American Peace Movement, 1941–1960

Contemporary American History Series

WILLIAM E. LEUCHTENBURG, GENERAL EDITOR

REBELS AGAINST

WAR The American

 Peace Movement,

1941–1960

Lawrence S. Wittner

COLUMBIA UNIVERSITY PRESS

 New York and London

Lawrence S. Wittner

is Assistant Professor of History

at Vassar College.

Copyright © 1969 Columbia University Press
Library of Congress Catalog Card Number: 69-19464
Printed in the United States of America
ISBN 0-231-03220-X
10 9 8 7 6 5 4 3 2

To My Parents

All I ask is that, in the midst
of a murderous world, we agree to reflect
on murder and to make a choice.

ALBERT CAMUS, 1946

(*Neither Victims Nor Executioners,* p. 23)

Preface

This study attempts to describe and analyze the shifting pattern of support which the ideal of world peace elicited within the United States between 1941 and 1960. "Peace," however, has been reduced gradually to its Orwellian genre by professional propagandists. Consequently, while most sectors of public opinion consider a commitment to peace acceptable, they do not welcome the abolition of international violence. The peace movement has distinguished itself from the rest of American society not because it has desired the establishment of peace, but because it has opposed the means of war.

The struggle against war has traditionally encompassed diverse viewpoints. While all participants in the peace movement have opposed militarism, some have opposed it more than others. Pacifists, for example, have refused to engage in or prepare for war under any circumstances, although peace-oriented non-pacifists have considered warfare a conceivable, if distasteful, possibility. In its structure, then, the peace effort, like other social movements, has resembled an onion, with the absolutists at the center and the less militant forming the surrounding layers. At times of popular enthusiasm for war, the less committed outer layers peel off, leaving the pacifist core; in times of strong aversion to the military, new layers are added and the onion grows in size. This structural fluidity accounts both for the peace movement's repeated weakness in times of international tension and for its peculiar resiliency.

Throughout its existence the peace movement has been plagued by a central problem, which Reinhold Niebuhr correctly assessed as its greatest dilemma: how to bridge the gap between the ideal and the real? Despite the popular appeal of peace, a military response, given the context of armed and competing nations, often seems to provide the only "realistic" policy. Pacifists have replied that each nation's "security" ensures other nations' insecurity, and that, consequently, national defense policies frequently lead to the very war and destruction they are alleged to prevent. And yet if an arms race is ultimately disastrous, is pacifism any more "realistic"? Must peace, of necessity, be reserved for inspirational sermons and sentimental poetry while the crucial decisions are left to "tough-minded" politicians, professional officers, and paramilitary scientists? Or can men of good will recapture influence over the destiny of mankind in the name of a more sophisticated "realism"? From the history of the peace movement at midcentury, an answer begins to emerge.°

I have been assisted in the preparation of this study by many people who were more than generous with their time and effort. Professor William E. Leuchtenburg of Columbia University supervised the entire project, providing me with painstaking and incisive criticism which often prevented my straying from the hard and rocky path of historical objectivity. Dr. Robert D. Cross, now president of Hunter College, reviewed the manuscript in detail and made many helpful suggestions. This study was first proposed five years ago by Professor Merle E. Curti in his graduate seminar at the University of Wisconsin, and has finally reached book form through the advice and encouragement of Mr. Bernard Gronert of the Columbia University Press. Many other individuals were kind enough to reply to my inquiries or to offer suggestions for research, including: Dr. Arthur Waskow, of the Institute for Policy Studies; Professor Charles Chatfield, of Wittenberg University; Professor James P. Shenton, of Columbia University; Professor Charles A. Barker, of Johns Hopkins University; and Dr. Harold Taylor, former president of Sarah Lawrence College. I am indebted to Professor George Landow and Professor Helen Mustard of Columbia University for their assistance on questions of style and translation, to Miss Naomi Aschner of Columbia University Press for her editorial re-

---

° A chapter on the 1930's and a brief epilogue have been added to place the midcentury decades in a broader historical context.

visions, and to Miss Anne Darneille of Vassar College for assistance in the preparation of the index.

My thanks go also to those who facilitated my research. Many of the participants in the peace activities with which this study is concerned offered vital information, granted me access to out-of-print materials, or submitted to long interviews. Among them are: Mr. David Dellinger, editor of *Liberation;* Mr. Ralph DiGia and Mr. James Peck, of the War Resisters League; the late Reverend A. J. Muste; Mrs. Mercedes M. Randall, of the Women's International League for Peace and Freedom; Dr. Theodore Roszak, former editor of *Peace News;* and Mr. Norman Thomas. The librarians and archivists of the Swarthmore College Peace Collection, Columbia University, the MacArthur Memorial, the Peace Information Center of the New York Friends Group, and Union Theological Seminary aided me in many ways. A grant from the Institute for International Order, patiently administered by Mr. Earl D. Osborn, did much to make this study possible.

Finally, I would like to thank my wife, Patricia, who shared the typing, note-taking, and proofreading entailed by this project and who nonetheless managed to tolerate it and me.

I am solely responsible for any errors of fact or judgment.

LAWRENCE S. WITTNER

Poughkeepsie, New York
November, 1968

Contents

I   The Peace Movement in the Thirties   1

II   Wartime Collapse   34

III   Men against the State   62

IV   The Best of All Possible Wars   97

V   Hiroshima: The Good News of Damnation   125

VI   Organizing for a New World, 1945–1948   151

VII   Retreat, 1948–1950   182

VIII   Midcentury Nadir, 1950–1956   213

IX   Breakthrough, 1957–1958   240

X   The Peace Movement Reborn, 1959–1960   257

    Epilogue   276

    Conclusion   282

    Bibliography   287

    Index   329

REBELS AGAINST WAR

The American Peace Movement, 1941–1960

CHAPTER I

The Peace Movement
in the Thirties

I am a pacifist. You, my fellow citizens . . . are pacifists, too.

FRANKLIN D. ROOSEVELT, 1940 [1]

In 1910, when Andrew Carnegie set aside ten million dollars in bonds "to hasten the abolition of international war," the optimistic Scottish immigrant assured his trustees that "when war is abolished," they could "consider what is the next most degrading evil." A quarter century later, although that contingency had not yet arisen, the cause of world peace could boast an unprecedented organization and popularity in the United States. One writer estimated at the time that the peace movement had twelve million adherents and an income of over one million dollars.[2]

The pacifist ideal, while possessed of a long and distinguished history, never took hold in the United States until the aftermath of World War I, when a wave of disillusionment with that conflict swept across the country. A series of gruesome books, often written by the participants themselves, turned Wilsonian rhetoric on its head. Henri Barbusse's *Under Fire,* Siegfried Sassoon's *Counter-Attack,* Ernest Hemingway's *A Farewell to Arms,* John Dos Passos' *Three Soldiers,* Laurence Stallings' *What Price Glory?,* and the most popular war story in America, a translation of Erich Maria Re-

---

[1] *New York Times,* May 11, 1940.
[2] Stanley High, "Peace, Inc.," *Saturday Evening Post,* CCX (March 5, 1938), 8; Merle E. Curti, *Peace or War: The American Struggle, 1636–1936,* p. 262; Robert H. Ferrell, "The Peace Movement," *Isolation and Security,* ed. Alexander DeConde, pp. 82–83; Marcus Duffield, "Our Quarrelling Pacifists," *Harper's,* CLXVI (May, 1933), 688–96.

marque's *All Quiet on the Western Front,* portrayed a gory and senseless slaughter. The redeeming features of this bloodshed were undermined for the public by scholars and publicists who pointed to selfish war aims and deception on the part of the Allies. Arthur Ponsonby's *Falsehood in Wartime,* Harold D. Lasswell's *Propaganda Technique in the World War,* and Sir Philip Gibbs' *Now It Can Be Told* helped to convince Americans that their emotions had been skillfully manipulated by the masters of war.[3]

As the circle of discontent widened, many Americans, convinced of their betrayal, found the culprit in the villain of the depression-scarred decade—the avaricious businessman. In the spring of 1934 an article entitled "Arms and Men," appearing in the conservative *Fortune* magazine, together with two books, George Seldes' *Iron, Blood and Profits* and Helmuth Engelbrecht and Frank Hanighen's *Merchants of Death,* stimulated interest in the machinations of munitions makers. *Merchants of Death* soon became a best seller and a Book-of-the-Month Club selection, while the thesis that traffic in armaments led to war gained widespread currency. It was thereafter repeated by the President of the United States, two former Secretaries of State, the *Christian Science Monitor,* the *Wall Street Journal,* and members of Congress. When the Nye Committee investigations, born themselves of popular outrage, were completed, the new mood had received its official sanction.[4]

It did not require many publicists to show that the war's aftermath failed to measure up to wartime promises. As the black-shirted legions drilled in Europe who could believe that the war had made the world safe for democracy, or that it had ended war? William

[3] Earl Charles Chatfield, Jr., "Pacifism and American Life, 1914 to 1941" (unpublished Ph.D. dissertation), pp. 72–73; Curti, *Peace or War,* pp. 268–70; Ferrell, "The Peace Movement," pp. 83–84; Robert E. Osgood, *Ideals and Self-Interest in America's Foreign Relations,* p. 330.

[4] John E. Wiltz, *In Search of Peace: The Senate Munitions Inquiry, 1934–1936,* pp. 19–23, 227–31; Walter Johnson, *The Battle against Isolation,* pp. 14–15. Seldes' book was a sensational account, which proclaimed itself "An Exposure of the World-Wide Munitions Racket," while its jacket carried a blurb telling of "the Frenzied Years of 1914–17 when . . . a peace-loving democracy, muddled but excited, misinformed and whipped to frenzy, embarked upon its greatest foreign war. . . . Read it and blush! Read it and beware!" George Seldes, *Iron, Blood and Profits;* R. E. Osgood, *Ideals and Self-Interest,* pp. 365–68.

Allen White, the Kansas newspaper publisher, wrote in an editorial of November 11, 1933:

Fifteen years ago came the Armistice and we all thought it was to be a new world. It is! But a lot worse than it was before.

Ten million men were killed and many more maimed, fifty billion dollars' worth of property destroyed, the world saddled with debts.

And for what? Would it have been any worse if Germany had won? Ask yourself honestly. No one knows.

. . . The boys who died just went out and died. To their own souls' glory, of course—but what else? . . . Yet the next war will see the same hurrah and the same bowwow of the big dogs to get the little dogs to go out and follow the blood scent and get their entrails tangled in the barbed wire.

And for what?

. . . . .

War is the devil's joke on humanity.[5]

In the early Thirties, stunned by the new perspective on World War I, millions of Americans vowed "never again." The Reverend Harry Emerson Fosdick recalled that he "went through the disillusionment of its aftermath, confronting with increasing agony the anti-Christian nature of war's causes, processes and results." He concluded that he would "never again put" his "Christian ministry at the nation's disposal for the sanction and backing of war," and consequently "became a pacifist." Clergymen "committed a sin when they blessed war banners," Rabbi Stephen Wise told a Paterson audience in 1931, "and I for one will never again commit that sin." The Jewish leader, who had deliberately taken a job in a naval shipyard during World War I, now declared that "war never ends war. War ends nothing but peace." In February, 1937, when Americans were asked, "If another war like the World War develops in Europe, should America take part again?," 95 per cent answered "no." [6]

With war and the military under fire, thought of disarmament flourished and achieved unprecedented respectability. "Secretary [of

[5] William Allen White, *The Autobiography of William Allen White*, p. 640.

[6] Harry Emerson Fosdick, *The Living of These Days: An Autobiography*, p. 293; *New York Times*, November 16, 1931; Hadley Cantril (ed.), *Public Opinion, 1935–1946*, p. 966; Francis Sill Wickware, "What We Think about Foreign Affairs," *Harper's*, CLXXIX (September, 1939), 404.

the Navy] Wilbur says the Navy is unready for war," laughed the *New Yorker* in 1929, and "by an amazing coincidence there is no war ready for the Navy." A total of 22,165 different plans for world peace were submitted in one year in the Bok Peace Award Contest. Albert Einstein told a pacifist meeting: "You must convince the people to take disarmament into their own hands and to declare that they will have no part in war or in the preparation for war." Young men who resisted conscription and refused arms served as "the pioneers of a warless world." Scientists should "refuse to co-operate in research for war purposes," while every newspaper should "encourage its readers to refuse war service," Einstein declared. This was "not the time for temporizing. You are either for war or against war." [7]

In reality the issue was far less sharply defined than the distinguished mathematician thought. Participants in the peace movement found unity solely in their collective opposition to war, although, even on this point, disagreement existed between pacifists and those, no less sincere, to whom military force represented a dreadful, but possible, alternative. On other issues the peace movement, like other mass movements, was hopelessly divided. And yet, despite their many differences, peace activists frequently shared a common faith, often unspoken, in the potentialities of a disarmed world. They saw feuding nations displaced by international authority, economic and racial injustice giving way to a more equitable social order, and fear and hatred replaced by harmony and joy. When Americans dreamed of a world without war, the vision shimmered hazily before them of the restoration of the human community.

A social cause with a variegated constituency, the peace movement appealed perhaps most strongly to women. In the decades following the granting of women's suffrage, politicians kept a wary eye on the peace issue, convinced that it exercised a strong influence over the feminine ballot. When the President hedged in 1935 on

[7] Thomas A. Bailey, *The Man in the Street: The Impact of American Public Opinion on Foreign Policy*, p. 69; Edith Wynner and Georgia Lloyd, *Searchlight on Peace Plans: Choose Your Road to World Government*, p. 9; Otto Nathan and Heinz Norden (eds.), *Einstein on Peace*, pp. 141–42. A collection of the early pacifist writings of Einstein is: Albert Einstein, *The Fight against War*.

neutrality legislation, Representative Fred Sisson of New York angrily informed the White House that "thousands and thousands of women's votes have been lost by this stalling." A visit to Washington in the cause of world peace by Mrs. Carrie Chapman Catt, who represented the eleven largest women's organizations in the country, occasioned considerable attention and respect from the uneasy legislators. Nor was the legend of Lysistrata primarily a matter of folklore. Frederick J. Libby, a leading figure in pacifist circles during this period, argued in 1930 that women "constitute the backbone of the peace movement in America," while a more recent student of the era has maintained that a large percentage of individuals involved in the peace effort were women. As one of their number has observed: "They were not women of the leisure class but professional women—doctors, lawyers, professors, editors of periodicals, journalists, social workers, reformers, and some public officials." [8]

In the decade before the European war clouds darkened the horizon, the American peace movement experienced some of its most dazzling successes within the Protestant churches. A conference on the Churches and World Peace of the Federal Council of Churches resolved in 1929 that "the churches should condemn resort to the war-system as sin and should henceforth refuse . . . to sanction it or to be used as agencies in its support." In 1931, when the religious pacifist magazine *The World Tomorrow* polled Protestant ministers in the United States on the question of military service, 12,076 of the 19,372 respondents declared that the church should never again sanction any war. Three years later, a similar poll found pacifism among the clergy on the rise.[9]

---

[8] Ferrell, "The Peace Movement," p. 104; William E. Leuchtenburg, *Franklin D. Roosevelt and the New Deal, 1932–1940*, p. 219; Frederick J. Libby, *The American Peace Movement*, p. 2; Robert Edwin Bowers, "The American Peace Movement, 1933–1941" (unpublished Ph.D. dissertation), p. 242; Mercedes M. Randall, *Improper Bostonian: Emily Greene Balch*, pp. 309–310; personal interview with Mercedes M. Randall, April 26, 1965. Mrs. Catt, a strong believer in the unique responsibility of women on the question of war or peace, told a women's delegation at the 1939 New York World's Fair that "we are responsible for the continuation of war, and for not making this a better world." *New York Times*, July 14, 1939.

[9] Doniver A. Lund, "The Peace Movement among the Major American Protestant Churches, 1919–1939" (unpublished Ph.D. dissertation), p. 107; Devere Allen, *The Fight for Peace*, p. 50; "The Church Pacifist," *Nation,*

As pacifism swept through the Protestant churches in the Twenties and Thirties, condemnations of war also increased in Catholic literature. Arguments developed by Catholic peace proponents usually questioned whether modern warfare could be compatible with the requirements in natural law for a just war. Outright pacifism remained weak, however, for few took the position that Catholics should refuse participation in all wars.[10]

Jewish religious opinion, formerly not as concerned as Protestant theology with the question of peace, veered sharply toward pacifism in these years. In 1935, when the Central Conference of American Rabbis was canvassed by mail on whether it should "recommend to its members that they refuse to support any war in which this country or any country may engage," 91 voted "yes," 31 voted "yes" with reservations, and only 32 voted "no." Until the late Thirties, the Central Conference of American Rabbis, the National Council of Jewish Women, and the National Federation of Temple Sisterhoods belonged to a militant peace organization.[11]

College students joined women and the clergy as the third great force in the peace effort of the mid-Thirties. In 1933, when the Brown University *Daily Herald* polled 21,725 students in 65 colleges on the issues of peace and war, it found that the largest number, 8415, pledged themselves to absolute pacifism; another 7221 would bear arms solely in the event of an actual invasion of the country; and only 6089 would serve in any war involving the United States. The following year, nationwide "strikes" against war commenced on American campuses. In April 500 Vassar College girls in caps and gowns, led by the president of the college, paraded through the Poughkeepsie streets, chanting "no more battleships, we want schools." This antiwar demonstration represented a radical turn-

---

CXXXII (May 6, 1931), 494; Kirby Page, "20,870 Clergymen on War and Economic Injustice," *World Tomorrow*, XVII (May 10, 1934), 222–56.

[10] Vernon Howard Holloway, "American Pacifism between Two Wars, 1919–1941" (unpublished Ph.D. dissertation), pp. 176–82.

[11] Holloway, "American Pacifism," p. 200; Allan A. Kuusisto, "The Influence of the National Council for Prevention of War on United States Foreign Policy, 1935–1939" (unpublished Ph.D. dissertation), pp. 55–56. A compilation of statements by religious bodies illustrating the development of pacifist sentiment within the church is: Walter Van Kirk, *Religion Renounces War*.

about from 1917, when undergraduates had similarly paraded, but in favor of war.[12]

On April 12, 1935, 60,000 students in the nation's colleges participated in a "strike" against war. Sponsored by religious pacifist and left-wing student groups, the demonstrations drew large numbers, especially in New York, where an estimated 10,000 gathered for denunciations of war and fascism. At Columbia University 3000 students cheered speeches by Roger Baldwin of the American Civil Liberties Union (A.C.L.U.), Professor Reinhold Niebuhr of Union Theological Seminary, and James Wechsler, editor of the Columbia *Spectator*, many taking the Oxford Oath of absolute refusal to serve in the armed forces. In November demonstrations in New York drew 20,000 students. At City College 3500 crowded into the Great Hall, booing the college president when he objected, unsuccessfully, to a reading of the Oxford Oath. At Columbia a meeting of 2000 students on South Field heard Professor Harry J. Carman, chairman of the college history department, urge "spreading the anti-war gospel." New York University's two campuses played host to 4500 cheering demonstrators. "It will take more than flagwaving and bugle calls to empty the colleges for another war," reported one observer of the campus protests.[13]

If the peace movement appealed strongly to professional women, clergymen, and college students, it found less support in other elements of the population. American farmers had displayed moderate interest in opposition to war since the days of William Jennings Bryan, and the three major agricultural organizations accordingly endorsed the work of peace groups. In the autumn of 1934 petitions to the President against increased armaments were signed by ninety-six thousand farmers within three weeks. Nonetheless, rural pacifism, perhaps because it clashed with another agrarian tradition of insular pride and bellicose nationalism, remained only lukewarm. The peace movement stirred even less fervor within business circles,

---

12 *Nation*, CXXXVI (May 24, 1933), 571; "A Student Strike against War," *Literary Digest*, CXIX (March 23, 1935), 17; Joseph P. Lash, *The Campus Strikes against War*, p. 3.

13 *New York Times*, April 13 and November 9, 1935; Harold Seidman, "The Colleges Renounce War," *Nation*, CXXXVI (May 17, 1933), 554–55.

while veterans' organizations regarded it with unveiled hostility. American labor, perhaps repelled by the upper middle class tone of the typical peace worker, exhibited only the mildest of interest, although a few left-wing unions occasionally participated in antiwar demonstrations.[14]

Arguing that wars merely reflected the imperialism of the capitalist order, American radicals became prominent proponents of peace in the mid-Thirties. At its 1934 convention the Socialist Party adopted a resolution by a 99 to 47 vote declaring its opposition to "militarism, imperialism, and war." Neither war nor "preparedness for war" could "be tolerated by Socialists," proclaimed the convention, and if war came, Socialists would attempt to break it up by "massed war resistance" in the form of "a general strike." American Communists took a similar position, emerging as the loudest advocates of a "united front" of the working class against war. Large numbers of liberals and unaffiliated radicals, members of neither left-wing party, nevertheless believed that wars were nothing more than the expression of an exploitative economic system.[15]

Unlike the Communists, however, many American Socialists had a strong ethical commitment to pacifism. As the peace movement moved left in the radical climate of the Thirties, pacifism and democratic socialism increasingly overlapped. Socialists who also belonged to absolute pacifist organizations included Devere Allen, Socialist candidate for the United States Senate in Connecticut; Jessie Wallace Hughan, Socialist candidate for several state offices in New York; Harry Laidler, director of the League for Industrial Democracy; Clarence Senior, national secretary of the Socialist

[14] Kuusisto, "The Influence of the National Council for Prevention of War on United States Foreign Policy," p. 92; Libby, *The American Peace Movement,* p. 2; Bowers, "The American Peace Movement," pp. 428–29; Curti, *Peace or War,* p. 288; M. M. Randall, *Improper Bostonian,* p. 310. One pacifist wrote in dismay: "Labor's leadership is working-class, but inclined to ignore the values of organized peace effort; the peace movement is 'high hat' or upper middle class when not positively blue blooded." Allen, *The Fight for Peace,* pp. 163–64.

[15] Devere Allen, "The Peace Movement Moves Left," *Annals of the American Academy of Political and Social Science,* CLXXV (September, 1934), 154–55; John W. Masland, "Pressure Groups and American Foreign Policy," *Public Opinion Quarterly,* VI (Spring, 1942), p. 119; James Peck, *We Who Would Not Kill,* pp. 60–64. See also: Norman Thomas, *War: No Glory, No Profit, No Need.*

Party; Powers Hapgood and Darlington Hoopes, members of the Party's national executive committee; as well as Kirby Page, Sherwood Eddy, Vida Scudder, John Haynes Holmes, and Reinhold Niebuhr. Perhaps the leading pacifist Socialist of the period was the party's Presidential standard-bearer, Norman Thomas. Thomas had joined the Fellowship of Reconciliation, a religious pacifist organization, when, as a minister in New York, he perceived "an irreconcilable gulf between Christian ethics and participation in war." In 1917 he resigned his parish to become executive secretary of the organization, maintaining close connections with it thereafter as titular head of the Socialist Party.[16]

Attempting to give some form to burgeoning peace interest throughout the United States, thirty-seven peace organizations united in 1933 to form the National Peace Conference, a loose federative effort. On the political Right were the "conservative" peace organizations, headed by the Carnegie Endowment for International Peace, the World Peace Foundation, the Woodrow Wilson Foundation, and the Church Peace Union. Old, wealthy, and compromised by their support of World War I, they failed to draw the new generation of pacifist militants but instead continued their patient efforts through established channels in educational work, in the promotion of international good will, and in the strengthening of legal and judicial machinery for the peaceful resolution of international conflict. The League of Nations Association, usually classified with these groups because of the scope of its concern, differed in that it did not possess independent economic resources but maintained a membership as a source of income and support.[17]

Perhaps the most vigorous and effective of the groups in the peace

[16] Chatfield, "Pacifism and American Life," pp. 482–83; Philip G. Altbach, "The American Peace Movement, 1900–1962: A Critical Analysis" (unpublished), pp. 16–26; Vera Brittain, *The Rebel Passion: A Short History of Some Pioneer Peace-makers*, p. 110.

[17] Merle E. Curti, "The Changing Pattern of Certain Humanitarian Organizations," *Annals of the American Academy of Political and Social Science*, CLXXIX (May, 1935), 61; "A Brief Review of Thirty-Five Years of Service toward Developing International Understanding," *International Conciliation*, No. 417 (January, 1946), 17–39; Elton Atwater, "Organizing American Public Opinion for Peace," *Public Opinion Quarterly*, I (April, 1937), 114; Ferrell, "The Peace Movement," pp. 99–103; Bowers, "The American Peace Movement," pp. 12–25.

movement's militant wing was the National Council for the Prevention of War (N.C.P.W.), founded in 1921 by the Quaker pacifist
Frederick J. Libby. The organization had no membership of its own,
but brought together pacifist groups with such peace-minded but
non-pacifist ones as the American Federation of Teachers, the
Young Women's Christian Association, and the National Education
Association. Libby made the first concerted efforts to attract farmers
and organized labor to the cause of peace, efforts which were rewarded with a moderate degree of success in the form of organizational endorsements of the N.C.P.W. and printing of its press releases. *Peace Action,* the monthly newsletter of the N.C.P.W.,
achieved a circulation of over twenty thousand, while the
N.C.P.W.'s Washington headquarters distributed between one and
two million pieces of literature yearly throughout the Thirties. In
1935 the N.C.P.W. sent regular press releases to six hundred publications, maintained reliable newspaper contacts in over three hundred Congressional districts, and began a radio program for which
Congressmen and Senators came to its studios to deliver speeches
often written by the N.C.P.W. staff.[18]

Operating out of an old building across the street from the State
Department under Libby's tutelage, the N.C.P.W. in 1935 consisted
of twenty-one participating organizations and ten cooperating ones,
a staff of eighteen, five branch offices throughout the country, and
an annual budget of well over one hundred thousand dollars.
Jeannette Rankin, a former leader in the women's suffrage and Progressive movements, and a former member of the House of Representatives who had voted against American entry into World War I,
served as its well-known Congressional lobbyist. The largest and
most aggressive of the peace organizations, the N.C.P.W. enabled
the peace movement to exercise a moderate influence in Washington
affairs.[19]

[18] Kuusisto, "The Influence of the National Council for Prevention of War
on United States Foreign Policy," pp. 27, 70–72, 77, 81, 94; Atwater, "Organizing American Public Opinion for Peace," p. 118; War Resisters League,
"National Council for the Prevention of War," *Peace Calendar and Appointment Book, 1965;* High, "Peace, Inc." p. 91.

[19] Ronald Schaffer, "Jeannette Rankin, Progressive-Isolationist" (unpublished Ph.D. dissertation); Ferrell, "The Peace Movement," p. 93; Kuusisto,

Around the corner form the Washington headquarters of the N.C.P.W. stood the offices of the United States section of the Women's International League for Peace and Freedom (W.I.L.P.F.). Founded in 1915 by Jane Addams and other feminine reformers active in the quest for social justice and world peace, the international organization expanded rapidly, although the American section remained the most powerful and vigorous. Swept forward by the wave of pacifist sentiment among American women in those years, the W.I.L.P.F. in 1937 had a paid staff of eleven, one hundred twenty branches throughout the country, and over thirteen thousand members.[20]

Thanks to the efforts of its lobbyist and executive secretary Dorothy Detzer, the W.I.L.P.F. sparked a number of Congressional activities in the Thirties, including the famous investigation of the munitions industry. Miss Detzer successfully persuaded Senators Norris and Nye and even Secretary of State Cordell Hull, to his later regret, of the necessity of the investigation. Eventually, when the W.I.L.P.F.'s lobbyist was accorded the opportunity to select the Nye Committee's chief investigator, she chose the zealous and radical Stephen Rauschenbush, who did much to initiate the Committee's sensational revelations.[21]

If the W.I.L.P.F. catered to the women's constituency, the Fellowship of Reconciliation (F.O.R.) ministered to the Protestant churches. Founded in England in 1914 as an international Christian fellowship, this religious pacifist organization developed into one of the leading spokesmen for radical Protestantism in the United States. The membership, largely recruited from the younger clergy and the religiously motivated professional classes, reached over four thousand in 1935. F.O.R. leaders included John Haynes Holmes,

---

"The Influence of the National Council for Prevention of War on United States Foreign Policy," p. 61.

[20] Gertrude Bussey and Margaret Tims, *Women's International League for Peace and Freedom, 1915–1965: A Record of Fifty Years' Work*, pp. 77–78, 152; *History of the Women's International League for Peace and Freedom, U.S. Section, 1915–1940* (1940), Women's International League for Peace and Freedom Manuscripts, Swarthmore College Peace Collection (WILPF MSS), Box 1.

[21] Wiltz, *In Search of Peace*, pp. 24–25; Dorothy Detzer, *Appointment on the Hill*, pp. 151–68; Robert A. Divine, *The Illusion of Neutrality*, pp. 63–66.

Harry Emerson Fosdick, and John Nevin Sayre, but after 1936 it came strongly under the influence of its most brilliant and daring thinker, A. J. Muste.[22]

Time magazine referred to Muste in 1937 as "lean, sparse . . . America's Number One pacifist." After careers as a minister, union organizer, "labor-college" administrator, and Trotskyite, Muste returned to the F.O.R. refreshed, "knowing from experience in the revolutionary movement," he stated in 1936, "that he who denies love betrays justice." His shift from Marxism to pacifism represented not a turn to the Right, but a revival of the utopian Left—an attempt to reunite the diverging strains of love and justice through the conversion of pacifism into a radical action movement.[23]

The War Resisters League (W.R.L.), established as the outgrowth of a F.O.R. enrollment committee in 1923, was designed by its founder, Jessie Wallace Hughan, to unite political, humanitarian, and philosophical objectors to war. Developed as the secular counterpart to the F.O.R., the W.R.L. sought to enroll conscientious objectors with the credo: "War is a crime against humanity. We therefore are determined not to support any kind of war and to strive for the removal of all causes of war." By February, 1937, over twelve thousand Americans, many of them socialists, anarchists, and independent radicals, had signed the W.R.L. pledge. Throughout the decade the W.R.L., with its offices in New York, played a relatively insignificant role in the peace movement; annual income never reached five thousand dollars and the active membership lagged below one thousand.[24]

An organization with pacifist principles but rarely considered part

22 Fellowship of Reconciliation, *What Is the Fellowship of Reconciliation?;* Masland, "Pressure Groups and American Foreign Policy," p. 115; "Membership Statistics" (1954), Fellowship of Reconciliation Manuscripts, Swarthmore College Peace Collection (FOR MSS), Box 4.

23 R. Alfred Hassler, *Conscripts of Conscience*, p. 15; A. J. Muste, Columbia Oral History Collection (COHC); *Christian Century*, LIII (October 14, 1936), 1374; Nat Hentoff, *Peace Agitator: The Story of A. J. Muste*, p. 9.

24 Jessie Wallace Hughan, *Three Decades of War Resistance*, p. 15; Frank Olmstead, "A Brief Biography: The War Resisters League" (January, 1945), Devere Allen Manuscripts, Swarthmore College Peace Collection (Allen MSS), Section C4, Box 1; Chatfield, "Pacifism and American Life," pp. 255–58; Atwater, "Organizing American Public Opinion for Peace," pp. 120–21; Evan Thomas to Members, December 26, 1944, War Registers League Manuscripts, Swarthmore College Peace Collection (WRL MSS), Box 3.

of the Thirties peace effort was the Catholic Worker movement. Launched on New York's Lower East Side in 1933 by Peter Maurin, an itinerant French peasant philosopher, and Dorothy Day, a graduate of the University of Illinois, former Hollywood scenario writer, suffragette, and contributor to the Socialist *Call* and the *New Masses*, the Catholic Worker movement combined religious, radical, and anarchist concerns. By the mid-Thirties it maintained a remarkable newspaper the *Catholic Worker* (one cent per issue, circulation 110,000), Houses of Hospitality for the poor in thirty cities, and a series of Farming Communes. In 1935 members organized a branch of the English *Pax* movement at its Mott Street headquarters to study Catholic teachings on the morality of war. Catholic religious leaders lectured there and around the country, while the *Catholic Worker* began a long documentation of its peace position, interspersed with articles on the immorality of war and conscription. Although it devoted its prewar efforts largely to charitable works, the Catholic Worker movement provided the leading voice in American Catholic circles for militant pacifism.[25]

The so-called Historic Peace Churches contained the largest numbers of traditional religious pacifists. In 1936 there were 114,337 Mennonites, 93,697 Friends, and 188,290 Brethren residing in the United States. Their outlook on war was simply but firmly expressed by a group of Quakers (Friends) to Charles II, King of England, in 1660: "We utterly deny all outward wars and strife, and fightings and outward weapons, for any end, or under any pretence whatever; this is our testimony to the whole world. The Spirit of Christ by which we are guided, is not changeable. . . . Therefore, we cannot learn war any more." Yet despite the pacifist heritage of these churches and the ongoing humanitarianism of their action organizations—the American Friends Service Committee (A.F.S.C.), the Brethren Service Committee, and the Mennonite Central Committee —time and assimilation had gradually eroded much of their corporate peace testimony. For this reason, and because of a strong

[25] Histories of the Catholic Worker movement include: Dorothy Day, *Loaves and Fishes* and Dwight Macdonald, *Memoirs of a Revolutionist: Essays in Political Criticism*, pp. 349–68. Peter Maurin's biography is: Arthur Sheehan, *Peter Maurin: Gay Believer*, while an autobiography of Miss Day is: Dorothy Day, *The Long Loneliness*. *Pax* is discussed briefly in: Sheehan, *Peter Maurin*, pp. 127–28, and *Catholic Worker* (February, 1937).

strain of religious quietism among the Mennonites and the Brethren, they never constituted as great an influence in the Thirties peace movement as their numbers might suggest.[26]

Left-wing groups made their own attempts to develop "mass" action for peace. The American League Against War and Fascism, established in 1933 by a coalition of liberal and left-wing organizations, drew together a paper membership of several million Americans in a "united front" against war. Members of its arrangements committee of that year, for example, included Communist leader William Z. Foster, as well as pacifists Devere Allen and Ray Newton. Groups of such divergent tendencies found it difficult to cooperate, however, and in 1934 Communists broke up a Socialist demonstration at a League meeting in New York. Shortly thereafter, Socialist elements, the National Association for the Advancement of Colored People (N.A.A.C.P.), and most pacifists began withdrawing from the organization. Nevertheless, the League Against War and Fascism remained vigorous throughout the decade, maintaining close ties with the Communist-influenced American Student Union and the American Youth Congress, holding mammoth demonstrations, and sending press releases to eight hundred farm, labor, and Negro newspapers across the country.[27]

Although in no sense mass organizations, these groups exercised considerable influence during the mid-Thirties. Through a maze of supporting organizations and interlocking committees, and buoyed

[26] U.S. Bureau of the Census, *Religious Bodies: 1936,* I, 346–48; *Why They Cannot Go to War,* n.p. Studies of the pacifist witness of the Historic Peace Churches are: Howard H. Brinton, *Sources of the Quaker Peace Testimony;* William D. S. Witte, "Quaker Pacifism in the United States, 1919–1942" (unpublished Ph.D. dissertation); Rufus D. Bowman, *The Church of the Brethren and War, 1708–1941;* Guy Franklin Hershberger, *War, Peace, and Nonresistance;* John Horsch, *The Principle of Nonresistance as Held by the Mennonite Church.*

[27] Irving Howe and Lewis Coser, *The American Communist Party: A Critical History, 1919–1957,* pp. 448–55; Chatfield, "Pacifism and American Life," pp. 312–16; Altbach, "The American Peace Movement," p. 26; Hughan, *Three Decades of War Resistance,* pp. 16–21; Atwater, "Organizing American Public Opinion," p. 118. When Socialists left the organization they formed the Keep America Out of War Congress in 1938, which attracted a distinguished group of liberals, labor officials, and Socialists. It does not appear to have been very influential, however. Norman Thomas, COHC, pp. 136–37; Albert Horlings, "Who Are the Appeasers?" *New Republic,* CIV (January 27, 1941), 112.

up on a cushion of favorable public opinion, pacifists were able to reach out to some forty-five to sixty million Americans.[28] The American peace movement had reached its zenith. Yet probably after 1935, and certainly after 1937 the pacifist impulse began to ebb, its strength declining in direct proportion to the rise of European fascism.

Ironically, and tragically, the renunciation of war by Americans coincided with Mussolini's seizure of power in Italy, the Nazi triumph in Germany, and the growth of Japanese militarism. But the discrepancy proved short-lived, for as the Axis powers began their series of military conquests—China and Ethiopia, Spain and Albania, Austria and Czechoslovakia—successive layers of the American peace movement broke away in anguished response. Moreover, those with an ethical revulsion to war could not fail to reserve a special shudder for the peculiar horrors of facism. The destruction of individual liberty, the glorification of hatred, and, perhaps the ugliest of all, a series of anti-Semitic attacks that raised the ancient pogrom to the status of a State religion, sickened American peace activists, and led many to conclude that war represented the lesser of two evils.

Leading the assault upon the antiwar establishment was the brilliant ex-pacifist clergyman Reinhold Niebuhr. "History has so vividly proven" the "worthlessness" of war, he wrote in 1929, "that it can hardly be justified on any moral grounds." Chairman of the F.O.R. from 1932 to 1933, he resigned from that organization in 1934 because of his belief that violence on the part of the working class in its quest for a new social order was justifiable. War between nations, however, Niebuhr considered quite another matter, until the onset of Axis expansion. Blasting pacifist support of mandatory neutrality legislation in late 1937 at the time of Japanese aggression in Manchuria, Niebuhr declared: "We can justify the refusal to take such risks only if we believe that peace is always preferable to the exploitation of the weak by the strong." After the Munich settlement, he made his final break with pacifism. "Modern Christian and secular perfectionism, which places a premium upon non-participation in conflict, is a very sentimentalized version of the Christian faith," he

[28] Ferrell, "The Peace Movement," p. 101.

wrote in 1940. And "modern Christian pacifism" was "simply a version of Christian perfectionism." On February 10, 1941, Niebuhr published the first issue of his journal *Christianity and Crisis,* which was designed to combat pacifism and neutralism within the churches.[29]

Americans now renounced pacifism with the same fervor with which they had previously renounced war. "Present-day world political conditions demand . . . a new attitude toward the problem of peace," wrote Albert Einstein, an active pacifist since 1914. "The existence of two great powers with definitely aggressive tendencies (Germany and Japan) makes an immediate realization of movement toward disarmament . . . impracticable. The friends of peace must concentrate their efforts rather on achieving an alliance of the military forces of the countries which have remained democratic." Sherwood Eddy, one of the foremost propagators of religious pacifism until this period, abandoned his pacifist faith. "Nothing . . . could stop them," he later remarked sadly, "except the use of force." Rabbi Judah Magnes, a prominent pacifist during World War I but a convert to force in 1939, typified the despair in the ranks of the peace movement. War against Germany might be immoral, he observed with sorrow, but "we do not know what else to do." [30]

Those Americans who remained committed to peace were not unaware of the evils of fascism; indeed, they were among the first to

---

29 Reinhold Niebuhr, "The Use of Force," *Pacifism in the Modern World,* ed. Devere Allen, pp. 16–17; Reinhold Niebuhr, "Why I Leave the F.O.R.," *Christian Century,* LI (January 3, 1934), 17–19; Lund, "The Peace Movement among the Major American Protestant Churches," pp. 119–20; Reinhold Niebuhr, *Christianity and Power Politics,* pp. ix, 4; Donald B. Meyer, *The Protestant Search for Political Realism, 1919–1941,* pp. 360–61; R. E. Osgood, *Ideals and Self-Interest,* pp. 381–83.

30 Albert Einstein to Jessie Wallace Hughan, August 12, 1933, WRL MSS, Box 15; Sherwood Eddy, *Eighty Adventurous Years: An Autobiography,* p. 104; Judah L. Magnes, "A Tragic Dilemma," *Christian Century,* LVII (March 27, 1940), 406–407; *New York Times,* October 28, 1948. A member of the War Resisters League wrote to Jessie Wallace Hughan: "I know that the Treaty of Versailles was a terrible mistake. I know that Britain, France, and others are responsible for the rise of Hitler. I know that he is a symptom and not a personal devil. My deepest sympathy goes out to the German people, as to all others of the world. Having said this, however, I must add that I do not see how the Allies can now lay down their arms." Edwin L. Clarke to Jessie Wallace Hughan, May 27, 1940, WRL MSS, Box 14.

warn of them. In the spring of 1933 the first large-scale protest in the United States against Hitlerism was led down Broadway by pacifist leader John Haynes Holmes.[31] When the Reverend Harry Emerson Fosdick spoke on Nazi crimes in 1933 at the Riverside Church, some of his parishioners grew extremely upset, contending that he was too politically aggressive. He recalled with irony, several decades after the incident: "Later they were ready enough to go to war with Hitler; in 1933 they . . . begged me to speak more softly even in talking about him." With the opening of the anti-Semitic drives of the Nazi regime, leaders of the peace movement worked desperately to overcome public opposition and save the helpless victims. "America is big enough to find a refuge for persecuted Jews," argued Peter Maurin in the *Catholic Worker*. Norman Thomas, urging that the United States serve as the asylum for European refugees, was sharply criticized. Polls in 1938 and 1939 reveal that less than 8 per cent of the American people were willing to admit Hitler's victims into the country. Thomas later remarked ruefully: "I learned first hand how many Americans preferred to fight or have their countrymen fight for the rights of Jews in Europe than to give them asylum in America."[32]

Nor did pacifists advocate or applaud the appeasement of the fascist powers. Oswald Garrison Villard, the pacifist editor of the *Nation*, labeled Chamberlain's pressure upon France to close its borders to Spanish Loyalists "an act so undemocratic, so base, and so perfidious as to deserve the bitterest condemnation." It was

[31] Rabbi Stephen Wise had arranged the anti-Hitler protest as an all-Jewish event, thinking that few other Americans would be interested, but he was joined, to his surprise, by his friend John Haynes Holmes. Down Broadway, from Columbus Circle to Union Square, marched the silent parade of thousands of Jews, preceded by Stephen Wise and pacifist minister John Haynes Holmes, the only Christian present. Carl Hermann Voss, *Rabbi and Minister: The Friendship of Stephen S. Wise and John Haynes Holmes*, pp. 285–86.

[32] Fosdick, *The Living of These Days*, p. 282; *Catholic Worker*, July–August, 1939; Harry Fleischman, *Norman Thomas: A Biography*, p. 195; Bailey, *The Man in the Street*, p. 25; Cantril, *Public Opinion*, p. 1150. A particularly shocking display of American indifference came in response to a poll of January, 1939. Americans were asked if the United States should permit the admission of "10,000 refugee children from Germany—most of them Jewish"; only 30 per cent replied "yes," while 61 per cent said "no." Cantril, *Public Opinion*, p. 1081. Thomas wrote in 1938: "The American who has studied the vogue of the Ku Klux Klan should understand some of the sources of Nazi strength." Norman Thomas, *Socialism on the Defensive*, pp. 85-86.

merely "another proof of the utterly heartless and ruthless way in which he pursues his shameful and stupid policy of keeping peace in Europe by wholesale surrenders to the dictators." "Has any British government in all history sunk so low?" asked Villard. Chamberlain's course was not one of pacifist humanitarianism, he wrote, but "of cowardly compromise, of buying off the dictators and thereby confirming them in their wrongdoing." [33]

Munich, the litmus test of appeasement, found peace workers astonishingly hostile, considering that President Roosevelt, the paragon of collective security, reported himself "not a bit upset over the final result" of the negotiations. Dorothy Detzer, scornful of the pact, asserted that "anyone who knows the nature of fascism knows that fascism must expand and Hitler has obligingly laid out his plans for all to read in *Mein Kampf*." Norman Thomas termed it "a logical kind of deal for capitalist powers." It was A. J. Muste, however, who presented the complete pacifist position, replete with all its difficulties. "Those people are probably right who think the four-power deal at the expense of Czechoslovakia and other lands is unlikely to accomplish any good," he wrote. "They lapse into sentimentalism, however, if they think war would accomplish more. There is only one course that will not lead to practically certain disaster: It is a renunciation of the game of power politics." [34]

Pacifists harbored no sympathies for fascism, but remained unconvinced that war represented a solution to the problem which it posed. Villard contended that the "cure" of military resistance resembled the disease. "Great armaments" are the "Road to Fascism," he warned. "They bring with them increased worship of the State, increased nationalism, increased State service, and therefore play into the hands of those like Hitler and Mussolini who declare that the citizen is made for the State and not the State for the citizen." Kirby Page, a leading pacifist publicist, feared that "the very nature of modern war necessitates the abrogation of democracy as an es-

[33] Oswald Garrison Villard, "Issues and Men," *Nation*, CXLVII (July 2, 1938), 18.

[34] Elliott Roosevelt (ed.), *F.D.R.: His Personal Letters, 1928–1945*, II, 818; Dorothy Detzer, "Dirge for Collective Security," *Fellowship*, IV (November, 1938), 6–7; Fleischman, *Norman Thomas*, p. 191; A. J. Muste, "Forth—to War?" *American Scholar*, VII (Autumn, 1938), 402n.

sential condition of success." The pacifist wanted security and peace, too, remonstrated John Haynes Holmes, "but how will they be attained through fighting? Where runs the connection between this violence and hate and the constructive policies which hold mankind together?" War might stop Hitler, they admitted, but would it stop Hitlerism? [35]

The organized peace movement underwent the beginning of a disastrous split in 1935, when the obvious collapse of the League of Nations and heightened European militarism presaged another great war. The N.C.P.W., the W.I.L.P.F., and staunchly pacifist groups, realizing their inability to prevent war in Europe, turned their attention to insulating America from that war; "conservative" elements, on the other hand, including the Carnegie Endowment for International Peace, the Church Peace Union, the World Alliance for International Friendship through the Churches, the Catholic Association for International Peace, the League of Nations Association, and Mrs. Catt's Committee on the Cause and Cure of War, gradually shifted to doctrines of collective security. In the heated neutrality debates, the former groups supported the maintenance of mandatory neutrality, while the latter worked for the modification of the neutrality provisions and, eventually, for their repeal.[36]

Joining the conservatives in the collective security camp after 1937 were important elements of the peace movement's left wing. The Spanish Civil War, the resurgence of German militarism, but especially the quest by the Soviet Union for a military alliance with

[35] Oswald Garrison Villard, *Our Military Chaos: The Truth about Defense,* p. 124; Kirby Page, *How to Keep America Out of War,* p. 39; John Haynes Holmes, *Out of Darkness,* p. 83. The chairman of the A.F.S.C. later explained: "Friends may sympathize with the alleged ends of a war; they may recognize as fact the situation which seems to others to recommend war. But that war is the way to deal with this situation or to strive toward these ends does not automatically follow. If flagrant abuse of its own citizens or of other peoples is practiced by a foreign power, violence on our part may involve other innocent persons and may not reduce the evil results." Henry J. Cadbury, "Peace and War," *The Quaker Approach to Contemporary Problems,* ed. John Kavanaugh, p. 10.

[36] Divine, *The Illusion of Neutrality,* pp. 93–94, 182; *New York Times,* January 30, 1937; Ferrell, "The Peace Movement," pp. 104–105; Kuusisto, "The Influence of the National Council for Prevention of War on United States Foreign Policy," pp. 103–262; Bowers, "The American Peace Movement," pp. 301–423.

the Western powers, signaled the end of the pacifist phase for American Communists. They now became dutiful New Dealers and supporters of the President's foreign policy, deftly swinging the League Against War and Fascism around to a collective security stance, and changing its name to the American League for Peace and Democracy. One of the leading sponsors of the campus protests, the American Student Union, captured by a coalition of Communist elements and the followers of its nominally Socialist secretary, Joseph Lash, veered from pacifism to collective security, dropping the Oxford Pledge. Student demonstrations thereafter repudiated the Oxford Oath and lauded President Roosevelt's handling of the international situation, although a sizable minority, led by the non-Communist Youth Committee Against War, clung to the pacifist faith.[37]

Other segments of the American Left, while straying from the absolute pacifist position, nonetheless proved more steadfast in opposing the participation of the United States in war. During the Spanish Civil War the Socialist Party recruited the Eugene V. Debs Column for service with the Loyalists. Replying to pacifist critics, Norman Thomas explained that the party would "use to the uttermost non-violent methods consistent with true democracy. But . . . it will not yield to fascism anywhere without a struggle and . . . non-violence is not its first and last commandment." Thomas personally gave up his pacifist commitment at this time, both because he could not bear the prospect of a Spanish Republican defeat and because of a turn toward what he considered greater sophistication in his religious faith. Although he did not desire American intervention, he castigated the Roosevelt Administration for its embargo of arms for the Loyalists. In January, 1937, he wrote: "The whole record shows that with impunity and without rebuke established governments if they are conservative or Fascist have been allowed to buy what they needed . . . when not actually at war with another nation. It is only when the Spanish Government

37 Howe and Coser, *The American Communist Party*, pp. 348–55; Daniel Bell, "The Background and Development of Marxian Socialism in the United States," *Socialism and American Life*, Vol. I, ed. Donald Drew Egbert and Stow Persons, pp. 360–61; Masland, "Pressure Groups and American Foreign Policy," p. 119; *New York Times*, April 21, 1939.

fights against Fascism for the peace and freedom of mankind that the President's scruples are suddenly aroused." [38]

The outbreak of war in Europe, however, cooled Socialist ardor, wrecking the Party in the bargain. In 1940 a Socialist Party convention supported absolute neutrality and opposed military appropriations, arguing that although "the cause for which Hitler has thrown the German masses into war is damnably unholy," the "war of Chamberlain and Reynaud is not thereby rendered holy." As a result of the Party's firm anti-interventionist position, it rapidly disintegrated after 1939. Leading Socialists broke with the Party's antiwar position or resigned in what is referred to in Socialist circles as the "silent split." Half of the *Call* editorial board spoke out for full economic aid to Hitler's opponents. One group of New York Socialists joined the Committee to Defend America by Aiding the Allies, while another formed the Union for Democratic Action, which later became Americans for Democratic Action.[39]

The Party's leader, Norman Thomas, was torn by conflicting beliefs. A longtime opponent of fascism, he watched its military victories with horror. "I felt terrible when France fell," he recalled. "It shook me as very few things ever shook me." Yet, the suffering of modern warfare appeared to him as a poor palliative. "The certain evils of American involvement in war seemed greater than the uncertain good we might accomplish in a war which was still without . . . positive aim," the Socialist leader declared. In the 1940 election campaign, "we still thought we ought to keep out of war and we still said so." Members of his family disagreed, and Thomas and his wife sadly packed their youngest son off to the American Field Service a month before Pearl Harbor.[40]

[38] Norman Thomas, "Norman Thomas Replies," *Fellowship,* III (February, 1937), 13; personal interview with Norman Thomas, October 4, 1966; Murray B. Seidler, *Norman Thomas: Respectable Rebel,* pp. 203–205; Norman Thomas, COHC, pp. 124, 135.

[39] David A. Shannon, *The Socialist Party of America: A History,* p. 255; Bell, "Background and Development of Marxian Socialism," pp. 393–94; Fleischman, *Norman Thomas,* p. 199; Seidler, *Norman Thomas,* pp. 210–11; Norman Thomas, COHC, p. 77.

[40] Norman Thomas, COHC, p. 127; Fleischman, *Norman Thomas,* pp. 194–95, 201. Thomas was extremely suspicious of the war aims of the parties involved in the European struggle. See, for example: Norman Thomas and Bertram D. Wolfe, *Keep America Out of War.*

Pacifism in the churches, relatively strong until 1939, began a slow decline thereafter. With the outbreak of war in Europe, Dr. George A. Buttrick, president of the Federal Council of Churches, asked Americans to maintain their neutrality "because . . . war is futile and because we are eager through reconciliation to build a kindlier world," while the executive committee of the Federal Council denounced war in a unanimous resolution one month later as "an evil thing contrary to the mind of Christ." Fear of succumbing to patriotic frenzy, as in World War I, led most clergymen to take a disinterested stance in the initial months of the conflict. Gradually, however, clerical pacifism waned. Although pacifists could still rally the religious figures with greatest prestige, many prominent churchmen now commenced taking an active role in the various aid-to-the-Allies committees. As in World War I, Episcopalians and clergy with British and Canadian ancestry appear to have been most involved in these ventures.[41]

After 1939 the conflict between "radical" and "conservative" peace groups heightened. The N.C.P.W., the W.I.L.P.F., and the small pacifist groups vigorously opposed the Roosevelt Administration's foreign policy, aid to Britain, and conscription. The "conservatives," on the other hand, of the opinion that peace could be achieved only by curbing the "aggressor nations," worked closely with the Roosevelt Administration in sponsoring programs of American military assistance to the British and in securing Congressional passage of the Selective Service law. Firmly committed to collective security policies, they formed the nucleus of the Committee to Defend America by Aiding the Allies.[42]

Symptomatically, the director of the Committee, William Allen White, was a former pacifist, while he was recruited for the post by Clark Eichelberger, the director of the League of Nations Association. "With many a conflict, many a doubt," White wrote to his niece, "I who am a philosophical pacifist have yielded to my practi-

41 Ray H. Abrams, "The Churches and the Clergy in World War II," *Annals of the American Academy of Political and Social Science*, CCLVI (March, 1948), 111–14; Meyer, *The Protestant Search for Political Realism*, pp. 350–54; *New York Times*, December 31, 1939.

42 W. Johnson, *The Battle against Isolation*, pp. 31–32, 41–42, 59; Divine, *The Illusion of Neutrality*, p. 304; John W. Masland, "The 'Peace' Groups Join Battle," *Public Opinion Quarterly*, IV (December, 1940), 664–73.

cal sense of the realities of a terrible situation." Indeed, although he sought to convince himself that aid to Britain was not, in fact, war, he had already grimly and unhappily accepted America's inevitable participation in the struggle. In May, 1941, White wrote to his old friend Oswald Garrison Villard: "I hoped I would never see another war. I shall never encourage the coming of another war. But if it comes, this summer or next summer . . . I see nothing to do but to fight it with all our might and all our hearts. And that's not a pleasant prospect for a man who realizes the utter futility of wars in the past and who can only hope rather vainly that, out of this war, men may learn wisdom in the end." [43]

With the signing of the Molotov-Ribbentrop Pact of August, 1939, American Communists, seriously embarrassed by their former bellicosity, launched another peace campaign, this time under the slogan "The Yanks Are Not Coming." The conflict in Europe, now an "Imperialist War," was not the business of the workers, and Communists obediently scuttled the American League for Peace and Democracy to make way for the American Peace Mobilization. The comrades proceeded to carry out crippling strikes against the Vultee Aircraft Corporation, the tank-producing Allis-Chalmers plant in Milwaukee, and the North American Aviation factory in California. Dalton Trumbo's antiwar novel *Johnny Got His Gun* (1930) was serialized in the Party press. Antiwar pickets ringed the White House on June 21, 1941, as the American Peace Mobilization called for National Peace Week. [44]

This proved to be strategically poor timing, however, for on the very day, Hitler's armies invaded Russia, thereby transforming the "Imperialist War" into a "People's War for National Liberation." The *Daily Worker* proclaimed the change of line to the faithful the following morning, but the organized campaign for peace and dis-

---

[43] W. Johnson, *The Battle against Isolation*, p. 150; W. A. White, *The Autobiography of William Allen White*, p. 642; Divine, *The Illusion of Neutrality*, p. 304.

[44] Howe and Coser, *The American Communist Party*, pp. 348–55; Earl Browder, *The Second Imperialist War*; Masland, "Pressure Groups and American Foreign Policy," p. 119; Basil Rauch, *Roosevelt: From Munich to Pearl Harbor*, p. 351; Bell, "Background and Development of Marxian Socialism," p. 396; Daniel Aaron, *Writers on the Left: Episodes in American Literary Communism*, p. 386.

armament was not disposed of quite so easily. Meeting the challenge, the Party announced two weeks later that the American Peace Mobilization would henceforth be known as the American People's Mobilization and would begin an intensive campaign "for all-out aid to the Soviet Union and Britain." The new slogan: "Victory over Fascism." National Peace Week, of course, was never mentioned again.[45]

The rapid shifts of the Communist Party from war to peace to war again had little effect upon the peace movement, although they disillusioned many intellectuals closer to the Party itself.[46] Most pacifists had had nothing to do with the Communists' latest "peace front," and consequently were relatively untouched by its collapse. "It was not possible," wrote one peace worker, "for pacifists to associate themselves with a group whose peace-mindedness depended upon the policy of a foreign dictator." A. J. Muste warned in 1940 against the "Communists' fake anti-war campaign and its dangers." Some Party members, like Bayard Rustin, a member of the Young Communist League, turned to pacifism.[47]

In their resistance to the armaments apparatus of war, peace workers had as little in common with their temporary allies, the isolationists, as with the Communists. America First never advocated disarmament, but consistently endorsed the growth of American military power; its statement of principles called upon the United States to "build an impregnable defense for America. With such a defense no foreign power, or group of powers, can successfully attack us." "Keep Out, Keep Ready" ran the isolationist American Legion's slogan. Isolationist Senators, inflamed by any thought of entering "Europe's wars," usually voted for American military appropriations. America First opposed the Roosevelt Administra-

[45] Howe and Coser, *The American Communist Party*, p. 395; *Daily Worker*, June 23, 1941; Masland, "Pressure Groups and American Foreign Policy," p. 119; Earl Browder, *Victory—And After*, p. 29.

[46] Norman Holmes Pearson, "The Nazi-Soviet Pact and the End of a Dream." *America in Crisis*, ed. Daniel Aaron, pp. 327–48; Aaron, *Writers on the Left*, pp. 309–90; Bell, "Background and Development of Marxian Socialism," p. 395.

[47] *Conscientious Objector*, February–March, 1941; A. J. Muste to Jessie Wallace Hughan, February 6, 1940, WRL MSS, Box 18; Hentoff, *Peace Agitator*, p. 113.

tion's foreign policy, explained its program director, because it allegedly squandered American resources upon foreign nations, thus failing to put America first. Isolationists, Communists, and collective security advocates, unlike pacifists, all believed in a strong military defense; they simply advocated different defensive lines.[48]

Furthermore, pacifists were alienated by isolationism's right-wing aura. Led for the most part by conservatives, financed by businessmen, and cheered by the reactionary Chicago *Tribune* and the New York *Daily News*, the forces of isolation seemed the epitome of the "masters of war." [49] Even more odious in the eyes of pacifists were isolationism's links to anti-Semitism and racism. Christian Front members poured into America First, despite the efforts of its leaders, while other neo-fascist groups seriously infiltrated isolationist ranks. Many of America First's leaders held strikingly racist views. Explaining his anti-interventionist position, Charles Lindbergh wrote that a European war was "not a question of banding together to defend the White race." Although America First contained a sprinkling of prominent liberals, its tone smacked of the political Right.[50]

American peace groups, on the other hand, generally promoted relatively advanced social and economic doctrines. A 1934 W.I.L.P.F. convention announced that "a real and lasting peace and true freedom cannot exist under the present system of exploitation, privilege and profit," and that consequently it would seek "a new system under which would be realized social, economic and political equality for all without distinction of sex, race, or opinion." In 1939

[48] Wayne S. Cole, *America First: The Battle against Intervention, 1940–1941*, p. 95; Alexander DeConde, "On Twentieth-Century Isolationism," *Isolation and Security*, p. 24; Bailey, *The Man in the Street*, p. 293; Selig Adler, *The Isolationist Impulse: Its Twentieth Century Reaction*, p. 274; Leuchtenburg, *Franklin D. Roosevelt and the New Deal*, p. 287; radio interview with Charles A. McLain, former Program Director, America First Committee, WBAI-FM, New York City, September 6, 1966; R. E. Osgood, *Ideals and Self-Interest*, pp. 377–80.

[49] Cole, *America First*, pp. 32, 60; Adler, *The Isolationist Impulse*, pp. 265–74, 283–84; Rauch, *Roosevelt*, p. 10; Leuchtenburg, *Franklin D. Roosevelt and the New Deal*, p. 311; Foster Rhea Dulles, *America's Rise to World Power, 1898–1954*, p. 200.

[50] Morris Janowitz, "Black Legions on the March," *America in Crisis*, p. 316; W. Johnson, *The Battle against Isolation*, pp. 161–67; Cole, *America First*, pp. 131–54; Paul Comly French (ed.), *Common Sense Neutrality: Mobilizing for Peace*, p. 178.

it declared: "There can be neither peace nor freedom without justice. The existing economic system . . . is a challenge to our whole
position." During the depression years pacifists were extremely
active in the labor movement—although the concern was not
reciprocated—leading strikes, marching on picket lines, and cam-
paigning for social justice. While some elements in the Historic
Peace Churches tended toward a more conservative position, or were
simply apolitical, most pacifists tied themselves closely to radical
causes. When F.O.R. members were polled in 1932 on their choice
for President, 75 per cent favored the Socialist candidate.[51]

Finally, at the core of much isolationism lay a belligerent nationalism, indifferent or hostile to the existence of foreign nations. The
leading newspaper of Los Angeles boasted in 1927 that "a change of
Ministers in France is of less importance to the residents of Los Angeles than a change of grade on an important thoroughfare." Paralleling isolationist indifference was often an attitude that suggested
disdain for alien societies. "To hell with Europe and the rest of those
nations!" declared a Senator from Minnesota during a 1935 debate
on the World Court.[52] Isolationists rather appropriately named their
leading organization America First.

The peace movement marched to a different drummer. During
the Thirties, when the country turned fervently isolationist and even
Franklin Roosevelt stated his opposition to the League of Nations,
every major American peace organization supported American entry
into the World Court and the League of Nations (although some
favored restrictions on the latter's warmaking powers).[53] Frederick J.
Libby estimated that 90 per cent of the movement's adherents
favored this policy. In 1925 Kirby Page undertook a twelve-week

[51] Mercedes M. Randall, High Lights in W.I.L.P.F. History: From the Hague
to Luxembourg, 1915–1946; "Principles and Policies" (1939), WILPF MSS,
Box 1; Chatfield, "Pacifism and American Life," pp. 459–83; Bowers, "The
American Peace Movement," pp. 153–236; Altbach, "The American Peace
Movement," pp. 16–26; J. B. Matthews, "Pacifists Prefer Thomas," World
Tomorrow, XV (October 26, 1932), 402.

[52] Bailey, The Man in the Street, pp. 121–22, 213.

[53] Ferrell, "The Peace Movement," pp. 85–90, 94–98; Norman Thomas,
COHC, pp. 124–25; Kuusisto, "The Influence of the National Council for Pre-
vention of War on United States Foreign Policy," p. 48; The History of an
Idea: The Women's International League for Peace and Freedom (1955),
WILPF MSS, Box 1; Schaffer, "Jeannette Rankin," pp. 163–64.

speaking tour on behalf of the World Court, and he was joined by John Nevin Sayre for five weeks and Norman Thomas and John Haynes Holmes for shorter periods. The Peace Section of the American Friends Service Committee promoted the League idea so assiduously that in 1934 the League of Nations Association financed two of its New England peace caravans. Meeting in October, 1941, the national board of the W.I.L.P.F. reported itself "deeply concerned by a spirit of isolationism on the part of a large body of American public opinion—an isolationism which manifests itself in a narrow and hard nationalism, an unscientific racism, a disastrous militarism and an unthinking acceptance of an armaments economy." It added: "We believe . . . that the world has developed into a single economic unity, and that only as nations develop . . . political world organization can we be spared from the continuance of war and violence." [54]

Obviously, then, the peace movement, despite its anti-interventionist position, was not "isolationist." This is a recurrent theme in the movement's literature. "The neutrality policy," observed Florence Brewer Boeckel of the N.C.P.W. in 1938, is "a policy of isolation from war, not of isolation from world affairs." Norman Thomas wrote in 1939: "Neutrality is concerned solely with avoiding war." In July, 1938, Oswald Garrison Villard told readers of the *Nation* that pacifists "are isolationists *only as to war,* and are opposed only to such measures of international cooperation as would lead to war." There is "no form of activity . . . in which we are not willing to cooperate with all nations, save . . . war." [55]

Yet in spite of their extreme ideological differences, a few members of the peace movement tried unsuccessfully to cooperate with isolationists in their common struggle to keep America out of war. When the America First Committee was organized in September, 1940, pacifists Albert W. Palmer and Oswald Garrison Villard were on its national board. Within a month, however, they had resigned,

---

[54] Chatfield, "Pacifism and American Life," pp. 288–95; Libby, *The American Peace Movement,* p. 6; *Four Lights,* I (December, 1941); C. B. Marshall, "Organized Groups," *Public Opinion Quarterly,* IV (March, 1940), 154.

[55] Florence Brewer Boeckel, "The Peace Movement in the U.S.A.," *Peace Year Book 1938,* p. 159; French, *Common Sense Neutrality,* p. 221; Villard, "Issues and Men," p. 18.

objecting to the Committee's endorsement of military defense measures. This, in addition to Villard's pacifism, prompted Secretary of the Interior Harold Ickes to include him in a list of "Nazi Fellow Travelers" in a speech given in April, 1941. Norman Thomas spoke at meetings sponsored by America First, although he refused to join and emphasized his differences with the organization's backing of "armament economics." After Lindbergh's Des Moines speech containing anti-Semitic overtones, Thomas would have nothing further to do with the Committee. With these few exceptions, most pacifists stayed clear of America First.[56]

Of all the peace groups, the N.C.P.W. strayed furthest down the isolationist path. "With the defeat of the World Court in the Senate," Libby wrote in 1935, "those who believe in the collective system began searching with the isolationists for temporary expedients to keep the United States out of war." In 1939, carried away by an almost fanatical opposition to the Administration, the N.C.P.W. veered sharply into the isolationist camp. It distributed hundreds of thousands of copies of speeches by isolationist Senators Borah, La Follette, Nye, McCarran, and Walsh, as well as by the very symbol of nationalist isolationism, Charles Lindbergh. America First donated $1000 to the N.C.P.W. in 1941 for its assistance in opposing the President's Lend-Lease program.[57]

The only other peace group to receive a large contribution from isolationist sources was the W.I.L.P.F., to which the America First Committee donated $500. Hard-pressed for funds in the lean days after 1939, the W.I.L.P.F. accepted this assistance from its anti-interventionist ally with discomfort. Three weeks before Pearl Harbor, when a local chapter president of the W.I.L.P.F. reported her members uneasy about any link with the America First Committee,

---

[56] Cole, America First, pp. 75, 78, 90–91, 147–48; Michael Wreszin, Oswald Garrison Villard: Pacifist at War, pp. 265, 269; New York Times, May 24, 1941; Norman Thomas, What Is Our Destiny, p. 36; Chatfield, "Pacifism and American Life," p. 680; Masland, "Pressure Groups and American Foreign Policy," pp. 116–17. According to the leading student of America First, some pacifists were found on the local chapter level of the organization, as well as in the national speakers bureau. None appear to be figures of any prominence in the peace movement, however. Cole, America First, pp. 75, 90.

[57] Schaffer, "Jeannette Rankin," p. 201; Kuusisto, "The Influence of the National Council for Prevention of War on United States Foreign Policy," p. 228; Cole, America First, p. 227; C. B. Marshall, "Organized Groups," pp. 154–55.

Miss Detzer assured her that there was none whatsoever. An executive committee member pointed out that the stand of the two organizations so clearly diverged on such matters as national defense and international cooperation that no connection was possible.[58] A close analysis of the ties between isolationists and the peace movement proves her essentially correct.

After 1935 pacifists took heart at the strong opposition of public opinion to American participation in war, but it is evident that this opposition was both on the decline and indicative of isolationist rather than pacifist motivations. A poll in November, 1935, found 75 per cent of the American people in favor of obtaining the approval of a national referendum before any declaration of war; by March, 1939, support for this plan dropped to 58 per cent of respondents. Although at no time prior to the attack upon Pearl Harbor did more than 25 per cent of the American people wish to enter the war, perhaps more reflective of popular sentiment were polls indicating that 68 per cent thought it more important to defeat Germany than to stay out of the conflict.[59] That pacifists comprised but a small percentage was evident from a *Fortune* poll in 1939, which found only 2.1 per cent of the country opposed to maintenance of armed forces by the United States. Indeed, throughout the late Thirties, but especially with the outbreak of war in Europe, polls recorded Americans consistently in favor of enlarging the country's military forces. The President faced only the mildest of legislative opposition to his army and navy appropriations bills. In 1940, alone, Congress appropriated seventeen billion dollars for the military.[60] Thus despite their desire to avoid war Americans readied themselves for it.

Analyzing this situation, Evan Thomas, a pacifist leader in the

[58] "Minutes of the W.I.L.P.F. Executive Board, February 26, 1941," WILPF MSS, Box 11; "Minutes of the Executive Committee Meeting, Women's International League for Peace and Freedom" (November 19, 1941), WILPF MSS, Box 11.

[59] Cantril, *Public Opinion*, pp. 969–77, 1025–26; Wickware, "What We Think about Foreign Affairs," p. 406; Hadley Cantril, "Opinion Trends in World War II: Some Guides to Interpretation," *Public Opinion Quarterly*, XII (Spring, 1948), 37; R. E. Osgood, *Ideals and Self-Interest*, pp. 408–409; William A. Lydgate, *What America Thinks*, pp. 32, 35.

[60] Cantril, *Public Opinion*, pp. 939–43; Dulles, *America's Rise to World Power*, p. 191.

W.R.L. and brother of the Socialist Party chieftain, sought to understand why people armed and went to war, although most "hate war
and believe no good can come from it." The "answer," he contended,
was that "the world is organized on the acceptance of war as the
only possible court of last appeal." Too many opponents of war
accepted the fact that "if all else failed, militarism must be met with
militarism." Yet what else could be done? It was with more than a
little justice that a 1941 editorial in the *Presbyterian Tribune* asked
"what practicable alternative" pacifists "have to offer to the political
courses framed . . . by statesmen which they condemn." "What do
pacifists propose," the journal inquired, "while the world is under
the German terror?" [61]

Unfortunately, by 1941 American pacifists had no "practicable
alternative" in the tragic context of the time. Their message had a
moral but not a political relevance. "Positively," Norman Thomas
recalled, pacifists "had nothing to offer in the problem of stopping
Nazism. . . . Nothing that is, except for a religious faith." In Germany, at least, there was no evidence that ethics were honored by
the conquerors; thousands of pacifists had already been placed in
concentration camps. Nor, in the last analysis, did the pacifist belief
demand political success. As William Penn had once declared, the
pacifist choice was "not fighting, but suffering." Such a creed had its
moral advantages, but surely could not be judged a "practicable
alternative." "Pacifism is an obligation, not a promise," conceded the
Friends Peace Committee in 1940. "We are not guaranteed that it
will be safe. We are sure that it is right." [62]

Only the faintest stirrings of political interest broke the surface of
moral concern [63] among pacifists in the years before Pearl Harbor.

[61] *Conscientious Objector*, November, 1939; "What Do Pacifists Propose?"
Presbyterian Tribune, LVI (August, 1941), 4.
[62] Bell, "Background and Development of Marxian Socialism," p. 401; Cadbury, "Peace and War," p. 9; Witte, "Quaker Pacifism," p. 310. Dr. Emil
Maurer, chairman of the Socialist Party in Vienna, told a London newspaper
reporter that when he was sent to the Buchenwald concentration camp in
September, 1938, one fifth of the inmates were pacifists, placed there for their
refusal to serve in the *Wehrmacht*. Reprinted from the *London Tribune*, April
27, 1945, in: Jan Levcik, "Buchenwald before the War," *Politics*, II (June,
1945), 173–74.
[63] One writer has succinctly phrased it: "Some people . . . tend to ask first,
'What kind of world would I like to make?' and these we may call 'political'

In 1918 John Haynes Holmes discovered Mohandas Gandhi, whom he lauded three years later in his widely discussed address "Who Is the Greatest Man in the World Today?" Gandhian *satyagraha*, or soul force, thereafter attracted considerable attention among pacifists interested in non-violent change. English pacifist Aldous Huxley commended it to public attention as the only option for oppressed people in the modern industrial age. Pamphlets of the F.O.R. made mention briefly of its use, while a W.R.L. pamphlet by Jessie Wallace Hughan argued in 1939 that resistance tactics could successfully halt an invasion of the United States. The only occasion on which non-violent resistance was actually tried by the theorists came in November, 1936, when two pacifist members of the American Federation of Full-Fashioned Hosiery Workers organized a "lie down" by members of their local in front of the factory gates. Despite an excellent response on the part of the workers, the strike failed when local law officials imprisoned all the strikers. A. J. Muste was exultant, especially after the national union appointed "a standing commission to study the merits and possibilities of using non-violent resistance in labor disputes"; however, nothing appears to have come of it.[64] *Satyagraha* remained a matter for talk and not for action.

The leading theorist of non-violent resistance was a Quaker lawyer, Richard Gregg. One day, quite accidentally, he read an article about Gandhi, and was greatly impressed with the few excerpts of the Indian leader's writings. After studying Gandhi's works, Gregg traveled to India in 1925, where he remained for the next four years, seven months of which he passed at Gandhi's *ashram*, or spiritual retreat. Arriving home, Gregg gave up his law practice and began to write and lecture on the subject of non-violence. His pioneering

---

people. Others ask first, 'What kind of action is right for me to undertake?' and these we may call 'moral' people." Arthur I. Waskow, *The Worried Man's Guide to World Peace*, p. 49.

[64] Voss, *Rabbi and Minister*, pp. 198–208; John Haynes Holmes, *My Gandhi;* Hentoff, *Peace Agitator,* p. 102; Aldous Huxley, *Ends and Means;* Fellowship of Reconciliation, *As War Comes Nearer,* p. 6; Fellowship of Reconciliation, *What Is the Fellowship of Reconciliation?,* p. 5; Jessie Wallace Hughan, *If We Should Be Invaded;* Herbert G. Bohn, "We Tried Non-Violence," *Fellowship,* III (January, 1937), 7–8; A. J. Muste, "Sit Downs and Lie Downs," *Fellowship,* III (March, 1937), 5–6.

study *The Power of Non-Violence* proved immensely influential; he followed it by a series of short pamphlets sketching in details on non-violent discipline and modes of living. The message of the book was revolutionary: non-violent resistance had a political and social significance. Not only was non-violence "right," but it "worked." [65]

Strangely enough, despite the popularity of Gregg's book, pacifists were slow to see that he had given them an alternative to violence in conflict situations. Perhaps the idea seemed too new; perhaps the task of converting the world to a different kind of struggle appeared too awesome. In any event, even Gregg, when attempting to answer the question "How Can Hitler Be Stopped?," omitted any mention of non-violent resistance. His outlook was pessimistic. "Now the fat is in the fire," he wrote, "and European peoples and governments are paying for previous obstinate mistakes of their ruling classes. Our country will have to pay its share." Non-violent resistance represented at least an alternative, however problematical, but one which was never explored. [66]

That pacifism remained almost solely a moral imperative is evident from the ebb and flow in the strength of peace organizations during the last years before the war. In general, those with absolute pacifist constituencies grew, while those with a broader membership rapidly faded. The religious pacifist F.O.R. increased from 4271 to 12,426 members between 1935 and 1941, with 4000 of the new members entering between August, 1940, and August, 1941. Similarly, the secular pacifist W.R.L. had its busiest year just before the war, enrolling the greatest number of new members, employing its largest staff, and spending the most money in its history. The N.C.P.W., which had garnered the support of many non-pacifist

[65] Chatfield, "Pacifism and American Life," pp. 548–49; Hassler, *Conscripts of Conscience*, p. 50; Richard B. Gregg: *The Power of Non-Violence; The Value of Voluntary Simplicity; Training for Peace: A Program for Peace Workers; Pacifist Program in Time of War, Threatened War, or Fascism; A Discipline for Non-Violence.* Another work that became a textbook for non-violent actionists at this time was: Krishnalal Shridharani, *War without Violence: A Study of Gandhi's Method and Its Accomplishments.*

[66] Richard B. Gregg, "How Can Hitler Be Stopped?" *Fellowship*, V (October, 1939), 6. Emily Balch later acknowledged that World War II was inevitable, given mankind's "failure to have ready any effective technique for constructive non-violent *action*, such as Gandhi had arrived at." M. M. Randall, *Improper Bostonian*, p. 341.

groups, saw them gradually fall away as the European crisis heightened; its income drastically declined, forcing it to pare salaries and drop staff members. Especially hard hit was the reformist W.I.L.P.F., whose chapter membership melted away in interventionist areas of the country. Between April, 1940, and April, 1941, membership in Manhattan dropped from 426 to 160, in Brooklyn from 334 to 146, in Santa Barbara from 125 to 55. Only in pacifist centers did it retain strength; in heavily Quaker Delaware County membership rose from 613 to 621, while in Philadelphia it fell only slightly from 1490 to 1432.[67] As Pearl Harbor approached, the peace movement grew increasingly pacifist.

The peace movement's dilemma of the late Thirties thus centered about the problem of the rise of fascism. Although the peace movement offered a long-term program of disarmament and social justice, it had no immediate solutions to cope with the aggresive world of angry power relationships it confronted. Its position was never adopted by any of the "great" nations, of course, but it seems unlikely that it could have met the military challenge posed by Hitler; pacifists would almost certainly have perished in the fiery hatred of the black-shirted legions. And while this may have been an ethically superior position, it was a bleak choice for men and nations.

On the other hand, pacifists quickly spotted the flaw in the logic of the collective security advocates. If the enemy was the cult of violence, nationalism, and racism, then war was obviously an inadequate method for its defeat. A world war might suffice in the short run, deposing Hitler, Mussolini, and their followers; but in the long run it offered little hope for a new type of relationship among men. Indeed, the hatred, brutality, and chauvinism churned up by modern warfare exacerbated the long-term problem as it alleviated the short-term one. Wars did not end this way, the peace movement understood; but then, how did they end?

[67] "Membership Statistics" (1954), FOR MSS, Box 4; Brittain, *The Rebel Passion*, p. 58; War Resisters League, *Our Busiest Year!* (1940), WRL MSS, Box 3; Kuusisto, "The Influence of the National Council for Prevention of War on United States Foreign Policy," pp. 54–56, 63, 65, 226–27; "Local Branches and Their Membership," WILPF MSS, Box 11; personal interview with A. J. Muste, June 2, 1966.

CHAPTER II

Wartime Collapse

The difference between being out of step with a dictator and being out of step with the democratic majority is practically negligible. The important thing is to be in step.

HENRY MILLER, 1941 [1]

When the Japanese government launched its attack upon Pearl Harbor in December, 1941, the tottering American peace movement collapsed. "Perhaps no war has ever produced so many individuals who at one time or another in their lives had vowed never to fight again, and then with the first trumpets found reasons as to why *this* war was different," commented two pacifists in retrospect. An imprisoned war resister urged, with a touch of bitterness, that in peacetime the names of conscientious objectors (C.O.'s) be filed with the Red Cross, and that if any subsequently went to war, *they* be prosecuted. [2]

Before December 7, peace activists found it relatively easy to cast discredit upon the war in Europe. Pacifists could flay Nazi atrocities and British imperialism with impunity, often garnering applause from their fellow citizens. But with the United States at last in the thick of that struggle, criticism of war became un-American and suspect as treason. The new climate of nationalism quickly scattered the already decimated legions of peacemakers.

The attack upon Pearl Harbor radically altered American opinion, which had formerly been divided over the merits of intervention. A poll on December 10 found that 96 per cent of the nation approved Congress' declaration of war, while only 2 per cent disapproved. Local Committees on Foreign Relations of the Council on

[1] Henry Miller, *Remember to Remember,* Vol. II of *The Air-Conditioned Nightmare* (New York: New Directions, 1947), p. 130.

[2] Arthur and Lila Weinberg (eds.), *Instead of Violence,* p. 134; Curtis Zahn to Abraham Kaufman, August 7, 1947, WRL MSS, Box 10.

Foreign Relations chronicled the dramatic shift. "The Detroit public was not ready for total war. It took Pearl Harbor to blast away the obstacles," reported the Detroit Committee. "The impact of that fateful December 7th seriously shook the opinions and convictions . . . within the Nashville Committee," reported another. In Louisville one observer contended that "the Japanese had done us a great service in that they united the country in the war effort," while another noted that the attack had "the gratifying effect of uniting the country along my line of thought, which at one time had been extremely unpopular." The Houston Committee stated that America "seemed to repossess overnight the integrity and resolution of national will, which many feared lost beyond recovery by dissension and partisan strife." [3]

Despite the widespread hostility to American intervention before December 7, far fewer opponents of war appeared after that date than during World War I. Representative Jeannette Rankin, who had a chance to vote against American participation in both world wars, recalled that the Congressional atmosphere departed radically from that in 1917. In the earlier conflict, "a week of tense debate" preceded the vote, while fifty members of the House voted "no." Claude Kitchen, the floor leader of the Democratic majority, "voted 'No' and wept unashamedly," but was retained in the leadership in spite of this, while Champ Clark, Speaker of the House, refrained from voting. The roll call on World War II revealed the change in Congressional and popular temper. The Pearl Harbor attack occurred on Sunday; the vote was scheduled for Monday. Miss Rankin wrote: "This time I stood alone. It was a good deal more difficult than it had been the time before." Six months after the bombing of Pearl Harbor, Jessie Wallace Hughan noted: "The general public, in the opinion of our veteran pacifists, is much more nearly unanimous in support of the war than in 1917." [4]

[3] Dulles, *America's Rise to World Power*, p. 207; Cantril, *Public Opinion*, p. 978; Percy W. Bidwell (ed.), *Our Foreign Policy in War and Peace: Some Regional Views*, pp. 5–6, 8, 12.

[4] Jeannette Rankin, "Two Votes against War—1917, 1941," *Liberation*, III (March, 1958), 4–7; Jessie Wallace Hughan, "Our U.S.A. Movement Since Pearl Harbor" (May 27, 1942), WRL MSS, Box 17; H. C. Peterson and Gilbert C. Fite, *Opponents of War, 1917–1918*, pp. 3–138; Weinberg, *Instead of Violence*, p. 134; M. M. Randall, *Improper Bostonian*, p. 339.

To a considerable degree, the sudden ground swell of support for the war represented a closing of ranks behind the flag. Illustrative of this move was the conversion of the isolationists to superpatriotism and war. The America First Committee, through its chairman Robert E. Wood, urged "all those who have followed its lead to give their full support to the war effort of the nation." Wood, Lindbergh, and many of its leading figures raced to enlist in the armed forces. "The only thing now to do," declared isolationist Senator Burton K. Wheeler, "is to lick hell out of them." Arthur Vandenberg, one of the Senate's leading isolationists, recalled that "that day ended isolationism for any realist." Seven months after America's entry into the war, Archibald MacLeish complained that isolationists "have appropriated the war. . . . Their newspapers have become the most chauvinistic, their speeches the most flamboyant, the country affords. They hate the enemy with a public hatred rarely surpassed in any vocabulary." [5]

The nature of the Japanese attack added a quality of emotionalism to the nation's response. Normally scholarly and analytical men were incensed. "The foully treacherous attack at Pearl Harbor gave every citizen, East and West, a sense of the deepest outrage," recalled historian Allan Nevins years later. "On December 7th we were all of one mind about the war," wrote MacLeish, the "war against the Japanese who had tricked us." The Houston Committee on Foreign Relations reported: "We found ourselves grievously smitten by a treacherous foe." Others viewed the attack in more apocalyptic terms. "With fire and brimstone came December 7," wrote Archbishop Francis Spellman. "America's throat was clutched, her back was stabbed, her brain was stunned; but her great heart still throbbed." Could America recover? Yes! "America clenched the palms of those hands oft-stretched in mercy to the peoples of the nations that struck her. America's brain began to clear. America began the fight to save her life." [6]

[5] "Fallen Citadel," Time, XXXVIII (December 22, 1941), 33; Cole, America First, p. 196; Thomas A. Bailey, A Diplomatic History of the American People, p. 740; Herbert Agar, The Price of Power: America Since 1945, p. 17; Archibald MacLeish, American Opinion and the War, p. 25.
[6] Allan Nevins, "How We Felt about the War," While You Were Gone: A Report on Wartime Life in the United States, ed. Jack Goodman, p. 11;

Many members of the peace movement, surprised by the attack upon Pearl Harbor, were convinced that, under the radically altered conditions, it was necessary to support a policy of military defense for the United States. Typical of these reluctant converts to force was Norman Thomas. "After Pearl Harbor there was no political alternative to carrying on the war to a point where the Nazi and Japanese warlords could not dominate the world," he wrote to friends. "The choice before us was a choice between circles of hell but the lowest and worst circle of hell would have been that imposed by a Nazi victory." Socialists had little interest in protecting the Western colonial empires, Thomas believed, but national defense was quite another matter. "When Socialists supported the war in Europe," Thomas told an interviewer in 1949, "you will notice that it is usually when their own countries were invaded." [7]

The churches, formerly a primary repository of the peace witness, now rallied to the flag. In December, 1941, just nineteen months after the Methodist Church, the largest Protestant denomination in the United States, proclaimed that it would never "officially support, endorse or participate in war," its bishops voted that "the Methodists of America will loyally support our President and our nation." Not to be outdone, Dr. William A. Elliott, president of the Northern Baptist Convention, reported that "Baptist ministers are 'all out' to win." The Synagogue Council of America called upon its congregations "to offer prayer for a speedy victory," while the administrative board of the National Catholic Welfare Conference sent a letter to President Roosevelt pledging "our institutions and their consecrated personnel" to the nation's wartime service. [8]

Since the country did react so strongly to Pearl Harbor, pacifists in sensitive positions were given powerful incentives to conform to the national mold. In California intense pressure was put on pacifist

---

MacLeish, *American Opinion and the War*, p. 14; Bidwell, *Our Foreign Policy*, p. 12; Francis J. Spellman, *The Road to Victory*, p. x.

[7] Personal interview with A. J. Muste, June 2, 1966; "Confidential Memorandum from Norman Thomas for Your Criticism and Advice, May 1, 1944," FOR MSS, Box 11; Norman Thomas, COHC, p. 127; Norman Thomas to Henry Geiger, December 11, 1944, Norman M. Thomas Manuscripts, New York Public Library (Thomas MSS), Box 47.

[8] "The Churches and the War," *Time*, XXXVIII (December 22, 1941), 67–68; Abrams, "The Churches and the Clergy," pp. 116–17.

schoolteachers. The local F.O.R. office received reports of two who were told they would not be rehired, one who resigned when about to be fired, and two others on the way out—all within one month of the commencement of hostilities. When Chalmer Johnson, a member of the Church of the Brethren, declined to sell "defense stamps" to his sixth grade class, his principal warned him that if he did not sell the stamps he would be fired. Johnson still refused and was brought to his school board on two hours' notice for a hearing, after which he was suspended. Others, like Miss Florence Auernheimer, a kindergarten teacher who refused to sell defense stamps to her five-year-old pupils, were forced out. In an attempt to discourage employment of pacifists in public service, the state legislature of California passed a bill which would require all applicants for employment to state their views on participation in war; Governor Earl Warren later vetoed it.[9]

Despite a generally good wartime civil liberties record, the nation often made life difficult for pacifists. In Kentucky the Assistant Attorney General ruled that a teacher who had accepted the Selective Service System's alternative service program could not be reappointed by the public schools. Such service, he declared, indicated "that at least he has been guilty of an offense involving moral turpitude, and that his conduct has been such that an orderly society must remove him from circulation." The Illinois Bar Association denied a lawyer admission to the bar for his pacifist beliefs, while in Miami, Florida, a schoolteacher was dismissed from his position when it was learned that he had registered as a C.O. In early 1943 Representative Carter Manasco of Alabama introduced a bill to deny federal employment to C.O.'s.[10]

Most Americans, although not personally hostile to pacifists, disapproved of their proselytizing in wartime. Dorothy Day recalls that

[9] Caleb Foote to A. J. Muste, January 16, 1942; Caleb Foote to Ernest Besig, American Civil Liberties Union, January 16, 1942; Caleb Foote to A. J. Muste, February 4, 1942, FOR MSS, Box 8; American Civil Liberties Union, *Liberty on the Home Front: In the Fourth Year of War*, p. 37.

[10] American Civil Liberties Union, *Liberty on the Home Front*, p. 39; Julien Cornell, *The Conscientious Objector and the Law*, pp. 113–14; Julien Cornell, *Conscience and the State*, pp. 52–57; *New York Times*, June 12, 1945; National Service Board for Religious Objectors, *Congress Looks at the Conscientious Objector*, p. 52.

the *Catholic Worker* printed a box urging men not to register for the draft, until she was called to the Chancery and told to cease this policy, which she then did. President Roosevelt, in a White House conference with Rabbi Stephen Wise, asked: "Can't you do anything with John Haynes Holmes? What's the matter with him?" Wartime polls reported that 87 per cent of a national sample opposed the expression of pacifist opinions. In the face of this negative public reaction, many peace workers undoubtedly fell silent, thereby adding to the country's sense of "national unity." [11]

Perhaps most important, the fascist horror, particularly the Nazi treatment of the Jews, undermined the peace effort even among the firmest of its adherents. "In the last war I was an uncompromising Pacifist," one correspondent told a War Resisters League official. Arrested for participating in antiwar meetings, denounced as an obstructer of the draft, her mail opened by the government, she remained "serene, for I saw *that* war as a war of Imperialisms." Yet after World War I she witnessed "the steady rise of . . . the idea that Force was a god to be worshipped; that nothing short of a world conquest of this idea was to be achieved, expressing itself in territorial conquest by a 'master race' under whose tyranny the masses, unarmed and helpless . . . would accept it as the truth"; it seemed "an evidence of the dark power rising everywhere." She concluded: "I cannot oppose this war effort," but "I confess my soul is sick within me because my feeling against war . . . and my honest intellectual conclusions are at variance." A Jewish pacifist, born in Germany, told Evan Thomas: "Although I detest war, conscription, the hypocrisy with which this war is being fought by the Allies, etc., still it seems to me that conditions would be even worse under Hitler, and that despite the dark future which is being planned by the Allies I have to cooperate with them because under Hitler there is no future at all." The W.I.L.P.F. reported heavy defections from

[11] Day, *Loaves and Fishes*, p. 60; Voss, *Rabbi and Minister*, p. 309; Leo P. Crespi, "Public Opinion toward Conscientious Objectors," *Journal of Psychology*, XIX (1945), 291. Diplomatic historian Thomas Bailey contends that "pacifists have been energetic in time of peace, although forced to soft-pedal their zeal in time of war." The general trend which Merle Curti finds is similar; he argues that instead of the peace movement putting an end to war, wars generally put an end, at least temporarily, to the activities of the peacemakers. Bailey, *The Man in the Street*, p. 293; Curti, *Peace or War*.

its membership because of the Nazi persecution of minority groups.[12]

Those who remained opposed to the war perceived Nazi fanaticism with disgust, but did not believe that war provided an answer to it. The Nazi persecution turned a number of his "best friends who were formerly staunch pacifists" into supporters of World War II, remarked Evan Thomas. "Emotionally, I can understand fully why they did this, and I have felt myself that evil such as Hitler represents must be resisted." But the question is, he added, "how we are to resist. Following the last war, I saw enough discrimination and actual brutality in this country to realize that people like Hitler were not unique. I had to make up my mind at that time what I considered to be the best form of resistance to that sort of thing. . . . I came to the conclusion . . . that violence is no answer to tyranny, exploitation, or brutality." He found this "especially true of organized war," which he thought represented "something far more complex . . . than a simple problem of resisting Hitler." [13]

Some pacifists took the position that only an immediate end to the war could save the Jews, since the conflict itself exacerbated their plight. Disturbed in 1942 by rumors of Nazi extermination plans, Jessie Wallace Hughan worried that such a policy, which appeared "natural, from their pathological point of view," might be carried out if World War II continued. "It seems that the only way to save thousands and perhaps millions of European Jews from destruction," she wrote, "would be for our government to broadcast the promise" of an "armistice on condition that the European minorities are not molested any further. . . . It would be very terrible if six months from now we should find that this threat has literally come to pass without our making even a gesture to prevent it." When her predictions were fulfilled only too well by 1943, she wrote to the State Department and the *New York Times,* decrying the fact that "two million [Jews] have already died" and that "two million more will be killed by the end of the war." Once again, she pleaded for

[12] Sarah Bard Field to Frank Olmstead, December 5, 1942, WRL MSS, Box 15; Moshe Kallner to Evan Thomas, July 22, 1943, WRL MSS, Box 17; *The History of an Idea: The Women's International League for Peace and Freedom* (1955), WILPF MSS, Box 1.

[13] Evan Thomas to Moshe Kallner, July 26, 1943, WRL MSS, Box 17.

the cessation of hostilities, arguing that German military defeats would in turn exact reprisals upon the Jewish scapegoat. "Victory will not save them," she insisted, "for dead men cannot be liberated." [14] However ineffectual her suggestion might have been in halting Nazi extermination policies, the war did not stop them either; in the end, despite the Allied war effort, the European Jews perished.

Yet despite the melting away of millions of peace adherents with the arrival of war, a substantial core of Americans remained pacifists during World War II. The United States government classified as C.O.'s 42,973 of the 10,022,367 males ordered to report for induction. If this same ratio is projected to the nation's population, omitting children, then the number of absolute pacifists in the nation must have numbered in the hundreds of thousands.[15] Oddly enough, although more general opposition to war prevailed in the country during World War I than during World War II, the number of absolute pacifists was much larger in the second great conflict than in the first. The percentage of young men inducted as C.O.'s by Selective Service tripled, while the percentage of those imprisoned (and classified as C.O.'s) quadrupled.[16]

[14] Jessie Wallace Hughan to John Nevin Sayre, November 27, 1942, WRL MSS, Box 17; Jessie Wallace Hughan to the Editor, New York Times, February 27, 1943, WRL MSS, Box 17; Richard W. Marin, Acting Chief, Division of Public Liaison, Department of State, to Jessie Wallace Hughan, April 29, 1944, WRL MSS, Box 17.

[15] Although the Selective Service System did not keep accurate or complete records on conscientious objection, it estimated that during the 6½-year life of the Selective Training and Service Act of 1940 it ordered the induction of 25,000 men classified I-A-O (noncombatant), 11,887 classified IV-E (alternative service), and imprisoned 6086 C.O.'s who either refused induction or did not meet the narrow requirements of the law. Thus, 42,973 of the 10,022,-367 males ordered to report for induction into the armed forces were C.O.'s. If this same ratio is projected to the nation's population of about 130,000,000, then over 556,400 Americans, including infants, remained pacifists during World War II. U.S. Selective Service System, Conscientious Objection, I, 105, 115, 117, 263; U.S. Selective Service System, Selective Service and Victory: The 4th Report of the Director of Selective Service, p. 348. See also: Vernon H. Holloway, "A Review of American Religious Pacifism," Religion in Life, XIX (Summer, 1950), 369.

[16] During World War I, 3989 out of a total of 2,810,296 men inducted were C.O.'s, or .14 per cent. This is but one third of the World War II record of .42 per cent. Even more striking is the increase in the number of imprisoned C.O.'s during World War II, which jumped from 450 to 6086, or from .016 to .060 per cent—an increase of four times—despite the provisions in the 1940

While the sizable number of absolute pacifists during World War II provided a modest monument to the peace proselytizing of the Thirties, it must be remembered that they comprised, in fact, less than one half of one per cent of the population. For the first time, pacifists grew conscious of how terribly isolated they were. "Today we are a 'Remnant,' " wrote President Dorothy Medders Robinson to the members of the W.I.L.P.F., "but we should never forget that every great idea at one time belonged to a Remnant." [17]

The receding tide of pacifism is evident in the reaction of the Protestant clergy to the coming of war. Perhaps the most outspoken of the religious journals, the *Christian Century*, accepted World War II as a "guilty necessity." "The war itself is the wages of our sin and injustice," wrote the editor, Charles Clayton Morrison. "It is a catastrophic tragedy . . . leaving us no choice save to decide on which side we shall fight." On the other hand, although it supported the war, the *Christian Century* did so with exceptionally little enthusiasm. "Let maddened men and blinded nations claim what they will for what they do," wrote Morrison. "The church of Christ cannot speak their language." This compromise position pleased neither pacifists nor interventionists; the editor admitted receiving four to five thousand letters by 1943 from pacifists critical of the magazine's view on the war.[18]

---

conscription law designed to avoid the pattern of imprisonment suffered by C.O.'s in World War I.

Draft evasion during World War II increased to 348,217 cases, as compared with 171,000 in World War I. As the number of inductees more than tripled and the number of evaders merely doubled, this actually represents a proportionate decline in this type of Selective Service violation. However, government figures make no distinction between the large number of purely technical violations (e.g., filling out a form incorrectly or reporting for examination on the wrong day) and complete desertion. A more efficient bureaucracy, greater familiarity with the system on the part of the public, and better means of publicizing Selective Service regulations could easily account for the decline in the percentage of draft violations. Conscientious objection therefore appears to serve as a more reliable indicator of antimilitary sentiment. U.S. Selective Service System, *Conscientious Objection*, I, 53, 60, 263; U.S. Selective Service System, *Selective Service and Victory*, pp. 198–99; Norman Thomas, *The Conscientious Objector in America*, pp. 14–15; Holloway, "A Review of American Religious Pacifism," pp. 368–69.

[17] Dorothy Medders Robinson to Members, January 3, 1942, WILPF MSS, Box 11; *Four Lights*, I (January, 1942).

[18] Abrams, "The Churches and the Clergy," pp. 114–15; "Modified Pacifism," *Christian Century*, LXI (July 26, 1944), 872; "Unnecessary Sectarianism,"

The pacifist victories in the Protestant churches were not entirely abortive. The clergy, in general, waxed far less belligerent during World War II than in World War I. Although most aggressive pacifism came to a halt, ministers hesitated to proclaim another "holy war," and their sermons concentrated upon matters of personal ethics. The Federal Council of Churches announced that "all share in responsibility for the present evils. There is none who does not need forgiveness. A mood of genuine penitence is therefore demanded of us—individuals and nations alike." [19] Indeed, some church leaders grew uneasy with their colleagues' lack of patriotic zeal. The repentant soldier, complained Paul Ramsey, should not "blubber over his gun-powder," but "get on with the shooting." Such protests, nevertheless, went largely unheeded, and the churches conspicuously attempted to instill a tone of sober, unsentimental piety into their pronouncements. *Time* magazine found it significant that although most religious leaders endorsed the war, "not one of them directly answered TIME's question as to whether most ministers feel America is fighting for the cause of righteousness." [20]

Although most Protestant religious leaders supported the war, however weakly, thousands held steadfast to the peace testimony. Several thousand Protestant clergymen remained pacifists, considerably more—both absolutely and proportionately—than during World War I. These included such prominent figures as Harry Emerson Fosdick, Walter W. Van Kirk, Ralph W. Sockman, Ernest Fremont Tittle, Allan Knight Chalmers, Georgia Harkness, John

Christian Century, LIX (November 11, 1942), 1382–85; "Is the Church Aloof?" *Christian Century*, LIX (October 14, 1942), 1249; "The Pacifist Conscience," *Christian Century*, LX (September 8, 1943), 1006. A pacifist reply to the views of Dr. Morrison is: Edward Yoder, *Compromise with War*.

[19] F. Ernest Johnson, "The Impact of the War on Religion in America," *American Journal of Sociology*, XLVIII (November, 1942), 354–55; Federal Council of the Churches of Christ in America, Commission to Study the Bases of a Just and Durable Peace, *A Righteous Faith for a Just and Durable Peace* (October, 1942), p. 101; Abrams, "The Churches and the Clergy," p. 116.

[20] Roland H. Bainton, *Christian Attitudes toward War and Peace*, p. 221; Stanley High, "Church Unmilitant," *New Republic*, CVI (June 22, 1942), 850–52; Stanley High, "What, Then, Should the Church Do?" *Christian Century*, LIX (September 23, 1942), 1146–48; "The Churches and the War," p. 67. In 1942 polls found that six out of ten clergymen believed the church should actively support the war, but many of these agreed that although it should build morale, it should not be used again for recruiting or the selling of war bonds. Bailey, *The Man in the Street*, p. 206.

Haynes Holmes, Methodist Bishop Paul B. Kern, and Episcopal Bishops Walter Mitchell and W. Appleton Lawrence. Illustrative of their attitude was the minority report of the General Council of Congregational Christian Churches, signed by 135 of the 544 delegates, which stated that "they cannot in loyalty to their Christian consciences, accept the way of violence and bloodshed. . . . They believe that the way of the cross requires them to endure suffering, if necessary, but not willingly to inflict it." [21]

In contrast to the irresolution of the spokesmen for Protestant denominations in supporting World War II, relatively few pacifists were found in the Catholic or Jewish faiths. Roman Catholic doctrine left room for the "just war," and Catholics, like most other Americans, accepted Pearl Harbor as the verdict in the controversy over intervention. Although many remained critical of certain aspects of the war, few Roman Catholics came out openly as full pacifists.[22] American Jews gave the war their overwhelming support, tempered only by the fear of becoming too prominent, thereby lending substance to anti-Semitic charges of a "Jewish War." For Jews, pacifism was undoubtedly a difficult discipline in a war with Germany. A chapter of the W.I.L.P.F. in Rockaway, New York, consisting primarily of Jewish members, was disdained by the neighborhood's Christians and anathema to its Jews.[23]

Continuing their long-term pacifist witness, the Historic Peace Churches once again rejected war. After the conflict commenced, a Brethren Church conference resolved that "the church's historic conviction that violence in the relations of men is contrary to the spirit

[21] A. J. Muste, *Not by Might*, p. 198; Bainton, *Christian Attitudes toward War and Peace*, p. 220; *Conscientious Objector*, January, 1942; "The Churches and the War," p. 68; Johnson, "Impact of the War on Religion," p. 356.

[22] Kenneth Latourette, "Christianity and the Peace Movement," *The Church, the Gospel and War*, ed. Rufus M. Jones, p. 107; Ralph Luther Moellering, *Modern War and the American Churches*, pp. 53–54.

[23] H. M. Kallen, "National Solidarity and the Jewish Minority," *Annals of the American Academy of Political and Social Science*, CCXXIII (September, 1942), 26–28; Abrams, "The Churches and the Clergy," pp. 117–18; M. M. Randall, *Improper Bostonian*, p. 361. A Jewish Peace Fellowship was established during the war, but its membership by August, 1942, consisted of only 50 members, with chapters in New York, Los Angeles, and Philadelphia. *Conscientious Objector*, August, 1942. Of an estimated 11,950 C.O.'s assigned to Civilian Public Service camps, Selective Service reports that only 162 were Catholic and 50 were Jewish. U.S. Selective Service System, *Conscientious Objection*, I, 318.

of Christ must be reaffirmed," while a statement of Rufus Jones, Quaker historian, was adopted as wartime policy by the American Friends Service Committee: "There must be amidst all the confusions of the hour a tried and undisturbed remnant of persons who will not become purveyors of coercion and violence, who are ready to stand alone, if it is necessary, for the way of peace and love among men." [24] Yet despite the official position of the peace churches, their corporate peace testimony exhibited considerable erosion.

The Mennonites provided the best pacifist record, with three out of five of their young men serving as C.O.'s. Nevertheless, Mennonite leaders were discouraged by the fact that such large segments of their flock now accepted wartime combat duty. "We can all see that the picture with regard to the stand taken by many of our brethren is not a flattering one," observed a local church conference, "and should give us . . . grave concern." The position of the Brethren young was particularly distressing in pacifist eyes, for less than one eighth rejected military service. A survey revealed that 62 per cent of the Brethren churches had dropped the pledge to refuse war service as a covenant of membership. A church official wrote: "The reports show that propaganda, the economic problem, and the influence of friends and community have been stronger in motivating action than the program of the church." The Quaker record also boded poorly for retention of a church peace testimony. Although throughout World War II not a single Yearly Meeting failed to state its opposition to war, most Quaker colleges in the United States accepted military training programs, while three fourths of all Quakers drafted declined to claim C.O. status.[25] Thus, although the Historic Peace Churches continued to provide the largest numbers of absolute pacifists in wartime, they, too, did not fail to succumb to the social pressures of a nation at war.

The social group with fewest ties to the traditional peace move-

[24] Rufus D. Bowman, *Seventy Times Seven*, p. 34; "Quakers Affirm Peace Witness," *Christian Century*, LVII (July 17, 1940), 909.

[25] Guy Franklin Hershberger, *The Mennonite Church in the Second World War*, p. 39; U.S. Selective Service System, *Conscientious Objection*, I, 321–22; Moellering, *Modern War and the American Churches*, p. 77; Bowman, *Seventy Times Seven*, p. 45; Ruth Freeman, *Quakers and Peace*, pp. 52–53; Holloway, "American Pacifism between Two Wars," p. 78.

ment and perhaps most disaffected by the war was the American Negro community. As a black journalist commented: "The Negro . . . is angry, resentful, and utterly apathetic about the war. 'Fight for what?' he is asking. 'This war doesn't mean a thing to me. If we win I lose, so what?' " A black army officer, home on furlough during Christmas, told friends in Harlem that he had been in "hundreds of bull sessions with other colored fellows" and none expressed any interest in the war. "What the hell do we want to fight the Japs for anyhow?" he asked. "They couldn't possibly treat us any worse than these 'crackers' right here at home." In 1942 Walter White, secretary of the N.A.A.C.P., related a conversation between a friend, a teacher at a well-known Southern Negro college, and one of his students. After a brief discussion of the war, the student exclaimed bitterly: "I hope Hitler wins!" That would be "the only thing that will teach these white people some sense—their knowing what it means to be oppressed." "But don't you realize," interjected the teacher, "that conditions would be even worse under Hitler?" "They can't possibly be any worse than they are for Negroes in the South right now," the student replied. "The Army jim-crows us. The Navy lets us serve only as messmen. The Red Cross refuses our blood. Employers and labor unions shut us out. Lynchings continue. We are disenfranchised, jim-crowed, spat upon. What more could Hitler do than that?" To his embarrassment, White found that the student's views were not unique. Some months later, he related the anecdote to a black audience of several thousand in a Midwestern city, utilizing it to warn his listeners against such attitudes. But after recounting the student's remarks, he recalled: "To my surprise and dismay the audience burst into such applause that it took me some thirty or forty seconds to quiet it." As Robert C. Weaver, a Negro prominent in the Roosevelt Administration, observed in an understatement, the black man's attitude toward the war was "certainly not enthusiastic support." [26]

In spite of the smoldering discontent of America's Negro population, however, it is indicative of the peace movement's isolation and debilitated state that it was unable to turn this rebellion into antiwar activity. Surprisingly few black men became C.O.'s; only 400 were

[26] Earl Brown, "American Negroes and the War," *Harper's*, CLXXXIV (April, 1942), 546–47; Walter White, "What the Negro Thinks of the Army," *Annals of the American Academy of Political and Social Science*, CCXXIII

classified as C.O.'s out of 2,427,495 registrants between the ages of 18 and 37, although another 167 Negro Moslems as well as a few Negroes refusing to serve in a Jim Crow army were imprisoned during World War II. Even black draft evasion remained low, with Negro registrants comprising only 4.4 per cent of Justice Department cases.[27] Negro acceptance of World War II appears to have stemmed not from any favorable commitment to it, but rather from the age-old patience of the Negro in tolerating the indignities of American society.

The war years witnessed the virtual disappearance of peace sentiment within the American working class. Morris Milgram, executive secretary of the Workers Defense League, informed peace workers bluntly in 1945 that pacifist activity in the labor movement was "almost non-existent." The few pacifists in positions of leadership within trade unions were almost all drained off to the Civilian Public Service (C.P.S.) camps and prisons during the war. He contended

---

(September, 1942), p. 67; Robert C. Weaver, "With the Negro's Help," *Atlantic Monthly*, CLXIX (June, 1942), 707. In January, 1943, a "Draftee's Prayer" appeared in a Negro newspaper:

> Dear Lord, today
> I go to war:
> To fight, to die,
> Tell me what for?
> Dear Lord, I'll fight,
> I do not fear,
> Germans or Japs;
> My fears are here.
> America!

Merze Tate, "The War Aims of World War I and World War II and Their Relation to the Darker Peoples of the World," *Journal of Negro Education*, XII (Summer, 1943), 530. Further evidence of Negro indifference to World War II is found in: Kenneth B. Clark, "Morale of Negroes on the Home Front: World Wars I and II," *Journal of Negro Education*, XII (Summer, 1943), 417–28; Adam C. Powell, Jr., "Is This a 'White Man's War'?" *Common Sense*, XI (April, 1942), 111–13; Roi Ottley, "A White Folks' War?" *Common Ground*, II (Spring, 1942), 28–31; P. L. Prattis, "The Morale of the Negro in the Armed Forces of the United States," *Journal of Negro Education*, XII (Summer, 1943), 355–63.

27 U.S. Selective Service System, *Selective Service and Victory*, p. 631; U.S. Selective Service System, *Conscientious Objection*, I, 143, 264. Other minority groups which contributed small numbers of C.O.'s were Puerto Rican Nationalists and American Indians. American Civil Liberties Union, *Conscience and the War: A Report on the Treatment of Conscientious Objectors in World War II*, pp. 40–41. Near the end of the war the F.O.R. executive committee, sensitive to pacifism's weakness among racial minorities, urged redoubled efforts to recruit them. "Minutes of Executive Committee Meeting, February 8, 1944," p. 2, FOR MSS, Box 3.

that "workers were sold on the war because of what they went through during the depression, and they wanted to support the administration which had given them some relief." The power of domestic policy approval in securing compliance with foreign policy was also stressed by A. J. Muste to explain labor's virtually complete endorsement of the war, symbolized by its no-strike pledge. As a result of labor's defection, pacifist groups were left without a lower class base. "It has become almost trite to point out that the FOR remains entirely too white and white collar," wrote the organization's West Coast field secretary. "The preponderance of upper and middle class persons . . . in our leadership and general membership make me seriously question whether the FOR as now constituted can ever accomplish a wholesale scaling of the racial and especially class walls which now enclose it." [28]

In contrast to the vanishing of lower class support, certain sectors of the middle class persisted as devoted adherents of pacifism in wartime. Over half the assignees to the Friends Civilian Public Service camps were of professional status, as compared with only 2.2 per cent of the inductees of the armed forces. The largest numbers represented were formerly employed as teachers and college instructors, social workers, artists, and actors. Two psychologists who measured the vocational interests of C.O.'s found that they tended to be "more interested in artistic and social service occupations . . . and distinctly less interested in . . . business" than non-pacifists of comparable age and education. Another psychological study of C.O.'s found them to be "idealists" and "radicals." Typical of this new breed of pacifist was Lowell Naeve, a twenty-four-year-old artist and former pupil of Diego Rivera, sentenced to prison for tearing up his draft card and mailing it to Secretary of War Stimson.[29]

The conjecture that the World War II pacifist constituency con-

[28] Morris Milgram, "Pacifist Activity in the Labor Movement" (February 1, 1945), FOR MSS, Box 6; Social Action News, Allen MSS, Section C4, Box 7; personal interview with A. J. Muste, June 2, 1966; Caleb Foote to A. J. Muste, John Nevin Sayre, and John Swomley, March 23, 1945, FOR MSS, Box 8. While about 46 per cent of Mennonite men inducted by Selective Service accepted alternative service, only 32 per cent of Mennonite factory workers and day laborers did so. Hershberger, The Mennonite Church in the Second World War, p. 45.
[29] Adrian E. Gory and David C. McClelland, "Characteristics of Conscientious Objectors in World War II," Journal of Consulting Psychology, XI

tained an inordinate number of middle class intellectuals is buttressed by examination of the educational level of C.O.'s While 89 per cent of the men in Friends C.P.S. had graduated from high school, only 24.4 per cent of the American population had done so. A significant 69 per cent of the same C.O.'s had attended college as compared with 10.1 per cent of the nation's population, 11 per cent of the army, and 7 per cent of the navy. In fact, 20.5 per cent of the men in Friends C.P.S. had done graduate work, as compared with .4 per cent of army inductees. Although 8.4 years of schooling was the median for the population of the United States, 96 per cent of the C.O.'s in Friends camps had received more than 8 years of education.[30]

Nor was this intellectual difference merely a matter of formal training; tests found pacifists registering considerably higher intelligence levels than comparable groups:

Table 1
*Comparative Standing of C.P.S. Assignees and Army Enlisted
Men in an Army Intelligence Test*

Army Grade	Percentage Army Men	Percentage C.P.S. Men
I	9.0	70.0
II	36.4	27.0
III	29.0	3.0
IV	17.0	0.0
V	8.6	0.0

Adapted from Gory and McClelland, "Characteristics of Conscientious Objectors," p. 250.

The exceptional strength of wartime pacifism among middle class intellectuals is not an easily explicable phenomenon. Most political

---

(September–October, 1947), 252–54; U.S. Selective Service System, *Selective Service and Victory*, p. 614; Ray R. Kelley and Paul E. Johnson, "Emotional Traits in Pacifists," *Journal of Social Psychology*, XXVIII (1948), 279–80. *Conscientious Objector*, August–September, 1941. Poet Robert Lowell was sentenced to a prison term for refusing induction in 1943. *Ibid.*, November, 1943.

[30] American Friends Service Committee, *Projects and Incentives*, p. 5; Gory and McClelland, "Characteristics of Conscientious Objectors," pp. 248–49; U.S. Selective Service System, *Selective Service and Victory*, p. 607. Among the Mennonites, college-educated draftees had a higher percentage of C.O.'s than any other educational level. Hershberger, *The Mennonite Church in the Second World War*, p. 43.

activists in American society have been middle class; but it may be the case that intellectuals are more immune than others in society to shifts of public opinion. They are not as subject to the influence of the mass media and have their own small-circulation journals of independent criticism and revolt. Relatively free of the danger of economic reprisal, and secure in their own communities, they find it easier than most other Americans to take positions of lonely dissent.[31] Moreover, many of the intellectuals were also radicals, and a number of left-wing organizations clung to a near-pacifist position throughout the war years.

When the United States entered the war, the various American socialist parties withheld their support. The Socialist Party, the largest and most influential of the group, was divided over the issue at its 1942 convention in Milwaukee. About half of the delegates wanted to go on record for "political non-support of the war," while the other half favored "critical support." The party finally adopted a compromise which tacitly permitted both positions, announcing that the Socialist Party "does not give its blessing to this war or any war." As Norman Thomas later recalled: "The result was that the party . . . never adopted a clear-cut statement of anything except general condemnation of wickedness." Despite the vagueness of the mandate, however, a significant number of Socialists became political objectors. The May Day, 1944, issue of the *Call* contained "greetings" from more than twenty Socialist C.P.S. groups, while a straw ballot of thirty-two Friends C.P.S. camps in 1944 gave Thomas 67 per cent of the vote.[32]

[31] The politically dissenting role of the intellectual in American society is explored in: Seymour Martin Lipset, *Political Man: The Social Bases of Politics*, pp. 310–43. C.O.'s were fairly welcome among educated people in wartime as compared with their acceptance among the less-educated strata in American life. Crespi, "Public Opinion toward Conscientious Objectors," pp. 217–22, 246–47, 249–50. An interesting parallel is the lonely steadfastness of middle class intellectuals in the Communist Party, even in its disastrous postwar years. For a probing analysis of the loyalty of the middle class to the Party, see: Nathan Glazer, *The Social Basis of American Communism*, pp. 130–68.

[32] N. M. Thomas, *What Is Our Destiny*, p. 11; Norman Thomas, COHC, p. 182; Shannon, *The Socialist Party of America*, p. 256; *New York Times*, June 2, 1942; *Conscientious Objector*, August and December, 1944; personal interview with Norman Thomas, October 4, 1966. Dwight Macdonald wrote: "This failure to split on the war issue has always seemed to me an indication of a certain lack of political seriousness in all the S.P. factions." Dwight Macdonald, "Thomas for President?" *Politics*, I (October, 1944), 279.

Socialists, anarchists, and humanitarian radicals opposed the war from a variety of motives. Ammon Hennacy, anarchist, tax refuser, and imprisoned C.O. during World War I, notified the United States District Attorney in May, 1942, that he would once again refuse to register for the draft. Citing Socrates, Christ, Thoreau, and Gandhi, he explained: "I speak for the time when all shall realize that they are Sons of God and brothers. When all the world is filled with hatred, this is the time when I must not be silent." Others, such as Milton Mayer, publicity director of the University of Chicago, argued that World War II was not a just war:

The Nazi purpose has always been fascism. We were so indifferent to it that we would not even admit its victims into our country before the war. We still will not admit them. We are still indifferent. Nor did we go to war with the Japanese fascists because their purpose was fascism. Far from it: we abetted their purpose for profit, and when we went to war with them it was not because their purpose was fascism; it was because they tried to steal from us what we had stolen forty-three years earlier from Spain. Our only announced purpose in this war, apart from the same old slogans is victory. Victory is not the same as justice.

Among the radical journals taking a non-interventionist position during the war were the *Call* and the *Progressive*.[33]

Stripped to little more than its pacifist hard core, the organized peace movement disintegrated. Especially hard hit were the umbrella organizations which maintained no memberships of their own, but rather depended upon the support of a war-weary public or on a coalition of peace-oriented but non-pacifist groups. The Keep America Out of War Congress and the Youth Committee Against War disappeared. The once prominent National Peace Conference faded away to meaninglessness upon the declaration of war because of the divergent positions of its constituent organizations. Consequently, it took no official stand on the war, but voted its support for "a just and enduring peace." By far the most dramatic demise was that of the N.C.P.W. As most of its supporting groups turned away to back the war, the organization could only depend

[33] Ammon Hennacy, *Autobiography of a Catholic Anarchist*, p. 57; Milton Mayer, *Conscience and the Commonwealth*, p. 18; Cole, *America First*, pp. 70–71. The outlook of American Trotskyites during World War II is expressed in: James P. Cannon, *Notebook of an Agitator*, pp. 127–42.

upon a handful of pacifist and minor religious societies. By the end of 1941 the facilities of the N.C.P.W. had been greatly reduced; for all intents and purposes, it was defunct by the end of World War II.[34]

Predictably, the "conservative" peace groups, which had spearheaded the drive for defense policies, did not hesitate to rally behind the government when war began. The day after Pearl Harbor, the trustees of the Carnegie Endowment condemned the Japanese attack and placed all its facilities at the disposal of the American government. United States agencies using the Endowment's facilities during the war years included the Department of State, Department of War, Lend-Lease Administration, National Resources Planning Board, Army Air Forces, Office of Strategic Services, and the Office of War Information. As in the first world conflict, the "conservative" peace groups consistently supported the government's war program.[35]

Maintaining its pacifist position undaunted by events, the W.I.L.P.F. lost about half its membership with American entry into the war. Dorothy Detzer wrote: "As pacifists, we can never yield our inalienable right to affirm and declare that war between nations or classes or races cannot permanently settle conflicts or heal the wounds that brought them into being." But other members were less sure of pacifism's soundness in a world at war. "We have lost members," reported the head of the W.I.L.P.F.'s Maryland Branch, "who, after years of loyal support of our work, came reluctantly to the conclusion that our attitude is no longer realistic." A major part of the membership as well as many of the most respected leaders of the American section remained absolute pacifists, including Dorothy Detzer, Dorothy Medders Robinson (president during the war years), and Hannah Clothier Hull (an influential Quaker and former president). Yet others, including Emily Greene Balch, who

[34] *Conscientious Objector*, February, 1942; Altbach, "The American Peace Movement," p. 38; "The National Peace Conference in a Second World War" (1942), FOR MSS, Box 10; Masland, "Pressure Groups and American Foreign Policy," p. 122n; file marked "Libby, Frederick," FOR MSS, Box 9; Jessie Wallace Hughan, "Our U.S.A. Movement since Pearl Harbor" (May 27, 1942), WRL MSS, Box 17.

[35] "A Brief Review of Thirty-Five Years of Service," p. 35; Jessie Wallace Hughan, "Our U.S.A. Movement since Pearl Harbor" (May 27, 1942), WRL MSS, Box 17.

was later to receive the Nobel Peace Prize, supported the war. "I realize that my position is neither very definite, nor very consistent," admitted Miss Balch; nevertheless, she was determined to persist in it and to remain active in the W.I.L.P.F., which is exactly what she did.[36]

Yet few withstood these tensions with Miss Balch's tenacity; most supporters of the war simply dropped out of the League. Although one member has written that the story of the war years was "a record of faith triumphantly kept," it was, in fact, being kept by a rather small group of intensely devoted women. At a general pacifist conference in February, 1946, Dorothy Detzer reported that the W.I.L.P.F., whose membership formerly totaled just under fifteen thousand, now had probably but one third of that. In that same year, when the first postwar international congress of the W.I.L.P.F. met in Luxembourg, dissolution of the organization was hotly debated by the delegates.[37] The W.I.L.P.F. emerged from the war considerably weakened in membership and influence.

The arrival of war found the Catholic Worker movement undaunted. "We are still pacifists," declared a *Catholic Worker* editorial. "Our manifesto is the Sermon on the Mount, which means that we will try to be peacemakers." Nevertheless, the commencement of hostilities initiated a decline in the movement. Many of its Houses of Hospitality were forced to close because of the C.P.S. system's drain on pacifist manpower, while the circulation of the newspaper dropped to half the former number. Readers of the *Catholic Worker* complained of its militant pacifism; union members, especially, found such ideas difficult to reconcile with their war industry employment. In 1940, with the passage of the Selective Service Act, *Pax* was transformed into the Association of Catholic Conscientious Objectors, "to develop a fellowship among Catholics

[36] Bussey and Tims, *Women's International League for Peace and Freedom*, p. 173; Dorothy Detzer, "Our Future Policies" (December 28, 1941), WILPF MSS, Box 11; "Report of the President for the Year 1941–42," Maryland Branch, W.I.L.P.F., WILPF MSS, Box 11; John Herman Randall, Jr., *Emily Greene Balch of New England: Citizen of the World*, p. 9; M. M. Randall, *Improper Bostonian*, pp. 349–51.

[37] M. M. Randall, *High Lights in W.I.L.P.F. History*, inside back cover; "Proceedings at Atlantic City Conference, February 12–14, 1946," Allen MSS, Section C4, Box 7; Bussey and Tims, *Women's International League for Peace and Freedom*, pp. 187–88.

who are conscientiously opposed to participation in modern war." It established forestry and hospital camps in New Hampshire, Illinois, and Maryland. The hard life endured by the men in these camps because of the Catholic Worker movement's precarious finances eventually led Selective Service to close them when their lack of an adequate food supply became painfully obvious.[38]

Paradoxically, as the broad front of peace organizations crumbled with American participation in World War II, the small pacifist groups mushroomed. By the end of the war, pacifists were at the apex of their organizational strength.[39] The income of the F.O.R. rose gradually over the war years from $60,000 in 1941 to $100,000 in 1945, while its membership reached a new high of slightly less than 15,000. In 1944 the F.O.R. had more than 20 paid staff members and 400 local chapters in the United States, as well as functioning groups in 125 of the 133 C.P.S. camps. After undertaking a field trip through the major American cities, the Reverend John Nevin Sayre reported that "the state of the F.O.R. appeared on the whole to be good." [40] He could have said "excellent." Like the F.O.R., the W.R.L. thrived during World War II. In 1939 the W.R.L. could count less than 900 "active" (dues-paying) members and an income of less than $5000. But war apparently quickened pacifist activity, for in 1945 the W.R.L. had more than 2300 active members, located primarily in New York City and several Eastern states, and an income of $20,000.[41]

[38] *Catholic Worker*, January, 1942; *ibid.*, March, 1942; Day, *Loaves and Fishes*, pp. 63–64; Day, *The Long Loneliness*, pp. 182, 258–59; Sheehan, *Peter Maurin*, pp. 127–28.

[39] Personal interview with A. J. Muste, June 2, 1966; Kirby Page, *Now Is the Time to Prevent a Third World War*, p. 160; Muste, *Not by Might*, p. 199; Bainton, *Christian Attitudes toward War and Peace*, p. 220.

[40] "Financial Report for 1941 to Members of the F.O.R.," *Fellowship*, VIII (January, 1942), 31; "Minutes of the Executive Committee Meeting, January 8, 1946," FOR MSS, Box 3; John M. Swomley, Jr., "Composite Staff Report" (September 23, 1944), FOR MSS, Box 3; "Membership Statistics" (1954), FOR MSS, Box 4; "Field Trip of John Nevin Sayre—New York to Mexico and Return, March 11 to April 21, 1944," FOR MSS, Box 3.

[41] Evan Thomas to contributors, December 26, 1944, WRL MSS, Box 3; "Minutes of Executive Committee Meeting, 12/26/45," WRL MSS, Box 2; *WRL News*, February 4, 1946, WRL MSS, Box 3; "Membership Summary, 1944" WRL MSS, Box 4; "Membership Inventory, December 31, 1942," WRL MSS, Box 4; also see file marked "Membership Committee, 1942–1947," WRL MSS, Box 4.

The phenomenon of pacifist growth amidst the wreckage of the larger peace movement appears to have resulted from the unique and uncomfortable position of the peace advocate in time of war. In peacetime the pacifist found himself in general accord with the professed ideals of his community. With the coming of war, however, he was increasingly isolated by hostile social pressure. He therefore sought out his pacifist brethren for encouragement in maintaining an otherwise exceptionally lonely stance. The Reverend E. Stanley Jones recalled that "when I saw that so many were slipping away from their pacifist stand . . . I decided I needed all the outer bolstering I could get to hold me to my declared convictions." In addition, with the arrival of conscription and war, the issue was joined; a decision for peace or war could not be avoided. While most chose war, those opting for peace were no longer satisfied with a vague expression of interest in a world without war. The "great influx in membership," the F.O.R. stated, "resulted from young people being forced to make up their minds about taking the pacifist position." Jones wrote that he "joined the Fellowship because, at this juncture, one cannot be equivocal." The president of the Federal Council of Churches, Dr. George A. Buttrick, became a member of the F.O.R. the day after Pearl Harbor.[42]

Solidification of a pacifist hard core, while comforting for the pacifist leadership, was not necessarily a sign of health in the peace movement. The coalescence of Thirties' converts in the wartime period indicated stabilization, not growth. As the F.O.R. noted in distress, "practically no new pacifists have been made all during the war years."[43] The scattered few still committed to peace had regrouped in pacifist cadres, but the peace movement's army had gone to war.

With the attack upon Pearl Harbor and the collapse of the organized peace movement, pacifist survivors were understandably less than eager for further conflict. "Pacifists . . . are a rather feeble

---

[42] Personal interview with Ralph DiGia, April 21, 1966; personal interview with A. J. Muste, June 2, 1966; E. Stanley Jones, "I Join the Fellowship," FOR MSS, Box 5; "Minutes of the Executive Committee Meeting, June 13, 1947," FOR MSS, Box 3.

[43] "Minutes of the Executive Committee Meeting, June 13, 1947," FOR MSS, Box 3.

folk," observed John Haynes Holmes in 1942, "feeble not only in numbers but in their capacity to do much in such a crisis." They could not end the war, he concluded, but "like a signpost, they can point the way in which men and nations may walk." Pacifists also felt inhibited by the "undemocratic" nature of any obstruction of the nation's war effort. "The people of our country—through their elected representatives—had spoken by a declaration of war," wrote Dorothy Detzer. "Therefore, in this terrible ordeal for our nation, we would do nothing which could circumvent the will of the people." Leaders of the Historic Peace Churches believed that, in wartime, they should stress the "positive" part of the pacifist program rather than "negative" opposition to the war—a witness to the way of love in a world of hate. Only a few, like Evan Thomas, the fiery new chairman of the W.R.L., raised the standard of full-scale revolt against war. "If one must dabble with labels such as positive and negative, constructive etc., I challenge many of those who are using these words all the time to show me wherein they are positive and constructive," he told A. J. Muste in 1942. "As a pacifist I want to end war and I want to bring it to the attention of the conscience and reason of my fellow men that war is the greatest evil of our time. Consequently I must do what I can to end it. . . . They seem to think that opposition to war is negative." [44]

By early 1943 the shock of Pearl Harbor had receded, and the peace movement reasserted itself to a moderate degree. Saturation bombing of European cities and the first American demands for unconditional surrender suddenly seemed to provide verification for the pacifist contention that war was but a euphemism for mass slaughter. A new restlessness swept the C.P.S. camps, clergymen criticized saturation bombing, and demands for immediate peace were first voiced.

In the Newark slums an ex-divinity student and Socialist, Dave Dellinger, and a handful of other revolutionary pacifists organized the People's Peace Now Committee to press for an immediate end to the war. Plans were laid for a militant, if modest, campaign. Thirty-five or forty pickets descended upon Washington, but, although

[44] Holmes, *Out of Darkness*, p. 84; Detzer, *Appointment on the Hill*, p. 239; Evan Thomas to A. J. Muste, February 10, 1942, FOR MSS, Box 11; John Haynes Holmes to Abraham Kaufmann, December 9, 1941, WRL MSS, Box 17.

police seized their signs and stopped the picketing, they were not arrested. The following weekend, members of the People's Peace Now Committee distributed leaflets in the slum areas of several cities demanding peace. This time many were arrested, ostensibly for their numerous, and very real, Selective Service violations. A small amount of assistance to this short-lived campaign was provided by the F.O.R. Answering the opposition of some staff members to the action, A. J. Muste argued that even if the picketing had no significance in stopping the war, it was, nevertheless, a prophetic witness that might stir up the movement.[45]

What was stirred up proved considerably less palatable to the pacifist leadership. In July, 1943, George W. Hartmann of the W.R.L. and a few other pacifists organized the Peace Now Movement. Unlike Dellinger's quasi-revolutionary committee, by this time defunct, the Peace Now Movement appealed to conservative elements of the America First type. Pacifists were horrified and, as the well-intentioned Dr. Hartmann sadly remarked, virtually "excommunicated" him from the fellowship. Pacifists could not "hesitate for a moment as to what the attitude is to be toward an organization whose leaders tried to get Harrison Spangler, Clare Hoffman, the Patterson-McCormick press interests, General Wood . . . to lead a movement for peace now," wrote A. J. Muste. "Actually to go to the ultranationalist and near fascist elements for support in a movement to end the war, seems to me to jeopardize the political effectiveness of pacifism in the profoundest sense." Pacifists wanted no links "with appeasement, ultranationalism, the Patterson-McCormick type of imperialism, labor baiting, etc." None of the peace groups supported or assisted the Peace Now Movement in any way.[46]

Actually, the organization proved far less dangerous than was

[45] Personal interview with Dave Dellinger, May 16, 1966; "Non-Violent Action Committee Meeting, June 12, 1943," FOR MSS, Box 5; John M. Swomley, Jr. to George Houser, April 5, 1943, Congress of Racial Equality Manuscripts, Swarthmore College Peace Collection (CORE MSS), Houser Correspondence.

[46] George W. Hartmann to A. J. Muste, September 15, 1943, FOR MSS, Box 20; A. J. Muste to Caleb Foote, May 9, 1944, FOR MSS, Box 8; A. J. Muste to Bishop William Appleton Lawrence, December 29, 1945, FOR MSS, Box 9; A. J. Muste to Shirley Walowitz, October 14, 1943, FOR MSS, Box 20; "Statement of F.O.R. Executive Committee" (January 25, 1944), FOR MSS, Box 3.

feared by pacifists, or by the House Committee on Un-American Activities, which labeled it "an un-American group" that was "clearly seditious," designed to "serve the interest of Goebbels' Nazi propaganda machine." The statement of purpose of the Peace Now Movement merely called upon "the United Nations, and especially the United States, [to] publish to the world fair and reasonable peace aims." The demerits of the organization seemed to have arisen not from intention but from choice of personnel. The Peace Now Movement's field secretary, for example, was a young Norwegian, John Collett, whom Muste feared to be mentally unbalanced and a possible Nazi agent. Subsequently arrested on a trip for the organization, Collett was involved in a crime, stated the Dies Committee report, "too disgusting to be recounted," which the New Republic later revealed to have consisted of climbing a tree overlooking a sorority house shower. Dr. Hartmann's trials were not over, for he was soon engaged in countless libel suits and investigations. George Hartmann is "a very nice guy," jibed civil liberties lawyer Morris Ernst, "but he certainly has no wisdom." [47]

Although pacifists kept their distance from the Peace Now Movement, a number remained very much concerned with halting the war raging about them. "When . . . I read in the Dies report that most pacifists are willing to do nothing but maintain a personal pacifist position during time of war," groaned Harrop Freeman, a pacifist lawyer, "I have to ask myself whether I am not a coward to fail to come out every day and say 'stop this awful slaughter now.'" The American Friends Service Committee sponsored commendable projects, one Quaker remarked, but why was it not peacemaking? With the defeat of Germany, the tempo of peace calls intensified. Fearful of the consequences of demands for unconditional surrender, the F.O.R. called upon the American government to "state publicly specific terms of settlement with Japan," while the W.R.L. pleaded for "An Immediate Settlement with Japan." Only an end to

[47] U.S. Congress, House Committee on Un-American Activities, Report on the Peace Now Movement, 78th Cong., 2d Sess., 1944, pp. 3–4; "General Statement of the Peace Now Movement," FOR MSS, Box 20; Helen Fuller, "Peace Now," New Republic, CX (February 14, 1944), 203–204; Morris Ernst to A. J. Muste, April 27, 1946, FOR MSS, Box 8; George W. Hartmann to Norman Thomas, November 1, 1944, Thomas MSS, Box 47.

the devastation of war, argued the F.O.R., would enable Americans to get to their real task of "healing the wounded, feeding the hungry, clothing the naked, [and] building homes for the homeless." [48]

Many other pacifists remained unconvinced of the wisdom of public demands for immediate peace. Their contention was not that a speedy end to the war was undesirable, but rather that in a society geared for war, prudence dictated silence. A campaign for immediate peace, argued Harry Emerson Fosdick, "would not only come to nothing; it would, I think, postpone the day of possible peace by the violence of the reaction it would arouse." It would "deprive the peace movement of a large part of the all too small influence it has today." [49]

But Fosdick was united with his more rebellious colleagues in their critique of Allied saturation bombing of European cities. In late 1943 the F.O.R. published a vigorous denunciation of this practice, *Massacre by Bombing*, written by the English pacifist Vera Brittain. This eloquent statement of twenty thousand words calling attention to the bombing of women and children, was signed by twenty-eight religious leaders and widely distributed in a plea for compassion toward noncombatants. "The response," Fosdick recalled, "was an outburst of vitriolic denunciation." The Reverend Daniel Poling called the appeal a "squawk" and accused the signers of being "mushy." Miss Brittain estimated that she was condemned in two hundred articles, while the *New York Times* reported letters arriving fifty to one opposed to the pacifist appeal. Support for an end to obliteration bombing came almost solely from Quaker and Roman Catholic newspapers. But one prominent internationalist, an ardent supporter of the war, privately told Fosdick, "Ten years from now almost everybody will be glad that someone said that." [50]

Unable to halt the course of the war, pacifists turned the bulk of

[48] Harrop Freeman to A. J. Muste, March 3, 1944, FOR MSS, Box 8; Dorothy Hutchinson, *A Call to Peace Now: A Message to the Society of Friends;* "V-E Day Statement, May 8, 1945," FOR MSS, Box 3; Theodore D. Walser, "An Immediate Settlement with Japan" (May 14, 1945), WRL MSS, Box 2.
[49] Harry Emerson Fosdick to A. J. Muste, April 27, 1944, FOR MSS, Box 8.
[50] Brittain, *The Rebel Passion*, p. 60; Fosdick, *The Living of These Days*, pp. 297–300; Harry Emerson Fosdick to A. J. Muste, February 23, 1944, FOR MSS, Box 8; George E. Hopkins, "Bombing and the American Conscience during World War II," *Historian*, XXVIII (May, 1966), 464–69.

their energies to mitigating its consequences. Peace groups worked in Congress to secure authorization to send shipments of food and relief supplies to famished European nations occupied by German troops. Although the plan made some headway in political circles, the Administration eventually decided to bury it, arguing that Germany should be made to bear the responsibility for the maintenance of her captive lands.[51]

Closely connected with this tentative project was the activity of the Historic Peace Churches in administering relief and rehabilitation programs both during and after the war. By 1942 the Mennonite Central Committee had provide over $300,000 in assistance to war-torn areas in France, Poland, India, China, and England, while the Brethren Service Committee sent relief workers and supplies to France and China. Originally, the peace churches had been training assignees in their camps for overseas work, but wartime hatred of C.O.'s induced Congressmen to attach a rider to an appropriation bill making this illegal. Despite these restrictions upon their activities, the Friends as of 1945 were operating the Friends Ambulance Unit in China, aiding in relief in India, caring for war victims in France, assisting the United Nations Relief and Rehabilitation Administration (U.N.R.R.A.) in the Mediterranean area, and working on problems of unemployment and race relations in the United States.[52]

Pacifists concentrated much of their attention upon racial and minority group problems. The plight of European refugees called forth efforts on the part of Emily Balch and the W.I.L.P.F. to assist them and to further their plans for immigration to the United States. Eventually, as a W.I.L.P.F.-supported bill to expand the number of refugees admitted to the country neared victory in Congress, the President accepted the plan and established the War Refugee Board

[51] Detzer, *Appointment on the Hill*, pp. 244–51; Clarence E. Pickett, "They Cry for Help!" *Peace Is the Victory*, ed. Harrop A. Freeman, pp. 88–106; Theodore Paullin, *Comparative Peace Plans*, p. 75.

[52] Hershberger, *War, Peace, and Nonresistance*, pp. 181–86; Clarence E. Pickett, *For More than Bread*, pp. 165–210, 219; American Friends Service Committee, *The Experience of the American Friends Service Committee in Civilian Public Service*, p. 5; American Friends Service Committee, *An Introduction to Friends Civilian Public Service*, p. 15; Hershberger, *The Mennonite Church in the Second World War*, pp. 194–218.

by Executive Order. The government's policy of internment camps for Japanese-Americans drew very bitter protests from the peace groups. "We are doing exactly the same thing as . . . Germany," bristled C. Read Cary of the A.F.S.C. The F.O.R.'s West Coast field secretary expressed his belief that "nothing could be more Hitlerian than this inhuman treatment of thousands of innocent people." Indeed, it was the head of a F.O.R. youth group, Gordon Hirabayashi, who brought the case for his people, unsuccessfully, to the Supreme Court. The W.I.L.P.F. and the A.F.S.C. were especially active in support of civil rights legislation, notably in the unsuccessful drive to abolish the poll tax and to create a permanent Fair Employment Practices Commission. "The problem of our time," asserted A. J. Muste, is "to build . . . an integrated family of mankind with all discriminations wiped out." [53]

Yet while humanitarian programs provided an outlet for "positive" pacifism, they also represented a partial retreat from militant opposition to war. Not only had public support for the cause of peace largely evaporated after 1941, but the tiny peace movement itself was showing marked signs of caution and conservatism. Unlike World War I, World War II met little resistance. In fact, the war might well have provided the *coup de grace* to this once-flourishing social cause. The issues and hopes of the interwar period had clearly run their course, leaving in their wake a series of broken pledges. Only a revolution seemed able to save the peace movement from extinction.

[53] J. H. Randall, *Emily Greene Balch*, p. 10; M. M. Randall, *Improper Bostonian*, pp. 356–59; Detzer, *Appointment on the Hill*, pp. 239–43; Pickett, *For More than Bread*, pp. 374–87; Mercedes M. Randall, *The Voice of Thy Brother's Blood: An Eleventh Hour Appeal to All Americans; Conscientious Objector*, July, 1942; Caleb Foote to A. J. Muste, January 31, 1942, FOR MSS, Box 8; Women's International League for Peace and Freedom, *The W.I.L. in Wartime;* A. J. Muste, *Wage Peace Now*, p. 19.

CHAPTER III

Men against the State

Many people think of pacifism as simply a withdrawal from conflict, a passive refusal to go along with the warmaking State. . . . Pacifism to me is primarily a way of actively struggling against injustice and inhumanity. . . . My kind of pacifism may be called "non-violent resistance."

DWIGHT MACDONALD, 1947[1]

War came as a rude shock to peace activists and left in its wake the depressing realization that traditional pacifism had failed to move nations from their violent course. For many in the pacifist hard core, especially within the peace churches, the war was simply another illustration of the "sinfulness" of this world, but for others it stimulated considerable self-criticism. Pacifist poet Kenneth Rexroth observed: "Many people . . . feel that orthodox pacifism in the US has very little sense of the reality of disaster which has swept over mankind, and is content to dodge the issues by clinging to a philosophy of life which is really only official interbellum propaganda of the Have Nations . . . Harding Pacifism, so to speak." Pacifists were in "a very compromising position," another pacifist admitted, with neither "the power to effectively resist the war on the one hand, nor to effectively resist fascism on the other." [2]

The dilemma of pacifists seeking a world of justice as well as love was particularly acute, for while they found no answer to their quest in war, they remained similarly dissatisfied with the passivity of traditional non-resistant pacifism. A Union Theological Seminary stu-

---

[1] Dwight Macdonald, "Why Destroy Draft Cards?" *Politics*, IV (March–April, 1947), 54–55.
[2] Kenneth Rexroth to A. J. Muste, October 16, 1942, FOR MSS, Box 16; George Houser, "Bases of Pacifism," *Pacifica Views*, II (July 28, 1944), 1–2.

dent, George Houser, imprisoned in Danbury Correctional Institution for refusal to register for the draft, wrote anxiously to A. J. Muste: "It seems to me that the time has definitely arrived for those of us who are opposed to war, and who favor the creation of a society with greater justice for all, to create a movement which can take us in that direction." The "political alternatives offered by majority groups in society" were obviously unsatisfactory, he noted. "We must raise up a movement based on non-violence as a method." [3]

Houser found a sympathetic correspondent in Muste. "I was not impressed with the sentimental, easygoing pacifism of the earlier part of the century," the secretary of the F.O.R. recalled. "People then felt that if they sat and talked pleasantly of peace and love, they would solve the problems of the world." Society was "in the midst of a revolution," Muste declared in 1942, and "the only chance that that revolution will really get somewhere and will not simply devolute into a general breakup of Western civilization, is that a non-violence movement should be built." Such a movement, he asserted, would have to "make effective contacts with oppressed and minority groups such as Negroes, share-croppers, [and] industrial workers." [4]

In early 1941 Muste assisted in the establishment of a "Non-Violent Direct Action Committee," which set up headquarters in a "Harlem ashram." About twenty New York pacifists met regularly, using Shridharani's War without Violence as a text. The chairman of the committee, the Reverend Jay Holmes Smith, who had been a member of an underworld gang until experiencing a religious conversion, had worked with Gandhi in India. "Efforts to prevent war, plus individual conscientious objection, plus works of mercy and reconstruction are indispensable but obviously inadequate," Smith wrote in a call for non-violence volunteers. "Total pacifism" necessitated "a new revolution, in which we seek to transform society by the method of non-violent action. . . . We envision the application of this method, developed by Mahatma Gandhi, to such areas of injustice and consequent conflict as race discrimination, denial of

[3] George Houser to A. J. Muste, June 11, 1941, FOR MSS, Box 17.
[4] Hentoff, Peace Agitator, p. 23; A. J. Muste to James Farmer, January 3, 1942, FOR MSS, Box 7; A. J. Muste, The World Task of Pacifism, p. 25.

civil liberties, exploitation of labor" and "any other entrenched social evil." Yet Smith's expectations far exceeded his leadership qualities, and this promising enterprise consequently came to naught.[5]

Race relations, Muste observed in 1942, was a field in which organizations existed that pacifists might enter to "play some such role as Gandhi and his satyagraha volunteers . . . played in the India National Congress." Several new members of the F.O.R. staff agreed. James Farmer, a recent graduate of Howard University's School of Religion, who worked as race relations secretary, was a vigorous proponent of pacifist action in the struggle for racial justice, as was Bayard Rustin, a young Negro Quaker employed as youth secretary, who would later succeed Farmer in the race relations post. They had their eyes particularly on A. Philip Randolph's burgeoning March on Washington Movement (M.O.W.), which in 1941 had wrung out of the Roosevelt Administration an Executive Order establishing the Fair Employment Practices Committee through the threat of a mass Negro protest in the nation's capital. Randolph, the dynamic president of the Brotherhood of Sleeping Car Porters, had been one of those to break with the Socialist Party in 1940 over the war issue, but he remained on close terms with pacifists because he found them more steadfast in their support of civil rights than his friends in the collective security camp. "I agree with your interpretation of Mrs. Roosevelt's statement that Negroes 'ought not to do too much demanding,' " he wrote bitterly to Muste. "If we don't demand now, when are we to demand? But it is apparent that the New Deal liberals are in retreat on every front."[6]

In late 1942 and 1943 Randolph—with the assistance of Farmer and Rustin, loaned to him by the F.O.R.—began to steer the March

[5] *Conscientious Objector*, February–March, 1941; Theodore Paullin, *Introduction to Non-Violence*, p. 2; "Memo #420 on J. Holmes Smith, September 7, 1944," FOR MSS, Box 10; J. Holmes Smith, "A Call for Non-Violent Volunteers" (February, 1942), FOR MSS, Box 5; A. J. Muste to Stanley Jones, July 3, 1942, FOR MSS, Box 8; Evan Thomas to A. J. Muste, September 13, 1943, FOR MSS, Box 11.

[6] A. J. Muste to James Farmer, January 3, 1942, FOR MSS, Box 7; James L. Farmer, Jr., "The Race Logic of Pacifism," *Fellowship*, VIII (January, 1942), 24–25; Bayard Rustin, "Non-Violence vs. Jim Crow," *Fellowship*, VIII (July, 1942), 120; Herbert Garfinkel, *When Negroes March: The March on Washington Movement in the Organizational Politics for FEPC*, pp. 27, 60–61; A. Philip Randolph to A. J. Muste, October 18, 1943, FOR MSS, Box 12.

on Washington Movement into Gandhian lines. His keynote address at a Detroit conference in September, 1942, gave the first indications of new emphases; in it, he called the Movement's attention to "the strategy and maneuver of the people of India with mass civil disobedience and non-cooperation." Rustin reported to Muste in February on a black conference in Columbus, Ohio: "A. Philip Randolph spoke in a way that convinced me that he is really concerned to develop an understanding and use of non-violence by the American Negro. *After the statements he made here, he is committed to follow thru,*" wrote the exultant young pacifist.[7]

Randolph did follow through; at the March on Washington Movement's first national convention in the summer of 1943, his opening address urged the audience of 1200 to adopt a policy of "non-violent good will direct action" for the organization. The following evening, Rustin spoke to the assemblage on the power of non-violence, while a session the next day, chaired by Dean William Nelson of Howard University, was devoted to its practical application. By the last day of the convention, the delegates had been taken by storm; the decision to adopt non-violent direct action tactics was unanimous. Projects were scheduled in the 26 cities of the nation with M.O.W. chapters.[8]

But pacifist hopes for non-violent resistance were again unfulfilled. The black press, relatively conservative, expressed its hostility. "The 'March on Washington' plan was bad enough," remarked the *Pittsburgh Courier,* "but alongside a call to civil disobedience, it seems quite sane." A newspaper poll found that Negroes rejected a "non-violent, civil disobedience campaign" by an almost three to one

[7] "March on Washington Movement: Proceedings of Conference Held in Detroit, September 26–27, 1942," FOR MSS, Box 21; "Minutes of Non-Violent Action Committee Meeting, January 25, 1943," FOR MSS, Box 5; Bayard Rustin to A. J. Muste, February 22, 1943, FOR MSS, Box 10. A. J. Muste was asked to deliver the opening address at the first national March on Washington Movement conference in 1943, but declined because of a previous engagement. His offer of pacifist material for Negro churches was gratefully accepted by Randolph, however, who remarked that "we are making a great drive among Negro ministers to win them over to the philosophy of non-violent solutions." A. Philip Randolph to A. J. Muste, May 25, 1943, FOR MSS, Box 21.

[8] John M. Swomley, Jr. to A. J. Muste, July 9, 1943, FOR MSS, Box 11; *Conscientious Objector,* August, 1943; Garfinkel, *When Negroes March,* pp. 135–37; J. Holmes Smith to A. J. Muste, July 8, 1943, FOR MSS, Box 21; personal interview with A. J. Muste, June 2, 1966.

ratio. Of even greater significance was the chilling effect of the 1943 Detroit race riot, which influential voices in the white community were quick to lay at the door of black protest. The Michigan Governor's committee investigating the riot blamed "the positive exhortation by many so-called responsible Negro leaders to be 'militant' in the struggle for racial equality." In case black leaders missed the point, the *New York Times* offered an article headlined: "CHICAGO CONVENTION DEFERS PROPOSED MASS APPEAL FOR REDRESS OF NEGRO GRIEVANCES, RACE TENSIONS RELIEVED, MOVEMENT HAD EXCITED FEARS OF OUTBREAK CLIMAXING FEELING FOLLOWING DETROIT RIOTS." The March on Washington Movement, already declining because of the war's dampening of Negro protest and because of conservative fears of Randolph's appeal to working class militancy, was moribund by 1944.[9]

But pacifist civil rights efforts were already meeting success elsewhere. In July, 1942, George Houser, now a F.O.R. staff member, reported to A. J. Muste that "there is another development in our Chicago action program about which you should know. . . . We have started our own committee." This Committee of Racial Equality (CORE) was "attempting to deal non-violently with cases of discrimination wherever they take place. . . . Just where everything will lead, we do not know," admitted Houser, "but sooner or later we are likely to hit upon something big." In the fall of 1941 a small number of Negro and white students from the University of Chicago and from local theological seminaries had begun meeting weekly on Saturday afternoons for discussions. Members of this group, composed primarily of pacifists, were greatly influenced in their conversations by the success of Gandhi's *satyagraha* campaigns. Concerned with racial tensions in their own community,

[9] Garfinkel, *When Negroes March*, pp. 47–124, 135–37, 144–46, 208; *New York Times*, July 4, 1943. Some Negro leaders later changed their minds about the direct action emphasis. The city editor of the Baltimore *Afro-American*, for example, who had been appalled by the idea of a non-violent resistance campaign when Rustin had met him at a M.O.W. conference, unexpectedly wrote to the F.O.R. leader: "Ever since I heard you . . . I have been thinking that what Baltimore needs is a non-violent, direct action campaign about which you spoke." He urged him to "lay the groundwork for such a campaign, in Baltimore." B. M. Phillips to Bayard Rustin, October 8, 1943, and Bayard Rustin to A. J. Muste, October 18, 1943, FOR MSS, Box 10.

they listened eagerly as James Farmer outlined a plan for the establishment of a non-violent direct action movement.[10]

In March, 1942, the students set up a preliminary organizing committee, which decided to experiment with a direct action project before continuing any further toward the formation of a new group. The White City Roller Rink in Chicago was chosen as the target area for an interracial team of twenty-four persons. Although the project failed to integrate the rink, it generated enthusiasm among the participants and among a number of others who heard of the experiment. Thus, on a Sunday afternoon in April, 1942, a group of fifty people met to form a permanent organization committed to the use of non-violent direct action in erasing racial discrimination. Bernice Fisher, a F.O.R. member, was appointed the first chairman. In June the name "Committee of Racial Equality" was adopted, primarily because "CORE" served both as a convenient abbreviation and as an indicator of the attempt to get at the roots of discrimination. Within the first year of its operation, CORE participated in sit-ins at two Chicago restaurants.[11]

Word of the activities of Chicago CORE spread rapidly to other cities, and the formation of new groups was spurred by organizing visits of James Farmer. When the Chicago group decided to hold a conference of local CORE organizations in June, 1943, delegates arrived from Baltimore, New York, Syracuse, Detroit, Colorado Springs, Columbus, Philadelphia, and Indianapolis. The convention voted to establish a loose federation and adopted Chicago CORE's constitution and statement of purpose. James Farmer was elected national chairman and Bernice Fisher secretary-treasurer. A second convention in June, 1944, changed the name to "Congress of Racial Equality." [12]

Technically, CORE was entirely independent of the F.O.R. As

[10] George Houser to A. J. Muste, July 13, 1942, FOR MSS, Box 8; George Houser, *CORE: A Brief History*, pp. 1–3; Carleton Mabee, "Evolution of Non-Violence," *Nation*, CXCIII (August 12, 1961), 78–79.

[11] Houser, *CORE*, pp. 3–6; Helen Buckler, "The CORE Way," *Survey Graphic*, XXXV (February, 1946), 50–51, 60.

[12] Houser, *CORE*, pp. 6–8; Report on the Third Annual CORE Convention, June, 1945 (July, 1945), CORE MSS; Buckler, "The CORE Way," pp. 50–51; George Houser to A. J. Muste, June 8, 1943, FOR MSS, Box 8.

Houser explained it: "We thought we could get a larger group of people in the work with an independent organization. . . . If the FOR name were attached to the group, it would tend to lessen the possibilities of expansion." Nevertheless, CORE remained under the protective wing of F.O.R. for many years. A. J. Muste served as its principal fund raiser, while George Houser, its executive secretary, operated the CORE national headquarters from his F.O.R. staff desk in New York. Attempting to define the relationship between the two groups, a F.O.R. memorandum in 1944 contended that CORE "is organizationally completely independent of F.O.R.," although "in practically every instance it is the F.O.R. members in a locality who have taken the initiative in forming the CORE groups and in carrying forward the CORE work." [13]

In wartime CORE chapters proved active in utilizing the new tools of social struggle. Despite Colorado's civil rights law, the larger movie theaters of Denver followed policies of racial discrimination until CORE sit-ins in 1943 brought them to an end. In Detroit a local CORE group confronted an all-white cafeteria with direct action tactics in the form of a non-cooperative standing line, and here, too, discriminatory practices collapsed. CORE activities in other cities yielded notable successes.[14]

Perhaps the most dramatic confrontation occurred in Chicago during the first national CORE convention. Chicago CORE, learning of racial discrimination at Stoner's, an upper middle class restaurant near the heart of the Loop section, had negotiated with the management, but to no avail. Thus, on an evening in June, 1943, sixty-five CORE members from the convention arrived to begin the project. White groups went inside first and were seated. After about half an hour of this infiltration, the first interracial group entered. Its members were ignored by the staff, but they stood at the front of the restaurant, waiting. Finally, after about half an hour, they were seated, Mr. Stoner, the owner, venting his irritation by kicking

[13] George Houser to John M. Swomley, Jr., July 1, 1943, FOR MSS, Box 8; personal interview with A. J. Muste, June 2, 1966; Hentoff, *Peace Agitator,* pp. 16–17; "Memo on CORE and Relation to F.O.R." (July 21, 1944), CORE MSS.
[14] James Peck, *Cracking the Color Line: Non-Violent Direct Action Methods of Eliminating Racial Discrimination,* p. 11; George Houser, *Erasing the Color Line,* pp. 15–17, 41–45.

George Houser in the shins. The second interracial group now entered; this time Stoner refused to seat them and restaurant business came to a halt. The police, called three times by Stoner, refused to make the expected arrests, and finally threatened to lock up Stoner if he bothered them again. Everyone in the restaurant, about two hundred persons, sat watching, while the CORE standees made plans to stay the night. Suddenly, an elderly white woman, unconnected with the demonstrators, stood up and asked one of the Negro girls if she would like to join her at her table. When she accepted, the seated white CORE members followed a similar policy until only two of the interracial group were left standing. Unexpectedly, the hostess stepped forward and escorted them to a table near the center of the dining room. Spontaneously, wild applause swept the restaurant, from CORE members and casual diners alike.[15] Here, at last, American pacifists found practical demonstration of the fact that their pacifism need not betray justice.

Not all pacifists, however, were pleased by CORE's militant tactics. One termed them "utterly unnecessary and highly undesirable," while CORE projects appeared to him as "futile and foolhardy experiments." A Southern college president on the F.O.R.'s national council objected to "what some of us feel is an unrealistic attitude toward the racial problems in the south." "Hasty actions of 'nonviolent' rebellion," warned a Southern lady active in the F.O.R., "would indeed . . . defeat our dearest interests." But most seem to have approved of the new pacifist venture in the field of civil rights, if only because they agreed with Bayard Rustin that "the issue of human rights takes many forms: race relations is one such form, and international relations is another, but beneath the formal differences these issues are really inseparable." [16]

While new directions in race relations were of great interest to many pacifists, a cause that struck closer to home for almost all

[15] J. Peck, *Cracking the Color Line*, pp. 1–4; George Houser to A. J. Muste, June 8, 1943, FOR MSS, Box 8; Houser, *Erasing the Color Line*, pp. 21–24; George Houser, "We Say No to Jim Crow," *Fellowship*, XI (April, 1945), 61–63.

[16] A. J. R. S. to John Haynes Holmes, August 11, 1944, FOR MSS, Box 8; N. C. M. to A. J. Muste, January 28, 1944, FOR MSS, Box 9; M. C. M. to A. J. Muste, July 12, 1943, FOR MSS, Box 9; Martin Oppenheimer and George Lakey, *A Manual for Direct Action*, p. x.

involved the rights of conscientious objectors. On January 10, 1940, apprehensive about the possibility of Congressional enactment of a draft law, the leaders of the Historic Peace Churches met with President Roosevelt to propose a program for C.O.'s. "We were in a dilemma," recalled Clarence Pickett of the A.F.S.C. "We were against conscription," but "were also concerned that any conscription measure adopted by our country should evince as much progress as possible in the way it dealt with conscientious objectors." They suggested the establishment of an alternative service program, under their direction, in which C.O.'s could perform work of a humanitarian nature. The A.F.S.C., as it later declared, "welcomed the opportunity in the midst of the war's destruction to render constructive national service through which it could promote human welfare, foster tolerance and goodwill, and contribute to the building of a free and peaceful world society." At the first conference the President seemed interested and agreeable.[17]

The actual establishment of the alternative service system, however, forced a number of compromises on the pacifist leaders. During Congressional hearings pacifist organizations, joined by the American Civil Liberties Union, sought enactment of provisions similar to those under the British law. In two important respects, however, the American law departed from the British precedent: it recognized conscientious objection solely on religious grounds and it failed to provide complete exemption for those who in good conscience could not accept compulsory government service. Section 5 (g) of the Selective Training and Service Act of 1940 simply declared that persons "by reason of religious training and belief" who were "conscientiously opposed to participation in war in any form" would be assigned "to work of national importance under civilian direction." In further conferences with President Roosevelt and with the Director of Selective Service, Clarence Dykstra, the former president of the University of Wisconsin, a series of Civilian Public Service camps under the direction of the Historic Peace Churches was agreed upon. Final plans were being worked out when, accord-

[17] Hershberger, *War, Peace, and Nonresistance*, pp. 166–67, 382–83; Pickett, *For More than Bread*, p. 311; American Friends Service Committee, *The Experience of the American Friends Service Committee in Civilian Public Service*, pp. 6–7; Philip E. Jacob, *The Origins of Civilian Public Service*; Bowman, *Church of the Brethren and War*, pp. 278–79.

ing to Clarence Pickett, the President suddenly expressed opposition to the proposed system and "advocated putting all the men to work under army direction." Frightened by this conversation, and fearful of what a Congressional appropriation for the camps might entail in the way of government or even military control, the leaders of the Historic Peace Churches agreed to assume all costs of the alternative service program. Thus, when the National Service Board for Religious Objectors (N.S.B.R.O.), representing the Historic Peace Churches and several other pacifist organizations, opened their Civilian Public Service camps in late 1940, several significant compromises were already embedded in the alternative service system.[18]

Nevertheless, at the time of its commencement the C.P.S. program drew the praise of almost all pacifists. The N.S.B.R.O. announced that pacifists now had "an opportunity to demonstrate . . . their faith in a different type of life." Quakers saw in the alternative service system a replication of the voluntary work camps which they had sponsored since 1920. Many of the men entering the program did so without realizing that they were in fact conscripts and under the ultimate authority of Selective Service; instead, they believed that they were about to embark upon a program of voluntary relief work under supervision of their pacifist peers. Only Evan Thomas, of all the pacifist leaders, expressed skepticism over the nature of alternative service. "There are worse places than jail under the circumstances," he told A. J. Muste. Muste did not agree. The responsibility of pacifism, he argued, "is to say to the world in Christ's name not only 'War is not the way,' but 'This is the way, walk ye in it.'" Most pacifists thought of the program, perhaps naively, as a service of love in a world at war.[19]

[18] U.S. Selective Service System, *Selective Service and Victory*, p. 177; American Civil Liberties Union, *Conscience and the War*, pp. 7–8; John W. Masland *et al.*, "Treatment of the Conscientious Objector under the Selective Service Act of 1940," *American Political Science Review*, XXXVI (August, 1942), 697–701; U.S. Congress, House, Committee on Military Affairs, *Compulsory Military Training and Service: Hearings on H.R. 10132*, 76th Cong., 3d Sess., 1940, p. 202; American Civil Liberties Union, *Liberty's National Emergency: The Story of Civil Liberty in the Crisis Year 1940–41*, p. 30; Pickett, *For More than Bread*, p. 320; Hershberger, *The Mennonite Church in the Second World War*, p. 50; Hershberger, *War, Peace, and Nonresistance*, pp. 168–69; Bowman, *Church of the Brethren and War*, p. 296.

[19] National Service Board for Religious Objectors, *The Conscientious Objector under the Selective Training and Service Act of 1940*, p. 9; R. Freeman, *Quakers and Peace*, p. 60; Mulford Q. Sibley and Philip E. Jacob, *Conscrip-*

In fact, the 12,000 pacifists in the 151 C.P.S. camps rendered the nation much valuable service between 1940 and 1946. C.O.'s put in over 8,000,000 man-days of free work for the United States, at an administrative cost to the Historic Peace Churches of well over $7,000,000. Much of the activity involved conservation and other endeavors of a fairly routine nature, but other employment entailed great sacrifice and risk-taking. Over 500 C.O.'s served as "guinea pigs": in typhus experiments, in which they wore lice-infested clothing; in jaundice research; in malaria research, in which C.P.S. volunteers were injected with the disease; in pneumonia research, in which they became infected by inhaling throat washings of persons who had the disease; and in nutrition research, in which C.O.'s were placed in conditions of starvation, extreme thirst, and extreme temperatures. More than 2000 C.O.'s worked as attendants in 41 mental hospitals and 17 schools for the mentally deficient, and were notably effective in developing methods of non-violent treatment of patients and in leading crusades for reforms in mental health facilities. "It may be regrettable that there should arise the necessity for the formation of such a group as the C.P.S.," wrote a state mental hospital director to Selective Service, "but . . . the group certainly was a godsend to us." [20]

And yet perhaps even more significant for the future of pacifism was the evolution of a widespread rebellion against the inadequacies of the C.P.S. system and against the traditional pacifists who administered it. The first of a series of disappointments arose when the assignees learned that the projects charted for them by Selective

tion of Conscience: The American State and the Conscientious Objector, 1940–1947, pp. 120–23; American Friends Service Committee, An Introduction to Friends Civilian Public Service, pp. 52–53; Hershberger, War, Peace, and Nonresistance, p. 244; Evan Thomas to A. J. Muste, October 29, 1940, FOR MSS, Box 11; Muste, World Task of Pacifism, pp. 32–40.

[20] U.S. Selective Service System, Conscientious Objection, I, 190, II, 279, 283–88; Pickett, For More than Bread, pp. 324–27; Melvin Gingerich, Service for Peace; Leslie Eisan, Pathways of Peace; Sibley and Jacob, Conscription of Conscience, pp. 134–40, 143–49, 538; American Friends Service Committee, The Experience of the American Friends Service Committee in Civilian Public Service, p. 9; New York Times, July 27, 1945; Harold S. Guetzkow and Paul H. Bowman, Men and Hunger; Frank Olmstead, They Asked for a Hard Job: CO's at Work in Mental Hospitals; Lowell E. Maechtle and Hans H. Gerth, "Conscientious Objectors as Mental Hospital Attendants," Sociology and Social Research, XXIX (September–October, 1944), 11–24.

Service were almost entirely in the field of rural conservation. C.O.'s engaged in "practically the same work the C.C.C. did," a Selective Service official explained to a Senate subcommittee. While forestry work may have utilized the skills of unemployed adolescents, pacifists found it considerably less suited to the older and better-educated C.P.S. population. The A.F.S.C. noted that of the 55 per cent of its men with professional training, 60 per cent were employed as unskilled laborers; another 30 per cent of its assignees had had skilled training, but 61 per cent of this group was similarly engaged in unskilled labor. "Civilian work is on the whole less satisfactory than the farm labor and reconstruction work of the first World War," noted the American Civil Liberties Union. Clarence Pickett recalled that C.O.'s in the A.F.S.C. camps "had been assigned to work which did not affect the wartime social emergencies of the nation and which could . . . have been largely suspended." Conscious of this fact, C.O.'s grew restless. "It had been necessary to struggle with a feeling of futility," recollected one camp assignee. "How can we be content day after day to manicure mountains," groaned another, "when the world has such crying need for practical real help and help that we want to give." [21]

The case of Dr. Don DeVault is illustrative of the rigidity of the C.P.S. system and of the gathering frustrations among C.O.'s. Assigned to digging ditches, DeVault, a research chemist and teacher at Stanford University with ten published papers, did research on penicillin molds in his spare time until dispatched to a special government camp for "rebellious" objectors. Here he continued his penicillin studies, which had reached a promising stage, and begged Selective Service to allow him time to complete them. Ordered to report for further dirt-shoveling, DeVault rebelled, announcing that he would work full time in his homemade laboratory at the camp; consequently, he was prosecuted and imprisoned. "If there is any sense in this wasting of a man's skills," declared the *Washington*

---

[21] U.S. Congress, Senate, Subcommittee of the Committee on Military Affairs, *Conscientious Objectors' Benefits*, 77th Cong., 2d Sess., 1942, p. 4; American Friends Service Committee, *Projects and Incentives*, p. 21; American Civil Liberties Union, *Conscience and the War*, p. 11; Pickett, *For More than Bread*, p. 329; Victor Chapin, *The Hill*, p. 5; Stephen G. Cary to A.F.S.C., July 29, 1942, quoted in Sibley and Jacob, *Conscription of Conscience*, p. 259.

Post, "we cannot see it. If there is any justice in this punishment of a man because of his conscience, it is beyond our discernment." [22]

Selective Service, however, despite a concession on the issue of work in mental hospitals, remained generally adamant in its narrow employment policies, making it perfectly clear to the C.P.S. assignees that their hopes for a humanitarian mission in a world at war were completely unfounded. "The program is not being carried on for the education or development of individuals to train groups for foreign service or future activities in the post-war period," Lieutenant-Colonel Franklin McLean of Selective Service explained in December, 1942. "There is no obligation to provide an assignee with work for which he has been particularly prepared, wishes to do, or regards as socially significant. Neither is there any intention of engaging in . . . the social welfare field," he continued. "The impression that camps are democracies to be run by the assignees is entirely erroneous." [23]

Further friction developed when C.P.S. assignees discovered that, unlike draftees into the armed forces, they would receive no wages and would thus be forced to support themselves and their families from their own resources. The situation was aggravated for C.O.'s by the fact that those drafted before Pearl Harbor, who had expected to serve but one year, now found themselves and their families plunged into destitution for the duration of the war. Although polls reported the public overwhelmingly in favor of providing remuneration for C.O.'s in government service, Selective Service vetoed all income proposals, apparently on the theory that pacifists would be deterred from accepting C.P.S. if it were made particularly intolerable. "Several things have helped" keep down the number of C.O.'s, General Hershey, the new Director of Selective Ser-

22 *Washington Post*, November 22, 1944.
23 American Civil Liberties Union, *Conscience and the War*, p. 25. The American Civil Liberties Union ascribed this rigidity to pressures by veterans' organizations. Indeed, Selective Service tacitly admitted that, as a result of pressure, it had not fully complied with the intent of the law. "While many Americans felt that the objector was entitled to the rights provided him in the 1940 law," it later wrote, "there were just as many who believed he was being treated as a member of a 'privileged class.' Consequently, additional projects were difficult to develop." American Civil Liberties Union, *Liberty on the Home Front*, p. 36; U.S. Selective Service System, *Conscientious Objection*, I, 168.

vice, told Congressmen, including "the fact that they get no pay, and that they have to be financed." Senator Mon Wallgren of Washington gasped: "You are treating these fellows worse than the Japs." Representative John Coffee of Washington observed: "A conscientious objector is granted legal standing by the Selective Service Act, but at the same time is fined, in effect, for his views." [24]

The unexpectedly military character of C.P.S. caused considerable resentment among assignees. Although Congress had declared that the Selective Service program was to be under civilian direction, C.O.'s noted the growing number of army officers in top administrative positions, the military appropriations for their salaries, the military awards for their part in C.P.S. administration, and the military rules for the camps themselves. The A.C.L.U. pointed with irritation to "the control of the camps and all Presidential appeals by military offices in Selective Service, apparently contrary to the express provisions of law." Congress settled the matter by amending the law to the effect that military officers directing Selective Service were to be regarded as working in a civilian capacity. No doubt this pleased the legal purists, but to the angry C.O.'s in alternative service, it was but one more proof that the Historic Peace Churches had sold them into bondage to the warmaking State. [25]

Had pacifists erred in compromising with conscription? As the nature of the C.P.S. system manifested itself, a flood of letters and resolutions poured forth from the camps charging that they had. "We consider conscription to be a process of involuntary servitude, which denies the freedom for occupational choice basic to democracy," read an open letter signed by a majority of the members of one camp. In a letter to "those concerned with CPS," David S. Richie, a member of the A.F.S.C. board of directors, wrote:

[24] American Friends Service Committee, *An Introduction to Friends Civilian Public Service*, p. 62; Crespi, "Public Opinion toward Conscientious Objectors," p. 289; National Service Board for Religious Objectors, *Congress Looks at the Conscientious Objector*, pp. 34, 56–57; U.S. Senate, Committee on Military Affairs, *Conscientious Objectors' Benefits*, p. 6; U.S. *Congressional Record*, 78th Cong., 2d Sess., 1944, XC, A654.

[25] Sibley and Jacob, *Conscription of Conscience*, p. 261; Hershberger, *War, Peace, and Nonresistance*, pp. 252–53; American Civil Liberties Union, *Liberty on the Home Front*, p. 38; American Civil Liberties Union, *Freedom in Wartime: A Report of the American Civil Liberties Union in the Second Year of War*, p. 37.

I believe that CPS does not represent a program promoted purely by the spirit of universal love. If so, there would be much more consequential work being done. . . . We have . . . assented to the right of the state . . . to take the individual out of the work he believes is right, as God gives him to see the right, in order to use him in whatever work the state determines. The fact that CPS is actually an aspect of military conscription and would not exist except for the decision on the part of the government to conscript for total war only makes our cooperation with the government program the more untenable. Our cooperation appears to me to be an almost traitorous denial of our basic faith.

In late 1942 a West Coast conference of C.P.S. campers resolved that "acceptance of conscription in C.P.S. has compromised our position as pacifists," while a young Quaker assistant director of a camp argued that "the Civilian Public Service program should be turned over to its rightful owner, the state." [26]

As rebellion brewed in the camps, Selective Service aggravated pacifist fears that C.P.S. was not a "service of love," but an integral part of military authoritarianism. A Selective Service memorandum announced that "from the time an assignee reports to camp until he is finally released he is under control of the Director of Selective Service. He ceases to be a free agent and is accountable for all of his time, in camp and out, 24 hours a day. His movements, actions and conduct are subject to control and regulation." Furthermore, "he ceases to have certain rights and is granted privileges instead. These privileges can be restricted or withdrawn without his approval or consent as punishment, during emergencies or as a matter of policy." As one pacifist rather aptly observed, C.P.S. seemed to hinge on the theory that "the individual is at the government's disposal." [27]

[26] "Open Letter from Camp #14," August 12, 1942, FOR MSS, Box 14; *Action* (October 5, 1943), Allen MSS, Section C4, Box 7; "West Coast C.P.S. Conference" (October 8, 9, 10, 11, 1942), FOR MSS, Box 6; Denny Wilcher, "Shall the C.P.S. Camps Continue?" *Christian Century*, LIX (December 16, 1942), 1558. One C.P.S. camper complained to interviewers: "Nothing is significant under conscription. The great loss is individual, voluntary action. Coerced sacrifice is no sacrifice." H. Otto Dahlke, "Values and Group Behavior in Two Camps for Conscientious Objectors," *American Journal of Sociology*, LI (July, 1945), 27. A young historian in one of the camps extensively compared Negro bondage in the antebellum South with C.P.S. and concluded that "the parallels between C.P.S. and slavery are clear." Arthur A. Ekirch, Jr., "C.P.S. and Slavery," *Pacifica Views*, II (August 25, 1944), 1, 4.

[27] American Civil Liberties Union, *Conscience and the War*, pp. 22–23; Weinberg, *Instead of Violence*, p. 137.

The very process of conscientious objection in a nation at war tended to exclude all but the strongly individualistic from pacifist ranks, except among followers of the Historic Peace Churches, and consequently a rebellion against the heavy-handed bureaucratic authority that plagued C.P.S. was almost inevitable. Walkouts from the camps began in 1942. "CPS is a compromise I cannot tolerate," announced a departing C.O., George Kingsley, on the second anniversary of the Selective Service law; "it is an insignificant witness against war and conscription." Joining him was Lewis Taylor, who told his fellow pacifists that "this program does not permit us to realize the social responsibilities that brought us here." Francis Bates, a C.O. at the C.P.S. camp in Stoddard, New Hampshire, left with a message for General Hershey: "Conscription is fundamentally wrong and an evil I can no longer cooperate with or submit to." It "violates man's rights, interferes with his God given vocation, robs him of the merit or consequences of a voluntary act, and makes of him a slave." He went on to "acknowledge my share in the guilt of having submitted to it." Paton Price of the F.O.R., another who walked out, stated that "the Peace Churches have entered a field in which they obviously have no business: that of administering a portion of the military program." C.P.S., he contended, "should be quickly abandoned as a hapless error." After three years in C.P.S., Corbett Bishop left his camp and journeyed to Washington, where he informed Selective Service, the Department of Justice, and the Federal Prison Bureau that he had ceased cooperation with them. He announced in a postcard to the F.O.R.: "I plan to receive the State as the tyrant it is, non-violently, non-cooperatively and non-servilely." [28]

The walkouts, begun spontaneously by a few individuals, soon assumed larger proportions. "Hardly a day passes when this paper does not receive from some conscientious objector a statement giving his reasons for choosing to go to prison rather than . . . work in a Civilian Public Service Camp," reported the *Christian Century*. Pacifist Denny Wilcher told readers of the journal in 1944 that "at

[28] *Conscientious Objector*, November, 1942, January, 1943, and October, 1944; Mulford Q. Sibley and Ada Wardlaw, *Conscientious Objectors in Prison, 1940–1945*, pp. 18–19; *Catholic Worker*, May, 1942; Corbett Bishop to A. J. Muste and John M. Swomley, Jr., July 3, 1944, FOR MSS, Box 14.

least one hundred men" had ceased cooperation with the church camps, among them "some of the most sensitive men in the peace movement." Evan Thomas rejoiced that pacifists no longer evaded the "issue of coercion." C.O.'s who chose prison, he wrote, "are rendering a great service to the struggle for freedom in America and the entire world." But the C.O.'s involved also took comfort in the new pattern of action rapidly evolving. "Western pacifism has too long depended on individual conscience," read a statement by seven pacifists, about to leave their camp. "We must now develop group non-violent action to effectively build a peaceful society." [29]

Resistant C.O.'s who remained in the camps set about sabotaging the system. "Forced labor," they contended, "can be made to be the world's most inefficient way of getting work done." The Germfask, Michigan, C.P.S. camp, one of the experimental government-operated camps established for men who would not work under the direction of the Historic Peace Churches, was the site of a particularly dramatic program of non-cooperation. Pacifists "were often quite adept when trying to 'botch their jobs,'" recalled Selective Service. "They carried dirt with shovels by spoonful-sized loads. Or they required a separate order for each movement on a job." Government officials noted that to get an assignee to chop down a tree, "it was necessary to order every blow, every withdrawal of the ax, and point to the exact spot the ax was to fall each time," while "the men would drive staples on the fencing project, not over the wire but beside it, above or below it . . . putting in 50 staples when one would have done the trick." According to Selective Service, C.O.'s "made life as miserable as possible for the supervisory personnel, thinking they would quit and the camp would eventually break up." Germfask exhausted five cooks, four camp managers ("not counting the one who stayed only a half day"), two project superintendents, three foremen, and five doctors. Campers ritually reported in as sick, and about four thousand of the twenty thousand man-days of the camp were consumed by alleged illness. The project superintendent recalled the "assignees' sense of humor" in planning concurrent sick-

29 "Pacifists Prefer Prison," *Christian Century*, LXI (January 26, 1944), 100–101; Denny Wilcher, "Conscientious Objectors in Prison," *Christian Century*, LXI (March 8, 1944), 302; Evan W. Thomas, *The Way to Freedom*, pp. 23–25, 30; *Conscientious Objector*, July, 1943.

nesses of men whose last names began with the same letters of the alphabet.

Of the twenty thousand man-days put in on the Germfask C.P.S. project, work consumed less than one fifth. Moreover, about one third of this project labor was devoted to cutting "2 miles of roadside brush," most of which "was done by the foremen in charge." Overall, concluded the wretched project superintendent, "the relative efficiency of the objector labor (plus the help of the working foremen) was one-twelfth." Potentially, "the group had the makings of a very fine community," he reported, citing the large numbers of "engineers, artists, professors, lawyers and what not." Actually, though, "these dormant talents were to be exercised in raising Hell." As one pacifist journal reported, "no socially conscious CPS man wishes to make this conscript system an extraordinary success, for he can no longer assume that it is an honest program." Slowdowns were illustrative of a "growing feeling that the increasingly irresponsible power of the State is a Very Bad Thing." Eventually, twenty-two objectors at Germfask were sentenced to federal prison terms and twenty-one were discharged for varying reasons. The bewildered project superintendent claimed that "no one who has not been closely associated with them for a substantial period of time could believe that such people could exist outside an insane asylum." [30]

Yet while the walkout and the slowdown had their devotees among outraged C.P.S. campers, by far the most popular and effective resistance tactic developed was complete non-cooperation, drawing its inspiration from both Gandhi and the labor struggles of the Thirties. Early direct action was on a small scale and sporadic. At the Quaker camp in Cooperstown, New York, the announcement by Selective Service of an increase in hours brought on a strike of five men in March, 1943. Armenag James Manoukian, assigned to a government camp in Mancos, Colorado, refused to labor for the State. "To perform this work without pay," he argued, "is to accede to the principle of slave labor." Twenty-eight men at the camp joined in a fast and fourteen began a work strike. In 1944 C.O.'s

[30] Sibley and Jacob, *Conscription of Conscience*, pp. 274–77; U.S. Selective Service System, *Conscientious Objection*, I, 232–40; George B. Reeves, *Men against the State*, pp. 12–14; " 'War Without Violence,' " *Pacifica Views*, II (May 25, 1945), 1–2, 4.

organized the "CPS Union" to protect the "rights" of assignees. Five hundred members joined in sixty-four camps and units, forming seventeen locals. Selective Service refused to recognize the union, of course, and exhibited an attitude of uneasy hostility toward its increasingly rebellious wards.[31]

The shaky situation broke open six months after the end of the war, when their continued incarceration, despite the release of military draftees, convinced many C.O.'s that Selective Service indeed regarded them as slave laborers. In February, 1946, assignees at a camp in Glendora, California, addressed an open letter to the new government managers of their camp. "We are concerned, not so much for ourselves who have been enslaved," they wrote, "but because CPS threatens the democratic society we know." They chronicled the growing sense of frustration and rebellion. "For several years we in Glendora have done as little work as possible because we did not like being slaves. During the last year, however, we have come to see clearly the threat CPS offers to society." They now felt "a responsibility to our country and to mankind to make a totalitarian-breeding system unsuccessful. . . . Our goal is not to fight you; our goal is to destroy CPS." In an aside to C.O.'s, the rebels charged that "the greatest difficulty that we pacifists have is that we are apt to talk and have meetings rather than act." The time had come, they proclaimed, for "RESISTANCE NOW!" [32]

Resistance began on April 24, when in response to the transfer of two leading C.O. agitators to another camp, twenty-five Glendora assignees began a work strike. As time passed, the strike widened, until by the middle of the following month eighty-two assignees at the camp had ceased all cooperation with the system. During this period, organized non-violent resistance began in the C.P.S. camps at: Cascade Locks, Oregon; Three Rivers and Minersville, California; Mesa, Arizona; Philadelphia, Pennsylvania; Gatlinburg, Tennessee; Bowie, Maryland; and Lapine, Oregon. In Big Flats, New York, forty C.O.'s refused to perform assigned duties after May 1.

31 Hershberger, *War, Peace, and Nonresistance*, p. 254; "The Manoukian Case," *Pacifica Views*, I (September 10, 1943), 2; Reeves, *Men against the State*, pp. 11–12; Sibley and Jacob, *Conscription of Conscience*, pp. 269–72; *Conscientious Objector*, November, 1944.

32 U.S. Selective Service System, *Conscientious Objection*, I, 244–45.

"That there is a growing resistance movement developing within CPS cannot be questioned," a pacifist observer reported. Discipline broke down completely at Glendora, where C.O.'s passed their time sending relief packages to Europe, mailing 3575 pounds of food in the first month. Rebellious strikers roamed the camps, lustily singing to the tune of "Pistol Packin' Mama":

> We labored lo! these many years
> For all those hazy goals;
> The Forest Service got our sweat
> And the Brethren got our souls.
>
> Break the system down, boys
> Strike the lick that does the trick
> And break the system down. [33]

The wave of non-cooperation found Selective Service unexpectedly helpless. On May 18, 1946, six C.O.'s were arrested. When others merely heightened their opposition, another fifty-one were arrested at Glendora on May 27, and six at Big Flats. But all attempts at discipline failed to move the unruly pacifists, now gaining their first exhilarating experience in the power of non-violent action. Only the promise of discharges within two weeks persuaded some of the men to return to work. The fate of the arrested C.P.S. strikers remained uncertain until March, 1947, when twenty-two of them were tried, convicted, and given suspended sentences.[34]

Although the activities of novice *satyagrahis* in C.P.S. provided a source for considerable discussion within pacifist ranks, the effect of their revolt upon American life should not be overestimated. Indeed, secreted away in geographically isolated camps, competing with the dramatic events of the war, and receiving virtually no publicity from the mass media, the activists created scarcely a ripple in public opinion. Outside pacifist circles only a few harried government offi-

---

[33] *Ibid.*, I, 245–46; *Conscientious Objector*, June, 1946; Sibley and Jacob, *Conscription of Conscience*, p. 272; Herbert Wehrly, "CPS Resistance," *Pacifica Views*, III (May 24, 1946), 1; "The C.P.S. Strikes," *Politics*, III (July, 1946), 177–80; "Statement of Aims of Assignees Striking at Civilian Public Service Camp #76, Glendora, California, April 30, 1946," FOR MSS, Box 13.

[34] U.S. Selective Service System, *Conscientious Objection*, I, 246–47; Sibley and Jacob, *Conscription of Conscience*, pp. 272–73, 339; American Civil Liberties Union, *In Times of Challenge: U.S. Liberties, 1946–47*, p. 54.

cials were aware of their existence. When C.O.'s received attention at all in wartime, it was generally to mention what a fine job they did in the army medical corps, as "guinea pigs" in medical experiments, and occasionally in the camps.[35]

Nor was this playing down of pacifist rebellion merely a product of the tastemakers' wartime discretion; most pacifists did not rebel or follow the lead of the new radicals, but dug many a fine ditch for Selective Service between 1940 and 1947. The Historic Peace Churches proved particularly acquiescent, cheerfully ready to "walk the second mile." Mennonites, with their philosophy of non-resistance that accepted suffering as a logical concomitant of this world, posed no threat to the alternative service system. One of their camp newspapers contained an editorial declaring: "Civilian Public Service is a privilege! . . . We intend to serve our country to the best of our ability. And we intend to do that without the unjustified grumbling and complaining that has been evidenced among some conscientious objectors." A bit more dissent occasionally crept into Brethren and Quaker pronouncements, and the A.F.S.C., after a crisis of conscience, eventually withdrew from administrative responsibility under the alternative service program; nevertheless, for most of the war, their position was virtually indistinguishable from that of the Mennonites. The A.F.S.C. lauded C.P.S. as "a positive approach" which "places the emphasis on service rather than on the negative element of protest and objection." Pacifism's luminaries consistently supported policies of cooperation with Selective Service. "Our job is to take things as they are, thank God that so much has

[35] General Hershey explained in 1943 to the Senate Military Affairs Committee that "the conscientious objector, by my theory, is best handled if no one hears of him." In 1944 the American Civil Liberties Union wrote angrily of the general's "determination to continue" keeping "those in civilian service out of sight in the work camps. . . . Selective Service evidently figures that the less public notice of objectors the better." The A.C.L.U. observed that publicity affecting C.O.'s was "on the whole favorable," describing guinea-pig experiments and other feats of courage. "But publicity as to the injustices inherent in the system," it noted, "has been difficult to get, even in liberal journals." National Service Board for Religious Objectors, *Congress Looks at the Conscientious Objector*, p. 61; American Civil Liberties Union, *In Defense of Our Liberties: A Report of the American Civil Liberties Union in the Third Year of the War*, p. 35; American Civil Liberties Union, *Liberty on the Home Front*, p. 40.

actually been won," remarked John Haynes Holmes. But "if the present situation goes on much longer," he warned, "we are going to lose everything." [36]

The radicals, drawn in good part from the ranks of political objectors, traditionally non-pacifist denominations, and even atheists within the generation of C.O.'s activated by the draft, were bitter at what they regarded as betrayal by the older "Pacifist Establishment." One of these rebels explained that they found themselves quite unlike "more conservative, more quietistic pacifists. Indeed they feel that they have far more in common with certain non-pacifist radicals and progressives." The point at issue, he contended, was whether "pacifism" or "non-violent 'revolutionism'" would serve as the "touchstone." If the latter, "clearly we cannot maintain effective unity with otherwise 'reactionary' pacifists." The peace churches' compromise on conscription was bitterly attacked. "If you represent the church," a young man told an elder statesman of the Historic Peace Churches, "we have no use for the church. Your chief concern is to enforce a military conscription law." Joining the militants was Bayard Rustin, who scored the pacifist leadership for cooperating with the government in the execution of conscription and himself refused to enter C.P.S. Even A. J. Muste, as a member of the wrong generation and an early supporter of C.P.S., was thought to be too concerned with prestige and the regard of men in high places; only Evan Thomas, of all the recognized pacifist spokesmen, drew the respect and admiration of the Young Turks.[37]

[36] Hershberger, War, Peace, and Nonresistance, pp. 235–40; American Friends Service Committee, An Introduction to Friends Civilian Public Service, p. 30; John Haynes Holmes to Frank Olmstead, December 16, 1942, FOR MSS, Box 8. The official Brethren church magazine affirmed that "the vast majority of the men in C.P.S. . . . are now rendering greater service to humanity than they were in their pre-induction occupations," while a report of the Brethren Service Committee claimed that C.P.S. was "the most outstanding protest in the United States against military service and against war." Hershberger, War, Peace, and Nonresistance, pp. 341–43; Sibley and Jacob, Conscription of Conscience, p. 325.

[37] Personal interview with Dave Dellinger, May 16, 1966; personal interview with Ralph DiGia, April 21, 1966; Roy Finch to A. J. Muste, May 20, 1944, FOR MSS, Box 7; Frank Olmstead, "The HPC and the CO," WRL MSS, Box 3; Conscientious Objector, November, 1942. "One unique problem fraught with somber difficulty is the prospect of seeing, talking with, working with,

But despite the barriers separating the militants from the traditional pacifist movement, the experience with non-violent struggles in C.P.S. added a new and vital element to that movement's dimensions. In future years, many in the older generation would catch up and those in the new one would mellow; yet in the meantime the groundwork for a new tradition in American life had been laid. "It is no longer necessary to look to India for examples of successful non-violent resistance to tyranny," commented a pacifist at the end of the war. "We can look right here in America at what has happened in the . . . camps." [38]

Paralleling the fermentation in C.P.S. was a program of resistance that developed in prison. During World War II, every sixth man in the federal prisons was a C.O. These incarcerated pacifists, comprising about 15 per cent of the World War II C.O. population, were of three types: Jehovah's Witnesses, who refused any classification other than ministerial exemption; men unable to qualify for C.P.S. either because of the narrowness of the legal provisions or due to an error in enforcement of the law on the part of the authorities; and those Americans opposed to conscription itself, including non-registrants and C.P.S. walkouts. [39]

Many of the opponents of conscription chose prison in an attempt

---

and even eating at the same table with Quakers," wrote one of the C.P.S. radicals with tongue in cheek. A policy of "Jim Quake" might be "misunderstood," he remarked, but he equally rejected the contention that "Quakers should be treated just like everyone else—even to the point of intermarriage." He urged, instead, a "Middle Way," a "dramatic demonstration that C.O.'s can conciliate themselves with all mankind—even Quakers." Wallace Hamilton, "Jim Quake," *Pacifica Views,* III (June 15, 1945), 2. But fiction was no stranger than fact. One C.O. wrote frankly in another pacifist journal: "In this camp it is literally an emotional strain to be associated with the Friends or the Service Committee. Enough people in the camp feel distrust and resentment toward them that we are constantly aware of the feeling." "An Open Letter to Friends," Newsletter of Civilian Public Service Camp 53, Gorham, New Hampshire (April 15, 1943), Allen MSS, Section C4, Box 7. Pacifist Julius Eichel angrily rejected Holmes' plea. "Conscription for any purpose can be justified only by despots or individuals with a slave psychology," he retorted. "Dr. Holmes and Conscription," *Fellowship,* IX (February, 1943), 39.

[38] George B. Reeves, "It Happened Here," *Pacifica Views,* III (September 21, 1945), 1.

[39] American Friends Service Committee, *The Experience of the American Friends Service Committee in Civilian Public Service,* p. 11; American Civil Liberties Union, *In Defense of Our Liberties,* p. 9; U.S. Bureau of Prisons, *Federal Prisons, 1944,* pp. 40–41.

to safeguard their freedom of conscience, much as Thoreau had done a century before. "Prison seems to be the mother of civil rights," wrote one pacifist. "As long as the state defines conscience, prison becomes a place where conscience can be maintained." Another perceived their sojourn behind bars as following directly in the American tradition of civil disobedience: "Thoreau spoke truly when he said, 'under a government which imprisons any unjustly, the true place for a just man is also a prison.'" Out from under the demoralizing wing of the peace churches, and in direct confrontation with their antagonist, the State, pacifists underwent a curious surge of exhilaration. "The authorities have the power to seize my body," wrote Corbett Bishop upon his departure from a C.P.S. camp, but "that is all they can do—my spirit will be free." [40]

Yet, ironically, following the demands of conscience and rejecting the claims of the State, pacifists were placed in the maw of an even more thorough system of institutionalized coercion than they found on the "outside." Nothing in this country "could be so totalitarian as the prison system," noted a young C.O. Others, grown skeptical of government intentions, were not so sure. "For those who want a preview of the American police state in action," wrote an imprisoned C.O., "thirty-two Federal correctional and penal institutions offer unlimited research facilities." One pacifist found his experience "the most perfect expression of the full implications of Statism. In the Prison the population is subjected to the type of control that State functionaries aspire to impose on the population 'at large.'" In such a context resistance had a positive role, pacifists concluded, for it maintained individual values in the face of authoritarian dehumanization. The importance of resistance, noted two pacifists, "lies not so much in the end to be attained, as in the act itself. It is one way, and in some cases, the only one, in which the individual can assert himself as an individual . . . rather than remain a mere ob-

---

[40] "Extracts from Letters Written by Roger Axford from Federal Correctional Institution, Milan, Michigan, August 17, 1944," FOR MSS, Box 7; George Reeves, "Why They Went to Prison," *Pacifica Views*, I (April 7, 1944), 4; *Conscientious Objector*, October, 1944; Sibley and Jacob, *Conscription of Conscience*, p. 360. Debs maintained a similar outlook toward his "time" during World War I: "I was never more free in my life, so far as my spirit was concerned, than I was in that prison cell." Eugene V. Debs, *Walls and Bars*, p. 70.

ject." [41] Not all imprisoned C.O.'s held such markedly existential views, but it would surely have been surprising to find these most uncompromising of pacifists deterred from obeying their social consciences at the behest of the State, even in prison.

The first act of organized resistance occurred in Danbury Correctional Institution on April 23, 1941, when sixteen prisoners, having had permission withdrawn by the warden to abstain from lunch to hold an antiwar demonstration, refused to report for work or obey the prison routine. The pacifists were immediately placed in solitary confinement, only to be freed after a short time because the warden desperately needed the pitching abilities of one of the incarcerated C.O.'s to bolster his prison baseball team. When the released strikers returned together to the prison dining hall, the reception by the other prisoners was tumultuous. [42]

Despite isolated acts of non-cooperation, planned pacifist resistance did not break out into the open again until early 1943. On February 12, Stanley Murphy and Lewis Taylor, two C.P.S. walkouts, began a spectacular "fast unto death" in Danbury against the terms afforded C.O.'s under the Selective Service Act. After the eighteenth day, prison officials force-fed the men by tube, keeping them tightly wrapped in sheets to prevent self-induced vomiting, but their fast and absolute non-cooperation continued for eighty-two days. Many pacifists were electrified by the action. At first, Lowell Naeve "couldn't see any sense to the idea," but "the more I thought about it the more I became convinced that their hunger strike was doing more for the men in jail than anything else." Naeve resolved to return to prison to join them, for "it appeared to me we had in a group of hunger-strikers our only way to freedom." Murphy and

[41] Charles R. Swift, III, *Prison Routine*, p. 9; Clif Bennett, "Resistance in Prison," *Prison Etiquette: The Convict's Compendium of Useful Information*, ed. Holley Cantine and Dachine Rainer, p. 3; "Introduction" to Cantine and Rainer, *Prison Etiquette*, n.p. Two pacifists contend that "surely it was slightly unreasonable to expect them to 'adjust' themselves to the abnormal life of a prison when they had, quite obviously, been unwilling to adjust themselves to certain aspects of the society outside." Sibley and Wardlaw, *Conscientious Objectors in Prison*, pp. 65–66.

[42] Howard Schoenfeld, "The Danbury Story," *Prison Etiquette*, pp. 12–26; Sibley and Wardlaw, *Conscientious Objectors in Prison*, p. 44; Sibley and Jacob, *Conscription of Conscience*, pp. 373–74; *Conscientious Objector*, June–July, 1941.

Taylor were later transferred to the federal prison system's mental hospital at Springfield, Missouri, where the inhumane treatment accorded them led to a federal investigation and a number of prison reforms.[43]

By mid-1943, the prisons were alive with pacifist activity; "nearly everyone . . . wanted to strike back and protest," reported Lowell Naeve during his second term. At Danbury the number of C.O.'s had increased from fifteen in early 1941 to two hundred, and they began to feel their strength. Initiating a sociology course of their own, Danbury pacifists discussed the social issue closest at hand—racial segregation in the prison dining halls. They formed a committee on the matter and conferred with the warden, who gave them liberal replies, but raised the argument that prison was not the place to change society. Pacifists disagreed; on August 11, they struck.[44]

Confined to their cells on a floor of their own, the eighteen C.O.'s involved managed to attain an astonishing degree of unity despite enormous difficulties. Strike meetings were held, "newspapers" printed and distributed, and morale maintained. Nevertheless, as Naeve observed, "winning the strike seemed impossible, much more impossible than it ever seemed before." Protests by pacifists, the A.C.L.U., and the N.A.A.C.P. failed to move the government hierarchy, headed by Federal Prisons Director James V. Bennett, a leading exponent of the "new penology." "After very thoughtful consideration," he wrote, "the prison authorities feel it [racial equality] can best be achieved through separation in line with generally accepted practice in the community at large." The "position which we have taken," Bennett continued, "is one approved by many leading

[43] New York Herald Tribune, May 6, 1943; Hershberger, War, Peace, and Nonresistance, pp. 246–47, 266; Lowell Naeve, in collaboration with David Wieck, A Field of Broken Stones, pp. 108–109; Cornell, The Conscientious Objector and the Law, pp. 70–74; American Civil Liberties Union, In Defense of Our Liberties, p. 37; U.S. Bureau of Prisons, Federal Prisons, 1944, pp. 21–22. Not all pacifists were pleased by the Murphy-Taylor non-cooperation. Albert W. Palmer, president of Chicago Theological Seminary, thought the fast "ill-advised on their part." Albert W. Palmer to A. J. Muste, March 13, 1943, FOR MSS, Box 18.

[44] Naeve, A Field of Broken Stones, pp. 133, 135; personal interview with Ralph DiGia, April 21, 1966; J. Peck, We Who Would Not Kill, pp. 101–30; Sibley and Wardlaw, Conscientious Objectors in Prison, pp. 44–45.

sociologists and idealists both white and Negro, as well as by society in general." He would not yield to "this small group of extremists," for racial segregation was "the most satisfactory way of handling the administrative and custodial problems involved." [45] Yet despite such discouraging responses the C.O.'s held out. The strike moved on into the winter months.

On December 22, after 135 days of non-cooperation, the pacifists were let out of their cells and escorted to conference with the warden. He told the bemused C.O.'s of his personal problems and then approached the topic of their strike. "Very shortly, seemingly out of nowhere," reported Lowell Naeve, "he proposed to end the racial policy in the mess hall if we would go off strike before Christmas!" The warden left to let them discuss the matter. Bewildered but jubilant, the men eagerly voted to end the strike, and Danbury became the first federal prison with racially integrated dining halls. "It's over, it's over," shouted an excited Jim Peck; "we've smashed 'em." [46]

The Danbury strike against segregation was but a beginning for an aroused pacifism. Symbolically, on the day the strike ended, five of the victorious C.O.'s notified the warden that they would not "submit to the prison's regimentation or work under the dictatorship of the prison authorities," and were immediately placed back in their old cells. At Lewisburg Penitentiary thirteen pacifists were on a work and hunger strike against racial segregation in their prison, which later evolved into an attack upon prison censorship. Prison officials, alarmed at their physical decline, had them force-fed, but finally capitulated in December, 1943, agreeing to modify literature regulations for the prison. In 1944 a large group of C.O.'s at Danbury began a hunger strike against restrictions on parole, with one striker added to the list every week. When prison authorities transferred some of the men to Lewisburg, seven immediately began a hunger strike there, too. After two of the strikers were released without penalties by the harried government officials, five others

---

[45] J. Peck, We Who Would Not Kill, pp. 101–30; James Peck, "The Ship that Never Hit Port," Prison Etiquette, pp. 67–69; Naeve, A Field of Broken Stones, pp. 135–44; James V. Bennett to A. J. Muste, October 1, 1943, FOR MSS, Box 19; James V. Bennett, "Racial Problems in Federal Prisons" (December 6, 1943), FOR MSS, Box 18.

[46] J. Peck, We Who Would Not Kill, pp. 101–30; Naeve, A Field of Broken Stones, pp. 143–144; Conscientious Objector, January, 1944.

joined the first five in a "rotation" strike. A sympathy fast commenced at Danbury. By October, 1944, prison authorities capitulated and rescinded the parole penalties hitherto imposed on strikers.[47]

Resistance spread to prisons around the nation. At Ashland, Kentucky, fourteen C.O.'s in the federal prison refused to eat in the dining hall so long as it remained segregated. Two of the pacifists were immediately transferred to another prison; the other twelve were placed in solitary confinement, where they remained for more than thirty-three weeks. In June, 1944, C.O.'s at the Petersburg, Virginia, Reformatory began a work strike against racial segregation and other prison conditions, while pacifists in the Milan Correctional Institution in Michigan commenced active resistance to the prison regime. By the end of the war C.O.'s at Danbury and Lewisburg followed a permanent policy of non-cooperation. The pacifists at Lewisburg announced to the F.O.R.: "We . . . are compelled to a non-violent revolutionary movement." [48]

The full potentialities of individual resistance to State authority were explored by the pacifist owner of a New York bookstore, Corbett Bishop. After causing Quaker officials a good deal of trouble in C.P.S., Bishop refused to return to his camp after a furlough in August, 1944, contending that C.P.S. represented a compromise of human freedom. During the subsequent legal proceedings he denied the government any cooperation and had to be carried by police to the court and to prison. Bishop posted no bond and prohibited others from doing so, and subsequently fasted 86 days in prison prior to his trial. Sentenced to a prison term for violation of the draft law, he continued his policy of complete non-cooperation, refusing to eat, move, or even leave his cot. Prison officials force-fed him for

47 Naeve, A Field of Broken Stones, p. 144; Sibley and Jacob, Conscription of Conscience, pp. 375–77; Sibley and Wardlaw, Conscientious Objectors in Prison, pp. 45–47; J. Peck, "The Ship that Never Hit Port," p. 67; "Hunger Strike at Lewisburg," Pacifica Views, II (October 27, 1944), 3; Conscientious Objector, November, 1943, January, 1944, and October, 1944; "Minutes of the Executive Committee Meeting, October 24, 1944," FOR MSS, Box 3.

48 "Pacifist Cons Fight Jimcrow," Pacifica Views, III (July 27, 1945), 2; Conscientious Objector, July, 1944, October, 1944, August, 1945, and February, 1946; Ernest Lefever, "U.S. Conscientious Objectors in Prison," WRL MSS, Box 3; Sibley and Wardlaw, Conscientious Objectors in Prison, pp. 47–48; Sibley and Jacob, Conscription of Conscience, pp. 376–77; "An Open Letter to the FOR, February 3, 1944," FOR MSS, Box 19.

144 days until July 13, 1945, when he was freed on parole. But Bishop refused to sign papers or accept the terms of parole, completely rejecting the government's authority over his person. As a result, on September 1 he was arrested for violation of parole and returned to prison. A full 193 days of continuous, complete noncooperation followed. On March 12, 1946, he was finally released unconditionally, having signed no papers and made no promises. Bishop had fasted and denied the State all cooperation for the incredible total of 426 days.[49]

Pacifists were dazzled by the rebellious C.O.'s performance. "Bishop came, through his words and actions, to be a living symbol of freedom," reported one of the more militant pacifist journals. His "victory," it contended, "is not merely a personal one." A policy of "non-violent resistance, applied in a small sphere today, tomorrow can be the bright, strong means of defeating—without war— imperial oppression and aggression throughout the world." "Corbett Bishop," the editor predicted, "is a forerunner." [50]

"You fellows do so much objecting," commented one prison guard to a C.O., "that if we opened the gate right now and told you to go home, some of you would get half way out and then come back and object about that." The irritated warder did not exaggerate. Increasingly, pacifists refused release from prison on any terms but complete freedom, and consequently would not accept parole. One pacifist explained that "altho technically I am guilty of violating the law, I am morally not guilty of any crime." Therefore, the "signing of papers which limit my range of activities and my freedom outside prison, is to me tantamount to admission that I am a criminal whose activities must be supervised." The imprisonment of men "for reasons of conscience" was "an injustice and I cannot condone it by signing papers, thus tacitly acknowledging the Government to be right in incarcerating me." [51]

Although government officials often retreated before the on-

[49] Purnell Benson, "Corbett Bishop Summary," FOR MSS, Box 14; *Conscientious Objector*, April, 1946; Sibley and Jacob, *Conscription of Conscience*, pp. 401–409; Sibley and Wardlaw, *Conscientious Objectors in Prison*, p. 42.
[50] *Conscientious Objector*, August, 1945.
[51] Curtis Zahn, "Notes on My Life among the Dead Men in Denims," *Prison Etiquette*, p. 80; Edward C. M. Richards, *They Refuse to Be Criminals: Parole and the Conscientious Objector*, pp. 33–34.

slaught of militant pacifism, it cannot be said that they really understood the men or the issues at stake. According to Federal Prisons Director James V. Bennett, C.O.'s showed "uncanny ingenuity at thinking up new issues to raise in connection with such matters as correspondence rules, visiting privileges, and race segregation." The "motivation" of the activist, Bennett asserted, was derived "from an overprotective home or a mother fixation, or from a revolt against authority as typified in the home and transferred to society at large." The militant pacifist was "a problem child—whether at home, at school, or in prison." A prison psychologist, too, revealed a tendency to view objection to war and authoritarianism as a disease to be cured rather than as a conflict between the State and individual ideals. He construed love for humanity, for example, as homosexuality, while Bennett concerned himself with the "rehabilitation" of the conscientious objector, surely an amusing consideration. But despite a lack of sympathy for their pacifist charges, federal officials clearly understood that they had encountered a new breed of convict, one they could well do without. The superintendent of a Western prison remarked to a pacifist on strike: "You C.O.'s may be glad when the war is over but not half as much as I who yearn for the good old days of simple murderers and bank robbers for prisoners!" [52]

With the end of the war, C.O. prison activities approached full-scale rebellion. On Lincoln's birthday, 1946, Danbury prison was picketed inside and outside by angry pacifists, who demanded the release of "political prisoners." Several dozen pacifists paraded in front of the prison and tried to enter, only to be barred from doing so by the guards. "First you . . . won't let me out—now you won't let me in," a demonstrator muttered. Three pacifists broke away

[52] U.S. Bureau of Prisons, *Federal Prisons, 1946*, pp. 13–14; U.S. Bureau of Prisons, *Federal Prisons, 1943*, p. 11; Robert M. Lindner, *Stone Walls and Men*, chapter 14; U.S. Bureau of Prisons, *Federal Prisons, 1946*, p. 10; Wilcher, "Conscientious Objectors in Prison," p. 303. The irony of prison "rehabilitation" for pacifists is illustrated by an encounter in jail between Louis Lepke, the boss of "Murder, Inc." and Lowell Naeve. Naeve tried to explain his crime, but Lepke failed to comprehend exactly what a C.O. was. Then, suddenly, the convicted murderer understood. "You mean they put you in here for *not* killing?" he asked incredulously, and laughed with gusto. J. Peck, "*The Ship That Never Hit Port*," p. 47; Naeve, *A Field of Broken Stones*, p. 29. Neither Lepke nor Naeve was "rehabilitated," however; the former was electrocuted, while the latter received another prison term—one because he killed and the other because he did not.

from the guards and raced up the hill toward the prison to bring the action within view of their counterparts inside but were eventually tackled by prison officials. Inside, two hundred prisoners staged a work strike and picketed the jail yard with clandestinely produced signs. Lowell Naeve reported: "As the slogans rose and the men's arms and heads began swaying with the slogans, it all began to suggest to me as never before what a real revolt might be like." [53]

Prison life provided a vital fund of experience that pacifists drew upon in postwar struggles. Jim Peck and other veterans of the Danbury upheavals found themselves quickly caught up in the activities of CORE and other radical pacifist enterprises upon their release from prison. "These demonstrations constituted our attempts to apply effectively on the outside the non-violent methods of protest which we had used in prison," he later explained. "Somehow it seemed a continuation of the same struggle." Peck "felt certain that non-violence would prove as effective in combatting racial discrimination on the outside as it had been in Danbury." Two pacifists, looking back upon the prison rebellions, concluded that C.O.'s "salvaged from their years of captivity ideas of immeasurable value to all of us who contemplate in the coming totalitarian days a continual warfare with the state—both in and out of its prisons." [54]

As pacifism evolved with the struggles of its practitioners, an interest in rebellion pervaded pacifist circles. A C.P.S. journal argued that "pacifism is the revolutionary movement of the twentieth century," while a Methodist minister observed that the only appropriate name for the pacifist was "revolutionist." Letters from the young militants took up the same theme in the demand for a new pacifism. George Houser proposed the creation of "a national organization of what we can call Non-Violent Direct Actionists." Another young activist looked to the formation of "a revolutionary pacifist group which renounces the class and caste structure of our society just as clearly as it renounces war." The F.O.R. responded to the radical ferment in 1944 by a call for "an imaginative and creative adapta-

[53] *Conscientious Objector*, March, 1946; Naeve, *A Field of Broken Stones*, p. 179.
[54] J. Peck, *We Who Would Not Kill*, p. 174; James Peck, *Freedom Ride*, p. 41; Cantine and Rainer, *Prison Etiquette*, n.p.

tion of the Gandhian method" in the United States. It would be "only in action that we shall actually be able to develop a philosophy and strategy of non-violence," noted a F.O.R. conference on "Revolutionary Pacifism." "Only by action and not talk can we teach pacifism . . . and gain the confidence of the masses." By the end of the war, pacifist academician Mulford Sibley had begun a theoretical review of non-violent tactics to "shake the present order to its foundations." [55]

Yet although the new non-violent radicals laid plans for social upheaval, they maintained their attitude of caution toward traditional revolution. "Pacifist revolutionaries . . . have learned their lesson," noted one of their journals. "The old formula, 'Kill the tyrants, write a constitution, and establish a new educational system,' doesn't work. Every tyrannicide is himself a potential Caesar; he has already acknowledged the superiority of the tyrant's method by using it." Pacifists were aware of the propensity of revolutions to turn sour. "It may be argued that a political elite which was fully imbued with pacifist principles would never resort to . . . betrayal," wrote one pacifist, but the "evidence" indicated otherwise. "We have seen, for instance, what happened to a regime that was devoted to the interests of the working class in Russia." Radical pacifists were forced to navigate the difficult course between the two shoals of non-resistance and Leninism.[56]

Convinced that they were developing a unique synthesis in revolution, radical pacifists perceived the European resistance movements as their natural allies in the struggle against the old order. A group of imprisoned activists noted their "feeling of kinship with the democratic resistance which has emerged under a socialist stimulus around the world." Yet pacifists should go "one step further," Dave

[55] "The Pacifist Revolution," *Pacifica Views,* I (June 11, 1943), 1; Caxton Doggett, "A Name for the Pacifist," *Christian Century,* LXI (October 11, 1944), 1164; George Houser to A. J. Muste, December 28, 1943, FOR MSS, Box 8; William Sutherland, Jr., to A. J. Muste, February 5, 1945, FOR MSS, Box 10; "Report on Study Conference on Revolutionary Pacifism, September 15–17, 1944," FOR MSS, Box 6; Dave Newhall, "Principles and Power," *Pacifica Views,* II (March 23, 1945), 1.

[56] "The Pacifist Revolution," pp. 1–2; H. R. Cantine, Jr., "The Political Goals of Pacifism" (February 1, 1945), FOR MSS, Box 6.

Dellinger argued. "We need a resistance that will renounce sabotage, sniping, deception, terrorism, and all other essentially violent acts." Pacifists "need to embrace a type of resistance that is equally unyielding to tyranny, but at the same time is humble, straightforward, and loving." [57]

As pacifists became more revolutionary, a small group of independent left-wingers centered about *Politics,* a radical journal published by literary critic and recent Trotskyite Dwight Macdonald, grew increasingly pacifist. In the first issue, appearing in February, 1944, Macdonald announced that he hoped "to create a center of consciousness on the Left, welcoming all varieties of radical thought." By the second issue, *Politics* had attracted contributions from a group of young, radical intellectuals, including Daniel Bell (editor of the *New Leader*), Frank Freidel (historian), Kenneth Stampp (historian), C. Wright Mills (sociologist), David Bazelon (economist), Milton Mayer (writer), and Paul Goodman (writer). Although he perceived World War II as "a clash of rival imperialisms," Macdonald rejected the pacifist position. "If I had to choose between becoming a C.O. and submitting to the draft . . . I should still choose the latter," he explained. Taking a fairly traditional left-wing position, he contended that the subversive soldier could do more to shatter the status quo than the "isolated" C.O. Yet the mechanical expediency of the traditional revolutionary, perennially "under wraps" until "objective" conditions "ripened," depressed Macdonald, while the vitality and activism of radical pacifism drew him despite his predilections. "The C.O., like the European anarchist or our own old-time Wobblies, at least reacts spontaneously, immediately against the evils he fights, and shapes his everyday behavior to fit his principles," Macdonald conceded. "This is a great thing." Moreover, the moral idealism of radical pacifism, when set against a background of revolutions betrayed, dazzled him. "After our experiences with the bureaucratic degeneration of the Bolshevik revolutionary movement," he admitted, "radicals must be more con-

---

[57] Rex Corfman, Henry Dyer, Roy Finch, Lewis Hill, Morris Horowitz, Byron Johnson, Igal Roodenko, and Stanley Rappeport, to a list of 60 radical pacifists, April 27, 1945, FOR MSS, Box 6; "Statement of Dave Dellinger, July 18, 1943," FOR MSS, Box 17.

cerned about individual morality than they have been in the past." [58]

By 1945 Macdonald was printing articles with a decidedly pacifist flavor. Typical of the rethinking being done among these independent radicals was the republication of French authoress Simone Weil's brilliant critique of traditional left-wing methods. "Revolutionary War is the grave of revolution," she asserted. "Not only would this mean to fight barbarous oppression by crushing peoples under the weight of even more barbarous massacre. It would actually mean spreading under another form the very regime that we want to suppress." History was "more and more forcing every political actor to choose between aggravating the oppression exercised by the various State apparatuses and carrying on a merciless struggle against those apparatuses in order to shatter them." Her conclusions were a striking parallel to those of the new pacifism:

Whether the mask is labelled Fascism, Democracy, or Dictatorship of the Proletariat, our great adversary remains the Apparatus—the bureaucracy, the police, the military. Not the one facing us across the frontier or the battle-lines, which is not so much our enemy as our brothers' enemy, but the one that calls itself our protector and makes us its slaves. No matter what the circumstances, the worst betrayal will always be to subordinate ourselves to this Apparatus, and to trample underfoot, in its service, all human values in ourselves and in others.

With the end of the war, to no one's surprise except perhaps his own, Macdonald found himself in the radical pacifist camp.[59]

The emergence of radical pacifism, then, resulted largely from

[58] Dwight Macdonald, "Why 'POLITICS'?" *Politics*, I (February, 1944), 6–8; *Politics*, I (March, 1944); Dwight Macdonald, "By Way of Rejoinder," *Politics*, I (July, 1944), 179–80.

[59] Simone Weil, "Reflections on War," *Politics*, II (February, 1945), 54–55; Christopher Lasch, *The New Radicalism in America, 1889–1963: The Intellectual as a Social Type*, pp. 324–26. Typical of Macdonald's disillusionment with war was his article of March, 1945, entitled "The Responsibility of Peoples," in which he contended that entire peoples are not accountable for the crimes of their rulers, thereby raising the delicate question of whether it was justifiable to wage indiscriminate war against the population of a nation, or, for that matter, to wage modern war at all. Dwight Macdonald, "The Responsibility of Peoples," *Politics*, II (March, 1945), 82–93. By the summer of 1946, *Politics* had contributed one hundred dollars to the Glendora strikers' fund and was supplying many of the packages for European relief handled by the men. "The C.P.S. Strikes," pp. 179–80.

social necessity, for despite a long-term interest in Gandhi, the peace movement did not develop the tactics of non-violent resistance until its youngest generation found them useful in dealing with injustices in American race relations, the C.P.S. camps, and the prisons. While at times overreacting and exaggerating the evils which they faced, the new crop of radicals nonetheless set the tone and strategy for future campaigns of non-violent action. Thus, although the historic pacifist impulse withered during the most destructive war in history, it harbored within itself the seeds of its own regeneration.

CHAPTER IV

The Best of
All Possible Wars

The problem is not how to get rid of the enemy, but rather how to get rid of the last victor. For what is a victor but one who has learned that violence works? Who will teach *him* a lesson?

NICCOLO TUCCI, 1945[1]

World War II witnessed a profound shift in public mood. The experience of almost four years of international conflict reshaped many of America's social values, but few were as profoundly affected as the popular attitude toward war. Just as the experience of the first World War had provided the context for a reevaluation of modern warfare, so the second great struggle proved influential in restructuring America's assessment of the value of a disarmed world. The result was ironic; for at the same time that pacifism was undergoing a surge of revival, most Americans were converted to the belief that their security rested upon preponderant military power.

Through their service in the nation's armed forces, large numbers of Americans became subject for the first time to the control of military officers, many of whom, quite naturally, desired the maintenance of a permanent military establishment to fight what they considered inevitable wars. In the spring of 1944, army and navy spokesmen agreed upon a program for universal military training to go into effect after the war and began a vigorous campaign to secure its legislative enactment. General Hershey explained that "the extent to which we can exercise influence after victory . . . depends . . .

[1] Niccolo Tucci, "Two Observations on World War III," *Politics*, II (July, 1945), 196.

upon the evidence we possess that we are prepared to back with force our recommendations." In June, 1945, General George S. Patton, Jr., addressed a Sunday school class in the Church of Our Savior, San Gabriel, California. "You are the soldiers and the nurses of the next war," the general told the children, most of whom were about eight years of age. "There will be another war. There always has been." Even supporters of the war grew uneasy at the opportunities that the unprecedented program of military training afforded army and navy chieftains to indoctrinate millions of young men with the military ethos. "How many are you conditioning permanently?" wondered historian Bernard DeVoto.[2]

Many servicemen resisted the military influence. The popular Bill Mauldin cartoons of the war years evidenced a definite distaste for officers, barracks life, and the apparent senselessness of much of army routine, while neither Norman Mailer's *The Naked and the Dead* nor James Jones' *From Here to Eternity* portrayed military life with much sympathy. Studies of combat during World War II found that, in a given action, fewer than one out of four soldiers, armed and in a position to fire their weapons at the enemy, actually pulled the trigger. Loneliness, boredom, and a thirst for civilian pleasures during their wartime sojourn led many soldiers to think poorly of the world of the "big brass."[3]

And yet, to a greater extent than they imagined, the men in the ranks tended to take on the military attitudes of their commanding officers. Although polls in December, 1938, found only 37 per cent of the population in favor of compulsory military training, 70 per cent of the men in the armed forces during World War II consistently favored universal military training for the postwar period. A warrant officer in the army who, according to his account, "took the Oxford Pledge" and reviled militarism during the Thirties, explained that his views and those of his comrades, also formerly pacifists, were reversed by military life. "We all see things a little more clearly now,"

[2] *New York Times*, April 27, 1944; *Washington Post*, May 11, 1944; Dwight Macdonald, "Atrocities of the Mind," *Politics*, II (August, 1945), 225; Bernard DeVoto, "The Easy Chair," *Harper's*, CLXXXVIII (March, 1944), 346.

[3] Merle Curti, *The Growth of American Thought*, pp. 733–34; S. L. A. Marshall, *Men against Fire*, pp. 50–63; Bill Davidson, "Why Half Our Combat Soldiers Fail to Shoot," *Collier's*, CXXX (November 8, 1952), 17.

he told the readers of a mass-circulation magazine in 1945. "I, who not so long ago regarded universal military training as a reactionary absurdity, think that it is essential for us to put such a program into effect right now." He had formerly been "ignorantly and prejudicially . . . ill disposed toward the standing Army," but now he understood that the men "who are building the future that others are discussing . . . are Regulars." This same attitude of reverence for the professional officer corps pervaded Herman Wouk's popular postwar novel *The Caine Mutiny*. Although a number of the newer veterans groups proved considerably less inclined to jingoism than their more powerful rivals, they drew only small numbers; by 1947 the American Veterans Committee consisted of only 100,000 members, while the American Legion had added 2,000,000 new members from the ranks of World War II servicemen. The veterans of World War II, like those of previous wars, showed a strong proclivity toward militarism in the postwar period; the major difference seems to have been that after 1945 there were more of them.[4]

On the home front, despite the frequent obeisance to internationalism, the war stimulated a relatively uncritical assessment of American power. "We know the facts," wrote Archbishop Francis J. Spellmen, Military Vicar of the Armed Forces. "We wanted no land. We committed no economic wrongs. We suppressed no civic liberties." Even America's enemies knew that "America is on the level and on the square." It was "for the sake of the righteous," one minister told a V-E Day audience, that "God has preserved our cities and kept them from harm." The second World War witnessed considerably less patriotic effusion than the first, but the tacit assumption of a unique American virtue nevertheless remained. World War II, for example, gave rise to the phrase and the concept of a "Free World"

[4] Cantril, *Public Opinion*, p. 458; Samuel A. Stouffer, *et al., The American Soldier: Adjustment during Army Life*, I, 446; E. J. Kahn, Jr., "A Soldier's Slant on Compulsory Military Training," *Saturday Evening Post*, CCXVII (May 19, 1945), 27, 94; Herman Wouk, *The Caine Mutiny;* Charles G. Bolté, "We're On Our Own," *Atlantic Monthly*, CLXXIX (May, 1947), 28–30; Willard Waller, *The Veteran Comes Back*. When, for example, an American Institute of Public Opinion poll in March, 1946, asked Americans if the United States should carry out the Bikini bomb tests, only 43 per cent of the nation's population thought it should—an opinion held by 65 per cent of the nation's World War II veterans. Cantril, *Public Opinion*, p. 24.

which, although already somewhat elastic, provided many Americans with the taste of a Manichean struggle between the forces of
Good and Evil. Most Americans, declared Allan Nevins in 1946, had
"been converted to a unifying moral conviction of the mission of the
United States during and after the war." The victory of better-
trained and better-fed troops, coupled with more and better arms,
became transmuted into a victory of "moral superiority," noted Hans
Morgenthau—a superiority "then taken to be a permanent quality
which not only explains past victories, but also justifies the national
claim to be the lawgiver and arbiter of mankind." [5]

The war contributed further to nationalism by vitiating the forces
of dissent which in the Thirties had served as a check upon an
uncritical celebration of "Americanism." Many of the most radical
young men of the depression years were exhausted by their wartime
experience. His generation had "forgotten" its "grandiose dreams,"
wrote Corporal John Higham from his army tent in Italy. The war
served "to enervate socially-conscious inquiry." Moreover, the new
college generation of the war years evidenced notable differences
from its radical predecessor of the Thirties. Polls of students at New
York's City College, the site of much previous antiwar activity,
found that 62.4 per cent desired "compulsory military training
after the war," and that 54 per cent predicted another world

[5] Curti, *The Growth of American Thought*, pp. 730–31; Spellman, *The Road
to Victory*, p. 123; Moellering, *Modern War and the American Churches*, p. 37;
Nevins, "How We Felt about the War," p. 13; Hans J. Morgenthau, "The
Pathology of Power," *American Perspective*, IV (Winter, 1950), 9. Spellman
contended that "America's contemporary position for international rectitude,
for international justice, for international generosity, is unparalleled in history."
Spellman, *The Road to Victory*, p. 129. In 1946 Commander Ben H. Wyatt of
the United States navy gave a group of Bikini natives, undergoing evacuation
from their homes for the testing of atomic bombs, his theory of how the war
came about. Japan "rose up and decided that they would occupy all this section of the world and overrun God's people," he explained. Japan attacked
America "without our having done one thing to her! . . . But, as I said, God
looks after his people. And America, weak as she was at the time, developed
a great army and navy and airforce." Meanwhile, "the great wise men of
America" were "working out the secrets of God. And under His guidance,
out of that study came the atom bomb." Commander Wyatt then told the
residents of Bikini to get off their island, since the United States was "trying
to make certain that if . . . any nations attack the peoples of God, . . . we
will have the force to protect us." The comments of the natives were not reported. *Kansas City Star*, June 20, 1946, clipping in FOR MSS, Box 12.

war by 1970. John Swomley of the F.O.R. wrote sadly in 1944 that student comprehension "of labor problems, economics, race tensions, and . . . war seems to be far below that of previous generations." If American society in the 1950's seemed dominated by a "silent generation's" bland acceptance of the status quo, more than a little of the responsibility rested upon the war's phasing-out of youthful dissent.[6]

During World War II, the belief developed that pacifists were responsible for Axis aggression. As columnist Walter Lippmann explained it: "The preachment and the practice of pacifists in Britain and America were a cause of the World War. They were the cause of the failure to keep pace with the growth of German and Japanese armaments. They led to the policy of . . . appeasement." Pacifists "thought they were 'keeping us out of war,'" argued a prominent clergyman, but "they know now they were keeping MacArthur out of ammunition." The Reverend Norman Vincent Peale took up the refrain in 1944: "Due to the popular feeling against war we allowed ourselves to get into such a position that we were totally unprepared, thus giving the Germans an opportunity to make this war."[7]

This belief in pacifist culpability developed as one of the strongest rationales for American faith in armaments. An advertisement for the Vultee Aircraft Corporation proclaimed the theme in July, 1945. "After Victory is won, if we forget some of the lessons we have learned so painfully in this war, we can easily drift back again to the status of a second-rate power in the air." This defense contractor asked: "Dare we rely on such a hit-or-miss air program *next* time?" The conclusion was obvious. "American . . . military planes must

[6] John Higham, "On Acquiring a Public Opinion," *Public Opinion Quarterly*, VIII (Winter, 1944), 497–98; *New York Times*, November 28, 1943; John M. Swomley, Jr., "Composite Staff Report" (September 23, 1944), FOR MSS, Box 3. For a sense of the wartime mood among young radicals, see: Karl Shapiro, "New Guinea Letter," *New Republic*, CIX (July 12, 1943), 46.

[7] Walter Lippmann, *U. S. Foreign Policy: Shield of the Republic*, p. 53; *New York Times*, August 19, 1942; Norman Vincent Peale to A. J. Muste, March 6, 1944, FOR MSS, Box 10. One historian writes: "For a time after the Second World War broke out, there was, among the people and leaders in the United States, a dogmatic conviction that the unwillingness to prepare and use military force in the 1920's and 1930's led to . . . the catastrophe of world conflict." J. Chalmers Vinson, "Military Force and American Policy, 1919–1939," *Isolation and Security*, ed. Alexander DeConde, p. 81.

excel those of any other nation." A book reviewer in the *New York Times* during 1945 grew incensed by Gertrude Stein's suggestion that wars were caused by public servants "believing what they are supposed to believe." The reviewer exploded: "Does it sound familiar? Wuxtry! Wuxtry! Read all about the parasites and warmongers in government offices!" It was "out of just this kind of thinking" that "the whole pseudo-pacifist doctrine between the two wars" developed, an attitude which "fostered unpreparedness by insisting that preparedness was the same as militarism" and "helped make the Munich pact inevitable." The path toward Munich "had been preordained by unthinking babblers who went around poking their parasols—usually pink—into diplomatic corners and holding their noses." The moral of the war, the reviewer warned, was that "evolution depends on the survival of the fittest." [8]

The pacifist-appeasement formula grew increasingly popular in the postwar period. Dwight Macdonald grumbled in 1946: "Already, the arguments are becoming horribly familiar: 'Isn't our imperfect democracy better than Stalin's (Hitler's) dictatorship? If Stalin (Hitler) is not 'stopped,' it will be our turn soon. Are you willing to face the prospect of a Communist (Nazi) world?" There were always, continued Macdonald, "only two Realistic alternatives: either 'appeasement' or resistance, by force if necessary." In 1948 the *Washington Star* rejected Albert Einstein's proposal for world government because it "ignores all of the lessons of our experience. Once before," the newspaper alleged, "after World War I, the United States discarded its arms." Indeed, "in doing so we came within a hair's breadth of losing World War II. We must not do it again. . . . World government will have to wait," concluded the journal. "The most mischievous word in the post-Hitlerian lexicon is 'appeasement,'" complained the *Nation* in 1961. "Every subsequent attempt, good or bad, to compose differences between nations has been tarred with this brush." As late as 1966 Secretary of State Dean Rusk told a convention of the Veterans of Foreign Wars that any withdrawal from Vietnam before complete victory would be as fatal

[8] "Let's Keep America Strong in the Air!" *Time*, XLVI (July 23, 1945), 14–15; Libby Benedict, Review of *Wars I Have Seen*, by Gertrude Stein, *New York Times Book Review* (May 20, 1945), p. 4.

as attempts to appease the fascist powers in the Thirties. The failure to meet the Japanese advance in Manchuria with armed force "led to World War II," he stated. But the Veterans of Foreign Wars, he noted, was "a group not confused about why we're fighting in Vietnam." The American objective, explained the Secretary of State, "is peace." [9]

Americans found one of the more encouraging aspects of World War II in the magnitude of their military victory. The Axis nations lay in ruins, with their governments destroyed, in one of history's most decisive defeats. "It meant that the enemy which had dealt us the foulest blow in our history had been compelled to the most abject capitulation," recalled Allan Nevins. "A wild passion of relief, pride, and joy shook a hundred and forty millions the night that news came of Japan's surrender." Americans confidently believed that they bore the largest share of responsibility for the victory; polls in mid-1943 found 55 per cent of the respondents naming the United States as the nation which had done most toward winning the war, although in Britain most chose the Soviet Union and only 3 per cent named the United States. "We have breathed the heady air of conquest; we have seen our flag everywhere triumphant, our enemies prostrate," declared *New York Times* military analyst Hanson Baldwin in 1949. "One cannot easily in a few months of history forget the high moments of yesterday, nor is it possible to turn at once—after . . . World War II—to other forces" and "other men than those who led us to victory." The United States and the Soviet Union, both at the peak of their military power, grew emboldened by their new strength. As a world federalist later observed: "It was hardly to be expected that, in the hour of their glory, they would fully grasp the fact that their sense of supreme sovereignty was an illusion." [10]

[9] Macdonald, *Memoirs of a Revolutionist*, p. 182; *Washington Star*, April 29, 1948; "Thou Shalt Not Appease," *Nation*, CXCIII (September 9, 1961), 129; *New York Times*, August 23, 1966.

[10] Nevins, "How We Felt about the War," p. 26; Cantril, *Public Opinion*, p. 1065; Hanson W. Baldwin, "When the Big Guns Speak," *Public Opinion and Foreign Policy*, ed. Lester Markel, pp. 98–99; Alan Cranston, "The Strengthening of the U. N. Charter," *Political Quarterly*, XVII (July–September, 1946), 188. General Douglas MacArthur recalled that with the end of World War II, "America, at the very apex of her military power, was the logical nation to

The fires of nationalism were further stoked by the hostilities which fighting the war inevitably encouraged. Abstractions, after all, rarely move men to combat, while fierce antagonisms toward foreigners stimulate action. "We must hate with every fiber of our being," Lieutenant-General Lesley J. McNair, director of the training program for all American ground forces, told a radio audience of servicemen in November, 1942. "We must lust for battle; our object in life must be to kill; we must scheme and plan night and day to kill." Civilians were not exempt from wartime hatreds. "The people in the community were beginning to get mad," reported the Detroit Committee on Foreign Relations. "The Japanese and Germans were . . . becoming . . . personal enemies." [11]

Theories of German racial depravity were common during the war years. Rex Stout, chairman of the Writers War Board, an affiliate of the Office of War Information, proclaimed in January, 1943, in an article entitled "We Shall Hate, or We Shall Fail:" "I hate Germans, and am not ashamed of it." Hitler arose, he explained, "as the culmination of the deep-rooted mental and nervous disease afflicting the German people." When the magazine *Common Sense* called attention to Stout's openly professed hatred for all Germans and his high position in the American propaganda apparatus, Elmer Davis, Director of the Office of War Information, angrily replied in defense of the mystery writer's viewpoint. Davis recalled "no evidence that any noticeable number" of Germans "ever displayed any dissatisfaction with the things their leaders were doing." [12]

Strangely enough, despite the revelations of Hitler's wholesale horrors, most Americans hated the Japanese far more than the Germans. Asked which of the two countries they thought the United States could "get along with better after the war," Americans were

---

which the world turned for leadership. It was . . . one of the greatest opportunities ever known." Courtney Whitney, *MacArthur: His Rendezvous with History*, p. 500.

11 Porter Sargent, *War and Education*, p. 276; Bidwell, *Our Foreign Policy*, p. 75.

12 "The Shame of American Writers," *Common Sense*, XIII (May, 1944), 187; "American Writers on Germany," *Common Sense*, XIII (June, 1944), 206–207. The editor of *Common Sense* retorted that Davis "must have noticed that more than half a million adult Germans were sufficiently dissatisfied with the Nazis to be sent to concentration camps to face torture and execution." *Ibid.*

nearly unanimous: 92 per cent chose Germany and only 8 per cent Japan. Racial epithets were particularly popular with the American people, who often described the Japanese as "rats" and "monkey faces." *Time*, which headed its account of the battle of Iwo Jima "Rodent Exterminators," declared: "The ordinary unreasoning Jap is ignorant. Perhaps he is human. Nothing . . . indicates it." An advertisement in the *New York Times*, approved by the War Production Board, showed a sinister Japanese face with the headline: "RAT POISON WANTED." The advertisement maintained: "There's only one way to exterminate the slant-eyes—with gunpowder!" A high official in the United States navy urged General Douglas MacArthur to "drive the monkeys into the Pacific Ocean." Indeed, the fighting in Asia reached a very ugly level after several years. American soldiers participated in the wholesale slaughter of Japanese prisoners and sent bones and skulls to the folks back home for souvenirs.[13]

Admiral William F. ("Bull") Halsey emerged as a particularly forthright hater of the people of Japan. *Time* magazine featured him on its cover in July, 1945, with his motto: "Kill Japs, kill Japs, and then kill more Japs." After the Japanese surrender ceremony on the *Missouri*, he remarked to reporters that he would "like to have kicked each Japanese delegate in the face." Dwight Macdonald reported hearing the admiral comment in a newsreel: "We are drowning and burning the bestial apes all over the Pacific, and it is just as much pleasure to burn them as to drown them." At an "off-the-record" dinner, Halsey allegedly told Washington newsmen: "I hate Japs. I'm telling you men that if I met a pregnant Japanese woman, I'd kick her in the belly."[14]

[13] Lydgate, *What America Thinks*, pp. 52–53; Bailey, *The Man in the Street*, p. 197; Norman Thomas, "Our War With Japan," *Commonweal*, XLII (April 20, 1945), 7–8; "Rodent Exterminators," *Time*, XLV (March 19, 1945), 32; "The Enemy," *Time*, XLII (July 5, 1943), 29; *New York Times*, September 20, 1943; W. C. to Douglas MacArthur, February 17, 1944, Supreme Commander for the Allied Powers in Japan Manuscripts, MacArthur Memorial (SCAP MSS), Box 12. Racial hatred also presented certain difficulties during World War II. One confused citizen complained that "it is hard to distinguish the Yellow Rat Japs sometimes from the Philippinos." C. T. to Douglas MacArthur, February 12, 1945, Douglas MacArthur Manuscripts, MacArthur Memorial (MacArthur MSS), Box 5.

[14] *Time*, XLVI (July 23, 1945), cover; "They Call Him 'Bull,' " *Time*, XLVI (September 10, 1945), 23; Macdonald, *Memoirs of a Revolutionist*, p. 93.

The attitudes of many Americans did not differ markedly from those of the commander of the Pacific fleet. Polls in 1944 found that 13 per cent of the population favored killing all Japanese at the end of the war. A writer from a small town in Massachusetts asked General MacArthur to "round up five or ten thousand Japs at a time and cremate them . . . every week until you put at least a million to death." A program of compulsory sterilization, often with racial overtones, appears to have enjoyed a particular vogue. "I would sterilized [sic] them all," declared a lady in Jersey City. "They hate our race—the white race—so it's up to us to get rid of them. And . . . God has shown us the way." Another concerned American suggested that only Japanese males be sterilized; Japanese females who wished to bear children could then "be accomodated [sic] by artificial insemination," with "virile blond Americans" utilized "so that the race will be really improved and humanized." When atomic bombs were dropped on two Japanese cities in August, 1945, few Americans were upset. No poll in late 1945 ever revealed more than 4.5 per cent of the respondents opposed to the use of atomic bombs under any circumstances, while 24 per cent told interviewers that they "would have tried to wipe out as many cities as possible before" the Japanese "had a chance to surrender." In short, after four years of war one out of four Americans tacitly admitted that his primary concern was not to secure surrender, but to kill as many Japanese as possible.[15]

After World War II, although Americans were obliged to learn that their former allies (Russians and Chinese) were now enemies and their former foes (Germans and Japanese) were now allies, overriding this reversal of roles was their long-term perception of an

[15] Cantril, *Public Opinion*, pp. 21, 23, 1118; M. M. to Douglas MacArthur, September 11, 1945, MacArthur MSS, Box 6; M. C. to Douglas MacArthur, August 16, 1945, MacArthur MSS, Box 5; E. W. to Douglas MacArthur, September 7, 1945, MacArthur MSS, Box 6; Bailey, *The Man in the Street*, p. 194; "The Fortune Survey," *Fortune*, XXXII (December, 1945), 305. The chairman of the Senate Committee on the District of Columbia commented: "If I had my way about it I think I would sterilize every damn one of them so in one generation there would be no more Japs." Theodore Bilbo to Douglas MacArthur, September 14, 1945, MacArthur MSS, Box 6. A "dream came true," wrote *Time* of the devastating firebombing of Tokyo; "properly kindled, Japanese cities will burn like autumn leaves." "Firebirds' Flight," *Time*, XLV (March 19, 1945), 32.

alien menace. For many, a bastardized version of the internationalist *Weltanschauung* prevailed—a virtuous America assailed by disagreeable foreigners who disturbed the peace. In 1962, when news analyst David Brinkley reported on the annual reunion of the 509th Composite Group, which had dropped the atomic bombs on Japan, a conversation of these servicemen ran as follows:

CARRON: Theirs was an awful lot worse—it was a sneak attack.

BESAR: We were dealing with Asiatics—not people like ourselves. . . .

. . . . .

LEVY: They had these Hiroshima maidens they brought in from Japan to take to New York to do plastic surgery on their faces. . . . Really, I never felt at all sorry for them or pitied them. They started it and we helped end it.

. . . . .

SHUMARD: My favorite saying was "I never lost any sleep over it" which is true—I was on a mission then and I would go on it again.

. . . . .

BESAR: Today's 50 megaton bombs don't bother me anymore than the 20 kilotons we carried at Hiroshima. . . .

SHUMARD: I think it would make a pretty loud bang.[16]

America's key role in the international conflict prompted a concern among foreign policy strategists for the virtues of power. An early promoter of a new role for America, publisher Henry Luce of *Time, Life,* and *Fortune* called for the creation of an "American Century" in early 1941. Arguing that the United States was already in fact deeply enmeshed in the war, he asked Americans to draw up plans to utilize their country's new position of power in world affairs. Others were less enamored than Luce of the "American Century" concept. The noted news analyst and scholar Quincy Howe observed that other nations might desire more than the "revolution" envisioned by the affluent Mr. Luce, and paraphrased the words of

[16] Virginia Naeve (ed.) *Friends of the Hibakusha,* pp. 91–92. At a Town Meeting of the Air debate in 1945, a member of the audience asked Major Erwin Lessner if it was fair to punish the German children, who were not, after all, responsible for the actions of their elders. The major replied that he felt that they should suffer, for "those innocent German children are the potential soldiers of World War III, just as the innocent German children who had been fed after 1918 later served in Hitler's army." Dwight Macdonald commented sardonically on the incident in 1953: "Today . . . it is a plus and not a minus for German kids that they are 'potential soldiers of World War III.'" Macdonald, *Memoirs of a Revolutionist,* p. 68n.

the Negro spiritual: "Everybody's talking 'bout revolution ain't goin' there." [17]

With American entry into the war, new voices were added to the cry for recognition of the part an armed America might play in the destiny of nations. In 1942, for example, two members of the Denver Committee on Foreign Relations pointed to the "rediscovery of the simple fact that our world position depends on power." Instead of "being ashamed of power and afraid to use it" and "following the vain hopes of some of the peace planners for a world free from war," the "new realistic attitude requires that we recognize that force has a place in our society and that our strength must be maintained at all costs." Americans, in their view, should work to "secure fundamental agreement that there shall be no disarmament and that we shall enforce world peace by force." The flavor of national interest was strong: "No one else is really anxious about us, nor should they be. They fear for themselves and we must watch out for ourselves." [18]

The writings of newspaper columnist Walter Lippmann epitomize the change in American thought. "In my youth," wrote Lippmann in 1943, "we all assumed that the money spent on battleships would be better spent on schoolhouses and that war was an affair that 'militarists' talked about." Now, however, he ridiculed hope for an international community, arguing that "the will of the most powerful states to remain allied is the only possible creator of a general international order." Consequently, he looked to a power alliance of the United States, Britain, and Russia to maintain the peace in the postwar world. International law, justice, morality, disarmament were chimeras. "We must consider first and last the American national interest. If we do not, if we construct our foreign policy on some kind of abstract theory of our rights and duties, we shall build castles in the air." "In short," concluded Lippmann, "we shall succeed in so far as we can become fully enlightened American nationalists." [19]

[17] Henry R. Luce, *The American Century.*

[18] Bidwell, *Our Foreign Policy*, pp. 84–85.

[19] Lippmann, *U. S. Foreign Policy*, pp. 8, 137, 166. The acceptance by Republican isolationists and by isolationist ethnic groups of the foreign policy

Those Americans seeking an end to international power struggles were aghast. "We've licked the Germans and in the process become so impressed with them that Nazism is likely to become the world system speaking another language," wrote newspaper columnist Dorothy Thompson. "Most journalism has turned into a claque for the New Realism, which is just a fancy name for the Old Nick." She found America "heading absolutely inevitably toward the next war"; World War II was "just the run-off for the ultimate championship." A. J. Muste presented the F.O.R. with a pessimistic report on expected postwar trends: "Expansion in Latin America and Pacific. More regimentation . . . ; big military establishment; quite possibly permanent conscription. A good many people with no illusions left about war but made hard, cynical, eager to 'get theirs.' " [20] For pacifists the message of World War II was the necessity of curbing the warmaking powers of the nation-State; but ironically, the moral drawn from the war by the "new realists" was just the reverse—that peace was contingent upon national "strength."

Peace activists had spoken much of the sufferings of war in the preceding decades, and had succeeded in convincing many Americans that war would prove an unmitigated disaster. Yet after four years of war numerous citizens found that this much-heralded picture of agony was not entirely accurate. World War II taught many Americans that war can have its compensations.

World War II's cost in the lives of men, according to an estimate by the United States War Department, reached eighty million casualties, of which the American dead, missing, and wounded accounted for about one million. Surely for these men and their families war brought bitter consequences, but for the United States as a whole, the casualty level remained gratifyingly light. The total of American battle deaths climbed to only about three times the automobile fatalities in the United States during the same period, while

---

sponsored by the Democratic Party in wartime and in the postwar period has often been cited as an example of a trend toward internationalism. This may, however, say more about the foreign policy than it does about any decline in nationalism.

[20] Dorothy Thompson to A. J. Muste, September 20, 1945, FOR MSS, Box 11; "Minutes of National Council Meeting, May 29–30, 1944," FOR MSS, Box 3.

the casualty level was markedly lower than that of any other major participant in the war:

Table 2
World War II Casualties

Country	Percentage of 1935 Population
United States	0.8
Great Britain	1.3
France	1.8
Japan	7.7
U.S.S.R.	8.3
Yugoslavia	12.2
Germany	14.3
Poland	17.5

Adapted from a table in: P. M. S. Blackett, Fear, War, and the Bomb: Military and Political Consequences of Atomic Energy, p. 220.

In October, 1945, a poll of American opinion revealed that the largest grouping of respondents—42 per cent—found wartime casualties lower than anticipated at the beginning of the war.[21]

For most Americans life on the home front proved unexpectedly free of hardship. The United States had still not recovered from its disastrous depression when the war began. In September, 1939, according to Works Progress Administration estimates, there were 9,500,000 idle workers in the United States; but by late 1941 the developing armaments economy which fed the European struggle had created 5,000,000 much-needed new jobs. As a Cornell University senior wrote: " 'Help Wanted' signs looked good, even if the job was carrying nitroglycerin." When the United States entered the war the lagging economy boomed, and suddenly, with 11,000,000 in the armed forces and 20,000,000 in war production jobs, an unprecedented period of full employment ensued. "In one sense," commented English author Aldous Huxley, "the current war in Europe was the politicians' solution to the unemployment problem." Historian Carl Becker noted: "In peacetime millions of men are out of

21 "A Brief Review of Thirty-Five Years of Service," p. 37; Blackett, Fear, War, and the Bomb, p. 78; Cantril, Public Opinion, p. 1074.

work, and they and their families lack food and clothes and other necessities of life. But as soon as war comes, all of these unemployed men find jobs, and when the war becomes 'total' the problem is . . . where to find men enough for the work that needs to be done." His conclusions were ominous: "We seem to live in a world in which the easiest and quickest way to abolish . . . unemployment and want is to practice on a grand scale . . . war." [22]

The war rejuvenated American captialism. In 1940 the gross national product of the United States stood at 90 billion dollars; by 1944 it had reached 200 billion. For the 56 American corporations holding 80 per cent of the defense contracts, the war offered unparalleled opportunities. Corporate profits after taxes rocketed to 8.5 billion dollars in 1943, the highest level in history. Dividends increased to abnormally large figures and the stock market boomed. "We had been told in the 1930's that the tradition of individual initiative and large-scale feats of production was ended," exclaimed Allan Nevins. "Multitudes of people" had "accepted those voices of discouragement which declared . . . that the nation had entered upon a tamer, more restricted phase of economic development." But the "home-front effort proved that they were false." He cited the enormous output of American industry in wartime and concluded: "The old, self-confident America was coming into its stride again." [23] Indeed it was. Enthused by the wartime bonanza the president of the General Electric Corporation, Charles E. Wilson, suggested a future alliance of business and the military to maintain "a permanent war economy." [24]

[22] Nels Anderson and Nathaniel H. Rogg, "Impact of the War on Labor and Industry," *American Journal of Sociology*, XLVIII (November, 1942), 364; Eliot Janeway, *The Struggle for Survival: A Chronicle of Economic Mobilization in World War II*, p. 245; " 'Safe Now in the Wide, Wide World': College Editors and Commencement," *Atlantic Monthly*, CLXVIII (August, 1941), 186; Broadus Mitchell, *Depression Decade: From New Era through New Deal, 1929–1941*, pp. 361–403; Aldous Huxley to John Nevin Sayre, January 31, 1945 (excerpts), FOR MSS, Box 8; Carl L. Becker, *How New Will the Better World Be?* p. 8.

[23] Donald M. Nelson, "What Industry Did," *While You Were Gone*, p. 216; Janeway, *The Struggle for Survival*, p. 259; Donald M. Nelson, *Arsenal of Democracy: The Story of American War Production*; Nevins, "How We Felt about the War," pp. 18, 23.

[24] Tristram Coffin, *The Passion of the Hawks: Militarism in Modern America*, p. 162; Fred J. Cook, "Juggernaut: The Warfare State," *Nation*, CXCIII (Oc-

But all social groups benefited from the wartime prosperity. The number of Negroes employed in manufacturing and processing increased from 500,000 to 1,200,000 between 1940 and 1944, and in government service from 60,000 to 200,000. Negroes employed as skilled craftsmen and foremen doubled in number as did those in semiskilled jobs, while the number of black women employed in industry quadrupled. More than 500,000 Negroes joined trade unions after 1940.[25] Farmers reached the highest level of prosperity they had ever attained. In 1940 the Bureau of Agricultural Economics estimated that agriculture attracted 2,500,000 people in excess of its labor requirements; but by the middle of the war, there was a drastic manpower shortage, and farm wages tripled. Between 1939 and 1945 farm prices rose 131 per cent. Net farm income climbed from 5.3 billion dollars in 1939 to 13.6 billion in 1944, while the farm mortgage debt dropped to half the 1920's figure.[26]

Throughout the country prosperity had returned. Between early 1940 and 1944 consumer income increased from 75 billion to 150 billion dollars, while liquid assets of individuals swelled from 50 billion to 140 billion dollars. The standard of living climbed accordingly. Despite the irritations of rationing, Americans were better fed than ever before. War Production Board Chairman J. A. Krug's report for 1944 stressed the fact that Americans were the best-fed, best-clothed, and best-housed people in the world. The *New York Times* commented that the findings of the report "will not be disputed . . . by anyone who stops to think about his own condition and compares it with what we know of conditions in other countries, even neutral countries." "When analyzed," stated the *Times*, American "hardships very often degenerate into mere irritations or shortages in goods that are luxuries and not necessities." And even lux-

---

tober 28, 1961), 285. Wilson suggested that every corporation employ an executive with reserve officer rank to serve as a liaison to the Pentagon—a policy put into unofficial practice during the 1950's.

[25] Carey McWilliams, "What We Did about Racial Minorities," *While You Were Gone*, p. 100; E. Franklin Frazier, "Ethnic and Minority Groups in Wartime, with Special Reference to the Negro," *American Journal of Sociology*, XLVIII (November, 1942), 369–77.

[26] Lowry Nelson, "Farms and Farming Communities," *American Society in Wartime*, pp. 85–91; Janeway, *The Struggle for Survival*, pp. 334–35; Walter W. Wilcox, *The Farmer in the Second World War*, pp. 95–96, 249–51.

uries were not forgone. Journalist Paul Gallico, describing American life in this period, painted a far from Spartan picture: "The home front shenanigans went on just the same, with night spots, bars, theatres, and places of entertainment jammed, silk shirts, fur coats, and diamonds moving off counters at a fantastic rate." [27]

The war provided social as well as economic benefits to some groups. Religious leaders were pleased to note the increase in church attendance and the beginning of the turn to religion that characterized the postwar period. "In spite of the fact that I hate war," wrote one Midwestern church leader, "I do believe it rallies folk around worthwhile activities more than . . . when they are allowed to go peacefully about their own affairs." Another religious prelate regarded soldiers as "missionaries as they depart to their posts in distant lands in conquest of souls for Christ." [28] Women found that wartime employment and the conscription of their husbands into the armed forces enhanced their social status. While many perceived the wartime period as drab and dispiriting, living as they were in poor housing and following their husbands about, others developed economic independence for the first time, and a larger share in the management of the home. A sociological study of 135 Iowa families deprived of their males by the armed forces during World War II revealed that a sizable number "did not miss their husbands at all, were glad to be free." Unlike the women of other nations, observed anthropologist Margaret Mead shortly after the war, American women "have suffered no important and catastrophic hardships of any sort. They have not been starved or bombed out, they have not been evacuated or had evacuees quartered upon them." Indeed, "here at home, they have been safe and their children have been

[27] Janeway, The Struggle for Survival, pp. 279, 335, 338; New York Times, July 6, 1945; Paul Gallico, "What We Talked About," While You Were Gone, p. 34. Compare this picture of American well-being with that of Europe at the end of the war, as reported by an American newspaper: "The average Greek man, woman, and child must live, this winter, on ⅓ of the American consumption of calories. . . . 10,000 Poles are dying monthly from tuberculosis caused by malnutrition; 75% of the adults and 85% of the children are without footwear. . . . 5000 die monthly in Vienna from tuberculosis, and the death rate is expected to double by Christmas." New York Times, November 13, 1945.

[28] F. E. Johnson, "The Impact of the War on Religion," p. 359; Spellman, The Road to Victory, p. 113.

safe. They have been asked to go on living pretty much as they did before." [29]

The available evidence suggests that Americans were conscious of their good fortune. Asked in August, 1943, if they personally had "had to make any real sacrifices" because of the war, 69 per cent of the country replied that they had made none. Two rechecks in subsequent polls revealed similar sentiments. The same question in January, 1945, found 64 per cent of the population contending that it had yet to make "any real sacrifices" for the war. When Americans were asked in March, 1940, if they thought they would be personally affected if the United States entered the war, 84 per cent of the population responded affirmatively, but in September, 1946, wiser after their World War II experience, only 51 per cent of the population reported its situation changed, while 48 per cent did not. Moreover, of this 51 per cent, a considerable segment reported changes for the better. Only 36 per cent of Americans believed their lives were any worse because of the war.[30]

Thus, after four years of conflict many Americans had learned that war was not an entirely unpalatable phenomenon. Few argued that it was a positive good, but many found, as sociologist Ruth Benedict wisely observed, that war "has its compensations." Indeed, peace was a risky business if it meant a return to the poverty of the Thirties. "This war has begotten one fear which seems altogether

[29] Janeway, The Struggle for Survival, p. 332; Ernest W. Burgess, "The Effect of the War on the American Family," American Journal of Sociology, XLVIII (November, 1942), 348–49; Reuben Hill, Families under Stress: Adjustment to the Crises of War Separation and Reunion, p. 59; Margaret Mead, "The Women in the War," While You Were Gone, p. 288.

[30] Cantril, Public Opinion, pp. 1121, 1171, 1178; Lydgate, What America Thinks, p. 70. Norman Thomas reported in 1947: "In the United States, to a degree that most Americans do not like to admit, war was accepted if not welcomed as a release from chronic depression and unemployment. In World War II for the last time in history Americans were exempt from the ruin which war brought to Europe. They found great compensation for war's sacrifices in the relief that first a defense boom, and then war itself, brought from the poverty and boredom of unemployment. I travel extensively in America, and few things have ever impressed me so much as the evidence I found, especially during the presidential campaign of 1944, that, despite growing casualty lists, many men and women rather easily reconciled themselves to an indefinite continuance of successful warfare so long as it brought them jobs, a sense of doing important work, and, in the aggregate, more food than they had had in peace." N. M. Thomas, Appeal to the Nations, pp. 5–6.

new," wrote Bernard DeVoto. "It is not often acknowledged. It has had little public expression, little direct expression even in private. It has to be sought in overtones, between the lines, as an implication and inference," but "it exists and it may well be the most truly terrifying phenomenon of the war. It is a fear of the coming of peace." [31]

Yet while World War II set many of the patterns of the postwar period, numerous crosscurrents emerged, the most significant of which was the widespread admiration for America's wartime ally, the Soviet Union. Subsequent charges and investigations of "twenty years of treason" have portrayed this strange love affair between Americans and the Red army as a typical case of liberal, New Deal perfidy. In fact, however, aside from the Communists, who were no doubt pleased by the turn of events, the prime movers in the wartime worship of the Soviet regime ran from slightly right of center to the forces of "archreaction."

Shortly after America's entry into the war, conservative spokesmen began to discover the virtues of the Soviet system. In early 1942 the Daughters of the American Revolution (D.A.R.) held their fifty-first "Continental Congress," in which they sang the national anthem and pledged allegiance to the flag nine times during five days, passed resolutions endorsing the Dies Committee, opposed joint income tax returns and foreign-language schools, and gave considerable praise to Russia. Mrs. Tryphosa Duncan Bates-Batcheller explained to the delegates that "Stalin is a university graduate and a man of great studies. He is a man, who, when he sees a great mistake, admits it and corrects it. Today in Russia, Communism is practically non-existent." Captain Eddie Rickenbacker, returning from a tour of the Soviet Union in 1943, told newsmen that he was impressed by the iron discipline in Russian industrial plants, severe punishments for absenteeism, compulsory overtime work, and the lack of "labor difficulties." "If they keep going on as they are," announced the jubilant airline executive, "you'll find Russia coming out of this war the greatest democracy in the world." Marshal Stalin's unwillingness to meet with other Allied leaders "should not be

[31] Ruth Benedict, "Primitive Freedom," *Atlantic Monthly*, CLXIX (June, 1942), p. 762; DeVoto, "The Easy Chair," pp. 345–47.

misunderstood," Captain Rickenbacker advised Americans. "The Soviet leader has been extremely busy." [32]

As if to make up for their past hostility, Americans of power and influence heaped tributes upon America's wartime ally. In 1941 American diplomat Joseph E. Davies wrote his apologia for the U.S.S.R. *Mission to Moscow* which was soon made into a Hollywood feature presentation. Philadelphia's conservative aristocracy flocked to the local concert hall to hear the Philadelphia Orchestra introduce the new Russian anthem, "Hymn to the Soviet Union." In 1943 Gardner Cowles, Jr., publisher of *Look* magazine, demanded that Americans make an "unequivocal commitment" to postwar cooperation with the Soviet Union. Stalin, he asserted, "wants just what the United States wants—security and peace." Columnist Walter Winchell told millions in 1944 that "fear of Russia" was a "bogey." At the end of the war General Eisenhower stated that "nothing guides Russian policy so much as a desire for friendship with the United States." [33]

The nation's political leaders were equally fulsome with their praise. Wendell Willkie's *One World* illustrates the degree to which Marshal Stalin captivated Americans of conservative leanings. Willkie reported happily that Russian leaders "talk little and listen well" and that "a surprising number of them are young, in their thirties." A result of Stalin's fanatical purges? No; the Soviet leader was just young at heart. "It would be my guess," wrote the Republican Party leader, "that Stalin likes a pretty heavy turnover of young people in his immediate entourage in the Kremlin. It is his way, I think, of keeping his ear to the ground." At a New York dinner on February

[32] "D.A.R. Makes History at Chicago Meeting," *Life*, XII (May 18, 1942), 34–35; *New York Times*, August 18, 1943; Paul Willen, "Who 'Collaborated' with Russia?" *Antioch Review*, XIV (September, 1954), 273. Business executives have frequently found much to admire in the Soviet system. A *Fortune* poll in 1945, for example, revealed that businessmen held more favorable views toward Russia than did the "poor and oppressed." Professor of industrial engineering Seymour Melman recounts this anecdote: "During a visit to Moscow, an American businessman suggested to me, that now that 'things are getting better between Russia and the United States, maybe we can learn something from them.' 'What is that?' I asked. He replied: 'Perhaps they can teach us how to take care of the unions.'" Peter G. Filene, *American Views of Soviet Russia, 1917–1965*, p. 161; Seymour Melman, *The Peace Race*, p. 40.

[33] S. Adler, *The Isolationist Impulse*, pp. 297–98; Willen, "Who 'Collaborated' with Russia?" pp. 260, 275; Agar, *The Price of Power*, p. 2.

23, 1943, Utah's Senator Elbert Thomas compared the Red army
with the forces serving under George Washington. "Freed by the
people's army, Russia today knows what she is fighting for," the
Senator exclaimed. "Men, women, and even children, have tasted
freedom." On the same day the New York State Senate passed a
special resolution commending the Red army, while some months
later former New York City Mayor James J. Walker told a cheering
mass rally that the Red army's "heartwarming gallantry" was an
inspiration to civilization.[34]

American mass-circulation magazines joined the love feast. *Reader's Digest* published a condensation of *Mission to Moscow* which,
among other revelations, including this analysis by Ambassador
Davies of the 1936–1938 purges: " 'What about the fifth columnists
in Russia?'—I replied, right off the anvil, 'There aren't any—they
shot them.' " *Reader's Digest* also carried a condensation of Sumner
Welles' *Time for Decision,* in which Welles observed that although
it was "superficially true" that the Soviet Union was a dictatorship,
"from the standpoint of the Russian people" that was "a hopelessly
inadequate appraisal." The *National Geographic Magazine* of May,
1943, contained a photograph of a father and son gazing reverently
toward the Kremlin. "There son," read the caption, "lives Marshal
Stalin, Head of the Government." [35]

To *Life* magazine, however, goes the prize for a degree of servile
admiration for the Soviet regime that would make even a hardened
Communist Party bureaucrat blush. Its March, 1943, issue, devoted
solely to Russia, exhibited an awesome but kindly picture of the
Soviet savior on its cover. The photograph was an exceptionally

---

[34] Wendell L. Willkie, *One World,* pp. 50–87; Willen, "Who 'Collaborated'
with Russia?" p. 271. British Prime Minister Winston Churchill followed a
similar course. On May 24, 1944, he told Parliament: "Profound changes have
taken place in Soviet Russia. The Trotskyite form of communism has been
completely wiped out." At this point William Gallacher, a Communist M.P.,
interposed: "There never was such a thing." Churchill continued. "The victories of the Russian armies have been attended by a great rise in strength of
the Russian state and a remarkable broadening of its views. The religious side
of Russian life has had a wonderful rebirth. The discipline and military
etiquette of the Russian armies are unsurpassed. There is a new national
anthem." Interrupting Churchill, an M.P. laughed and interjected a comment,
to which the Tory leader replied: "The honorable gentleman had better be
careful to keep in step." *New York Times,* May 25, 1944.
[35] Willen, "Who 'Collaborated' with Russia?" pp. 266–67, 269.

difficult one to take, according to the editors, since "Stalin's granite face kept breaking into a grin." A *Life* editorial set the tone. Russians "live under a system of tight state-controlled information," the editors conceded, "but probably the attitude to take toward this is not to get too excited about it." After all, "if the Soviet leaders tell us that the control of information was necessary . . . we can afford to take their word for it." *Life* apparently took the word of Soviet "leaders" on other matters, too. The N.K.V.D., reported the magazine, was "a national police similar to the F.B.I." A very necessary one, too, because after his exile from Russia Trotsky had left behind "a secret network of opposition which strove for years to undermine the government." Answering questions about Russia's religious freedom in the same issue, the ubiquitous Ambassador Davies pointed proudly to the 1936 constitution. Although there was some opposition to the adoption of provisions for religious freedom among a few Party members, he admitted, objections "were overcome by Premier Stalin's personal advocacy of their passage." [36]

Members of the non-Communist Left fought back against this glorification of totalitarianism. "Stalin's rule," stated Norman Thomas in 1944, was "the most comprehensive and amoral dictatorship on earth." In May, 1943, a letter to the *New York Times* from John Dewey and Suzanne LaFollette, who had served respectively as chairman and secretary of the international commission of inquiry into the Moscow Trials of 1937–1938, provided a devastating critique of the Warner Brothers film adaptation of Ambassador Davies' book. "The film 'Mission to Moscow,'" they charged, "is the first instance in our country of totalitarian propaganda for mass consumption." The country's independent radicals were particularly incensed by American-Soviet wartime agreements. "Teheran read backward spells nature," quipped Daniel Bell. Norman Thomas assailed "the type of liberalism which justifies in Stalin what it condemns in Hitler." American Socialists decried the Kremlin's execution of Polish Socialists and the Katyn Forest massacre, both of which were either ignored or distorted by the mass media.[37]

[36] *Life*, XIV (March 29, 1943), cover and pp. 8, 20, 36, 40, 49.
[37] N. M. Thomas, *What Is Our Destiny*, pp. 77–80; *New York Times*, May 9, 1943; Daniel Bell, Letter to the Editor, *Politics*, II (February, 1945), 62;

Pacifists, similarly appalled, once again struggled against the tide. The W.I.L.P.F. delegates at the San Francisco conference reported: "A new phenomenon has occurred. Any criticism of Russia is seen as a terrific danger and a way of encouraging war with Soviet! So those who were the most vocal in the past against any 'appeasement' . . . seem prepared to reverse themselves when the same situation arises in regard to Russia." Yet, "it seems to us here," noted the indignant pacifists, "that we serve not only our own country's best interests but Russia's when we continue to criticize the present Russian policy." A. J. Muste protested to Acting Secretary of State Joseph Grew over the State Department's claim that it had no knowledge of the sixteen Poles arrested by Russia on charges of divisive operations against the Red army. He suggested that the government was soft-pedaling the Polish issue to gain the favor of the U.S.S.R., and warned of "appeasement of the Russian government." When Senator Claude Pepper criticized Muste's "attitude of mistrust and apprehension toward a major nation," the pacifist leader gently replied that "we must be realistic and not deceive ourselves into thinking that good-will and trust exist when they do not." [38]

But the critics of Soviet policy were hopelessly outmaneuvered and outnumbered. A wartime poll revealed that 46 per cent of the American respondents were of the opinion that Russia had a government "as good as she could have for her people," while only 28 per cent held a contrary view. By the end of the war most Americans believed that Russia could be trusted to cooperate with the United States in the postwar period.[39] And while this honeymoon would endure for a short time, it was in the long run of little value to the cause of international reconciliation, for those Americans who most loved Marshal Stalin's grins merely reacted with the anger born of

Norman Thomas to Roger H. Soltau, March 23, 1945, Thomas MSS, Box 47; Willen, "Who 'Collaborated' with Russia?" pp. 278–79.

[38] Dorothy Detzer, Ruth Gage-Colby, and Mary Farquharson, "We Went to San Francisco" (1945), WILPF MSS, Box 30; A. J. Muste to Joseph Grew, May 28, 1945, FOR MSS, Box 8; Claude Pepper to John Nevin Sayre, April 25, 1945, FOR MSS, Box 10; A. J. Muste to Claude Pepper, May 9, 1945, FOR MSS, Box 10.

[39] Howe and Coser, The American Communist Party, p. 431; Cantril, "Opinion Trends in World War II," p. 39; Filene, American Views of Soviet Russia, p. 163.

betrayal when, in later years, they became aware that he was not the Soviet George Washington. Pacifists and independent radicals, assessing Russian policy more realistically in wartime, maintained their equilibrium far better during postwar crises involving the Soviet bloc.

Unlike World War I, the second World War produced no great wave of disillusionment. The former had been blessed with ludicrous encomiums which held up poorly over time, but the latter received only the most guarded praise, and consequently the American people never acquired that degree of idealism which demanded spectacular changes in international relations. "Actually nobody is fighting for any ideal at all," exclaimed a soldier in the South Pacific. "They're fighting for their lives and to get this damn mess over with so they can go back home and forget about the rest of the world." The noble principles of the Atlantic Charter were virtually unknown to Americans. In 1942, after the Atlantic Charter had been proclaimed by Roosevelt and Churchill and widely discussed by the press, 79 per cent of those polled in the United States admitted that they had never heard of it, and 90 per cent were unable to name any of its provisions. Another survey found 61 per cent of the respondents ignorant of the much-heralded Four Freedoms. In March, 1942, a majority of Americans polled admitted having no "clear idea of what the war is all about." Two years later, after exposure to the bulk of the nation's wartime "information," over 40 per cent of a national sample still maintained this position.[40]

The resulting tolerance for the war precluded disillusionment; shortcomings were expected. "While some thirty years ago the idea of a war to end wars could be taken seriously," wrote John Dewey in 1945, "we now indulge only in the modest hope of being able to establish a peace that will last a generation or two." Polls in 1946 reflected an astonishing split. Asked if they thought "the war helped to solve any of the problems the world faced before the war," 63 per cent of the respondents answered "no." In fact, 77 per cent agreed that the war brought "new problems for the world to solve that we

---

[40] Bailey, *The Man in the Street*, p. 164; Cantril, *Public Opinion*, pp. 1077, 1083; Cantril, "Opinion Trends in World War II," p. 38; Herbert Blumer, "Morale," *American Society in Wartime*, pp. 222–23.

wouldn't have if there hadn't been a war." But only 15 per cent thought it a mistake for the United States to have entered the war. Startled by the lack of disillusionment they found among soldiers, a group of social psychologists observed that "soldiers had no very pronounced expectations of anything coming out of the war" and "hence, a strong reaction of disillusionment after VE Day hardly should have been anticipated—one cannot be disillusioned if his initial expectations are not particularly high." The "lack of emotional 'letdown' seems best explained by the fact that there were very few illusions to be shattered," the psychologists concluded.[41]

The suppression of civil liberties during World War I had initi-ated a wave of disillusionment among liberals, but World War II occasioned few comparable outbreaks of repression. To be sure, the Japanese-American internment camps, the imprisonment of over 6000 conscientious objectors, the trial of Trotskyite leaders under the Smith Act, and the totalitarian aspects of Administration plans for a labor draft involved serious abridgments of constitutional guaran-tees. Nevertheless, formerly apprehensive for domestic freedoms in wartime, the liberals were now jubilant at the nation's compara-tively good record. Liberal journalist Michael Straight wrote proudly to a pacifist magazine in 1945: "You state that 'modern war . . . will in the end make fascists of us all.' Many people held this fear," but "it has proved to be groundless." Consequently, liber-als were far less disillusioned with the second World War than they had been with the first.[42]

Of all the elements that combined to render World War II a relatively satisfying conflict for Americans, perhaps the most signifi-cant involved the nature of the enemy. Unlike the Central Powers of World War I, the Axis nations of World War II "certainly did their best to provide . . . all the normal conditions of the just war," as one pacifist admitted. The brooding evil of Adolf Hitler would cast a ghastly pall over all future discussions of the war. John Cogley of

[41] John Dewey, "Democratic Versus Coercive International Organization: The Realism of Jane Addams," Introduction to Jane Addams, *Peace and Bread in Time of War*, p. xi; Cantril, *Public Opinion*, pp. 978, 1111; Stouffer, *The American Soldier*, II, 595–97.

[42] Michael Straight, "A Non-Pacifist Answers," *Pacifica Views*, I (January 26, 1945), 1; S. Adler, *The Isolationist Impulse*, p. 295.

the Center for the Study of Democratic Institutions wrote years later of World War II: "Those who fought it do not, a decade and a half after it was brought to a close, feel that they acted irrationally. They tend, rather, to think of Nazism as an aggressive force that had to be stopped and see their role in the war not as armed ideologues meeting rival ideologues," but rather "as defenders of national integrity, property and human life resisting by force those who were on a rampage of destruction." Walter Millis agreed: "As John Cogley observes, most of us still feel that the war on Nazism was a morally justified enterprise—it was better to have fought that evil, even at the price of a slaughter, than to have acquiesced in it." [43]

For many who lived through the late Thirties and the war years, the recollection of fascism served as a continuing rationale for the rejection of pacifism. "This general satisfaction that the U.S. did right to help win the second World War is one reason . . . why contemporary pacifism has so little appeal for us," Cogley acknowledged. "The very thought of a Hitler victory . . . still suggests more horror than can be elicited by even the liveliest memory of the war's anguish." It is "no love of violence . . . that keeps even religious men out of the pacifist's camp," he argued; "rather it is their recent experience with totalitarian evil." [44] The revival of pacifism as a significant social movement awaited the maturing of a generation with less emotional investment in the tragic world crisis that occasioned World War II—a generation that did not perceive this particular war as the prototype. For many who lived through them, however, the years of the struggle against fascism provided the frame of reference for their future assessment of war and peace.

The end of the war found Americans more committed than ever before to the use of armed force in international relations. Proposals for postwar conscription received overwhelming support from the nation. Although only 37 per cent favored compulsory military training in late 1938, approval varied between 67 and 75 per cent during the war, dipped to 65 per cent in August, 1945, and increased by

[43] Bainton, *Christian Attitudes toward War and Peace*, p. 220; John Cogley, "A World without War," *The Moral Dilemma of Nuclear Weapons*, ed. William Clancy, pp. 26–27; Walter Millis, "War As a Moral Problem," *The Moral Dilemma of Nuclear Weapons*, p. 31.

[44] Cogley, "A World without War," pp. 26–27.

late October again to 75 per cent; opposition never rose above 29 per cent of those polled. When asked in November, 1945, which they would rather do first—"pass a law requiring boys over eighteen to take a year of military training in the future, or try to get the world organization to abolish military training in every country in the world"—Americans overwhelmingly chose the former. Although the United States army had consisted of 190,000 men prior to the war, a poll in June, 1945, reported that the mean number desired by Americans for their postwar, peacetime army was 2,000,000. It may be argued, of course, that Americans were merely reacting to what they perceived as a Soviet military threat; but a June, 1946, poll found greater support for a peacetime draft among Americans with no fears of Russian aggression than among those who believed Russia desired world domination.[45]

International disarmament proposals found few proponents in the United States. Asked in October, 1945, if they favored a multilateral agreement to abolish standing armies and military training, 68 per cent of the respondents said "no" and only 24 per cent, "yes." A similar poll in March, 1946, asking if the United States, Great Britain, and Russia should "get together and do away with armaments and military training," received a reply two to one in the negative. In the immediate aftermath of the atomic explosions in Japan, only 14 per cent of a national sample favored turning the new weapon over to an international organization. A string of military bases circling the globe appealed to Americans far more than any disarmament proposals. In June, 1943, surely a time when popular fear of Soviet expansion after the war was at its nadir, 84 per cent of those polled believed the United States "should come out of this war with more military bases outside this country"; only 8.1 per cent disagreed. Sadly, Clarence Pickett of the A.F.S.C. observed: "We have emerged from World War II more fearful, more anxious, more committed to the use of physical violence for protection, than we have ever been before." [46]

In their confrontation with the world's most powerful military

[45] Cantril, *Public Opinion*, pp. 458–59, 466, 472, 944.
[46] *Ibid.*, pp. 21, 170, 1170; Stuart Chase, *American Credos*, p. 70; Pickett, *For More than Bread*, p. 336.

establishment, pacifists could expect little support from the public. The contest was surely a lopsided one. Yet, the final and most devastating stroke of the war—the great burst of flame that instantly consumed the cities of Hiroshima and Nagasaki—redressed some of the balance. For in the eerie half-light of its atomic glow, a new group of Americans, suddenly perceiving the end of the road, concluded that mankind had to be drawn back from the rim of the abyss.

CHAPTER V

Hiroshima: The Good News of Damnation

Leon Bloy, the French philosopher, referred to the good news of damnation, doubtless on the theory that none of us would be Christians if we were not afraid of perpetual hell-fire. It may be that the atomic bomb is the good news of damnation, that it may frighten us into that Christian character and those righteous actions and those positive political steps necessary to the creation of a world society, not a thousand or five hundred years hence, but now.

ROBERT M. HUTCHINS [1]

At 8:15 A.M. on August 6, 1945, a single American plane, flying high over the Japanese city of Hiroshima, released an atomic bomb. "Because of the lack of warning," noted the United States Strategic Bombing Survey, "the explosion came as an almost complete surprise, and the people had not taken shelter." The government agency estimated that seventy to eighty thousand were killed and an equal number injured; military troops represented less than 5 per cent of the casualties. In the United States the reaction to the news of the atomic devastation overshadowed even the celebration of the war's end nine days later. President Harry S. Truman, on board the U.S.S. *Augusta* in mid-Atlantic when word of the Hiroshima explosion arrived, proudly told the ship's crew: "This is the greatest thing in history." [2]

---

[1] "Atomic Force, Its Meaning for Mankind," *University of Chicago Round Table*, No. 386 (August 12, 1945), p. 12.

[2] U.S. Strategic Bombing Survey, *The Effects of Atomic Bombs on Hiroshima and Nagasaki*, pp. 3, 5; Arthur Holly Compton, *Atomic Quest*, p. 254n; Curti, *The Growth of American Thought*, p. 745; Michael Amrine, *The Great Decision: The Secret History of the Atomic Bomb*, p. 202.

The use of the bomb immediately initiated a public controversy. Churchmen, especially, questioned the wisdom and morality of the atomic attack upon Japanese cities. In a joint statement on August 9, 1945, Bishop G. Bromley Oxnam, president of the Federal Council of Churches, and John Foster Dulles, chairman of the Council's Commission on a Just and Durable Peace, called for "a temporary suspension or alteration of our program of air attack on the Japanese homeland." On the same day the Reverend Bernard Iddings Bell declared at a noonday service in Trinity Church, on Wall Street and Broadway, that any victory secured by the atomic bomb would be "at the price of world-wide moral revulsion against us." Dr. Bell stated that he doubted if Christian missions in the Orient under Western auspices would "ever again matter." American religion and democracy, he observed, "stand discredited in all Asia and elsewhere too." [3]

The clerical revolt against atomic warfare gathered momentum in subsequent months. Editors of Roman Catholic publications, spurred on by the Pope's criticism of the bombing of Hiroshima and Nagasaki, occasionally subjected the American decision to sharp attack. One wrote: "I think the use of the atomic bomb, in the circumstances, was atrocious and abominable, and that civilized people should reprobate and anathematize the horrible deed." On August 20, thirty-four church leaders of different faiths, mostly pacifists, assailed the use of the atomic bomb as "an atrocity of a new magnitude," and asked the President to order a halt to further bomb production. "Its reckless and irresponsible employment against an already virtually beaten foe will have to receive judgment before God and the conscience of humankind," they declared. "It has our unmitigated condemnation." The high-water mark of clerical discontent, however, was reached in March, 1946, when the Federal Council of Churches announced: "As American Christians, we are deeply penitent for the irresponsible use already made of the atomic bomb." The bombing of Hiroshima and Nagasaki were termed "morally indefensible." Americans had "sinned grievously against

[3] Richard Barnet, *Who Wants Disarmament?* pp. 5-6; *New York Times,* August 10, 1945.

the laws of God and against the people of Japan," this church organization concluded.[4]

Yet while indignation and dismay at America's use of atomic weapons held the initiative in religious circles during the postwar months, church leaders were far from united behind a pacifist banner. "You have certainly misrepresented the church in your condemnation of the government, and you have provoked some of our leading laymen to an extreme degree," one clergyman wrote to A. J. Muste. "So far, so good," the president of the World Alliance for International Friendship through the Churches commented on the use of the atomic bomb. He found the new weapon deplorable only when "in the hands of sinful men." Moreover, the report of the Federal Council of Churches, stern as it was on the bombing of Hiroshima and Nagasaki, refused to condemn the use of atomic weapons under all circumstances. Thus the ringing denunciation of the atomic bomb by this august church body in effect accomplished virtually nothing; it could not rescind the use of the atomic bomb in the past, and would not preclude its use in the future.[5]

Pacifists, jarred into action by the unexpected bombings, provided the hard core of American discontent. "When the bomb dropped on Hiroshima, we were in the midst of a project with tenant farmers and sharecroppers in South Carolina," recalled a Quaker pacifist, "but it almost seemed as though the bomb had dropped on us too. . . . I thought we had now just about reached . . . dead end." Dorothy Day grew unexpectedly sarcastic as she talked of the President. "He went from table to table on the cruiser which was bringing him home from the Big Three conference," she noted, "telling the great news, 'jubilant,' the newspapers said. *Jubilate Deo*. We have killed 318,000 Japanese." Christ, she asserted, had already

---

[4] Moellering, *Modern War and the American Churches*, p. 55; *New York Times*, August 20, 1945; Federal Council of Churches, *Atomic Warfare and the Christian Faith*, Report of the Commission on the Relation of the Church to the War in the Light of the Christian Faith (March, 1946), pp. 11–12; *New York Times*, March 6, 1946.

[5] Harold E. Nicely to A. J. Muste, October 1, 1945, FOR MSS, Box 9; G. Ashton Oldham, "A Message from the President of the World Alliance," *World Alliance News Letter*, XXI (September, 1945), 1; Muste, *Not by Might*, pp. 161–68.

given his judgment of the act: "What you do unto the least of these my brethren, you do unto me." [6]

They were joined by other elements of the peace movement who had given the war their support. "Our . . . use of two atomic bombs to destroy crowded cities" was an atrocity "of the first magnitude," recalled Norman Thomas. "We shall pay for all this in a horrified hatred of millions of people which goes deeper and farther than we think." Dwight Macdonald, jolted at last into an outright pacifist position, contended that the bombing of Hiroshima and Nagasaki "places 'us,' the defenders of civilization, on a moral level with 'them,' the beasts of Maidanek"; it represented, he remarked, "*Götterdammerung* without the gods." Many American intellectuals experienced a sickening sense of human decay and moral emptiness. The poet Hermann Hagedorn wrote:

> What have we done, my country, what have we done?
> Our fathers knew greatness.
> What shall the shrunken soul do to fill out and be itself again?
> Our fathers knew mercy.
> What will the wet stick do to burn once more?
> A sickness eats at our hearts.
> Our bodies have grown fat and our souls thin.[7]

Yet although public indignation at the use of the atomic bomb reached beyond the borders of the World War II pacifist constituency, it never represented a dominant current in public opinion. On August 8, 1945, a poll found that only 10 per cent of the population opposed the use of atomic bombs on Japanese cities, while 85 per

[6] Wilmer J. Young, *Visible Witness: A Testimony for Radical Peace Action*, p. 18; *Catholic Worker*, September, 1945. After the bombings, C. O. Bent Andresen walked out of his C.P.S. camp, asserting: "I will devote the time I have, til the prison doors close behind me, to awakening America to what she has done." As he hitchhiked through the country, he distributed the following statement on mimeographed handbills: "If we should be blind to the wickedness of a needless act of such horror, our minds and hearts would become . . . hardened. . . . What would be left to keep us from the political and ethical blackness that was Nazi Germany?" "Walkout," *Pacifica Views*, III (August 31, 1945), 2; Bent Andresen, "A Message to People of Goodwill," FOR MSS, Box 12.

[7] N. M. Thomas, *Appeal to the Nations*, p. 18; Fleischman, *Norman Thomas*, p. 215; Dwight Macdonald, Editorial, *Politics*, II (August, 1945), 225; Macdonald, *Memoirs of a Revolutionist*, pp. 27–28, 177; Hermann Hagedorn, *The Bomb that Fell on America*, p. 14.

cent approved. A more detailed breakdown of popular sentiment on the use of atomic bombs against Japan is provided by a *Fortune* poll of December, 1945, which revealed that 22.7 per cent of the respondents wanted to use "many more of them before Japan had a chance to surrender," 53.5 per cent favored the manner in which the bombs were actually utilized, 13.5 per cent advocated a test demonstration before use on cities, and that only 4.5 per cent "would not have used any atomic bombs at all." [8]

The massive support given the atomic holocaust by the American people was compounded from diverse and seemingly contradictory sentiments. On the one hand, hatred of the Japanese people provided strong motivation. "I have no feeling of guilt whatever in the use of the atomic bombs on Japan," wrote one lady. "I only regret that atomic bombs were not used to blast the four Jap islands into oblivion." Her solution to the war: genocide. "There may be innocent women and children, but they only in my opinion breed more of the same kind of soldiers to make us trouble in the future." Congressman Charles A. Plumley of Vermont expressed much the same attitude in a telegram of congratulations on the bombing to Secretary of State James Byrnes. "The American people are backing you and the president to the limit," he avowed, "determined that now is the time to exterminate the Yellow Peril for all time. . . . Let the rats squeal." Others, perhaps most, tied their support of the bombings to humanitarian considerations. "I am happy that the bomb was used to end the war and to save the lives of millions of Japanese as well as Americans," an atomic scientist wrote.[9]

A series of government reports in 1946, however, began to under-

---

[8] Cantril, *Public Opinion*, pp. 20, 23; Bailey, *The Man in the Street*, p. 194; "The Fortune Survey," *Fortune*, XXXII (December, 1945), 305.

[9] L.A.D. to Post War World Council, September 5, 1945, Thomas MSS, Box 48; *Burlington Free Press*, August 11, 1945, clipping in Thomas MSS, Box 48; Robert S. Stone to A. J. Muste, April 1, 1946, FOR MSS, Box 12. Pacifists grew incensed at the "humanitarian" justifications. Kirby Page wrote: "So thoroughly had the American people been indoctrinated with the idea of military necessity that for most of them the statement that the atomic bomb brought the war to an end more quickly and saved thousands of American lives was all the justification needed for its use. Atrocity had ceased to be atrocity when it saved American lives. Moral sensitivity had become so seared and deadened that the atrocity of massacring 50,000 human beings in the image of God was hailed as a supreme blessing to mankind." Page, *Now Is the Time*, p. 6.

cut the "humanitarian justification" by pointing to how close Japan was to surrender at the time of the bombings. "It cannot be said . . . that the atomic bomb convinced the leaders who effected the peace of the necessity of surrender," declared one government report. A carefully researched study by the Strategic Bombing Survey similarly concluded that "the Hiroshima and Nagasaki atomic bombs did not defeat Japan, nor . . . did they persuade Japan to accept unconditional surrender." Based upon a detailed investigation of the political situation in Japan and on interviews with Japanese leaders, the Survey proclaimed: "Certainly prior to 31 December 1945, and in all probability prior to 1 November 1945, Japan would have surrendered even if the atomic bombs had not been dropped . . . and even if no invasion had been planned or contemplated." Retired Secretary of State Byrnes remarked impatiently: "The military experts informed us that . . . our invasion would cost us a million casualties." [10]

Yet the real source of long-term guilt reactions was novelist John Hersey's "Hiroshima," which avoided a discussion of the necessity of the bombing and focused instead upon the tragedy it entailed. The *New Yorker* devoted its entire August 31, 1946, issue to an account by Hersey of the effect of the Hiroshima bombing upon the lives of six people. "The impact of this story on the American people was striking," observed two psychologists. Copies of the magazine issue were immediately at a premium, and newspapers reprinted the entire 30,000-word account, carrying editorials and news articles concerning its significance. "Hiroshima" was read over a major radio network and published in book form, whereupon it became an immediate best seller. Letters poured into the *New Yorker* office approving the story by ten to one. Typical was the agonized appraisal of one reader: "As I read I had to constantly remind myself that we perpetrated this monstrous tragedy. We Americans." An atomic scientist recalled: "I wept as I read John Hersey's *New Yorker* account. . . . We didn't realize." For decades thereafter, a strain of anxiety remained. Americans traveled to Japan in expiation, raised money to assist the victims of the bombing, and even fabricated the romantic

[10] U.S. Strategic Bombing Survey, *The Effects of Atomic Bombs on Hiroshima and Nagasaki*, p. 22; U.S. Strategic Bombing Survey, *Japan's Struggle to End the War*, pp. 12–13; James F. Byrnes, *Speaking Frankly*, p. 262.

legend of a "Hiroshima Pilot," plagued with remorse for his role in the dropping of the bomb. It is surely one of the curiosities of twentieth-century American life that this recurrent theme of America's collective guilt, so deeply moving and compelling for some, in fact touched so few.[11]

Yet if guilt did not mobilize any large sector of the populace in the struggle against war, the exigencies of survival did. "Hiroshima made me a pacifist," recollected Congresswoman Helen Gahagan Douglas. "Reason has made it clear that war is no longer usable as an instrument of foreign policy, and that war in the future would be senseless." President Truman told his neighbors at a fair in Caruthersville, Missouri: "We can't stand another global war. We can't ever have another war unless it is total war, and that means the end of our civilization as we know it. We are not going to do that." The atomic bomb "means the end of world war," announced Dr. Vannevar Bush, a leading atomic scientist. "Fear will prevent it." Robert M. Hutchins found "only one subject of really fundamental importance at the present moment, and that is the atomic bomb. Although it is not a cheerful subject," he admitted, "we must consider it, for the issue is that of survival, to which all other issues are secondary." [12]

[11] John Luft and W. M. Wheeler, "Reaction to John Hersey's 'Hiroshima,'" *Journal of Social Psychology*, XXVIII (1948), 135–40; John Hersey, "Hiroshima," *New Yorker*, XXII (August 31, 1946), 15–68; V. Naeve, *Friends of the Hibakusha*, pp. 44–63; Alice Kimball Smith, *A Peril and a Hope: The Scientists' Movement in America, 1945–47*, pp. 80–81; Gunther Anders and Claude Eatherly, *Burning Conscience*; William Bradford Huie, *The Hiroshima Pilot*. The *Fortune* survey of opinions on the bombing found that the well-to-do and the well-educated turned in larger minorities than average for the two mildest courses of action suggested, revealing a similar constituency to that of the peace movement. This is also, of course, the *New Yorker* constituency. Somewhat different results could have been attained had letters been received from the poor, whom *Fortune* found to have a proclivity for the more destructive attitudes. A prominent exception in their attitudes were American Negroes, who turned in strong minorities for the milder positions toward Japan, perhaps a reflection of the fact that they bore less racial hatred for the Japanese than their poor white counterparts. "The Fortune Survey," *Fortune*, XXXII (December, 1945), 305. Not all supporters of Hersey's were drawn toward pacifism. One reader declared: "I read Hersey's report. It was marvelous. Now let us drop a handful on Moscow." Luft and Wheeler, "Reaction to John Hersey's 'Hiroshima,'" p. 138.

[12] Weinberg, *Instead of Violence*, p. 3; Muste, *Not by Might*, p. 1; *Washington Post*, December 4, 1945; Robert M. Hutchins, *The Atomic Bomb Versus Civilization*, p. 5. A. J. Muste observed with some amusement: "The practical

The news of the atomic explosion sent a sudden wave of alarm across the globe. "This world is at the end of its tether. The end of everything we call life is close at hand," wrote the aging English author, H. G. Wells. "It is the end." In India, informed of the Hiroshima bombing, Gandhi thought: "Unless now the world adopts nonviolence, it will spell certain suicide for mankind." In the United States the reaction was no less apocalyptic. Books by scientists and scholars appeared with titles such as *One World or None, The Absolute Weapon,* and *Five Minutes to Midnight.* "The underlying populations should regard this new source of energy with lively interest— the interest of victims," advised Dwight Macdonald. "It is written that man may not look upon the face of God and live," an American Senator mused; "it remains to be seen whether man may usurp the power of God and survive." [13]

This immediate response to the atomic explosions was widespread. In September, 1945, 83 per cent of Americans admitted that there was a "real danger" of "most city people on earth being killed by atomic bombs" in the event of another world war. A poll in that same month found that 64 per cent of respondents believed the atomic bomb had made wars less likely. The reason supplied by the vast majority was "fear." Thus, "it was not an altogether unrealistic hope," one atomic scientist maintained in retrospect, "that mankind could be reasoned—or frightened—into entering a new, peaceful world." [14]

Traditional pacifists held ambivalent feelings toward this new phenomenon, later termed "nuclear pacifism." On the one hand, it smacked of a certain selfishness, and seemed to raise a banner of coarse pragmatism in place of pacifist humanitarianism. "Americans would do well to be less concerned about atomic bombs which may be dropped on them than about what the bombs they dropped on

politicians . . . are now saying what the pacifists and impractical idealists used to say, only to be smiled at, sometimes indulgently and often not so indulgently." Muste, *Not by Might,* p. ix.
[13] H. G. Wells, *Mind at the End of Its Tether,* pp. 1, 4; Weinberg, *Instead of Violence,* p. 20; Barnet, *Who Wants Disarmament?* p. 5; Macdonald, Editorial, *Politics,* II (August, 1945), 225; Cranston, "The Strengthening of the U.N. Charter," p. 189.
[14] Cantril, *Public Opinion,* pp. 21–22; Morton Grodzins and Eugene Rabinowitch (eds.), *The Atomic Age: Scientists in National and World Affairs,* p. 6.

Hiroshima and Nagasaki did to them," observed A. J. Muste. Another wrote: "The new 'psychology' . . . is not worthy of mention. It is fear psychology. . . . That is not pacifism. . . . Can you frighten people into being good?" But pacifists could not help but admire the way in which the logic of atomic devastation reinforced their traditional arguments. "It would seem to me," wrote John Swomley on the day after the destruction of Hiroshima, "that now is the time to point out that man has . . . invented an instrument for obliterating such a portion of the earth's surface that it is possible for life to be wiped out, and therefore disarmament is essential." [15]

The current of nuclear pacifism ran deepest among traditional "internationalist" groups—writers, intellectuals, university faculty, scientists, and other Americans of professional status—which had supported World War II. Typical of the peace movement's new recruits was Norman Cousins, the young editor of the *Saturday Review of Literature*. "It seemed . . . that man . . . had come face to face with the problems of human destiny," he wrote years later of the events at Hiroshima; the night of the bombing, he sat down to compose his famous editorial "Modern Man Is Obsolete." "On August 6, 1945, a new age was born," he declared; the dropping of the bomb "marked the violent death of one stage in man's history and the beginning of another." The "new age" created "a blanket of obsolescence not only over the methods and the products of man but over man himself." Cousins contended that Americans had to be made cognizant of the changes, the most awesome of which was that "man's survival on earth is now absolutely dependent on his ability to avoid a new war." Another convert was the liberal news commentator, Raymond Gram Swing. "I was as greatly affected by the atomic bomb as by any event in my lifetime," he recalled almost two decades later. "I felt that along with every member of the human race I was personally involved, and being involved had a personal responsibility. I was a news commentator with the duty of explaining the great issues of the times. This was, I knew, the greatest that had yet arisen." Swing decided to devote one out of five of

---

[15] Muste, *Not by Might*, p. 2; Curtis Zahn to A. J. Muste, October 9, 1945, FOR MSS, Box 12; John M. Swomley, Jr. to A. J. Muste, August 7, 1945, FOR MSS, Box 11.

his radio broadcasts to a discussion of the implications of atomic energy. "The weapons of war have now reached a power which can destroy us, so that if we wish not to be destroyed we must end the use of the weapons," he wrote in 1946. "And since the weapons cannot be effectively banned if war is to continue, there is no choice but to end war." [16]

In their search for a way to end war, however, the majority of nuclear pacifists veered away from the path trodden by most traditional pacifists; instead, they found the means to world peace in the quest for world government. The idea of extending sovereignty to the world community had attracted the attention of writers and scholars since the twelfth century, and had been a persistent theme of the literature of the American peace movement.[17] Yet it was not until the late Thirties that the world government concept had begun to gather momentum in the United States. In 1937 the Campaign for World Government, directed by Rosika Schwimmer and Lola Maverick Lloyd, commenced its pioneer work; it was soon publishing analyses of "the preliminary steps necessary for a representative World Convention to draft the . . . constitution for an all-inclusive . . . Federation of Nations." On June 5, 1939, California Congressman Jerry Voorhis introduced a resolution calling upon the President of the United States to prepare a plan for the calling of such a convention. Interest in world government, however, remained limited. The New York Times correspondent in Geneva covering the League of Nations, Clarence Streit, could not even find a publisher for a book he had written on the subject in 1935.[18]

[16] Norman Cousins, Who Speaks for Man? pp. 14–15; New York Times, May 10, 1966; Norman Cousins, Modern Man Is Obsolete, pp. 8–10; Raymond Swing, In the Name of Sanity, pp. vi–ix, 1; Raymond Swing, "Good Evening!" A Professional Memoir, p. 242.

[17] Lists and explanations of the many world government plans since the Middle Ages are found in: Wynner and Lloyd, Searchlight on Peace Plans, pp. 29–378; Harrop Freeman, Coercion of States in International Organizations, pp. 2–54.

[18] Lola Maverick Lloyd and Rosika Schwimmer, Chaos, War, or a New World Order? p. 3; Rosika Schwimmer, Union Now for Peace or War? The Danger in the Plan of Clarence Streit, pp. 14–15; Clarence K. Streit, The Need for Union Now, p. i.

The coming of war in Europe radically altered the fortunes of the world government movement. The former president of the National Press Club suddenly found Streit's book *Union Now* "the possible answer of the democracies to Adolf Hitler's '*Mein Kampf.*'" After publication in 1939, it immediately became a best seller and over the next few years sold more than 300,000 copies. In rapid succession Streit produced a remarkable number of pamphlets and condensations of his basic plan. Although his ideas varied to some extent with the fortunes of the wartime Allies, his most popular and striking conception envisaged a federal union of "the democracies," of which he counted fifteen. The popularity of his proposals prompted him to establish Federal Union, Inc. in 1943 to help enact the Streit program.[19]

Yet despite the sizable splash it created the Federal Union plan was far from utopian; indeed, in many respects it was positively reactionary. For one thing, it did not foresee a world government but only a union of a minority of nations, not very persuasively defined as "democracies" yet which included countries like the Union of South Africa. Streit boasted of the fact that the "fifteen democracies together practically own this earth"; *Fortune,* expressing strong approval of the plan, observed with delight the fact that "these states already produce 96 per cent of the world's nickel, 95 percent of the rubber, 73 per cent of the iron ore, 72 per cent of the gold, 72 per cent of the tin, 66 per cent of the oil, 65 per cent of the coal, and 65 per cent of the raw cotton." Why, however, one seventh of the world's population should, in Streit's words, "own almost half the earth, rule all its oceans, govern nearly half mankind" was never explained. Streit's program won the endorsement of numerous top corporation executives, including the former president of the United States Chamber of Commerce. Federal Union, wrote the editor of *Fortune,* would "help to develop the free libertarian economy, from which—imperfect as it is—mankind has already derived so much." But despite the plan's conservatism, even such a harsh critic as

[19] Clarence K. Streit, *For Union Now,* inside front cover; S. Adler, *The Isolationist Impulse,* pp. 330–31. Streit's other works include: *The Essence of Union Now; Of Freedom and Union Now; Union Now: The Proposal for the Inter-Democracy Federal Union; Union Now with Britain.*

Rosika Schwimmer had to admit that Streit's book had "given the idea of federal union of the world the greatest publicity it has had since the world campaign for the League of Nations." [20]

Union Now was followed in wartime by an avalanche of books and articles advocating various forms of world organization. [21] The most popular and least specific, Wendell Willkie's *One World*, sold over one million copies within two months of its publication, and two million within two years. Slightly less popular was the elaborate formula of bridge expert Ely Culbertson for an international police force. The most politically sophisticated and slashing indictment of the existence of independent nations was presented by a young writer, Emery Reves. Written near the end of the war, Reves' book, *The Anatomy of Peace*, reflects how far the world government principle had moved toward the millennial since Streit's cautious gropings. "Let us be clear about one thing," he wrote. "A league of sovereign nation-states is not a step . . . toward peace. Peace is law. The San Francisco league [i.e., the United Nations Organization] is the pitiful miscarriage of the second World War." He con-

[20] Streit, *For Union Now*, p. 10; Streit, *Union Now*, p. 104; "Business-and-Government," *Fortune*, XIX (April, 1939), 66–67; Federal Union, Inc., *Let's Not Make the Same Mistake Twice*, p. 17; Schwimmer, *Union Now for Peace or War?*, pp. 8–11, 14. An occupational breakdown of the 17 members of the national committee of Union Now in 1940 (excluding Streit) reveals: 4 corporation presidents, 1 corporation lawyer, 1 financial counselor, 1 former editor of *Fortune*, 1 millionaire philanthropist, 3 educational administrators, 3 in teaching or educational research, 1 doctor, 1 citizens union president, and 1 author. All in all, a rather respectable, upper class group. Vernon Nash, *It Must Be Done Again: Thirteen American States Point the Way for the Nations Now*, pp. 42–43.

[21] Among them were: Herbert Agar *et al.*, *The City of Man: A Declaration on World Democracy;* Leslie Balogh Bain, *Chaos or Peace;* Percy Bordwell, "A Constitution for the United Nations," *Iowa Law Review*, XXVIII (March, 1943), 387–421; G. A. Borgese, *Common Cause;* William C. Brewer, *Permanent Peace;* Nicholas Murray Butler, *Toward a Federal World;* Percy E. Corbett, *Post-War Worlds;* Nicholas Doman, *The Coming Age of World Control;* Howard W. Eaton (ed.), *Federation: The Coming Structure of World Government;* Robert M. MacIver, *Towards an Abiding Peace;* Otto Tod Mallery, *Economic Union and Durable Peace;* Scott Nearing, *United World: The Road to International Peace;* Oscar Newfang, *World Federation;* Oscar Newfang, *World Government: A Suggested Formula for Use at the End of the War;* Amos J. Peaslee, *United Nations Government;* Mario A. Pei, *The American Road to Peace: A Constitution for the World;* Ralph Barton Perry, *One World in the Making;* Abe Rogow, *A Plan for Immediate and Lasting Peace;* Wallace C. Speers, *Coorder Nations: A Proposal for World Coordination;* Michael Straight, *Make This the Last War: The Future of the United Nations*.

cluded: "Equal and sovereign power units can never, under any circumstances, under any conditions, coexist peacefully." [22]

During the war years, world government sentiment occasionally exhibited surprising strength on the local level. On March 13, 1941, a resolution memorializing Congress on world federation was adopted by the North Carolina state legislature; the legislature of New Jersey passed a similar resolution in May, 1942. Balloting in Massachusetts during November, 1942, on the question of calling a convention for the purpose of establishing a world government revealed 75 per cent of the state's voters in favor of the proposal. Under the leadership of fifteen-year-old Harris Wofford, Jr., Student Federalist groups sprang up in New York, Minnesota, and Florida, dedicated to the goal of a World State. "It is today the hall-mark of intellectual and moral respectability to say that one believes in 'world cooperation' or 'world government' after the war," Norman Thomas observed with some amusement.[23]

The formation of the United Nations Organization, however, put the advocates of world government in an awkward position. At the time of the Dumbarton Oaks agreements many in the United States believed the United Nations charter too weak to prevent war. Grenville Clark, a New York lawyer, published a long letter in the *New York Times* during late 1944 in which he warned that "this combination of a nearly impotent Assembly . . . and . . . a Council that is hamstrung, or at best hampered, by the right of any one of the Big Five to veto sanctions, must be a weak reed to support the peace of the world." Cord Meyer, a young world federalist who assisted one of the United States delegates at the San Francisco Conference, reported that he "left San Francisco with the conviction that World

[22] Willkie, *One World;* Eric F. Goldman, *Rendezvous with Destiny: A History of Modern American Reform,* p. 307; Edith Wynner, "Ely Culbertson's So-Called Plan for World Federation" (mimeographed); Theodore Paullin, Review of *The World Federation Plan* by Ely Culbertson, *Fellowship,* IX (February, 1943), 38; Ely Culbertson, *Total Peace: What Makes Wars and How to Organize Peace;* S. Adler, *The Isolationist Impulse,* p. 331; Emery Reves, *The Anatomy of Peace,* pp. 273–74.

[23] *The Declaration of the Federation of the World;* Lydgate, *What America Thinks,* p. 45; Stephen Benedict, "Breakers and Makers of Tradition," *Common Cause,* I (September, 1947), 107–108; Harris L. Wofford, Jr., *World Federal Democracy: A Plan for Action,* cover, inside cover, and p. 1; Norman Thomas, *World Federation: What Are the Difficulties?* p. 4.

War III was inevitable, if the U.N. was not substantially strength-ened." The more militant pacifists engaged in a bitter denunciation of plans for the United Nations. "It is an organization only in a nominal sense," announced the W.R.L., "the sense in which an alliance may be called an organization. It therefore misleads people who are anxious for a genuine world government." The F.O.R. contended that "the demand of the Big Nations that they be given veto power and thus left free from the controls which they insist other nations must accept" was indicative of the fact that the U.N. was "likely to prove . . . a camouflage for the continuation of imperialist policies and the exercise of arbitrary power by the Big Three for the domination of the world." [24]

But most Americans who considered the Dumbarton Oaks proposals and later the San Francisco Charter inadequate withheld their criticism, fearful lest the plans for world organization be killed in Congress by the same scissors action of dissidents on both extremes that had destroyed the League of Nations. Harry Emerson Fosdick, for example, worried that "we who wanted a better outcome will turn perfectionist, and . . . will join up with the isolationists . . . and that between us no world organization will be accepted by the Senate." The W.I.L.P.F., the Socialist Party, and the Federal Council of Churches, all disappointed by the concessions to nationalism in the new organization, nevertheless worked for its acceptance by Congress. Advocates of world federation generally urged Senate ratification, hoping that once the United Nations was created it could be transformed from a league of nations into a world government. As E. Raymond Wilson of the Friends Committee on National Legislation observed, the Charter was bad, but it left room for improvement.[25]

[24] Cranston, "The Strengthening of the U.N. Charter," pp. 191–93; *New York Times*, October 15, 1944; Cord Meyer, Jr., *Peace or Anarchy*, pp. 3–5; "An Open Letter from the War Resisters League to the Committee on Foreign Relations of the United States Senate" (August 12, 1945), WRL MSS, Box 2; "Draft Statement on San Francisco Conference" (June 29, 1945), FOR MSS, Box 3.

[25] Cranston, "The Strengthening of the U.N. Charter," pp. 191–93; Harry Emerson Fosdick to A. J. Muste, March 16, 1945, FOR MSS, Box 8; J. H. Randall, *Emily Greene Balch*, p. 11; "National Board Resolutions Re: United Nations Charter," WILPF MSS, Box 4; Norman Thomas, *A Socialist Looks at the United Nations*, p. 21; Federal Council of Churches, "Christian Standards

Hiroshima gave a new impetus to the movement. "What little confidence they had been able to work up in the just-being-refurbished league-of-nations went up in smoke," recalled a world government advocate. The atomic bomb "forced us to look at what we had all been trying not to see: namely that no agreements between sovereign *nations* to do something, or not to do something, are likely ever to amount to much. Of this sad fact we had been amply warned. . . . And yet—even yet, until Hiroshima—we continued to hope. Since Hiroshima, we have begun to see the fallacy of hoping, and have at last begun to demand something more." Robert M. Hutchins told the readers of a world federalist journal: "Time is of the essence. It is now or never. . . . The obstacles in the way of World Government and the unity of mankind are staggering. But the other way lies perdition." Norman Cousins observed that "the need for world government was clear long before August 6, 1945, but Hiroshima and Nagasaki raised that need to such dimensions that it can no longer be ignored." National sovereignty was "preposterous now." [26]

The message spread rapidly that, in Hutchins' words, "the survival of mankind demands a world community, a world government, and a world state." World government "must be given an honest try," wrote the essayist E. B. White; "otherwise our science will have won the day." Owen J. Roberts, retired associate justice of the United States Supreme Court, told 1500 publishers at the annual meeting of the Associated Press in New York that a "parliament of the world" must be established; the "alternative," he warned, would be "the constant peril of utter destruction." The "day the atomic bomb dropped on Hiroshima, a fearful obligation fell upon all who want to perpetuate civilization," wrote the historian Carl Van Doren. "We cannot afford the luxury of national rivalry and jealousy running wild in a world that holds the atom bomb." The "whole development culminating in the atomic bomb is terrible," remarked Rein-

---

and Current International Developments," *International Conciliation*, Number 409 (March, 1945), pp. 143–44; Latourette, "Christianity and the Peace Movement," p. 105; *Conscientious Objector*, June, 1945.

[26] Fremont Rider, *The Great Dilemma of World Organization*, pp. 11–12; Robert M. Hutchins, "1950," *Common Cause*, I (July, 1947), 2; Cousins, *Modern Man Is Obsolete*, pp. 20, 23.

hold Niebuhr. Yet "the fact that the instrument has been created may increase the fear of war sufficiently so that we can build a real world organization. Therein lies our hope." [27]

Diverse sources pooled their energies to give the world government movement an impressive spread of support: Robert L. Lund, former president of the National Association of Manufacturers; Philip Murray, head of the Congress of Industrial Organizations; scientists Albert Einstein and Harold Urey; industrialist Owen D. Young; educator Stringfellow Barr; Senator Glen Taylor and Representative Jerry Voorhis; writers Thomas Mann and Upton Sinclair; and Socialist leader Norman Thomas. Protestant religious spokesmen and organizations endorsed the world government idea. Although few members of the American Catholic hierarchy gave the fledgling movement their approval, a notable exception was the Most Reverend James A. Griffen, Roman Catholic Bishop of Springfield, Illinois. In October, 1945, a group of fifty influential persons were invited to a conference in Dublin, New Hampshire, by former Justice Roberts. Those in attendance included Robert P. Bass, former governor of the state, and Thomas H. Mahoney and Grenville Clark, prominent lawyers. Their conference report called for "a world federal government with limited but definite and adequate powers to prevent war." [28]

Despite the diversity of support attracted by the cause, the prototype world government advocate was generally an influential and "weighty" figure. As historian Dexter Perkins observed, although world government proponents were "not very powerful numerically," they were "a part of that elite opinion . . . which deserves to

[27] Hutchins, *The Atomic Bomb Versus Civilization,* p. 10; Elwyn Brooks White, *The Wild Flag,* p. 188; *New York Herald Tribune,* April 23, 1946; Carl Van Doren to "Friend" (form letter), September, 1945, FOR MSS, Box 12; Reinhold Niebuhr to A. J. Muste, August 21, 1945, FOR MSS, Box 12.

[28] "One Planet: America Ponders the Vision of a Federation of the World," *Newsweek,* XXVIII (October 14, 1946), 45; Mayne A. Harrington, "Recent Thought on World Peace" (unpublished Ph.D. dissertation), p. 34; "World Opinion on World Government," *Common Cause,* I (September, 1947), 101–103; Owen J. Roberts, "Real World Parliament to Keep Peace," *Vital Speeches,* XII (May 1, 1946), 426–28; Glen H. Taylor, "Why a World Republic?" *Free World,* X (December, 1945), 26–31; Clyde Eagleton, "World Government Discussion in the United States," *London Quarterly of World Affairs,* XII (October, 1946), 251–52.

be regarded as of more importance than mere numbers suggest." Another uniform trait was their support of World War II. Although pacifists were occasionally active at the local level of the movement, its leadership posts were filled almost entirely by men prominent in the nation's wartime endeavors. A typical activist was Grenville Clark, the author of the Selective Training and Service Act of 1940, and the drafter of the ill-fated Austin-Wadsworth bill for the total mobilization of manpower.[29]

The dissatisfaction of world government proponents with lesser sovereignties spilled over in the post war period. Raymond Gram Swing found the United Nations "suited only to the preatomic era"; it had "no validity in the atomic age." In a letter to the editor of the *New York Times*, twenty prominent Americans joined to demand the creation of a "Federal Constitution of the world." The U.N. charter, they wrote, "is a tragic illusion unless we are ready to take the further steps necessary to organize peace." The charter, "by maintaining the absolute sovereignties of the rival nation states . . . , resembles the Articles of Confederation," which "did not work." Given "the new reality of atomic warfare," they concluded, world government was an "immediate, urgent necessity, unless civilization is determined on suicide." Shortly after Hiroshima, Clarence Streit's Federal Union organization collapsed when most of its members concluded that regional alliances were dangerous and that only world government would do. Robert M. Hutchins expressed the new mood of grim determination in late 1945: "The task is overwhelming, and the chance of success is slight. We must take the chance or die." [30]

The sense of urgency occasioned by the atomic bomb stimulated a considerable degree of popular support for international authority. A Greenville, North Carolina, attorney, Robert Lee Humber, persuaded fourteen state legislatures to adopt a resolution urging Congress to establish a world government; by 1946 nineteen others were either considering it or had already passed the resolution in one

[29] Dexter Perkins, *The American Approach to Foreign Policy*, p. 113; Cornell, *The Conscientious Objector and the Law*, p. 87.

[30] Swing, *In the Name of Sanity*, p. 25; *New York Times*, October 10, 1945; Cranston, "The Strengthening of the U.N. Charter," p. 197; Hutchins, *The Atomic Bomb Versus Civilization*, p. 13.

house. During World War II there were only three periodicals throughout the world devoted to some form of federal union, but the end of the war witnessed the emergence of three national monthlies in the United states alone, as well as dozens of chapter bulletins. Books on world government multiplied. Emery Reves' *The Anatomy of Peace*, first published in June, 1945, had appeared in sixteen languages in twenty-one countries by 1949. The authors of one study of world federalism wrote that the number of postwar world government plans was "so great as to defy even listing." World government was "discussed in radio forums, student meetings and at cocktail parties," noted New York University professor of international law Clyde Eagleton in 1946. "The feeling that the United Nations is hopelessly weak . . . is widespread in the United States." Polls bore out his assertion; surveys in August, 1946, found that 54 per cent of the nation believed the "United Nations organization should be strengthened to make it a world government with power to control the armed forces of all nations, including the United States."[31]

The movement's political power rose accordingly. By mid-1946, of a total of ninety-six United States Senators, seven openly advocated world government, while a dozen others admitted privately that they supported it. Between fifty and one hundred of the 435 members of the House of Representatives favored some form of world government, as did Minnesota's Governor Harold Stassen, considered a leading contender for the Republican nomination for President in 1948. As early as the summer of 1945, President Truman told a Kansas audience: "We live in this country . . . in which we can get along with our neighbors. Now, we must do that nationally. It will be just as easy for nations to get along in a republic of the world as it is for you to get along in the republic of the United States." On October 24, 1945, Senator Glen Taylor of Idaho, introducing his first resolution in Congress, urged that "the Senate go on record as favoring the creation of a world republic." The resolution suggested that

[31] "One Planet," p. 44; O. K. Armstrong, "Grassroots Crusader," *Reader's Digest*, XLVIII (May, 1946), 45–49; Wynner and Lloyd, *Searchlight on Peace Plans*, p. 545; Eagleton, "World Government Discussion," pp. 254–55; Cord Meyer, Jr., *Peace or Anarchy*, p. 213n; U.S., *Congressional Record*, 80th Cong., 1st Sess., 1947, XCIII, Part 7, 8507.

"every possible effort of our delegates to the United Nations Organization be directed toward the ultimate goal of establishing a world republic based upon democratic principles and universal suffrage regardless of race, color, or creed." The former country banjo-player claimed that he had "studied the problem for a good many years," but "when the atomic bomb fell . . . the effect was something like that of a man turning around and seeing a grizzly bear on his tracks. It hurried me up a little."[32]

Of all the groups spurred to action by the atomic crisis, none seemed as profoundly converted as the atomic scientists. Their concern began with their role in the creation of the bomb during the war. Leo Szilard and Albert Einstein, frightened by the possibility of German development of atomic weapons, had persuaded the United States government to initiate the atomic bomb project. As the famous "Franck Report" noted: "The compelling reason for creating this weapon with such speed was our fear that Germany had the technical skill necessary to develop such a weapon and that the German government had no moral restraints regarding its use." Einstein later remarked that if he "had known that the Germans would not succeed," he "would never have lifted a finger." Even when confronted with the German danger, scientists did not accept the project with equanimity; Edward Teller, a young physicist, hesitated to join it because of his belief that science should not serve the needs of war.[33]

Thus, when Germany lay defeated and Japan seemed close to surrender, considerable consternation developed within the ranks of the atomic scientists. Szilard recalled: "In 1945, when we ceased worrying about what the Germans might do to us, we began to worry about what the government of the United States might do to other countries." Eugene Rabinowitch, a physicist at the Chicago Metallurgical Laboratory, noted that in 1945 "some of us walked the streets of Chicago imagining the sky suddenly lit by a giant fireball,

[32] Cranston, "The Strengthening of the U.N. Charter," pp. 195–96; U.S., Congressional Record, 79th Cong., 1st Sess., 1945, XCI, 9987.
[33] Ralph E. Lapp, Atoms and People, pp. 28–30; Robert Jungk, Brighter than a Thousand Suns: A Personal History of the Atomic Scientists, pp. 87, 357; Laura Fermi, Atoms in the Family: My Life with Enrico Fermi, pp. 220–21.

the steel skeletons of skyscrapers bending into grotesque shapes." Having made the successful appeal to President Roosevelt to build the bomb, Szilard now tried the same method to prevent its use against Japan. The scientist's letter, warning against an atomic armaments race, lay on the President's desk, untouched, when he died on April 12, 1945. Failing to secure an interview with his successor, Szilard, accompanied by physicists Harold Urey and Walter Bartky, journeyed to Spartanburg, South Carolina, to meet with President Truman's personal adviser, James F. Byrnes. According to the scientists' later description of the meeting, Byrnes told them that use of the bomb was necessary to demonstrate American military strength to Russia; he was also much concerned with justifying the expenditure for the bomb project of two billion dollars. Neither the accounts of the scientists nor that of Byrnes reveal that he understood the main point of their visit. Government officials shared a greater commitment to the actual utilization of the bomb than did many scientists, to whom the weapon had represented a deterrent. As Secretary of War Henry Stimson later wrote: "It was our common objective, throughout the war, to be the first to produce an atomic bomb *and use it.*" [34]

On June 11, 1945, the worried scientists in Chicago again attempted to influence the decision to use the bomb, this time by transmitting the "Franck Report" on "Social and Political Implications of Atomic Energy" to the Secretary of War. Three physicists, three chemists, and one biologist (James Franck, Donald Hughes, Leo Szilard, Thorfin Hogness, Glenn Seaborg, Eugene Rabinowitch,

[34] Jungk, *Brighter than a Thousand Suns,* pp. 171–79; Eugene Rabinowitch, "Five Years After," *Bulletin of the Atomic Scientists,* VII (January, 1951), 3; Linus Pauling, *No More War!* p. 157; Alice Kimball Smith, "Behind the Decision to Use the Atomic Bomb: Chicago, 1944–45," *Bulletin of the Atomic Scientists,* XIV (October, 1958), 296; James F. Byrnes, *All in One Lifetime,* p. 284; Grodzins and Rabinowitch, *The Atomic Age,* p. 9; Henry L. Stimson, "The Decision to Use the Atomic Bomb," *Harper's,* CXCIV (February, 1947), 98, emphasis added. According to Szilard, "Byrnes did not argue that it was necessary to use the bomb against the cities of Japan in order to win the war. He knew . . . that Japan was essentially defeated. . . . At that time Mr. Byrnes was much concerned about the spreading of Russian influence in Europe." Byrnes believed, noted Szilard, that "demonstrating the bomb would make Russia more manageable." Leo Szilard, "A Personal History of the Atomic Bomb," *University of Chicago Round Table,* No. 601 (September 25, 1949), pp. 14–15.

and J. J. Nickson) argued that the United States should forgo a temporary military advantage in order to prevent a postwar nuclear arms race. "We were all deeply moved by moral considerations," observed Rabinowitch, "but we did not think that in the necessarily amoral climate in which wartime decisions have to be made these would be effective." Shortly before this, President Truman had appointed an "Interim Committee" to study the problem of the use of the bomb against Japan; consequently, it was to the scientific panel of this committee, composed of Robert Oppenheimer, Arthur H. Compton, Enrico Fermi, and Ernest O. Lawrence, that the Franck Report was sent for review. As the Interim Committee had probably made its decision on June 1, it is doubtful that this report or subsequent efforts to prevent the use of the bomb were seriously considered. In any event, on June 16 the scientific panel reported to Stimson: "We can see no acceptable alternative to direct military use." [35]

The rejection of the Franck Report did not, however, put an end to the controversy. During the first two weeks of July, Szilard gathered signatures for a petition urging the Secretary of War to forgo use of the bomb. General Leslie R. Groves, who headed the Manhattan Project, allowed the petition limited circulation and passed the word to scientists that they were at liberty to organize counterpetitions, although none appears to have done so. Indeed, among the collection of letters relating scientists' views on the use of the bomb which was turned over to Stimson on August 1, only two urged using the new weapon without warning. The renewed agitation prompted Arthur H. Compton of the scientific panel to order a sounding of the sentiments of atomic scientists. On July 12 a poll of 150 scientists' views on the bomb was conducted at the Chicago Metallurgical Laboratory: 2 per cent favored withholding all use; 11 per cent desired an experimental demonstration without military use; 26 per cent wanted an experimental demonstration followed, if necessary, by full use; 46 per cent favored a "military demonstration in Japan," followed, if necessary, by "full use"; and 15 per cent

[35] "A Report to the Secretary of War," *Bulletin of the Atomic Scientists*, I (May 1, 1946), 2–4, 16; Pauling, *No More War!* p. 158; Smith, *A Peril and a Hope*, p. 153; Robert Gilpin, *American Scientists and Nuclear Weapons Policy*, p. 47; Smith, "Behind the Decision to Use the Atomic Bomb," pp. 306–307; Stimson, "The Decision to Use the Atomic Bomb," p. 101.

advocated the most effective use of the weapon to achieve surrender. Thus, only 13 per cent completely opposed use of the bomb against Japan, 39 per cent would have at least held an "experimental demonstration" before proceeding further, and a full 85 per cent would have sanctioned no more than a "military demonstration" before proceeding to "full use." A mere 15 per cent advocated using the weapon against Japan as military efficiency dictated—the position apparently adopted by the Interim Committee. Yet when asked on July 23 by government officials for the results of the poll, Compton gave them a most curious interpretation. He stated that the scientists agreed with the decision of the Interim Committee; in 1956 Compton declared it to be "a striking fact" that "the same points of view were presented with closely the same degree of relative frequency" by both the scientists and the members of the Interim Committee.[36]

Two weeks later, the bomb fell on Hiroshima. According to Eugene Rabinowitch, "the news of the Hiroshima strike was a terrible blow to many who had contributed most toward making the atomic bomb possible." Albert Einstein, who had known nothing of the bomb project since his initiating letter, remarked sadly when the news reached him: "Oh, weh!" (Alas!) And yet, recalled Rabinowitch, "a glimmer of hope appeared in the darkness. Was there not a chance—an off-side chance, but still a chance—that the fate of Hiroshima and Nagasaki would cause Man to turn a new leaf?" Could not scientists "spur this decision by buttonholing all who would listen and preaching to them our message of doom and our precept for survival: live in peace or perish?" The subsequent scientists' movement thus arose as a "conspiracy to preserve our civilization by scaring men into rationality."[37]

[36] Grodzins and Rabinowitch, The Atomic Age, pp. 10, 28–29; Lansing Lamont, Day of Trinity, p. 146; Smith, A Peril and a Hope, p. 57; Arthur H. Compton and Farrington Daniels, "A Poll of Scientists at Chicago, July, 1945," Bulletin of the Atomic Scientists, IV (February, 1948), 44, 63; Compton, Atomic Quest, p. 244. According to Stimson, the Interim Committee had decided that "the bomb should be used against Japan as soon as possible," on "a dual target" [i.e., both military and civilian], "without prior warning." Stimson, "The Decision to Use the Atomic Bomb," p. 100.

[37] Rabinowitch, "Five Years After," p. 3; Nathan and Norden, Einstein on Peace, p. 308. The extent of scientific disapproval of the Hiroshima bombing is indicated by a poll of the Manhattan Project scientists in September, 1945,

The pattern of wartime dissent carried over into postwar organization. The Atomic Scientists of Chicago grew out of James Franck's Committee on the Social and Political Implications of Atomic Energy. Groups sprang up at Los Alamos, Oak Ridge, New York, and wherever else the atomic scientists worked. The Atomic Scientists of Chicago claimed the support of "over 90 per cent" of the scientists from the bomb project. On November 16 and 17 a meeting of thirteen local groups formed the Federation of Atomic Scientists "to promote the use of scientific discoveries in the interest of world peace and the general welfare of mankind." The *Bulletin of the Atomic Scientists*, originally the journal of the Chicago group but later the organ of the new Federation of Atomic Scientists, first appeared, observed its editor, "to make fellow scientists aware of the new relationships between their own world of science and the world of national and international politics," as well as "to help the public understand what nuclear energy and its application to war meant for mankind." The scientists' crusade had begun.[38]

In the immediate postwar period, the atomic scientists led the struggle to secure civilian control of atomic energy. Oppenheimer and Compton, on increasingly good terms with military and political leaders, had assured their restless underlings that the Truman Administration was engaged in delicate and secret negotiations for the international control of atomic energy, which could be jeopardized by intervention or publicity from the rank-and-file scientists. Leo Szilard, however, once again taking the initiative, found that negotiations were indeed going on, not for international control, but for

conducted by a sociologist: 1.8 per cent would have wiped out as many cities as possible before the Japanese had a chance to surrender; 53.9 per cent would have used it on one city at a time until the Japanese surrendered; 38.9 per cent would have demonstrated the weapon to Japanese leaders in an uninhabited area, and then given them a chance to surrender; 3.6 per cent would have refused to use it on cities; and 1.8 per cent did not know what they would have done. Thus 55.7 per cent in effect approved of the manner in which the bomb was handled, while 42.5 per cent did not. Smith, *A Peril and a Hope*, pp. 78–79.

38 Smith, "Behind the Decision to Use the Atomic Bomb," pp. 111–12; "The Atomic Scientists of Chicago," *Bulletin of the Atomic Scientists of Chicago*, I (December 10, 1945), 1; "The Federation of American Scientists" (1946), FOR MSS, Box 12; "National Organizations of Scientists," *Bulletin of the Atomic Scientists of Chicago*, I (December 10, 1945), 2; Grodzins and Rabinowitch, *The Atomic Age*, p. v; Smith, *A Peril and a Hope*, p. 87.

control by the American military, through the device of secret and closed committee hearings on an Administration bill. The discovery that the military, in partnership with members of the President's Interim Committee, were rushing the top-secret May-Johnson bill through Congress outraged the restive scientists and galvanized them to action. Setting up headquarters in Washington, they buttonholed Congressmen, visited editors, gave lectures, and attended important social gatherings. Szilard worked his way in to testify against the bill at the House committee hearings, much to the irritation of Chairman Andrew May, who persisted in misunderstanding him and calling him "Mr. Sighland." By July, 1946, the battle had been won; Congress dropped the May bill and passed the McMahon Act for the civilian control of atomic energy.[39]

The prominence of atomic scientists in postwar peace efforts can be accounted for partially by misgivings over their wartime role. Once scientist, Cyril Smith, commented: "Sometimes I wake up at night feeling the plutonium metal in my hands—metal that I personally helped fabricate for the bomb—and realize that it killed hundreds of thousands of people. It's not a pleasant feeling." On December 10, 1945, Albert Einstein told a Nobel Anniversary dinner in New York:

Physicists find themselves in a position not unlike that of Alfred Nobel. Alfred Nobel invented an explosive more powerful than any then known—an exceedingly effective means of destruction. To atone for this "accomplishment" and to relieve his conscience he instituted his awards for the promotion of peace. Today, the physicists who participated in producing the most formidable weapon of all time are harassed by a similar feeling of responsibility, not to say guilt. As scientists, we must never cease to warn against the danger created by these weapons.

Sometimes they expressed their discomfort in an indirect manner. "Our country, the United States, has a peculiar responsibility," observed the Federation of Atomic Scientists. "We are committed . . . to assume the initiative. . . . *The bombs are marked 'Made in the U.S.A.'*" At other times their disquiet was naked and emotional.

[39] James L. Penick, Jr., *et al.*, *The Politics of American Science, 1939 to the Present*, p. 96; Gilpin, *American Scientists and Nuclear Weapons Policy*, pp. 49–50; Jungk, *Brighter than a Thousand Suns*, pp. 231–38.

"The physicists have known sin," wrote Robert Oppenheimer, "and this is a knowledge which they cannot lose." [40]

Moreover, the atomic scientists had an acute awareness of the threat posed to human existence by the new weapon. "When I first heard that atomic bombs had been exploded over Hiroshima and Nagasaki," wrote the chemist Linus Pauling, "I was shocked, as were many other scientists, by the terrible powers of destruction that had been made available to man by the progress of science." Harold Urey, Nobel Prize-winning chemist, contended that the existence of atomic weapons had created "the most dangerous situation that humanity has ever faced in all history." "Time is short," noted the Federation of Atomic Scientists, "and survival is at stake." [41]

For some scientists the conversion to the cause of peace represented little more than a superficial reaction. It was, after all, soothing to believe that a weapon causing such enormous damage also had its good side—that it made war obsolete. "Quite a few scientists believed deeply that the A-bomb, itself, would prove a powerful force for peace," noted physicist Ralph Lapp. "Man, they reasoned, would at last have to put an end to the dreadful succession of wars which have marked recorded history." The bomb "did not cause demoralization, it caused hope," recalled Laura Fermi. "These atomic bombs are too destructive, men said in Los Alamos after Hiroshima. They will not be used again. There will be no more wars." Scientist Luis Alvarez wrote to his son: "What regrets I have about being a party to killing and maiming thousands of Japanese civilians this morning are tempered with the hope that terrible weapon we have created may bring the countries of the world together and prevent further wars." In this sense, of course, the peace-as-necessity argument merely served as a comforting rationalization for men disturbed by an act of mass killing, the counterpart of the popular contention that the bombing "saved lives." In a private

[40] Lamont, *Day of Trinity*, pp. 300–301; *New York Times*, December 11, 1945; Federation of American (Atomic) Scientists, "Survival Is at Stake," *One World or None: A Report to the Public on the Full Meaning of the Atomic Bomb*, ed. Dexter Masters and Katherine Way, p. 79; "Expiation," *Time*, LI (February 23, 1948), p. 94.

[41] Pauling, *No More War!* p. 168; Harold C. Urey, "How Does It All Add Up?" *One World or None*, p. 58; Federation of American (Atomic) Scientists, "Survival Is at Stake," p. 79.

conversation on the development of the atomic bomb, one of the most prominent of the scientists asked in apparent sincerity: "Can you think of any single thing we might have done, better calculated to produce a more beneficial result for the human race?" [42]

Many others, however, regarded the establishment of a peaceful world as a desperate quest rather than as a cause for self-congratulation. In the postwar period they threw themselves into the struggle against war. Many were prominent in the burgeoning campaign for world government. It was "necessary that the individual state be prevented from making war by a supranational organization," Einstein maintained. In light of the "political mentality prevailing at present," he conceded, this might "seem illusory, even fantastic"; nevertheless, it was the "only . . . way out." Robert Oppenheimer noted that the atomic bomb required "a very real renunciation of the steps by which in the past national security has been sought." A new comprehension of the imperative nature of peace deeply affected the scientific community. As one physicist told a scientific gathering: "The atomic bomb is the final and conclusive proof of the fact that there must be no more wars." [43]

[42] Lapp, *Atoms and People*, p. 76; Fermi, *Atoms in the Family*, p. 245; Lamont, *Day of Trinity*, pp. 265–66; Swing, *In the Name of Sanity*, p. 90.
[43] Grodzins and Rabinowitch, *The Atomic Age*, p. 99; Albert Einstein, "Atomic War or Peace," *Atlantic Monthly*, CLXXX (November, 1947), 29–32; U.S., *Congressional Record*, 79th Cong., 1st Sess., 1945, XCI, 9989; Albert Einstein, "The Way Out," *One World or None*, p. 76; J. Robert Oppenheimer, "The New Weapon: The Turn of the Screw," *One World or None*, p. 25; Lee A. DuBridge, "Science and National Policy," *Bulletin of the Atomic Scientists*, I (May 15, 1946), 12.

CHAPTER VI

Organizing for a
New World, 1945–1948

They constantly try to escape
From the darkness outside and within
By dreaming of systems so perfect
that no one will need to be good.
T. S. ELIOT [1]

In the relatively friendly atmosphere of the immediate postwar period the American peace movement experienced a mild revival. Nonviolent revolutionaries and world government advocates, the radical vanguard in pacifist and "internationalist" ranks, took the lead in organizing a vigorous campaign against war among the American people. In retrospect the zeal with which they adhered to their theories and pursued their quarrels stands out as a trifle ludicrous, but in the early days of the postwar era, before the chill of the Cold War settled over the country, a climate of hope prevailed.

With the end of the war traditional pacifist organizations lost their "outlaw" status and began to recoup a bit of their fallen prestige. In 1946 the Nobel Peace Prize was awarded to Emily Greene Balch of the Women's International League for Peace and Freedom; in 1947 it went to the American Friends Service Committee.[2]

---

[1] T. S. Eliot, The Rock (New York: Harcourt, Brace and Company, 1934), p. 42. Reprinted by permission of Harcourt, Brace & World, Inc.

[2] Such success did not go to their heads. Henry Cadbury, chairman of the A.F.S.C., was designated to receive the prize for his organization in Oslo. As he neither owned nor desired to buy the dress suit with tails which the formality of the occasion required, he decided to borrow one from the A.F.S.C.'s used clothing warehouse in Philadelphia. Cadbury found a suit that fit, wore it to receive the Nobel Prize, and then returned it to the warehouse, from which it was baled and shipped with other old clothes to Budapest. Pickett, For More than Bread, p. 295.

One consequence of the postwar easing of pacifist-community tensions was a decline in organizational strength. In March, 1945, A. J. Muste noted that at the end of a war "centrifugal tendencies in organizations and movements tend to manifest themselves. The onset of the war draws people together; the end of the war drives them apart." He proved an accurate prognosticator. The Fellowship of Reconciliation, which had reached a peak of almost 15,000 members during the war, gradually fell to below 14,000 by 1948. Similarly, the tiny but burgeoning War Resisters League went into a period of decline in membership and finances after 1945. Most pacifists talked of a "postwar letdown." Engaged in peace action on the West Coast during 1946, Roy Kepler reported: "One thing which I feel is almost universally true this summer is that people are taking a vacation; the world looks safe until at least fall, so they are recuperating after 5 years of war." [3]

By 1946 and 1947 pacifist organizations faced another source of change: the return from the C.P.S. camps and prisons of thousands of young C.O.'s, many of whom held new and startling ideas about the functions of a peacemaker. George Houser told a meeting of the F.O.R. national council that he would "like to see a really revolutionary resistance program developed soon." Older pacifists in the Fellowship disliked the doctrines of the "new pacifism," and resented to some degree the growing influence of its young and militant following. By 1948 the struggle within the F.O.R. had been resolved in favor of the traditionalists. The organization announced that while individual members and staff could engage in radical action projects, "the actual organization of civil disobedience campaigns by the FOR . . . , which involves placing the FOR in a position of carrying on illegal activities, is not feasible under the

[3] A. J. Muste to Caleb Foote, March 28, 1945, FOR MSS, Box 8; "Membership Statistics" (1954), FOR MSS, Box 4; "Minutes of National Council Meeting, October 24–26, 1946," FOR MSS, Box 3; personal interview with Jim Peck, April 21, 1966; see file marked "Membership Committee, 1942–1947," WRL MSS, Box 4; Evan W. Thomas to Members of WRL, December 26, 1946, WRL MSS, Box 2; Roy Kepler to Frank Olmstead, July 22, 1946, WRL MSS, Box 17. Organizations accepting non-pacifists expanded slightly. The W.I.L.P.F., for example, grew from its wartime low to 4000 members by 1948; nevertheless, it had far to go to regain its strength of the Thirties, when it had had 15,000 members. Mildred Scott Olmstead, "Report of the Administrative Secretary" (November 19, 1948), WILPF MSS, Box 13.

pattern of an inclusive Fellowship to which we adhere." At the same
time the F.O.R.'s national council worried lest "the movement . . .
lose the 'cutting edge' of these young people who are willing to go
this whole way." [4]

The radicals experienced greater success within the War Resisters
League. Attracted by its wartime defense of rebellious C.O.'s against
the more conservative leadership of the peace churches, the militants poured into the organization at the end of the war. At the
time, its executive secretary for nineteen years, Abe Kaufman, was a
loyal adherent of the W.R.L.'s traditional function as an enrollment
and educational organization for C.O.'s. By 1947 and 1948, however,
the executive committee was sharply weighted against him; it included such C.P.S. and prison veterans as Dave Dellinger, Roy
Finch, George Houser, Jim Peck, Igal Roodenko, and Bayard Rustin, as well as such resistance advocates as Dwight Macdonald, A. J.
Muste, and George Reeves. In June, 1947, the committee adopted a
resolution declaring that the W.R.L. would "adapt its literature and
activities to the promotion of political, economic, and social revolution by non-violent means." Kaufman resigned in September, 1947,
and was succeeded by Roy Kepler, one of the most zealous of the
new proponents of direct action. Thereafter the W.R.L. served as a
radical action organization, although for purposes of retaining its
more conservative following it refrained from openly advocating
illegal positions, such as non-registration for the draft.[5]

Much of the postwar radicalism, however, stayed clear of traditional pacifist circles, and instead channeled itself through new institutions. Pacifist journals with a strong anarchist flavor flourished in
the aftermath of World War II. The best known and most widely
read was Dwight Macdonald's *Politics*, begun in 1944, but others

[4] "Minutes of National Council Meeting, November 20–22, 1947," FOR
MSS, Box 3; personal interview with Dave Dellinger, May 16, 1966; "FOR
Council Meeting, December 2, 1948," FOR MSS, Box 3; "FOR and Other
Organizations, Including Peacemakers" (1948), FOR MSS, Box 3; "FOR
Council Meeting, December 4, 1948," FOR MSS, Box 3.

[5] Personal interview with Ralph DiGia, April 21, 1966; personal interview
with Jim Peck, April 21, 1966; "War Resisters League Executive Committee,
1948," WRL MSS, Box 2; "Minutes of Executive Committee Meeting, June 16,
1947," WRL MSS, Box 2; Abraham Kaufman to the Executive Committee,
September 8, 1947, WRL MSS, Box 2; Roy C. Kepler, "Memorandum on
WRL Policy and Program" (1948), WRL MSS, Box 2.

such as *Retort* and *Resistance* sparked a good deal of discussion until their demise in the early Fifties. Because, as a matter of principle, the latter two periodicals financed their circulation solely from voluntary contributions, they appeared sporadically and never reached a wide audience, even among pacifists. The hardy *Catholic Worker* proved more successful, however, maintaining a sizable readership. Typical of the pacifist-anarchist euphoria was *Direct Action*, published in 1945 by Dave Dellinger. The first issue advocated "strikes, sabotage and seizure of public property now being held by private owners," as well as "civil disobedience of laws which are contrary to human welfare." One of the writers proposed a system of "radical banditry," whereby "we take rather than buy what we want" in stores; city workers would "seek to evade taxes, evade purchases, and evade rents." Another writer suggested that when people were hungry, "a mass invasion of A & P supermarkets by housewives with hungry families, for the express purpose of emptying the shelves, would be a good way of keeping down the profits of the masters." Pointing out the dangers in such methods, an editor observed that "taking goods *surreptitiously*" would imply that they belonged to the store owners, "thereby continually paying homage to capitalist ideals of property." [6]

Out of the wartime pacifist ferment emerged the Committee for Non-Violent Revolution (C.N.V.R.). In November, 1945, a group of radicals issued a "Call" to a conference in Chicago, stating that "the time has come for radical elements from the groups devoted to war-resistance, socialism, militant labor unionism, consumer cooperation and racial equality to attempt to come together in a common program of revolutionary action." From February 6 through 9, 1946,

---

[6] William Robert Miller, "The Mightier Pen: American Peace Journalism, 1815–1960," *Fellowship*, XXVI (May 1, 1960), 26; *Conscientious Objector*, December, 1945. "Radical Banditry" was the source of a good deal of amusement in pacifist circles. One C.O. described the band of radical pacifists bearing down on Macy's one Saturday afternoon with a banner aloft proclaiming: "It's Smart to Be Thrifty, but It's Smarter to be a Direct Actionist!" After the sacking of Macy's was well under way, Gimbel's would raise a sign hastily in self-defense:

DIRECT ACTIONISTS!!

Counter-revolutionary, capitalistic Lord and Taylor's has

NYLONS!! LONG LIVE THE REVOLUTION!!

Wallace Hamilton, "Robin Hood: Latest Model," *Pacifica Views*, III (January 18, 1946), 2.

this "Conference on Non-Violent Revolutionary Socialism" met in Chicago's Labor Center, with ninety-five radical pacifists attending its sessions. At its conclusion the delegates voted to establish C.N.V.R., a loose federation of local radical pacifist groups with a steering committee in New York.[7] C.N.V.R.'s founding statement of principles contained a remarkable fusion of socialism, anarchism, and pacifism. Rejecting "nationalization of industries," the conference called for local control of the means of production and distribution by the workers on the job, complete social and economic equality, and the development of cooperatives and even of private enterprise, providing that the individual did not employ labor or draw more than a given income. C.N.V.R. proposed "free choice of vocation," "democratic representation of workers in planning agencies," the right to organize and to strike, and "free choice in spending personal income." Unlike many other utopian plans such a society would guarantee "freedom of speech, press, movement, assembly, organization, education, religion, radio and cinema facilities." As for war, its members planned to "refuse to serve in the armed forces, give financial support to the government, work in war plants or cooperate with the conscription program," but instead would "appeal to workers to leave war jobs and to soldiers to desert." Indeed, for the conference participants, pacifism and socialism were intimately related. "As the instrument of mass revolution," non-violence would be utilized both to defeat aggression and to secure "the occupation of production facilities by direct action groups." C.N.V.R. concluded that "killing, maiming, and violent coercion of people is counter revolutionary, whenever and by whomever it is done."[8]

Like many a kindred left-wing experiment, the fledgling organization failed to live up to its revolutionary promises. During the next year, it did little more than picket the United Nations, denouncing it

[7] "Call to a Conference" (November, 1945), United States Peace Material, Miscellaneous, 1944–1949; *Conscientious Objector,* March, 1946; personal interview with Dave Dellinger, May 16, 1966; Don Calhoun, "The Non-Violent Revolutionists," *Politics,* III (April, 1946), 118–19; "Report of February Conference on Non-Violent Revolutionary Socialism, Chicago, February 6, 7, 8, 9, 1946," United States Peace Material, Miscellaneous, 1944–1949.

[8] "Report of February Conference on Non-Violent Revolutionary Socialism, Chicago, February 6, 7, 8, 9, 1946," United States Peace Material, Miscellaneous, 1944–1949.

as a cover for imperialist policies; the ruling class rather obstinately ignored these harbingers of its downfall, although the demonstrators were, to their surprise, arrested. By 1948 C.N.V.R. had been absorbed into a larger and more permanent organization, Peacemakers.[9]

Peacemakers grew out of a series of pacifist retreats at Pendle Hill in late 1947 which expressed concern for generating a more radical pacifist activity, to include civil disobedience and the development of "cells" which could engage in simplified living and devote time to peace action. One manifesto, written by A. J. Muste, Milton Mayer, and Cecil Hinshaw, called for a conference in early 1948 "of those interested in a more revolutionary pacifist movement." In February, 1948, a larger group of American pacifists issued a declaration announcing a conference in Chicago during April to consider "the idea of non-violence, based on a spiritual philosophy of life, as an effective social technique." Much of the impetus for the conference came from those pacifists who, finding even the W.R.L. in the hands of conservative, Old Guard elements at the time, sought a greater break with the warmaking State than was afforded through participation in traditional organizations. A. J. Muste recalled years later that "it was at the time when the peacetime draft was being introduced and many people felt the need of an organization that emphasized non-cooperation." [10]

In response to this call, about 250 men and women met in Chicago during early April, 1948, for a "Conference on More Disciplined and Revolutionary Pacifism." The meeting brought together two groups: potentially militant pacifists who had compromised their position to some degree during World War II, but who were now

9 *Catholic Worker*, November, 1946; *Conscientious Objector*, April, 1946; Macdonald, *Memoirs of a Revolutionist*, p. 297. Dwight Macdonald, a member of C.N.V.R., reported that he could not "see that the U.N. is either a hope or a menace; just a bore." Dwight Macdonald, "The Truth about U.N.," *Politics*, III (November, 1946), 338.

10 "FOR and Other Organizations, Including Peacemakers" (1948), FOR MSS, Box 3; Cecil Hinshaw, Milton Mayer, and A. J. Muste, "One World Groups" (late 1947), FOR MSS, Box 6; personal interview with Dave Dellinger, May 16, 1966; Peacemakers, *Introducing Peacemakers;* personal interview with Jim Peck, April 21, 1966; A. J. Muste to Margaret McCulloch, January 16, 1961, A. J. Muste Manuscripts, Swarthmore College Peace Collection (Muste MSS), Box 8.

ready for more radical action (e.g., A. J. Muste, Dwight Macdonald, Milton Mayer); and the militants from the prisons and C.P.S. camps, including about half of C.N.V.R. Together, they voted to establish Peacemakers, a network of local, radical pacifist cells. According to Peacemakers' first public announcement, "Groups or cells are the real basis of the movement, for this is not an attempt to organize another pacifist membership organization, which one joins by signing a statement and paying a membership fee." Instead, Peacemakers would attempt "to stimulate activity at the local level" through "a kind of 'lay order' of persons both in and outside of existing pacifist organizations . . . who have undertaken definite disciplines and responsibilities." Individuals would " 'belong' only as they are active in such groups." [11]

The Peacemaker program was more Gandhian and less Marxist than that of C.N.V.R. It called for the use of non-violent techniques to resolve conflicts, unilateral disarmament on the part of all nations, political and economic democracy, and "inner transformation" of the individual. As might be expected, great emphasis was placed upon "war-resistance" and a clear exposition of the non-registrant position. An early Peacemakers circular stated: "We call on youths to refuse to register or render any service under this iniquitous law and on all others to support youth in this non-violent non-cooperation." The "usual verbal protests and conventional campaigns for repeal are not enough now," it declared. "DISOBEDIENCE is therefore the most democratic and patriotic course." [12]

Tax refusal constituted the most unique of the Peacemakers programs. In 1947 several pacifists who had independently commenced tax refusal several years before had begun to correspond. When Peacemakers was formed the following year, they assisted in the

[11] Peacemakers, *Introducing Peacemakers;* "Report of Chicago Conference on More Disciplined and Revolutionary Pacifism," *Fellowship,* XIV (May, 1948), 26; "Minutes of Executive Committee Meeting held April 7, 1948," WRL MSS, Box 2; personal interview with Dave Dellinger, May 16, 1966. Members of Peacemakers' first executive committee included Dave Dellinger, Julius Eichel, George Houser, Roy Kepler, Dwight Macdonald, Milton Mayer, A. J. Muste, Bayard Rustin, and Charles Walker. Peacemakers, *A Declaration to the American People.*

[12] Peacemakers, *Introducing Peacemakers;* Peacemakers, "Refuse to Register" (ca. 1948), Allen MSS, Section C4, Box 8.

establishment of its Tax Refusal Committee, which vigorously promoted the idea through publications and public statements. Nonpayment took two forms: earning less than the minimum taxable balance, or earning more than the minimum but refusing to pay all or part. In both categories, a number refused to file income tax returns at all, despite the legal penalties. The motivation for tax refusal was generally based upon the fact that most federal tax revenue was used for military purposes. One pacifist explained to his tax collector: "My alliance has to be with the people of the world who suffer, not with the governments which make them suffer." Another wrote of his decision: "How can I in decency turn over money to pay others to make or use . . . atrocious weapons on other human beings and children of God?" Yet despite a strong stand on this matter by a handful, most pacifists continued to pay their taxes, largely because of the difficulties of avoiding withholding taxes and the reluctance of individuals and organizations to engage in illegal activities. By 1950 probably less than one hundred pacifists had emulated Thoreau's example of a century before.[13]

Some members of the postwar generation of radical pacifists sought a new way of life through the establishment of cooperative communities. This particular drive had much to commend it to young C.O.'s finally released from prison or C.P.S. camps. Cooperatives had always ranked high in pacifist theory for their ethic of non-competition, and served as a means whereby radicals could live in capitalist America without supporting what they believed to be its exploitative practices. Others argued that if they were to act as radicals in the outside world, they would need a self-sustaining existence to remain free of economic reprisal. Moreover, the mystique of a rural, cooperative, community appealed strongly to dissatisfied urban intellectuals. "All of us are aware of a widespread urge among pacifists to 'go rural,'" a writer remarked in one pacifist journal.

13 Peacemakers, "Handbook on Nonpayment of War Taxes" (mimeographed), pp. 6–7; Peacemakers, "Why We Refuse to Pay Taxes for War" (ca. 1950), Allen MSS, Section C4, Box 8; Robert C. Friend to Collector of Internal Revenue, March 15, 1948, WRL MSS, Box 15; A. J. Muste, "Why Tax Refusal?" (March, 1960), Muste MSS, Box 10; Theodore Paullin, "I'll Pay My Taxes," *Fellowship*, XIV (January, 1948), 12–13; "Report of Committee on Tax Problems to the National Council, 11/16/48," FOR MSS, Box 3.

Finally, the prison and C.P.S. camp experience had already welded a sense of community among small groups of pacifists formerly isolated from one another. "Having been forced to live together, and finding some comfort in this enforced solidarity against a hostile society, we perhaps feared the prospect of facing the world alone again some day," a communitarian remarked. "Anyway, we felt we should retain our accidental unity." [14]

As a result of this pacifist interest, cooperative communities sprang up in a number of areas across the country, including settlements near Glen Gardner and Frenchtown, New Jersey, and Americus, Georgia. The most successful of the pacifist utopias, the Macedonia Cooperative Community, took root in the Blue Ridge foothills of Georgia. Founded in 1937, Macedonia had collapsed during the war years but revived when its determined founder convinced a group of C.O.'s to settle there after the war. The eighteen pacifists worked at various forms of farming and at a small woodworking factory which they built. The wage system was discarded, and the entire operation was run on a communal, subsistence basis. In 1949 the Macedonia community applied for membership in Peacemakers as a local cell group. Members of this rural cooperative agreed with Dwight Macdonald, who publicized their activities, that in "limited, small-scale kind of activity some seeds may be planted now which will later produce larger changes." Despairing of traditional forms of social upheaval, they sought a direct and non-bureaucratic approach to social action, which would not substitute means for ends. An itinerant Communist Party organizer, stopping at Macedonia on his way north, was visibly impressed with their life but complained that they were not assisting the Party in furthering a more widespread revolution. "He may be right," a pacifist resident observed, "but we suspect that the way for men to become free is to begin to live as free men." [15]

[14] Muste, *Not by Might*, p. 212; Arthur E. Morgan, *Small Community Economics; Conscientious Objector*, December, 1944; personal interview with Ralph DiGia, April 21, 1966; Stanley Gould, "Advice to the Landlorn," *Fellowship*, XV (September, 1949), 8; David R. Newton, "The Macedonia Community," *Politics*, V (Winter, 1948), 27.

[15] Personal interview with Ralph DiGia, April 21, 1966; Newton, "The Macedonia Community," pp. 27–30; *Peacemaker*, I (September 7, 1949), 2; Macdonald, *Memoirs of a Revolutionist*, p. 192. Dave Dellinger, the mainstay

One aspect of the pacifist expansion into new areas resulted in the formation of the Pacifica Foundation, a series of listener-sponsored, non-commercial radio stations. In 1946 a group of C.O.'s in the San Francisco Bay Area set up the first of the local stations, KPFA-FM, taking the name for their parent body from the C.P.S. journal *Pacifica Views*. Pacifica's articles of incorporation declared that its stations would attempt to "engage in any activity that shall contribute to a lasting understanding between nations, races, creeds and colors; to gather and disseminate information on the causes of conflict between any and all of such groups;" and "to promote the study of political and economic problems, and of the causes of religious, philosophical and racial antagonisms." The first station proved so successful that a second, KPFK-FM was established shortly thereafter in Los Angeles, and a third, WBAI-FM, in 1960 in New York. A pacifist in California reported proudly: "KPFA is a real milestone in the history of the American mass media: a true revolution—and more than anything else it has turned this area into a real cultural and political community." [16]

In the postwar period CORE continued to grow as C.O.'s returned from the prisons and C.P.S. camps to participate in its projects and to establish chapters across the country. During its early years CORE's national and local leadership, comprised primarily of young pacifists such as Houser, Rustin, and Farmer, gave the organization much of its non-violent, interracial emphasis. In 1945 CORE had ten affiliated groups, thirteen in 1947, and fifteen in 1949. The national headquarters of the loosely structured organization followed George Houser, its unpaid executive director, from his post in the Cleveland F.O.R. office to his position with the national office of the F.O.R. in New York. [17]

---

of the Glen Gardner Community, wrote: "I think the need is not only to be sensitive to new ways of withdrawing our support from the war machines . . . but also to develop new ways of living in brotherhood. . . . It seems to me that the current growing edge of pacifism is the development of communities of sharing, and that those of us who want to attack the causes of war should begin in our own lives." A. J. Muste, "Of Holy Disobedience" (mimeographed), p. 20.

[16] *Fellowship*, XXVI (February 1, 1960), 3; "Facts about the Pacifica Foundation," *WBAI Folio*, VII (April 11–May 8, 1966), 31; Theodore Roszak to the Author, February 7, 1966.

[17] Mabee, "Evolution of Non-Violence," p. 79; Houser, *CORE: A Brief History*, p. 10.

Throughout this period CORE engaged in non-violent forays upon racial segregation. Sit-ins at Washington, D.C., lunch counters in the summer of 1947 assisted in finally opening up sections of that city's downtown area to Negroes, although the manager of the local Y.M.C.A. at first refused to bother the board of directors of his institution with such a "triviality." The successful sit-ins received wide acclaim from the Negro press across the country, as well as the mild interest of a local white newspaper.[18] During the summers of 1947 and 1948, CORE members attempted to desegregate the swimming pool at Palisades Amusement Park in New Jersey by forming standing lines that refused to leave when denied admission. Demonstrators were repeatedly beaten (Jim Peck received a broken jaw and rib), arrested by police, and brought to what was rather obviously rigged justice; one girl, arrested for passing out leaflets at the Park gate, was inadvertently found guilty by the court recorder before the defense took the stand. Although the Park's owner announced, "You'll all be dead before I change," newspaper stories of the incidents and critical editorials helped to enact New Jersey's 1949 Civil Rights Act and to end the color line at Palisades Park.[19]

In 1946 the Supreme Court's decision in the Irene Morgan case, which struck down state laws requiring segregated seating in interstate travel,[20] prompted the first "Freedom Ride," jointly sponsored by the F.O.R. and CORE. From April 9 to 23, 1947, an interracial team of sixteen men traveled on this "Journey of Reconciliation" through the Upper South to test compliance with the court decision. Although attacks upon the riders occurred only in Chapel Hill, North Carolina, local police arrested Journey participants on six different occasions. As a result three of the demonstrators, all pacifists, eventually served sentences of thirty days each on a Southern "road gang." One of them, Bayard Rustin, later wrote a pamphlet describing this experience, "Twenty-two Days on the Chain Gang at

18 *Washington Post*, July 18, 1947; *The Afro*, July 15, 22, and 29, 1947, *Norfolk Journal and Guide*, August 2, 1947, *Pittsburgh Courier*, July 23, 1947, clippings in FOR MSS, Box 5; "Interracial Workshop Progress Report" (1947), CORE MSS.
19 James Peck, "Bilboism in New Jersey," *The Crisis* (January, 1948), pp. 17–18, reprint in CORE MSS; J. Peck, *Cracking the Color Line*, pp. 11–12; *Pittsburgh Courier*, September 25, 1948, reprint in CORE MSS.
20 *Morgan v. Virginia*, 328 U.S. 373 (1946).

Roxboro, N.C.," which sparked an investigation and reform of the state's prison conditions.[21]

Pacifists spent much of their time in the postwar era attempting to secure amnesty for C.O.'s imprisoned during World War II. In this effort they were joined by the C.I.O., the Federal Council of Churches, the American Veterans Committee, and segments of the press. President Truman's appointment of an Amnesty Board, composed of Justice Owen J. Roberts, Willis Smith, former president of the American Bar Association (and later Governor of North Carolina after defeating the liberal incumbent, Frank Graham, by means of a highly racist campaign), and James F. O'Neil, subsequently National Commander of the American Legion, greatly disappointed these groups. After a year of study the Board disregarded the World War I precedent of general amnesty and recommended pardon in the cases of only 1523 of the 6000 imprisoned C.O.'s—those whose beliefs could be considered as fitting under the narrow definition of the 1940 draft act. The thousands whose convictions did not, such as Jehovah's Witnesses and humanitarian and non-religious objectors, were denied amnesty. This decision tended to confirm a number of C.O's in their militant anarchism. "If we are being refused amnesty for being thorns in the side of government," wrote one, "then I am rather proud to be left in that class." [22]

Radical and traditional pacifist alike joined in the struggle against proposals by the President to continue compulsory military training into the postwar era. The Truman Administration, assisted by an exceptionally active lobbying effort on the part of the War Department, sought to replace the 1940 selective service law, scheduled to expire in March, 1947, with a more inclusive program of universal military training (UMT). Pacifists, on the other hand, viewed any

[21] George Houser and Bayard Rustin, We Challenged Jim Crow! A Report on the Journey of Reconciliation, April 9–23, 1947; Houser, CORE: A Brief History, pp. 9–10; J. Peck, Cracking the Color Line, pp. 29–30; J. Peck, Freedom Ride, pp. 14–27; "Personalities and Projects," Survey, LXXXV (October, 1949), 553.

[22] Sibley and Jacob, Conscription of Conscience, pp. 388–98; American Civil Liberties Union, In Times of Challenge, pp. 53–54; American Civil Liberties Union, Our Uncertain Liberties: U.S. Liberties, 1947–48, pp. 59–60; U.S. Bureau of Prisons, Federal Prisons, 1947, pp. 20–21; New York Times, December 10, 1945; Robert Friend to Frances Rose Ransom, January 9, 1948, WRL MSS, Box 15.

peacetime revival of conscription, in A. J. Muste's words, as "a major turning point, a sinister development." Their opposition hinged not merely upon their own difficulties in the event of a new military draft—indeed, most pacifist groups, including the A.F.S.C., refused to ask special provisions for C.O.'s, and opposed the bill in its entirety—but upon their belief that it signaled the coming of a new military power struggle. The A.F.S.C. argued that "each step a nation takes to increase its own security thereby decreases the security of its neighbors." In this manner conscription would make "security impossible and war inevitable." The army did not "build men," Milton Mayer told the readers of the *Progressive*, but trained them for "killing. Killing, and nothing else, is what the army is for, and the only thing it can properly build is killers and killees." [23]

Pacifist opposition to the conscription law proposed by the Truman Administration took radical forms. In February, 1947, four pacifists burned their draft cards in San Francisco's Union Square, while in Los Angeles another thirty sent their own unwanted Selective Service credentials to the President. A New York gathering of about two hundred fifty persons in the same month witnessed the burning of sixty-three draft cards. The meeting, chaired by Bayard Rustin, heard addresses by Dwight Macdonald, Dave Dellinger, and A. J. Muste. Macdonald told the assemblage: "We have decided to attack conscription by the simplest and most direct way possible: that is, by refusing . . . to recognize the authority of the State in this matter." Altogether, between four and five hundred Americans destroyed their draft cards or mailed them back to the President during February, 1947.[24]

Far more successful in halting compulsory military training, however, was the support the anti-UMT campaign mustered among non-pacifist groups. Pacifists contributed the money and the staff to establish the National Council Against Conscription, which served as a nerve center and clearinghouse for a large variety of organiza-

[23] Clyde E. Jacobs and John F. Gallagher, *The Selective Service Act: A Case Study of the Governmental Process*, pp. 27–35; Muste, *Not by Might*, p. 151; American Friends Service Committee, *Peacetime Conscription: A Problem for Americans*, p. 12; Milton Mayer, *What Can a Man Do?* pp. 96–97.

[24] Orval Etter to George Houser, February 14, 1947, Houser Correspondence in CORE MSS; *Catholic Worker*, November, 1965; Dwight Macdonald, "Why Destroy Draft Cards?" pp. 54–55.

tions. Despite the approval of UMT by most veterans' groups, the United States Chamber of Commerce, and a sprinkling of prominent individuals, it drew the fire of almost every major religious, labor, farm, and educational organization in the nation. Some, like the labor unions, feared the element of compulsion in UMT. Others, like Robert M. Hutchins, viewed the adoption of any form of conscription as "an act of war." Republican control of Congress particularly hindered the Truman Administration's legislative efforts, for the House leadership proved hesitant to take the steps necessary to bring the proposal to the floor. Nor was there much sentiment among rank-and-file members of Congress, both Democrats and Republicans, for a vote on a politically volatile issue with the approach of the 1948 elections. As a result the bill for universal military training died a quiet death in the House Rules Committee, while conscription ground to a halt with the expiration of the Selective Service Act in March, 1947. Years later, A. J. Muste recalled the campaign as "the only case where a really effective coordination of pacifist forces and near pacifist was achieved." [25]

Pacifists viewed the heightening Cold War with alarm and sought to ease tensions between the United States and the Soviet Union. A pacifist conference declared that while "Russian expansionism, the existence of Communist divisive groups in other countries, and Russian nationalism are serious concerns," Americans "must see that U.S. policies are at least parallel, if not actually provocative." The American government's attitude toward the atomic bomb and its demand for military bases around the world, the pacifists explained, "are all carefully noted and weighed by those charged with the

[25] C. E. Jacobs and Gallagher, *The Selective Service Act*, pp. 31, 33, 39–42; R. Freeman, *Quakers and Peace*, pp. 65–65; "Minutes of the Executive Committee Meeting, October 24, 1944," FOR MSS, Box 3; John M. Swomley, Jr., *The Military Establishment*, pp. 19–33; Robert M. Hutchins, "Conscription—An Act of War," *Progressive*, XII (January, 1948), 9; A. J. Muste to Sidney Aberman, July 27, 1960, Muste MSS, Box 1. Pacifists had few illusions about their success. Frank Olmstead of the W.R.L., after interviewing several Republican members of Congress in 1947, concluded that "a victory of the moment may be ours," but "for political reasons and not on principle." Frank Olmstead, "Report of Interview with Sen. Bricker on Jan. 20, 1947," WRL MSS, Box 11. For the extent of the F.O.R.'s involvement, as well as that of its staff member, John Swomley, in the postwar battle against conscription, see file marked "Swomley, John," FOR MSS, Box 11.

conduct of Russian power diplomacy." Although "attempts to white-wash Russian shortcomings or crimes will not in the long run contribute to good will and reconciliation," the United States "must remove the fear of intervention and help to raise the Russian standard of living, and thus remove the causes which create and maintain the conditions which we criticize." Peacemakers advised America to "give unquestionable proof of its desire to build a world community" by exhibiting a willingness "to disarm completely now, and to share food, natural resources, and other goods with the needy peoples of the world." [26]

Like the radical pacifists, the atomic scientists mobilized their forces for a world without war. As of mid-1946 the Federation of American Scientists, which earlier absorbed the Federation of Atomic Scientists, had 2000 members. The basis of its program was simple: "The arms race must be stopped." Eugene Rabinowitch, editor of the Federation's *Bulletin,* has observed that the scientists were subsequently considered naive, "accused of not understanding that the Soviet Union is a totalitarian dictatorship, out to convert the world to its ideology, and, if opportunity appears, to conquer those who refuse to be converted." He replied: "As if we did not know this! . . . The aims were set, and the fight undertaken, not in idealistic blindness to reality, but in full realization that these aims were *almost* unattainable, and the fight *almost* lost, even before it began." Leo Szilard "used to say that the chances of avoiding atomic war with the Soviet Union were between 5 and 10 per cent." Scientists "knew all this," maintained Rabinowitch, "yet we . . . tried to work against the all but inevitable trend, because we saw only too clearly what the consequence of letting this trend take its course would be." [27]

The most militant of the scientific organizations was the Emergency Committee of Atomic Scientists, consisting of Albert Einstein, Harold Urey, Hans Bethe, Selig Hecht, Thorfin Hogness, Philip

[26] "Record of Proceedings Atlantic City Conference for Peaceworkers, December 4–7, 1945," Allen MSS, Section C4, Box 7; Peacemakers, *A Declaration to the American People.*
[27] "Council of Federation of American Scientists Meets," *Bulletin of the Atomic Scientists,* I (May 1, 1946), 16; Federation of American (Atomic) Scientists, "Survival Is at Stake," p. 78; Rabinowitch, "Five Years After," p. 3.

Morse, Linus Pauling, Leo Szilard, and Victor Weisskopf. Einstein, as chairman of the Committee, issued a series of startling political broadsides. "A world authority and an eventual world state are not just *desirable* in the name of brotherhood, they are *necessary* for survival," he announced in 1946. Addressing a rally of student federalists that same year, he charged that the United States had not made "a really serious effort" toward an understanding with the Soviet Union. "It seems to me that America had done just the opposite. . . . There was no need to keep on producing more and more atomic bombs." Indeed, he argued, "enduring peace will come about, not by countries continuing to threaten one another, but only through an honest effort to create mutual trust. One should assume that the desire to bring about decent conditions for mankind on this planet as well as the fear of unspeakable annihilation would render those in positions of responsibility wiser and more dispassionate." [28]

As the Cold War heightened in 1947 and 1948, the Emergency Committee again prophesied disaster if the trend toward military power were not reversed. On June 29, 1947, the Committee announced that it was "imperative" that the American people understand the failure to secure international control of atomic weapons, for the alternative was "the death of our society." It warned that "the Prussian disease of which the German and Japanese states have died is beginning to infect the conquerors." In April, 1948, it argued against the policy of "armed peace in a two-bloc world." This would "entail tremendous and steadily accelerating armaments expenditures over an indefinite period" and "might also betray our moral position by propping up antidemocratic regimes as counter-poise to the Soviet Union." Such a policy led "inevitably to a war which would end with the total collapse of our traditional civilization." The Emergency Committee of Atomic Scientists reiterated that there was but one hope for mankind—"world government." [29]

Yet after its first shudder at Hiroshima, public opinion began to desert the scientists. The Bikini bomb tests in the summer of 1946

28 Pauling, *No More War!* pp. 220–21; Albert Einstein, " 'The Real Problem Is in the Hearts of Men,' " *New York Times Magazine* (June 23, 1946), p. 7; Albert Einstein, *Out of My Later Years*, p. 138.
29 *New York Times*, June 30, 1947; Nathan and Norden, *Einstein on Peace*, pp. 410–11, 471–72.

were at least partially responsible. "Before Bikini the world stood in awe of this new cosmic force," wrote *New York Times* science reporter William Laurence, but "since Bikini this feeling . . . has been supplanted with a sense of relief." The average American "had expected one bomb to sink the entire Bikini fleet, kill all the animals aboard, make a hole in the bottom of the ocean and create tidal waves that would be felt for thousands of miles." As "none of these happened, he is only too eager to conclude that the atomic bomb is, after all, just another weapon." Opinion surveys confirm this analysis; a Gallup poll taken in the aftermath of the Bikini tests revealed that most Americans found the atomic bomb less destructive than expected. After watching the first explosion of the test series, a reporter remarked to Norman Cousins: "The next war's not going to be so bad after all." [30]

Atomic power also grew more tolerable to Americans because of a widespread faith in its "peaceful uses." Analyzing this relatively unfounded conviction, David Lilienthal, the former chairman of the Atomic Energy Commission (A.E.C.), contended that Americans believed "that somehow or other the discovery that had produced so terrible a weapon simply *had* to have an important peaceful use." They could then stand not only as world destroyers, but as world saviors. Lewis Mumford wrote that "the devil baited the atomic bomb very cunningly" with "the notion that the 'peacetime' uses of the atomic bomb far outweigh its dangers." Therefore, when a national poll following the Bikini tests asked, "How worried are you about the atomic bomb?" it was not altogether surprising that 50 per cent answered "not at all." [31]

Finally, the scientists' movement was undercut because their principal weapon—that of fear—cut two ways. As Robert M. Hutchins astutely remarked in 1946, if peace was to be based upon "fear of retaliation," then this meant "an armament race." Norman Thomas

[30] William L. Laurence, "The Bikini Tests and Public Opinion," *Bulletin of the Atomic Scientists*, II (September 1, 1946), 2; Cantril, *Public Opinion*, p. 25; Cousins, *Who Speaks for Man?* p. 25. The log kept by Dr. David Bradley during the Bikini tests illustrates the opposite reaction. David Bradley, *No Place to Hide*.

[31] David E. Lilienthal, *Change, Hope, and the Bomb*, pp. 109–110; Lewis Mumford to Frank Olmstead, March 8, 1946, WRL MSS. Box 18; Bailey, *The Man in the Street*, p. 123.

wrote: "Nobody can escape the logical conclusion that if our best hope is fear of retaliation, then our best defense is not disarmament, but scientific armament." The "One World or None" concept, after all, relied upon the atomic bomb as world government's ace in the hole—the guarantor of a warless world through its deterrent power. How easy, then, for even the most pacific of men to conclude that, for the good of the world, America's atomic arsenal had to be preserved! "The paradox of the present situation," observed Henry P. Van Dusen, president of Union Theological Seminary, "is that, so long as the United States possesses exclusively the secret of the atomic bomb, peace is secure. . . . There is even a faint hope that this instrument may actually accomplish what all of our decades of labor for peace have failed to accomplish—the abolition of war, because no nation will be fool enough to risk involvement in conflict." When David Lilienthal visited Los Alamos in 1946 a "distinguished staff member" briefed him on the feasibility of a new super-bomb (later called the H-bomb), explaining that such a weapon would frighten nations into finally accepting the necessity for world government. Lilienthal added that in 1963 he still heard this argument advanced by "present-day weaponeers and 'civilian strategists.' " [32]

Sensing, perhaps, the ebbing of support for their idealistic proposals, American scientists united behind the more conservative Acheson-Lilienthal proposals for the international control of atomic energy, subsequently presented to the U.N. by Bernard Baruch. Karl T. Compton, president of the Massachusetts Institute of Technology, argued that they represented "an effective compromise between the presently impractical suggestion of a world state, on the one hand, and the terrifying prospect of doing nothing, on the other hand." On April 14, 1946, the Federation of American Scientists announced that "American scientists are overwhelmingly in favor of the principles of the 'Acheson Report,' " while the secretary of the American Association for the Advancement of Science termed

[32] Robert M. Hutchins, Review of *The Absolute Weapon: Atomic Power and World Order*, by Bernard Brodie (ed.), *New York Times Book Review* (June 9, 1946), pp. 6, 27; N. M. Thomas, *Appeal to the Nations*, pp. 42–46; Henry P. Van Dusen to A. J. Muste, August 24, 1945, FOR MSS, Box 12; Lilienthal, *Change, Hope, and the Bomb*, pp. 35–36.

it "a great historic document distinguished alike for its scientific excellence and its statesmanship." Even the Emergency Committee of Atomic Scientists reported their complete agreement with the Baruch Plan; the Russian proposals, remarked the committee's vice-chairman, Harold Urey, were "inadequate." [33]

Few peace-oriented Americans found much to their liking in the Gromyko proposals, but a number expressed their reservations on aspects of the Baruch Plan. As Norman Cousins and Thomas K. Finletter, two supporters of the Plan, observed, while "all the nations in the world would be asked to surrender their sovereignty in the mining, processing, and manufacture of fissionable materials," the United States "would still be permitted to stockpile its own atomic bombs." Attacking this same point in the American plan, Cord Meyer, Jr., wrote that its rejection "would demonstrate nothing but the understandable reluctance of other nations to give up their means of making atomic weapons while the United States continues its monopoly." The best publicized of the Baruch Plan's critics, Secretary of Commerce Henry A. Wallace, predicted the Russian rejection on just these grounds. Then, asking what Americans would have done were they Russians, he answered: "I think we would react as the Russians appear to have done. We would have put up counter-proposals for the record, but our real effort would go into trying to make a bomb so that our bargaining position would be equalized. That is the essence of the Russian position." A. J. Muste noted one element of accord in both the American and Soviet proposals: "Both say to the other 'I don't trust you and will not take any chances, but I ask you to trust me and take the chances which that involves.'" [34]

[33] Gilpin, *American Scientists and Nuclear Weapons Policy,* pp. 57–62; "Scientists Comment on State Department Report," *Bulletin of the Atomic Scientists,* I (April 15, 1946), 12; *New York Times,* June 30, 1947.

[34] Norman Cousins and Thomas K. Finletter, "A Beginning for Sanity," *Bulletin of the Atomic Scientists,* II (July 1, 1946), 14; Cord Meyer, Jr., "What Are the Chances?" *Atlantic Monthly,* CLXXVIII (July, 1946), 42–43; Henry A. Wallace, "Letter to the President," *Bulletin of the Atomic Scientists,* II (October 1, 1946), 2; A. J. Muste to Felix Morley, August 1, 1946, FOR MSS, Box 9. Muste, unlike Wallace, did not want the United States to "share" the secret of the bomb with Russia; in fact, he thought this "dangerous." Instead, he suggested "an international agreement to abolish national military establishments and conscription." A. J. Muste to Harry S. Truman, November 7, 1945, FOR MSS, Box 12; A. J. Muste to Henry A. Wallace, September 26, 1945, FOR MSS, Box 12.

More successful than either the pacifists or the scientists in organizing a widespread social movement in these years were the world federalists. Books and articles on the subject of world government continued to arouse public discussion,[35] while political activists among its adherents secured startling victories. By 1949 seventeen state legislatures had passed resolutions urging Congress to begin planning toward world government. In the United States Senate, Glen Taylor introduced a world government resolution, cosponsored by Senators Dennis Chavez, Olin Johnston, Charles Tobey, Claude Pepper, and James Murray, that would ask the President to "immediately take the initiative in calling a general conference . . . for the purpose of making the United Nations capable of enacting, interpreting, and enforcing world law to prevent war." Taylor received the support of a number of influential individuals, including Harold Urey, Frank Graham, and James G. Patton, president of the National Farmers Union.[36]

The ready political support achieved by world federalism in the United States reflected not only the unique experience of the country with federation, but also, more significantly, the organizing efforts of the mushrooming world government groups. In late 1946 a letter in the New York Times declared that world government organizations were "swamped with applications for charters, requests for literature and new memberships." Reliable estimates placed their total membership at about 17,000. At the end of the war, three major world government groups had emerged in the country: Americans United for World Government, Student Federalists, and World Federalists, U.S.A. In addition there were many independent

---

[35] See, for example: Philip Jessup, A Modern Law of Nations; Frederick L. Schuman, "Toward the World State," Scientific Monthly, LIII (July, 1946), 5–19; Thomas K. Finletter, "Timetable for World Government," Atlantic Monthly, CLXXI (March, 1946), 53–60; Georg Schwarzenberger, "The Prospects for International Law," Review of Politics, VIII (April, 1946), 168–82; Emery Reves, "World Government Is the First Step," Reader's Digest, XLVIII (February, 1946), 109–117; Erich Kahler, "The Reality of Utopia," American Scholar, XV (Spring, 1946), 167–79; Quincy Wright, "Making the United Nations Work," Review of Politics, VIII (October, 1946), 528–32.

[36] Harrison Brown, "The World Government Movement in the United States," Bulletin of the Atomic Scientists, III (June, 1947), 166; Gerard J. Mangone, The Idea and Practice of World Government, p. 24; U.S., Congressional Record, 80th Cong., 1st Sess., 1947, XCIII, Part 7, 8506.

state organizations as well as a number of smaller national groups; among the latter were the Committee for a People's World Constitutional Convention and Campaign for World Government. In the spring of 1946 a group of students at Northwestern University formed still another organization, Students for Federal World Government. More a "cadre" than a membership organization, most of its adherents donated their personal savings to the group, left their jobs, and rotated employment in three shifts over a twenty-four-hour working day in the organization's combination dormitory-office building.[37]

Concerned about the lack of coordination between the various world government organizations, Students for Federal World Government, now World Republic, called a meeting in Chicago during November, 1946, to discuss the possibilities of unification. The groups meeting decided to plan for a larger gathering at a later date. The resulting convention of sixteen world government organizations in Asheville, North Carolina, held in February, 1947, resulted in the merger of most of them under the name "United World Federalists." The platform adopted committed U.W.F. to "work primarily to strengthen the United Nations into a world government." Ironically, World Republic and several of the smaller groups refused to join U.W.F. because of their desire for a "people's convention" rather than a conference of delegates appointed by sovereign governments to serve as the initiator of a world government.[38]

United World Federalists rapidly emerged as the leading spokesman for world government in the United States. As of mid-1947 it had about 17,000 dues-paying members, in 200 chapters scattered over 31 states. Its officers included Cord Meyer, Jr., president, with Grenville Clark, Norman Cousins, Thomas K. Finletter, W. T. Holliday, Robert Lee Humber, Raymond Gram Swing, and Carl Van Doren serving as vice-presidents. A study of the organization's social

[37] Mangone, *The Idea and Practice of World Government*, p. 31; *New York Times*, December 29, 1946; H. Brown, "The World Government Movement," pp. 156–57; S. Benedict, "Breakers and Makers of Tradition," p. 108; *New York Times*, June 15, 1947.
[38] H. Brown, "The World Government Movement," p. 157; *New York Times*, February 22–24, 1947; United World Federalists, *Unity and Diversity*, p. 1; George T. Peck, "Who Are the United World Federalists?" *Common Cause*, I (July, 1947), 28.

composition revealed that the leaders of U.W.F. were often of liberal Protestant extraction, residing largely in metropolitan areas on the East Coast; most came from well-to-do families, although few were businessmen. By the end of 1948 the membership of U.W.F. had grown to approximately 40,000, in 659 chapters. Rallies of thousands were addressed by liberal Democrat Chester Bowles, Norman Cousins, Representatives Brooks Hays (Dem., Ark.) and Walter Judd (Rep., Minn.), and by long-time "internationalist" James P. Warburg.[39]

Although not a membership organization like the U.W.F., the University of Chicago Committee to Frame a World Constitution developed as a second major focal point of world government concern. Following Robert Huchins' "Good News of Damnation" statement on August 12, 1945, two members of the faculty called upon the University of Chicago president to suggest that steps be taken immediately to draft a world constitution. Professors Richard P. McKeon and G. A. Borgese urged the university to establish an "Institute for World Government," pointing to the "symbolic" fact that "the University of Chicago played a decisive role in inaugurating the atomic age." Thereafter, the new Committee to Frame a World Constitution made the University of Chicago the stormy center of intellectual rigor and social action on the question of a world community. Hutchins alone became a one-man movement. "If we wish to be saved, we shall have to practice justice and love, however humiliating it may be to do so. These practices have long been commended to us by the very highest authority; they now appear to be our only alternative," he wrote in 1947. "Our Christian civilization will have to christianize itself in a hurry. It will have to dedicate itself to the proposition that men are men before they are Englishmen, businessmen, workingmen, or Americans, and that all men are brothers. . . . This proposition, always popular on Sundays, requires the subordination of Americanism to Humanity." [40]

[39] H. Brown, "The World Government Movement," p. 157; United World Federalists, *Unity and Diversity*, p. 4; G. T. Peck, "Who Are the United World Federalists?" p. 28; "UWF's Birthday Marks Half a Decade of Progress," *The Federalist*, I (February, 1952), 6.

[40] "Brief History of the Committee," *Common Cause*, I (July, 1947), 11–12; Hutchins, "1950," p. 1. At its inception in November, 1945, the Com-

Harrison Brown, one of the more outspoken of the atomic scientists, observed in 1947 that most of his friends, when asked for their prescription for the world's ills, "will state: 'a world government.' But there agreement ends." The largest area of disagreement between advocates of world government centered about the question of how much; "minimalists" wanted merely enough to achieve security against war, while "maximalists" argued that a world government had to have the power to ensure justice. The U.W.F. was admittedly minimalist, since it called for "a world government of limited powers, adequate to prevent war." On the other hand, the Committee to Frame a World Constitution, after an early struggle over the functions of a world authority, finally decided upon a maximalist standard. G. A. Borgese argued that "if the haves shall have what they have and the have-nots shall not lose what they don't have, if by security we mean that nobody shall disturb us in the enjoyment of our goods, pride, power, and nobody shall disturb them in the fruition of their destitution and abjectness," then the majority of mankind would obviously find world government unacceptable. Robert Redfield, also a member of the Committee, agreed: "The price of peace is justice." This split over the nature of world government represented a problem which its advocates generally avoided only by virtue of their lack of any real success.[41]

mittee included: Hutchins; Richard P. McKeon, professor of philosophy, University of Chicago; G. A. Borgese, professor of philosophy, University of Chicago; Mortimer J. Adler, professor of the philosophy of law, University of Chicago; William E. Hocking, professor of religion, Harvard; Wilber G. Katz, dean of the Law School, University of Chicago; James M. Landis, dean of the Law School, Harvard; Reinhold Niebuhr, professor of applied Christianity, Union Theological Seminary; Robert Redfield, professor of anthropology, University of Chicago; Beardsley Ruml, chairman of the Federal Reserve Bank of New York; and Rexford G. Tugwell, professor of political science, University of Chicago. Three members withdrew: Hocking and Ruml because of impediments of business or distance; Niebuhr because of theoretical disagreements. Subsequently added were: Albert L. Guerard, professor of literature, Stanford; Erich Kahler, lecturer, New School for Social Research; Stringfellow Barr, president, St. John's College; and Harold A. Innis, chairman, department of political economy, University of Toronto. "Brief History of the Committee," pp. 13–14.

[41] H. Brown, "The World Government Movement," p. 156; "Brief History of the Committee," pp. 15–17; *New York Times*, August 19, 1946; G. A. Borgese, "Of Atomic Fear and Two 'Utopias,'" *Common Cause*, I (September, 1947), 84–89; Robert Redfield, "The Price of Peace," *Common Cause*, I (September, 1947), 81–82. Borgese commented: "No sooner do we move from

In the years immediately following Hiroshima, American world federalists were critical of the foreign policies of both the United States and the Soviet Union. U.W.F. considered these nations "the main obstacles to the coming of federal world government." As the tension between the two countries heightened, with the Soviet Union increasingly assigned the role in the United States as instigator of the rift, world federalists did their best to fight against this trend. "It is at least inconsistent to declare that there can be no doubt as to the defensive nature of American preparations," wrote Cord Meyer, Jr., "while seizing upon every similar step by the Soviet Union as incontrovertible evidence of its insatiable imperialism." The U.W.F. leader argued that "Soviet policy in the Balkans is similar to American behavior in China and Greece. Each competitor seeks to insure by force that the other does not gain the controlling influence in areas each considers essential to its security." National rivalries of this type would inevitably occur, he insisted, unless the nations accepted a world authority.[42]

Yet despite the criticism world government proponents directed at American foreign policy, most accepted its underlying principle—military deterrence. This was strikingly demonstrated in a Town Meeting of the Air debate of December 30, 1947. The assistant editor of the *New York Herald Tribune* opened with a belligerent blast: "Let's have peace based on international respect for the power of America. Let's have the most powerful Army, Navy, and Air Force in the world. . . . Civilization preserved through force." Cord Meyer, Jr., labeled this a program of "peace by intimidation." Such a policy, the U.W.F. president argued, "may work for a time, but it will end inevitably in the collective suicide of a third war." A "peace among nations armed with the means of annihilating each other's cities, will be intolerable while it lasts and it will not last for

the comfortable area of generic propaganda to specific programs than we see how steep is the path." G. A. Borgese, "One World and Seven Problems," *Common Cause*, I (July, 1947), 3.

42 United World Federalists, *Unity and Diversity*, p. 3; C. Meyer, *Peace or Anarchy*, pp. 58, 77. The Soviet Union took to such criticism no better than the United States. *Pravda* branded world government plans as "reactionary utopias," while two Soviet scientists answered a letter from Albert Einstein on the matter with the remark that world government was "nothing but a flamboyant signboard for the world supremacy of the capitalist monopolies." Nathan and Norden, *Einstein on Peace*, p. 445.

long." But then, after an eloquent plea for world federation, he concluded: "Until this world federation is established and the nations agree to disarm under its protection, I would agree with Mr. Forrest [of the *Herald Tribune*] that we must maintain our defensive military strength." To make this point clear, he repeated it again later in the program: "I think we have to follow a policy of military preparedness now, given the fact that other nations are arming." Here lay the irony of the world federalist position: simultaneous support for the arms race and for world government.[43]

Pacifists were quick to spot a similar inconsistency in the position of the atomic scientists. If atomic warfare would be a catastrophe, then why prepare for it? "The scientists who made Hiroshima possible . . . are making the next Hiroshima possible," jibed Milton Mayer. Improvements upon the original bomb "have been made by the men who, on their night out . . . inform the Elks or the Eagles of the horrors of atomic war and the desperate necessity of world government." Bayard Rustin sharply criticized the "men who cry out that atomic weapons will destroy civilization [but] continue to make them, because national allegiances demand it." He told a Quaker gathering: "They announce that they work with 'heavy hearts and without enthusiasm' but they do not answer the heart. They answer the demands of the state." [44]

In a public reply to an "Emergency Appeal" by Einstein in 1946, A. J. Muste issued a brilliant critique of the scientists' position. If Einstein, Condon, Bethe, Szilard, Urey, and the Federation of American Scientists refused to make atomic weapons, Muste contended, "the American people would at last realize that you were deadly serious about the bomb. . . . What is infinitely more important," wrote the pacifist leader, "they would be shaken out of moral

---

[43] "Which Road to Peace in 1948?" *Town Meeting: Bulletin of America's Town Meeting of the Air,* XIII (December 30, 1947), 8–10, 21. Forrest, in his reply to Meyer, backed away a bit from his earlier conclusions, taking a more conventional Cold War line: "I think Mr. Meyers [sic] got a wrong idea of what I stand for. That is, I don't expect to build a tremendous powerful army and all that sort of thing. I expect to have the United States strong enough as a world leader on this side of the fence with Russia a leader on the other, to make an impression on the nations who want to be democratic nations and to play along with us in the United Nations." *Ibid.,* p. 21.

[44] Milton Mayer, "Vicarious Atonement," *Fellowship,* XIV (September, 1948), 14; Bayard Rustin, *"In Apprehension How Like a God!"* p. 16.

lethargy and despair and would become capable of inspired action to abolish war and build a democratic society, because they would behold the spectacle of men who do not try to shift the responsibility for their actions onto the military or the State, who refuse to make conscience subservient to them." There is "a deep cleavage in our souls and in our society because our moral and social development has not kept pace with technological advance," Muste stated. "That cleavage must be healed first and basically within the morally responsible human being. It will be healed in the scientist who becomes a prophet," he affirmed, "a man whose words and actions are in true accord." Mankind's destiny "is being decided by the scientists who take, or fail to take, upon themselves the awful responsibility of being prophets, conscientious objectors, persons, whole human beings, and not technicians or slaves of a warmaking State, albeit heavy-hearted and unenthusiastic ones." [45]

Muste's challenge brought confusion and dismay. W. A. Higinbotham, chairman of the Federation of American Scientists, replied uneasily that most of his acquaintances had left the Manhattan Project to return to peaceful employment, or were working on the peaceful uses of atomic energy. Moreover, he revealed that, in his view, the use made of the bomb during World War II was "very shortsighted." Yet "we believe in government by the people," the eminent physicist added. "If scientists were to walk out on all military projects they would be taking the law into their own hands just as surely as the Ku Klux Klan." This idea that a scientific walkout would somehow be undemocratic and illegal pervaded the replies of the scientists. A "strike," noted Hans Bethe, "would only antagonize the public of the United States who would rightly accuse us of trying to dictate the policies of the country." Harold Urey wrote: "I personally believe in obeying the laws of this country. . . . I exercise my right as a citizen in attempting to change the rules, not in frustrating the rules as they are laid down." Finally, most argued that such a stand by scientists would "weaken" the United States, accepting thereby the paradoxical position of other world government advocates. Scientists "have two clear-cut duties," said Edward Teller in 1947: "to work on atomic energy under our present admin-

45 A. J. Muste to Albert Einstein, May 28, 1946, FOR MSS, Box 12.

istration and to work for a world government which alone can give us freedom and peace." [46]

Yet while the public policies of the scientists' associations avoided "controversial" positions of this type, many scientists, as individuals, began to withdraw their support from the arms race. In late 1946 Robert M. Hutchins told A. J. Muste that "a movement is gaining ground among scientists . . . against working on anything that looks like a weapon." Illustrative of this attitude was the public letter of Norbert Wiener, a mathematician at the Massachusetts Institute of Technology since 1919 and a missile research expert for the United States government during World War II, which stated in emphatic terms his refusal to provide information to a large aircraft corporation. "The policy of the government . . . during and after the war, say in the bombing of Hiroshima and Nagasaki, has made it clear that to provide scientific information is not a necessarily innocent act," he noted. "I do not expect to publish any future work of mine which may do damage in the hands of irresponsible militarists." According to the *Atlantic Monthly*, Wiener's reaction was "typical of many scientists who served their country faithfully during the war." When asked for his opinion on the matter, Einstein asserted: "Non-cooperation in military matters should be an essential moral principle for all true scientists." [47]

This attitude, while not a dominant one, appears to have been

---

[46] W. A. Higinbotham to A. J. Muste, August 5, 1946, FOR MSS, Box 12; Hans Bethe to A. J. Muste, December 16, 1946, FOR MSS, Box 12; Harold C. Urey to A. J. Muste, June 10, 1946, FOR MSS, Box 12; Edward Teller, "Atomic Scientists Have Two Responsibilities," *Bulletin of the Atomic Scientists*, III (December, 1947), 356. Others were less negative. "Your criticism seems to me justified to a high degree," Einstein replied, while Szilard expressed his agreement "on the moral issue involved," but noted that "considerations of expediency" on the part of "the majority of scientists" would doom Muste's proposal to failure. Albert Einstein to A. J. Muste, October 11, 1947, Muste MSS, Series 1, Box 1; Leo Szilard to A. J. Muste, December 18, 1946, FOR MSS, Box 12.

[47] Robert M. Hutchins to A. J. Muste, November 4, 1946, FOR MSS, Box 8; Norbert Wiener, "A Scientist Rebels," *Atlantic Monthly*, CLXXIX (January, 1947), 46; Nathan and Norden, *Einstein on Peace*, pp. 401–402. Other physicists criticized Wiener's decision. Physicist Louis Ridenour found himself "in violent disagreement" with Wiener. While he regarded it "as deplorable that our nation is preparing for war, . . . I shall certainly not attempt to impede such preparations." Louis Ridenour, "The Scientist Fights for Peace," *Atlantic Monthly*, CLXXIX (May, 1947), 80–83.

widespread. In December, 1945, Dr. Theodore Hauschka, a biologist, appealed to Robert Oppenheimer and his associates to "pledge publicly, as a group, that you will desist from carrying your experiments further . . . until . . . safeguards against misuse have been devised." By the time of the Bikini tests, according to one influential scientist, most of the participants in the Manhattan Project were "back at their universities and their efforts are not going into the tests. (Some at least refused to participate because of their grave doubts of the value or propriety of the tests.)" Hanson Baldwin, the *New York Times* military expert, wrote in irritation that by such behavior the scientists "have tended to complicate and make difficult the task of staging atomic bomb tests in the Pacific. . . . The Army and Navy are admittedly handicapped." Scientific resistance to the military even percolated down to the comic strip level. In 1947 a scientist in the "Superman" series announced that "today we scientists must accept moral responsibility for what we produce," while Superman stated in reply: "The atomic world cannot really afford more innovations it doesn't know how to use." [48]

Often provoked by the timidity of the scientists' crusade, pacifists were only slightly less critical of world government. Although most pacifists accepted the idea of world government in theory, few actually became deeply involved in world federalist activities; the vast majority simply gave their new allies lukewarm support. To some degree this reflected the pacifist distrust of State power. "The development of political statism of a tyrannical variety has become so rapid that our job is to help maintain freedom for individuals without falling into the N.A.M., Chamber of Commerce, Hayek line," one radical asserted. Even the old-line leaders of the peace movement grew wary of expanded government authority. "I have a very considerable distrust of government as such," observed Emily Balch, "and see no reason to be sure that a world government would be run

[48] *New York Times*, December 5, 1945; Lee A. DuBridge, "What about the Bikini Tests?" *Bulletin of the Atomic Scientists*, I (May 15, 1946), 7; Hanson Baldwin to A. J. Muste, March 5, 1946, FOR MSS, Box 12; A. J. Muste to Jerry Siegal and Joe Shuster, October 6, 1947, FOR MSS, Box 7. Gallup polls, however, found that only small percentages of the country favored a halt to American manufacture of atomic bombs: 30 per cent on April 10, 1946, and 21 per cent on November 13, 1946. Cantril, *Public Opinion*, p. 25.

by men very different in capacity from those who govern national states." [49]

Moreover, a majority of pacifists took a "functionalist" rather than a federalist approach to international problems. Many argued that coercion of states by an international organization could not maintain peace. What the world needed, they insisted, was not more authority at the top, but rather greater cooperation of peoples at the bottom in solving their mutual problems. "Is it sufficient to write constitutions and to establish police powers," asked one, "or is unity to be achieved through the action of more intangible forces, the elimination of causes of friction, increasing the number of fields of cooperative endeavor." Borrowing from the "maximalist" argument, they asserted that justice, and not force, was the true cement of any harmonious international order; for this reason, wrote A. J. Muste, "we shall be well advised to concentrate on the economic, cultural and spiritual conditions of peace rather than the legal and military." This attitude manifested itself in strong support of the United Nations' social and economic activities, but in continued opposition to its role in "peacekeeping" operations. Most pacifists—although by no means all—rejected an "international police," since they did not consider the military coercion of nations analogous to the enforcement of law upon individuals. [50]

[49] "Excerpts of Comments Received from Members" (August, 1945), WRL MSS, Box 2; J. H. Randall, *Emily Greene Balch*, p. 11. One pacifist wrote that "the great problem presented by the atomic bomb is not . . . to discover some new device of government . . . but to diminish government altogether. The problem is to give power back to the individual, so that he may be responsible for his own actions. Humanity does not need to learn how to live together," but "how to live alone; to have private opinions, not a public opinion; to be men, not citizens." *Conscientious Objector*, December, 1945. On the other hand, even the most radical pacifists felt that, stripped of war, governments could prove to be tolerable. "We do spiritually aim at 'one world,' a common humanity," wrote A. J. Muste, and "that does require some means of communication and . . . widespread exchange, certainly of ideas, but also of certain kinds of goods, and of sociopolitical instrumentalities. How you can have these things without the organization to utilize them, I don't see." He added: "If the modern state no longer had war as its main preoccupation, with all the machinery that that implies, and the regimentation, it seems to me that all sorts of things would be possible which are not possible now." A. J. Muste to Richard Gregg, June 4, 1947, FOR MSS, Box 11.

[50] Harrop A. Freeman and Theodore Paullin, *Coercion of States: In Federal Unions*, pp. 1–2; A. J. Muste, "A Footnote on International Police," *Fellowship*,

Pacifists and non-pacifists directed a great deal of criticism at the schematic nature of world government plans. "Political unity," one pacifist argued, "develops from a sense of community." A. J. Muste held a similar position; to him world government seemed "a way to impose peace rather than growing out of it." Ironically, Reinhold Niebuhr, the old pacifist nemesis, agreed with this critique. "If the community does not exist in fact, at least in inchoate form, constitutional instruments cannot create it," he wrote in 1946. But "to say that there is no way of guaranteeing the peace of the world constitutionally," he added with characteristic pessimism, "is not to say there are other ways of guaranteeing it. There are none." [51]

Yet throughout the period from 1945 to 1948, in contrast to Niebuhr's dim appraisal of the possibilities for peace, influential sectors of American society did actively concern themselves with disarmament and the abolition of war. Lewis Mumford called them the "awakened ones," and reported their message to be this:

The madmen are planning the end of the world. What they call continued progress in atomic warfare means universal extermination, and

VIII (August, 1942), 136; Theodore Paullin, *Comparative Peace Plans*, pp. 76–77, 82; Harrop A. Freeman and Theodore Paullin, "Federalism and Force," *Fellowship*, IX (January, 1943), 5–6; Theodore Paullin, "A New International Order—Functional or Constitutional," *Peace Is the Victory*, ed. Harrop A. Freeman, pp. 120–37; Page, *Now Is the Time*, pp. 47–60; H. A. Freeman, *Coercion of States in International Organizations*, pp. 5–57; Julien Cornell, *New World Primer*, pp. 78–79. For a discussion of the conflict between federalists and functionalists in Quaker ranks, see: R. Freeman, *Quakers and Peace*, pp. 58–59; Bertram Pickard, *Peacemakers' Dilemma: Plea for a Modus Vivendi in the Peace Movement*.

[51] Personal interview with A. J. Muste, June 2, 1966; Reinhold Niebuhr, "The Myth of World Government," *Nation*, CLXII (March 16, 1946), 312–14. A. J. Muste told one world government advocate that he firmly believed that "if we have peace we shall have some form of genuine world government," but "it could be that peace is the horse and world government the cart." A. J. Muste to Vernon Nash, October 1, 1946, FOR MSS, Box 9. Other non-pacifist critiques of world government included: Waldemar Gurian, "World Government," *Commonweal*, XLII (September 28, 1945), 573; Edward R. Lewis, "Are We Ready for a World State?" *Yale Review*, XXXV (Spring, 1946), 491–501; Walter Lippmann, "One World of Diversity," *Vital Speeches*, XIII (December 15, 1946), 138–40; Nathaniel Peffer, "Politics Is Peace," *American Scholar*, XV (Spring, 1946), 160–66; N. A. Pelcovits, "World Government Now?" *Harper's*, CXCIII (November, 1946), 396–403; Stefan T. Possony, "The Atomic Bomb," *Review of Politics*, VIII (April, 1946), 147–67; James Quarles, "E Pluribus Unum: 1946 Model," *World Affairs*, CIX (September, 1946), 181–85; William B. Ziff, *Two Worlds: A Realistic Approach to the Problems of Keeping the Peace*.

what they call national security is organized suicide. There is only one duty for the moment: every other task is a dream or a mockery. Stop the atomic bomb. Stop making the bomb. Abandon the bomb completely. Dismantle every existing bomb. Cancel every plan for the bomb's use. . . . Either dethrone the madmen immediately or raise such a shout of protest as will shock them into sanity.[52]

"Nuclear pacifists," when added to the busy "radical pacifists," gave the peace movement a fairly wide array of support and scope of concern.

Indeed such breadth of support hinted at a certain shallowness. "We may disagree on some things," John Foster Dulles told A. J. Muste, "but I think, we agree on most." General Douglas MacArthur informed the Allied Council for Japan that "the progress and survival of civilization" were "dependent upon . . . the realization . . . of the utter futility of force as an arbiter of international issues." Yet how valid were the renunciations of war by men who still accepted the deterrence concept? Pacifists stirred uneasily. "Those who do not undergo a spiritual revolution," warned Muste, "will, after a period of protesting that atomic war 'simply must not be,' find a moral justification, or more accurately excuse, for engaging in it—always, of course, on the right side, 'our' side." [53] For the peace movement, the period from 1945 to 1948 seemed a promising beginning, but time and events would ultimately provide the test of its resolve.

[52] Lewis Mumford, "Gentlemen: You Are Mad!" *Saturday Review of Literature*, XXIX (March 2, 1946), 5–6.
[53] John Foster Dulles to A. J. Muste, June 10, 1946, FOR MSS, Box 7; Douglas MacArthur, "The Surrender of Right to Make War," *Vital Speeches*, XII (April 15, 1946), 390; Muste, *Not by Might*, p. 79. World government supporters were often less skeptical than Muste. The chairman of Students for Federal World Government invited MacArthur to address a World Youth Peace Conference, adding: "Your presence and your voice at this convention may well lead us out of chaos into a true peace." The chairman of the Campaign for World Government thought that the general had made a "great contribution." Rempfer L. Whitehouse to Douglas MacArthur, June 22, 1946, MacArthur MSS, Box 7; Georgia Lloyd to Douglas MacArthur, April 8, 1946, MacArthur MSS, Box 7.

CHAPTER VII

Retreat, 1948–1950

The President's speech . . . stirred strange echoes before him. For, just after he had declared that this country must above all keep itself strong, a formation of five B-36 bombers swept low over the vast crowds.

NEW YORK TIMES, 1949[1]

By 1948 relations between the United States and the Soviet Union had deteriorated to a marked degree, with the international situation hardening into East-West polarity. The political crisis which ensued, increasingly perceived in strategic and military terms, threw the American peace movement into disarray. As a result the movement commenced a retreat after 1948; although some elements held to their original policies, many grew more conservative and less independent of the American position in the Cold War, while still others abandoned the struggle completely. In this manner the retreat that began in 1948 grew to a rout by 1950.

In the postwar period both the American and the Russian governments, at the peak of their military and political power, sought to extend their influence over international events. The Truman Administration continued the development and stockpiling of the atomic bomb, established a chain of military bases around the world, and provided large-scale military and technical assistance to prop up the right-wing governments of Greece and China against Communist-led uprisings. The Soviet Union utilized the power and influence World War II afforded it in Eastern Europe to initiate a series of local Communist takeovers, which quickly resulted in the suppression of opposition parties and the creation of "people's democracies." For Americans, the most startling occurred in February,

[1] *New York Times,* January 21, 1949. The speech referred to was the President's inaugural address.

1948, when the Czech government of President Eduard Beneš and Premier Jan Masaryk, always careful to remain on good terms with its Russian neighbor, was ousted in a sudden coup d'état and replaced with a Soviet model. Communist-led revolutions in various parts of the world, coupled with the Party's electoral strength in Western Europe, frightened Americans, and convinced many that the Soviet Union had embarked upon a campaign to widen its control over ever-larger areas of the globe.

The Truman Doctrine, the first serious statement of American Cold War policies, presented pacifists, in Dwight Macdonald's words, with an "impossible alternative"—"American imperialism or Russian imperialism." Pacifists realized that the people of Greece and Turkey needed the aid called for by the President, but they disliked the framework provided by the proposal. "To skirt the United Nations by supplying the Greek and Turkish Governments with relatively permanent military and economic aid in the name of the United States alone is far too likely to endanger peace more than it could bolster freedom," the W.I.L.P.F. observed. Macdonald viewed the Truman Doctrine as "more a competitor than an opponent of the Kremlin Doctrine," and "at best . . . no more than a detour on the road to World War III." Seeking an acceptable alternative, A. J. Muste suggested that Americans "support the Truman proposal for relief to Greece—under civilian auspices. Reject the Truman proposals for political and military action." [2]

The European Recovery Program (E.R.P.), better known to Americans as the Marshall Plan, raised similar difficulties for opponents of a two-bloc world. Pacifists, who had long urged America to devote her resources to the reconstruction and rehabilitation of wartorn nations, found themselves in an embarrassing dilemma because of the obvious political implications of the assistance. The W.I.L.P.F., although it favored such aid through the United Nations, regretfully supported the Marshall Plan for lack of an alternative. It worried, however, that "our policy may strengthen reactionary private and governmental elements in Europe and thus bring

[2] Macdonald, *Memoirs of a Revolutionist*, pp. 187, 190; "Statement on U.S. Policy toward Greece and Turkey" (March 18, 1947), WILPF MSS, Box 30; "National Board Resolutions Re: Point Four," WILPF MSS, Box 4; A. J. Muste, "How to Stop Russia and Communism," FOR MSS, Box 28.

about the collapse of the socialist governments." Local branches, according to the organization's national policy committee, expressed "fear that Europe would be split into East and West, fear that the US would attach political conditions to her aid, fear that German industry would be restored to the detriment of the industry and security of her victims." The *Catholic Worker* staunchly opposed the Marshall Plan on the grounds that it violated "the Christian concept of charity," and represented an attempt "to take advantage of a people's destitution." One writer for the journal observed: "What we possess beyond our actual needs belongs of right and in justice to those who do not have it. They owe us nothing in return—certainly nothing of political or economic allegiance." [3]

Other pacifists refused to take a definite stand for or against the measure. "The Marshall Plan" is "substituted for WPA," charged Dwight Macdonald. "The basic issue is the same. U.S. capitalism must give relief to the European peoples for the same reason it had to give a dole to its own citizens in 1935: politically, to short-circuit revolution; economically, to enable the market to absorb goods." In both cases, "Communists are the feared leaders of the revolution." The only difference for Macdonald was that in 1935 he had "hoped they would make it," while in 1948 he did not. A. J. Muste approached the Marshall Plan with divided feelings. "Objectively considered . . . ERP is a means of buying or holding support for the United States in its power-struggle with Russia," he stated; moreover, as such, it did not assist all areas of the world in need. On the other hand, it would provide valuable assistance to some of these

[3] "Statement of the Policy Committee on the Marshall Plan, October 24, 1947," WILPF MSS, Box 30; "National Board Resolutions Re: Relief for Europe," WILPF MSS, Box 4; Bussey and Tims, *Women's International League for Peace and Freedom*, p. 191; Detzer, *Appointment on the Hill*, p. 251; *Catholic Worker*, December, 1947, and January, 1948. These fears were not entirely without foundation. The Administration utilized a conservative appeal to "sell" the Marshall Plan to powerful corporate pressure groups. Truman's liaison officers promised the National Association of Manufacturers that the E.R.P. would be managed on "sound business principles" and that it would help counteract the European trend toward socialism. Calling upon the business elite to administer the new program, the President appointed Paul G. Hoffman, president of the Studebaker Corporation, as its director. Hoffman soon earned the gratitude of American industrialists through advertisement of the alleged merits of the American "free enterprise" system. S. Adler, *The Isolationist Impulse*, p. 365.

countries, aid that could be obtained in no other way. To Muste, then, the government program seemed a "bitter dilemma." [4]

Non-pacifist elements divided on the matter. When Secretary of War Henry L. Stimson asked Einstein to join a committee in support of the Marshall Plan, the scientist replied that he could not endorse the plan "as it is presently formulated." E.R.P. was regarded, he warned, "as a political scheme directed against the Russian bloc and hence may serve to aggravate existing political tensions." The influential United World Federalists, however, strongly backed the measure, while noting at the same time that it would prove "inadequate *if this is all we do.*" Perhaps the most prominent opponent of the Marshall Plan, Henry A. Wallace, maintained that he was "for the plan until it became apparent that it was to be administered altogether outside the U.N., in the spirit of the Truman Doctrine." Wallace "opposed . . . its application as an instrument of cold war against Russia"; to the former Vice-President, E.R.P. looked like a "Martial Plan." [5]

The question of conscription, raised by a new Administration proposal in 1948, provided an issue around which most elements of the peace movement could rally. Although the international climate was less propitious for an antidraft fight than the preceding year, a new wrinkle was added to the situation by a threatened rebellion of American Negroes against racial discrimination in the armed forces. In the fall of 1947 the director of the National Council Against Conscription had conferred with Bayard Rustin and William Worthy, a black journalist, on the possibility of forming a committee to oppose racial segregation in the armed forces. As a result of this conference, the Committee Against Discrimination in Military Service and Training, organized as an independent entity in November, 1947, announced a campaign "to insure inclusion of equality amendments in pending legislation for universal training." Fearful that an antidiscrimination rider would result in the defeat of the conscrip-

[4] Dwight Macdonald, "Small Talk," *Politics,* V (Winter, 1948), 56; A. J. Muste, "ERP—Promise, Menace or Dilemma," *Fellowship,* XIV (February, 1948), 8–10.

[5] Nathan and Norden, *Einstein on Peace,* pp. 425–26; "Where UWF Stands," *World Government News,* VI (March, 1948), 7; Henry A. Wallace, *Toward World Peace,* p. 36; Agar, *The Price of Power,* p. 75.

tion bill, President Truman ordered studies made on the possibility of eliminating racial bias in the armed forces. When Secretary of the Army Kenneth Royall, to whom the assignment was given, reported that segregation was "in the interest of national defense," black leaders were furious. A. Philip Randolph told the Senate Armed Services Committee that he would "personally pledge . . . to openly counsel, aid and abet youth . . . in an organized refusal to register and be drafted." A poll of 2200 Negro college students on 26 campuses revealed that 71 per cent favored a policy of civil disobedience to the draft. The N.A.A.C.P. pledged its support for such a program.[6]

But with the passage of the draft act in the spring of 1948 after a bitter legislative struggle, at least partially over racial segregation, the threatened rebellion failed to materialize. To be sure, Randolph, now chairman of the League for Non-Violent Civil Disobedience Against Military Segregation, addressed a crowd in Harlem and urged men to refuse registration and induction. At the time, he stated that he planned to "oppose a Jim Crow Army" until "I rot in jail." Yet the issuance soon thereafter of the President's Executive Order of July, 1948, ordering an end to racial discrimination in the armed forces took the edge off black demands. Randolph and other prominent leaders now agreed to desist, although young militants like Rustin desired to continue the struggle.[7]

Pacifists staged a minor civil disobedience campaign of their own. The 1948 draft act represented, in pacifist eyes, an advance over the 1940 legislation because it granted C.O.'s complete exemption, and a regression for requiring a stricter religious test for C.O. status. Yet for many the particular provisions of the law were unimportant; pacifists could take little comfort in any measure requiring compulsory military service. Consequently, although the actual drafting of men was suspended during 1948 due to a manpower surplus, over forty pacifists had been sentenced to prison terms as of July 1, 1949, for refusal to register. The government also, on occasion, prosecuted

[6] Swomley, *The Military Establishment*, pp. 73–75; *New York Times*, April 1, 1948, and June 5, 1948.

[7] C. E. Jacobs and Gallagher, *The Selective Service Act*, pp. 43–102, 114–15; *New York Times*, July 18, 1948, and July 27, 1948; Bayard Rustin to Norman Thomas, July 27, 1948, Thomas MSS, Box 55; "Randolph Withdraws from Anti-Jimcrow League," *Fellowship*, XIV (October, 1948), 34.

those who counseled non-registration. When Larry Gara, a Quaker teacher in an Ohio Mennonite college who had served a prison term as a C.O. during World War II, advised a non-registrant divinity student at his school to stand by his principles, he was given an eighteen-month prison sentence for this action. Through writing, picketing, and preaching, pacifists advocated civil disobedience to conscription, although their efforts appear to have had little effect upon a nation accustomed to obedience to law and increasingly committed to the Cold War.[8]

Russia's aggressive moves in Eastern Europe during 1948 drove many in the American peace movement to a more bellicose stance. Norman Thomas, for example, although always bitterly anti-Communist, had previously been "very skeptical" of the Truman containment policy. But following the Czech coup he took a much stiffer position, supporting most of American foreign policy for the next decade. Like the Russian actions in Czechoslovakia, Soviet attempts to close off Berlin to the West brought on a rash of reappraisals among American peace activists. Raymond Gram Swing found himself "forced to recognize that the siege of Berlin . . . postponed any expectations I harbored of co-operation between the United States and the Soviet Union for the maintenance of peace." He "began to appreciate . . . that the spread of Communism . . . had to be curbed, [and] the free world . . . sustained and defended."[9]

[8] American Civil Liberties Union, *Our Uncertain Liberties*, p. 61; Sibley and Jacob, *Conscription of Conscience*, p. 480; American Civil Liberties Union, *In the Shadow of Fear: American Liberties, 1948–49*, p. 44; *Peacemaker*, I (June 28, 1949), 1–2; *Peacemaker*, I (August 9, 1949), 1. The tenor of public opinion is shown by the response of the *New York Times* to a sermon by the Reverend Donald Harrington, the successor to John Haynes Holmes in the pulpit of New York's Community Church. Harrington had demanded that the government free Gara or also arrest him, since he, too, had told young men seeking draft advice to "consult their consciences." "In other words," stated the young minister, "if Gara is guilty, I am guilty." The *Times* felt called upon to write a long editorial assailing Harrington's defense of civil disobedience to the draft. "To encourage the individual to obey only those laws that pleased him could only result in chaos," the *Times* editorial remarked. After this genuflection to community stability the editorial recited the litany of the Cold War: "The armed forces . . . were and are engaged in an effort to help preserve the peace. The considered judgment of the great majority of our elected national officials is that the way to help preserve peace is to keep our nation strong." *New York Times*, August 8 and 9, 1949.

[9] Personal interview with Norman Thomas, October 4, 1966; Swing, *"Good Evening!"* pp. 252–53.

Defections plagued even the ranks of the radical pacifists. After a trip to Eastern Europe, Evan Thomas became discouraged over the political possibilities of pacifism in the face of totalitarianism. In his letter of resignation from the War Resisters League, the former chairman explained that his "views about war" had not changed, "but I am less certain that I formerly was of the best ways to resist this worst of all mankind's evils." Nothing that pacifists "have done or can do now brings peace," he wrote sadly. "This is far and away the greatest disappointment of my life, but it is a fact." At this point, too, Dwight Macdonald abandoned pacifism as well as all political interest. He later wrote that he "lost faith" in pacifism because it could not solve the "problem of the Soviet Blockade of Berlin. . . . As a pacifist you can't believe in armies. And so, naturally, you should say that the American, the British, the French and Russian soldiers had no right to be in Berlin and should leave Berlin." But "if they had left . . . this would have meant turning over two million people or so to the Russians," people who "had indicated time and time again that they . . . didn't want to be turned over to them." Macdonald complained that "this is a real dilemma for all us Utopians." Finding no solution, he drifted out of the peace movement, abandoned *Politics*, and retreated in despair to cultural criticism.[10]

By 1948 the atomic scientists faced a similar dilemma. On the one hand, as the Cold War heightened, intense pressure was brought upon them to modify any commitments to unorthodox positions. As early as 1946, Harold Urey wrote that the scientists were "in danger of being accused of being internationally minded and not loyal" and were "afraid of being accused of being Communists, or something of that sort." Especially after President Truman's Loyalty Order of March 21, 1947 the tension heightened. A news story in the New York *Sun*, for example, charged that an article in the *Bulletin of*

[10] Personal interview with Dave Dellinger, May 16, 1966; personal interview with Ralph DiGia, April 21, 1966; Evan W. Thomas to Sidney Aberman, December 12, 1950, WRL MSS, Box 2; Dwight Macdonald, "Why I Am No Longer A Socialist," *Liberation*, III (May, 1958), 4; Macdonald, *Memoirs of a Revolutionist*, pp. 78, 193–97; Lasch, *The New Radicalism*, p. 324. Macdonald's resignation from the W.R.L. executive committee was tendered in the spring of 1949. "WRL Executive Committee Meeting, September 12, 1949," WRL MSS, Box. 2.

the Atomic Scientists advocated unilateral destruction of American atomic power plants, that its author was a member of the Lawyers' Guild, and that an editor of the journal was connected with the Communist-dominated United Electrical Workers; the charges were later retracted only upon the inception of legal proceedings. The deteriorating situation prompted eight of America's leading scientists to make public a message to both Presidential candidates in September, 1948, assailing the atmosphere of suspicion surrounding scientists in government employment.[11] On the other hand, it was all too obvious that the Soviet Union, behind a series of equivocations, had flatly rejected the Baruch Plan. As David Lilienthal, then chairman of the Atomic Energy Commission, recalled, the Russians "were obsessed by the knowledge that we had the Bomb while they did not," and had decided to develop their own. The hopes of the scientists for international control of the atom were consequently dashed.[12]

Confronted with this narrowing of maneuverability, the scientists' movement dissipated. A small minority, led by Philip Morrison, Linus Pauling, and Harlow Shapley, continued to seek means for the international control of atomic energy, calling for new approaches to the problem. A larger and far more influential group, however, began to argue that with the intensification of the Cold War, mili-

[11] Harold C. Urey to A. J. Muste, April 4, 1946, FOR MSS, Box 12; "The *New York Sun* Retracts Inaccurate Statements about the Bulletin," *Bulletin of the Atomic Scientists*, IV (February, 1948), 63; Walter Gellhorn, *Security, Loyalty, and Science*, p. 158. Indicative of the great fear that spread among government scientists was the fate of the *American Review of Soviet Medicine*. Founded in 1943 and published in the U.S. by the American-Soviet Medical Society, the journal contained translations of scholarly articles that had previously appeared in Russian medical periodicals. At the time of the Loyalty Order, the Society had 600 members in Washington, D.C., but within two years this number had dropped to 30. In Bethesda, Maryland, the site of the National Institutes of Health and the United States Naval Hospital, there were 150 subscriptions at the time of the Order; when the magazine suspended publication in October, 1948, none remained. During this period, the magazine received numerous requests that it be mailed to subscribers in a plain wrapper not bearing its name. Thus, despite its completely non-political, scientific character, the journal lasted but one and a half years after the issuance of the Truman Loyalty Order. Gellhorn, *Security, Loyalty, and Science*, pp. 161–62.

[12] Gilpin, *American Scientists and Nuclear Weapons Policy*, p. 35; P. M. S. Blackett, *Studies of War: Nuclear and Conventional*, pp. 75–76; Lilienthal, *Change, Hope, and the Bomb*, p. 26.

tary containment of the Soviet bloc took precedence over any plans for international control. Harold Urey, Robert Oppenheimer, Edward Teller, Arthur Compton, I. I. Rabi, James Conant, and Hans Bethe became prominent spokesmen for this school of thought. Although a few members of this group continued to hope that plans for controls and deterrence could be worked out simultaneously, little of the postwar élan, the overriding conviction that war was unthinkable, remained.[13]

Writing to Richard Gregg in mid-1947, A. J. Muste had remarked upon the "unreality" of "the choices with which we are confronted in a Presidential election."[14] Never was this more true than in 1948, when, despite the appearance of challengers seeking the peace vote, the movement could find no entirely satisfactory choice. In the end, instead of offering an alternative to the bipartisan foreign policy of containment, the election served to splinter and demoralize the peace forces, while reinforcing the drift to Cold War.

The year 1948 marked the Socialist Party's last stand. In 1944 the Party had reached a new low when Thomas garnered only 80,000 votes. But the death of Roosevelt and the declining fortunes of the Democratic Party, liberal and labor dissatisfaction with Truman, and the victories of the British Labour Party and the Canadian Cooperative Commonwealth Federation, raised hopes among Party stalwarts that labor could be persuaded to unite with the Socialists to form a third party. In 1946 a Chicago conference of 125 delegates organized a National Education Committee for a New Party, while a number of individuals, disaffected during the war years, returned to the Socialist fold. It was thought that a large Thomas vote in 1948 would generate a left-wing resurgence. During the course of the campaign the Party took a fairly stiff position toward Russia and approached, but did not reach, the Truman Administration's outlook on the Cold War. "The major, but by no means the only threat of war," its platform observed, "lies in the aggression of the Soviet empire and the international Communist movement." Nevertheless, Thomas also made a strong appeal to the peace constituency, calling for international disarmament, an end to

[13] Gilpin, *American Scientists and Nuclear Weapons Policy*, pp. 64–73; Wynner and Lloyd, *Searchlight on Peace Plans*, p. 543.
[14] A. J. Muste to Richard Gregg, June 4, 1947, FOR MSS, Box 11.

all forms of imperialism, and the scrapping of the Truman Doctrine.[15]

But the dramatic opening of Henry A. Wallace's campaign for the
Presidency quickly obscured the Thomas peace appeal, as well as
Socialist hopes for a new third party. On September 12, 1946, Secretary of Commerce Wallace had criticized the Truman Administration's foreign policy as unnecessarily "tough" with Russia, in a Madison Square Garden address; eight days later, after a considerable
furor, Wallace had been relieved of his cabinet post. Cut adrift from
the Administration, the former Vice-President became the editor of
the *New Republic,* assuming the leadership of a broad variety of
disaffected individuals on the Left. Wallace's prominence as a hard-
core New Dealer, coupled with his oft-expressed desire for a return
to friendly relations with Russia, made him the natural spokesman
for many idealistic liberals fed up with the Truman Administration,
as well as for those Americans still enamored of the Popular Front
days of the late Thirties and of the honeymoon of the war years. As
for the American Communist Party, it promptly scrapped Marx and
rushed to install Henry Wallace as its patron saint. These elements
united in the Progressive Party crusade of 1948.[16]

Although few observers have questioned Wallace's sincerity as a
non-Communist spokesman or, for that matter, Communist participation in the Progressive Party, there has been a great deal of dis-
pute as to the degree of Communist influence in the Wallace campaign, a problem not easily resolved. The complexity of this issue is
illustrated by the statements of Wallace himself. On occasion, the
Progressive Party nominee freely criticized Russia for its "rigorously
orthodox . . . thought control." After referring to abrogations of
civil liberties in the United States, he added: "The situation is a long

[15] Bell, "Background and Development of Marxian Socialism," p. 402;
Fleischman, *Norman Thomas,* p. 223; Seidler, *Norman Thomas,* pp. 231–33;
N. M. Thomas, *Appeal to the Nations,* pp. 138–70. Thomas disliked the role
of a Cold Warrior. He wrote somewhat testily in 1946: "I find it rather ironic
that so many of those who denounced me because although I abhorred fascism
I wanted to keep America out of war against Germany and Japan now de-
nounce me as a war-maker against Russia simply for wanting the truth known."
Norman Thomas to Albert Sprague Coolidge, May 7, 1946, Thomas MSS, Box
49.

[16] Agar, *The Price of Power,* pp. 61–63; Goldman, *Rendezvous with Destiny,* pp. 315, 319–22.

way from being as bad as it is in Russia." Moreover, for an alleged fellow-traveler, Wallace showed himself strangely free of reverence for the Communist Party. "Americans who accept Moscow or Marxian orthodoxy are foolishly giving up one of their own dearest possessions," he remarked in 1948. "The non-Russian communists act as though Moscow were the sacred custodian of all that is pure and holy and therefore they should defend everything Moscow does." Yet Wallace could often apologize for Soviet policy to a degree obviously unwarranted by the facts. The Czech coup, for example, he termed "practically predetermined by the announcement of the Truman doctrine"; in his view, "rightists" had "precipitated" the event with "American support." Wallace could also be most ingenious in justifying the peculiarly brutal nature of Stalin's regime: "Had not Stalin carried through his ruthless purge of Nazi-Trotskyist conspirators, Adolf Hitler might have found it possible to conquer the world in the years that followed." Both Communists and non-Communists must surely have wondered at some particularly embarrassing moment in the campaign just why they were supporting Wallace.[17]

If Wallace's evaluation of the Soviet Union seemed, at times, murky, his plea for peace rang out sharp and clear. "The thing which disturbs me most about the United States," he told Americans in 1948, "is the thing that also disturbs me most about the world—the dominance of faith in force as the ultimate arbiter." Russia and England were, in this respect, "equally sinners with the United States," he said. "Nothing . . . will save us but belief in the unity of all mankind." Such sentiments could not fail to evoke the admiration of thousands of Americans, as the new party made the peace issue its predominant theme. "The choice," asserted the keynote speaker at the Progressive Party convention, "is Wallace or war." [18]

Startled by the emergence of the Wallace phenomenon, the Socialist Party leveled a blistering attack at its new political rival.

[17] Wallace, *Toward World Peace*, pp. 3, 50, 63, 65. According to historian Eric Goldman, Wallace "was fellow-traveling." Goldman, *Rendezvous with Destiny*, p. 323. A more recent and intensive account of the Progressive Party, however, contends that it was Communist-supported but not Communist-controlled. See: Karl M. Schmidt, *Henry A. Wallace: Quixotic Crusade 1948.*

[18] Wallace, *Toward World Peace*, pp. 117–18; Alexander De Conde, "On Twentieth Century Isolationism," p. 28; Goldman, *Rendezvous with Destiny*, p. 322.

Norman Thomas charged the Progressive Party with "giving a blanket endorsement to the foreign policy of the aggressive Soviet dictatorship, the cruel masters of some ten million slaves, the men primarily responsible for the cold war, the ruthless seekers after universal power." The Socialist candidate argued that he "presented a program far more likely to lead to peace than the militarism of Harry Truman or the appeasement of Henry Wallace." As Thomas later explained, he considered the Progressive Party "mostly a front for the Communists—not that the majority of its members or voters were Communists, but the majority of the people who controlled it were Communists. . . . That was the great reason we would have nothing to do with it." Thomas told one of his supporters in the summer of 1948: "I am opposed to war with Russia . . . but I do not think we can successfully avert war by condoning a movement destructive of the things that . . . make life most worth living. And such a movement, alas, Communism under Stalin has become." [19]

Although Wallace appealed strongly to the nation's liberal community, influential segments were already mobilizing against him and his sources of strength. In March, 1947, the first official conference of Americans for Democratic Action (A.D.A.) drew together important leaders in the liberal camp opposed to cooperation with the Progressive Citizens of America, Wallace's principal backer. Unlike the liberals clustered around Wallace, most A.D.A. stalwarts approved of the Truman Doctrine. According to one of their number, James Wechsler, they "had come to grips with the reality of Soviet power and discarded the naivetés that had so often led many of them into the blind alley of international wishful thinking." At the national convention of the Progressive Party in Philadelphia, the A.D.A. position on Wallace's candidacy was expressed by James Loeb, who declared the new party to be a Communist front. Wechsler, one of two reporters to travel with the Wallace entourage throughout the campaign, considered it "a division of Stalin's foreign legion." [20]

[19] Seidler, *Norman Thomas*, pp. 231–33; Fleischman, *Norman Thomas*, p. 225; Norman Thomas, COHC, p. 180; Norman Thomas to Mr. and Mrs. Edward S. Allen, June 28, 1948, Thomas MSS, Box 54.

[20] James A. Wechsler, *The Age of Suspicion*, pp. 215–16, 218, 230; Goldman, *Rendezvous with Destiny*, p. 322. Yet despite his great hostility to the Wallace campaign, Wechsler acknowledged that it often appealed to an idealistic, non-

The portended liberal split during the campaign eventually ran three ways. At the New York State convention of A.D.A., Benjamin McLaurin of the Brotherhood of Sleeping Car Porters urged the liberal organization to endorse Norman Thomas for the Presidency. Scouting for bigger names, however, A.D.A. first tried to secure General Dwight D. Eisenhower or Justice William O. Douglas, then anybody, and finally settled for Truman. Columnists Max Lerner and Dorothy Thompson supported the Socialist candidate, as did Daniel Bell, Erich Fromm, C. Wright Mills, Richard Rovere, Edmund Wilson, and Bertram D. Wolfe. While the *New Republic* naturally embraced Wallace, the *Progressive* came out for Thomas.[21]

With a few exceptions, the campaign elicited little excitement among the atomic scientists and other world government advocates. Wallace's criticism of the Baruch Plan and his desire to "share" the bomb with Russia did not enhance his popularity among the scientists, and consequently only a few were active in his campaign; Harlow Shapley served as a delegate to the Progressive Party convention, while Einstein endorsed Wallace for President. According to an editorial in *World Government News*, "world federalists could expect little if anything . . . from the presidential candidates." Noting that the speeches of Truman and Dewey paid their respects to internationalism, the journal nevertheless labeled these as "weasel words." While the Socialist Party supported the eventual creation of a "democratic federal world government," and the Progressive Party accorded Senator Glen Taylor, sponsor of several Congressional resolutions on world government, its Vice-Presidential nomination, the editorial expressed slight interest. To some degree this probably reflected the scant hopes of minor parties for electoral success, but also, especially in the case of Wallace, the desire of world federalist leaders to avoid a controversial political "taint." Consequently, the

---

Communist constituency. "Especially in the early months," he noted, "there were good and gracious people enlisted under his banner; that was the sadness of the project." Wechsler, *The Age of Suspicion*, pp. 224–25.

[21] Fleischman, *Norman Thomas*, pp. 225, 229, 237; Goldman, *Rendezvous with Destiny*, pp. 325–26; Stationery of Independent Voters for Norman Thomas (1948), Thomas MSS, Box 55; Morris Rubin, "The Choice for President," *Progressive*, XII (September, 1948), 3–4.

journal concluded that "the presidential campaign will hardly afford the best opportunity to advance world federalism." [22]

Pacifists found the campaign exceedingly perplexing. On the one hand, Wallace criticized much that troubled them about American foreign policy. After the famous Madison Square Garden address, Clarence Pickett had written to Wallace: "Many of us who are closely involved in the peace activities of this country have been deeply moved by . . . your New York speech." A Quaker pacifist, responding to Norman Thomas' attack upon Wallace, told the Socialist candidate: "I find it hard to believe that Mr. Wallace is in the employ of Stalin or any other militarist dictator." Rather, the Progressive nominee "realizes . . . that in every country, including Russia and America, the vast electorate yearns for peace. He, as ardently as you, recognizes the stupid anachronism of war. Can you not . . . support each other in the things you agree on?" [23]

Others argued that only a Wallace vote would serve as an effective protest against the Cold War. Jim Peck, for example, told the readers of *Fellowship* that "the bigger the vote for Wallace, the

[22] Henry A. Wallace, "Whose Atomic Secret?" *New Republic*, CXVI (February 17, 1947), 26–27; Gilpin, *American Scientists and Nuclear Weapons Policy*, p. 53n; Goldman, *Rendezvous with Destiny*, p. 322; Nathan and Norden, *Einstein on Peace*, p. 469; "Politics as Usual?" *World Government News*, VI (August, 1948), 3–4. The world federalist fear of a Wallace "label" was dramatically illustrated when Mrs. Anita McCormick Blaine, a wealthy heiress in her eighties, decided to establish a Foundation for World Government with a gift of one million dollars. World federalist groups and the Emergency Committee of Atomic Scientists accepted the news joyfully, but the Wallace issue eventually poisoned the enterprise. Mrs. Blaine, a loyal supporter of the Progressive Party candidate, expressed her hope that the former Vice-President might at some time become associated with the foundation, although no commitments were made. Thereafter, controversy rapidly arose in world federalist circles as to whether a Wallace "taint" might not be extremely harmful to the movement. It reached a crisis when the Scripps-Howard newspapers made the story public in September, 1948, under the banner headline: "Angel's Million Assures Wallace Post-Election Job." Stringfellow Barr, chosen as the prospective director of the foundation, resigned, while the preparatory committee for the project disbanded. The U.W.F. dissociated itself from the foundation, as did the Emergency Committee of Atomic Scientists. Ironically, Henry Wallace never did establish any ties with the foundation. Gradually, over the next few years, links between world government groups and the foundation were renewed. Nathan and Norden, *Einstein on Peace*, pp. 499–501; "Uneasy Money," *World Government News*, VI (November, 1948), 7.

[23] Clarence Pickett to Henry Wallace, October 4, 1946, FOR MSS, Box 10; Mrs. F. B. to Norman Thomas, May 25, 1948, Thomas MSS, Box 54.

more definitely the powers that be will know that a large number of Americans do not support what Wallace describes as 'the bipartisan reactionary war policy.' " A series of letters in *Fellowship* propounded the same thesis. "Wallace is the only leader who is presenting at this time and through this campaign a cleancut issue on whether there will be peace or war," one writer declared. Another stated: "Whatever his past or future, and however phony his premises, he is at least clearcut and forthright on halting the Truman-Marshall march to catastrophe. Hence the only clearcut and forthright vote against war is a vote for Wallace." [24]

While Wallace evoked a modest ground swell of support in pacifist ranks, the majority, including almost all of the pacifist leaders, opposed the Progressive nominee. Dwight Macdonald, for example, flailed Wallace mercilessly throughout the campaign. "Henry Wallace has for years been the mouthpiece of American communism," the editor of *Politics* charged, "a great wind of rhetoric blowing along the prevailing trade route of Stalinoid liberalism." While "it is not true that Henry Wallace is an agent of Moscow," Macdonald observed, "it is true that he behaves like one." The "only sensible action for a pacifist in 1948," in Macdonald's opinion, was "no action: that is, don't vote." The readers of *Politics* generally agreed with its editor's unfriendly assessment of Wallace; a poll in 1948 of these leftists and pacifists, theoretically the stuff of which the Progressive Party should have been molded, found that less than one quarter responded favorably to Wallace's political views. [25]

[24] Personal interview with James Peck, April 21, 1966; James Peck, "Should Pacifists Vote for Henry Wallace?" *Fellowship*, XIV (March, 1948), 15; "That Man Wallace," *Fellowship*, XIV (May, 1948), 27–28. Peck did not skirt the Communist issue, but maintained that "if you were against everything the Communists endorse over here and in countries where they have not come into power with their totalitarian dictatorships, you would have to be against unionism, racial equality and civil liberties as well as against anything anti-war." J. Peck, "Should Pacifists Vote for Henry Wallace?" p. 15.

[25] Dwight Macdonald, "Should Pacifists Vote for Henry Wallace?" *Fellowship*, XIV (March, 1948), 7–9; Dwight Macdonald, "Henry Wallace," *Politics*, IV (March–April, 1947) and (May–June, 1947), 33–44, 96–117; Ruth Harper Mills, "The Fascinated Readers," *Politics*, V (Winter, 1948), 62. A survey by pacifists four years later concluded: "The Progressive Party . . . won support for Wallace's candidacy in 1948 from a considerable number of pacifists, though not from an appreciable number of leading pacifists." "Report of Subcommittee on Pacifist Political Activity in Connection with the 1952 Elections" (March 3, 1952), FOR MSS, Box 4.

A. J. Muste took a position similar to Macdonald's. The "lack of clarity" in Wallace's thought, he argued, "makes him *as a political figure* . . . the instrument and captive of his only organized support . . . the Communist Party and its front organizations." As a matter of "objective political reality," Muste insisted, "a vote for Wallace is a vote for the Communist Party." What the election needed was a "mediating" influence, "a non-Communist and non-appeasement force," the pacifist leader asserted. "Tragedy is piled on tragedy for our country and for the world because the progressives, liberals, unions, and farm organizations, which ought to be flatly opposing the nation's war-course, are so uncritically *anti-Russian* . . . and so ignorant of how really to overcome communism that they support the war-policy." These forces "line up with the Right, with reaction, with violence, though they do not mean to do that and try to make themselves believe they do not." For Muste, then, the election outlook was gloomy and all options "unsatisfactory." [26]

A majority of pacifists probably supported the Socialist candidate in 1948. Despite his shift toward the Truman containment policy, Thomas was, after all, the traditional pacifist favorite; one C.O., for example, had written in 1944: "Norman Thomas 'swept the country' —in CPS!" Among the supporters of the Socialists in 1948 were John Haynes Holmes, Bayard Rustin, George Houser, Constance Muste (A. J.'s daughter), and Milton Mayer. Donald Harrington urged the readers of *Fellowship* to support the Socialist Party because it "has always fought against the things that make for war—against military training, conscription, armaments races, balance-of-power politics, and a war-breeding capitalist-imperialist economy." According to Harrington, the Socialist Party had within its membership "a larger percentage of pacifists, and probably a larger number, than any other political party." One member of the New York F.O.R. revealed that of the seven voters in her household, one voted for Dewey, another for Truman, and five for Thomas.[27]

[26] A. J. Muste, "A Vote for Wallace Will Be—A Vote for the Communists," *Fellowship*, XIV (July, 1948), 7-9.
[27] Henry Geiger to Norman Thomas, December 19, 1944, Thomas MSS, Box 47; John Mecartney, Letter to the Editor, *Fellowship*, XIV (October, 1948), 38; Donald Harrington, "Pacifists Should Vote Socialist," *Fellowship*,

The comparatively poor electoral showings of Wallace and Thomas, with 1,150,000 and 140,000 votes respectively, coupled with the upset Truman victory, demoralized the peace effort. For American Socialists, it meant the end of the political road; "we realized that the Socialist Party's last hope of creating a new political alignment had gone down the drain," wrote Thomas' campaign manager. "The results of the election," Thomas acknowledged, "made it certain that labor and liberal forces will now try to go along with the Democratic Party." The outlook in the Progressive camp seemed no less hopeless. Although the Wallace movement had drawn together large numbers of unaffiliated individuals opposed to the Cold War, the size of the electoral defeat made future efforts along this line appear futile. Wallace's pet liberal journal, the *New Republic*, sank from a circulation of 100,000 to 20,000. While the Truman Administration's military containment policy could by no means be considered to have received a mandate, as one study has indicated, "the fact that it had failed to arouse significant opposition meant endorsement of a negative sort." [28] The Cold War had acquired legitimacy.

In the aftermath of the election President Truman moved from the advocacy of a mixed economic-military answer to the Soviet challenge to one based primarily upon military power. "If we can make it sufficiently clear . . . that any armed attack affecting our national security would be met with overwhelming force, the armed attack might never occur," he stated in his inaugural address. "I hope to send to the Senate a treaty respecting the North Atlantic Security Plan." The NATO Pact, as it came to be called, passed the

XIV (May, 1948), 9–12; Florence D. Hamilton to Norman Thomas, December 5, 1948, Thomas MSS, Box 56. The author has found no other evidence of pacifist support for either Truman or Dewey.

[28] Shannon, *The Socialist Party of America*, pp. 255–56; Fleischman, *Norman Thomas*, p. 237; Norman Thomas to Luigi Antonini, November 15, 1948, Thomas MSS, Box 54; Altbach, "The American Peace Movement," p. 48; Schmidt, *Henry A. Wallace*, p. 251. Figures do not reveal the complete story of the Progressive disaster. Wallace did well only among minority groups, indicating that his stand for peace probably had less to do with his total vote than did other issues, such as Palestine and civil rights. According to Samuel Lubell, "probably three fourths of Wallace's vote came from Negroes and Jews," with New York State alone giving Wallace about half his total vote. Samuel Lubell, *The Future of American Politics*, p. 220.

Senate on July 21, 1949, by an overwhelming vote. Pacifists naturally deplored the Administration's return to the time-worn arts of power-diplomacy. The W.I.L.P.F. charged that the North Atlantic Treaty would weaken the United Nations and other international institutions, hence making war more, rather than less, likely. Al Hassler, editor of *Fellowship*, argued that as "a military alliance" the NATO Pact "writes *finis* . . . to the so-recent dreams of 'one world,' and chooses instead a two-world division." [29]

Proponents of world government found less cause for gloom. Few criticized NATO; some, indeed, thought it rather promising. In 1949 a group of the nation's most distinguished statesmen, academicians, and industrialists joined to form the Atlantic Union Committee. Founded by former Justice Roberts, and promoted by pollster Elmo Roper, former Secretary of War Robert P. Patterson, and Undersecretary of State William L. Clayton, the Committee saw in NATO the possible realization of the Streit plan. Only a few world government advocates seriously questioned the major premises of the defense pact. One of these, James P. Warburg, argued that "the proposed treaty creates an ineffective defense against the secondary danger of military aggression at the price of weakening the defense against the primary danger of political penetration." Warburg maintained that the pact "raises the question of whether we are not placing too little emphasis upon our constructive efforts for peace and too much emphasis upon a purely negative policy of strategic containment." [30]

The Truman Administration's proposal in 1949 to develop the hydrogen bomb occasioned the final revolt of the scientists against

[29] *New York Times,* January 21, 1949, and April 18, 1949; "Resolutions Adopted by the Annual Meeting, U.S. Section, May 5-8, 1949," WILPF MSS, Box 13; Alfred Hassler, "Pact with Death," *Fellowship,* XV (May, 1949), 10.

[30] Theodore W. Olson, "Peace and the American Community" (mimeographed), p. 189; S. Adler, *The Isolationist Impulse,* p. 331; Wynner and Lloyd, *Searchlight on Peace Plans,* p. 544; James P. Warburg, "Memorandum on the Proposed Atlantic Alliance" (February 1, 1949), WILPF MSS, Box 31. Streit maintained that his refurbished "Federal Union of the Free" would "remove the danger of war with Russia" by "uniting so much power . . . that the communist dictatorship would not dare to attack." He then asked himself the logical question: "Isn't this power politics?" After marvelous circumlocutions, he concluded that it was not. Clarence K. Streit, *Federal Union of the Free,* pp. 11, 15–16.

military policies. In October the General Advisory Committee of the Atomic Energy Commission voted unanimously against an all-out program to produce the H-bomb. At the long and solemn meeting, the scientists present—James B. Conant, Robert Oppenheimer, Enrico Fermi, Cyril Smith, Lee DuBridge, and I. I. Rabi—opposed the idea on moral and technical grounds. Rabi and Fermi stated that the bomb should not be manufactured by the United States under any circumstances, while Conant cryptically remarked in a widely-read article that "we must deliberately refrain from taking out all the forms of military insurance that may come to mind." Sensing the new level of destructiveness within mankind's grasp, scientists stiffened their resistance in a fashion not seen even in the dramatic wartime conflict over the A-bomb. "I believe the most important question is the moral one," wrote Hans Bethe, expressing the views of many of his colleagues. "Can we, who have always insisted on morality and human decency, introduce this weapon of total annihilation into the world?" [31]

One sector of scientific opinion, however, took a very different position on the moral responsibility of the scientist, and eventually prevailed. Edward Teller, the driving force behind the H-bomb project, argued: "It is not the scientist's job to determine whether a hydrogen bomb should be constructed, whether it should be used or how it should be used. This responsibility rests with the people and with their . . . representatives." Although "the people" had no more opportunity to decide upon the development of the H-bomb than they had had upon the development of its predecessor, in January, 1950, President Truman announced that he had "directed the Atomic Energy Commission to continue its work on all forms of weapons, including the so-called hydrogen or super-bomb." Many scientists continued to fight against the H-bomb program, only to be rewarded in later years with political attacks upon their patriotism. An atmosphere of despair settled over the once-spirited scientists' movement. Under the leadership of Teller, and with the assistance

[31] Joseph and Stuart Alsop, We Accuse! The Story of the Miscarriage of American Justice in the Case of J. Robert Oppenheimer, p. 11; James B. Conant, "Force and Freedom," Atlantic Monthly, CLXXXIII (January, 1949), 22; Coffin, The Passion of the Hawks, p. 199; Ralph E. Lapp, Kill and Overkill: The Strategy of Annihilation, pp. 19–20.

of MANIAC, a high speed computer, scientists commenced work upon the first thermonuclear weapon. Einstein commented morosely: "General annihilation beckons." [32]

Truman's H-bomb decision triggered pacifist protests and demonstrations across the country, none of any great size or impact. "From flame-thrower to blockbuster to atomic bomb to Hell–Bomb—the nations, including the United States, march straight on," read one particularly bitter antibomb appeal. "No one draws a line and says: 'This is too much. We are pulling out of this march of death.' If the time has not come now to draw such a line," it asked, "will it ever come?" [33]

The outbreak of fighting in Korea during June, 1950, dealt the final hammerblow to the fragile postwar peace movement. World government organizations almost universally accepted the American role in the conflict. U.W.F. chapters in about thirty cities and towns across the country ran an advertisement proclaiming: "United World Federalists are wholeheartedly behind our nation in this and every fight that may darken the nation's future." Much of the world federalist resolve sprang from their perception of America's participation in an "international police" action. "We are not fighting this war under our own flag," a member of the Committee to Frame a World Constitution explained, "but, morally if not technically, under the flag of the United Nations." Thus, he believed that although "the Koreans are fighting a civil war, in their own country, which has been divided against their will," the "conception of a world police . . . implies the right of intervention." Federalists could take comfort in the fact that although the conflict was indeed war, it did not smack of a narrow nationalism. Minnesota World Federalists found it "gratifying . . . that our government moved with U.N. sanction and is flying the U.N. flag." Still, there were limits to federalist tolerance, even for "police" action. "As the agents of the United Nations, we are fighting aggression, not communism," declared a

---

[32] Gilpin, *American Scientists and Nuclear Weapons Policy*, pp. 73–122; "H-Mystery Man: He Hurried the H-Bomb," *Newsweek*, XLIV (August 2, 1954), 25: Lapp, *Atoms and People*, pp. 108–109; H. Agar, *The Price of Power*, p. 105.

[33] "We Must Draw the Line Now" (1950), FOR MSS, Box 28; *New York Times*, February 12, 1950; *Washington Post*, April 7, 1950; *Peacemaker*, I (March 15, 1950), 2–4 and (April 25, 1950), 1.

Chicago Committee member. "We should have been just as ready to stop the South Koreans, if they had been the first to break the peace. . . . The ideal we serve is 'the great republic of humanity,' " he added, "not the Truman Doctrine." [34]

Pacifists found it "astonishing how completely the concept of 'police action' . . . dominated American reaction" to the Korean War. The staunchest of their allies fell in line behind the Truman policy. Immediately after the dispatch of American troops, the Federal Council of Churches rushed word of its support into print, while the Socialist Party's National Action Committee voted unanimously to back the action, "despite the mistakes of our government in the past." Norman Thomas became a strong supporter of efforts to "beat back that aggression." A number of Progressive Party leaders, including Henry A. Wallace and O. John Rogge, repudiating their party and its Communist support, affirmed their faith in America's war role. Even the traditionally antiwar *Progressive* expressed approval of the Truman move, and criticized "true-blue pacifists," whose devotion to peace "robs them of the capacity to see how meeting force with force can result in anything but war." A few Communists and die-hard isolationists, whom pacifists found unacceptable allies, comprised the only other vocal opposition to the war. As a result, according to one pacifist leader, pacifists were "reduced pretty much to talking to themselves." [35]

The pacifist conception of the Korean War varied greatly from that of their former world federalist, Socialist, and liberal allies.

[34] "Grim Lesson," *World Government News*, VIII (September, 1950), 3–5; Albert Guerard, "The Meaning of Victory," *Common Cause*, IV (November, 1950), 169–71. For other examples of this attitude, see: "Embattled Peacemaker," *World Government News*, VIII (August, 1950), 3–6; G. A. Borgese, "Still It Is Korea," *Common Cause*, IV (October, 1950), 113–15. World federalists probably overemphasized even the symbolic role of the United Nations in the conflict. General MacArthur observed that in Korea the U.N. flag was flown "only on rare occasions." Douglas MacArthur to Mike Lally, November 14, 1950, SCAP MSS, Box 34.

[35] Alfred Hassler, "Cops in Korea," *Fellowship*, XVI (September, 1950), 4; *New York Times*, July 7, 1950; Bell, "Background and Development of Marxian Socialism," pp. 225, 397; Norman Thomas, COHC, p. 215; personal interview with Norman Thomas, October 4, 1966; Norman Thomas to Richard Harrington, August 23, 1950, Thomas MSS, Box 60. Wallace, for one, was bitterly disillusioned. He wrote A. J. Muste: "If our Left Wing friends were interested in peace they would write Stalin to end the Korean conflict." "Interim Administrative Committee" (August 7, 1950), WRL MSS, Box 2.

"What is taking place in Korea is not 'police action,'" declared a
F.O.R. pronouncement. "Calling it that does not change the fact
that armies are fighting against each other and bombing and shelling
civilian populations." Korea represented "restraining action by a
world organization only on the most superficial and legalistic basis,"
wrote Al Hassler. "Practically, it is part of the formerly 'cold' war
between the United States and the USSR, in which Korea and the
Koreans, as well as the United Nations itself, have been and are
being manipulated with complete callousness by both sides as their
'national interests' seem to dictate." Hassler maintained that the
"police interpretation" pivoted on a "two-dimensional view of the
United Nations," since that institution was not, in fact, "a world
organization created and functioning in the interests of world peace,"
but "the cockpit of the struggle" between the United States and the
Soviet Union. The American call for intervention, he observed, had
been accepted by the U.N. only because of the absence of Russia
and the de facto government of China, "both frankly partisans of
North Korea." Thus, "what the 'police action' really means," he concluded, "is that a truncated UN has been conscripted as an ally of
the United States in its struggle against the Soviet Union and world
communism." Pacifists received little comfort from the U.N. presence, since the organization functioned as a belligerent in the conflict, rather than as a mediator.[36]

As a result of its deepening involvement in the Cold War, the
Soviet Union launched a series of massive "peace offensives"
throughout the world after 1948. Utilizing its resources in the Communist parties and "front groups" of non-Communist nations, it
sought thereby to hinder the military efforts of the Western bloc,
particularly of the United States. The American Communist Party
apparatus accordingly jumped from the ill-fated Progressive Party
campaign into command of a series of bogus peace ventures: the
Cultural and Scientific Conference for World Peace, the American

[36] Fellowship of Reconciliation, *The Meaning of Korea;* Hassler, "Cops in
Korea," pp. 5–7; A. J. Muste, *Korea: Spark to Set a World Afire?;* Women's In-
ternational League for Peace and Freedom, "Korea—A Reaffirmation," Allen
MSS, Section C4, Box 1; Bussey and Tims, *Women's International League for
Peace and Freedom,* pp. 204–205; *Peacemaker,* II (July 11, 1950), 2; "Execu-
tive Committee Meeting, War Resisters League, July 10, 1950," WRL MSS,
Box 2.

Peace Crusade, and finally the Stockholm Peace Petition campaign. An official Party statement proclaimed:" The Party's Peace Campaign is our major task. . . . It is primary and transcends all other issues and struggles." Other "struggles" would not be forgotten, but transformed. "For example, the fight to free Eugene Dennis must feature his role as the Party's outstanding fighter for peace; his imprisonment as a war preparation; his freedom as a blow for peace. Every issue before us . . . must be thought through and presented in terms of the over-riding issue: PEACE." [37]

While there is little doubt that Communists planned, managed, and directed these campaigns, many participants were undoubtedly sincere in their concern for world peace, and cannot be classified as either Communists or fellow-travelers. The Stockholm peace pledge, for example, received 1,350,000 signatures in the United States, largely because it represented a statement of beliefs that many non-Communist Americans could endorse:

> We demand the outlawing of the atomic weapons as instruments of aggression and mass murder of peoples.
> We demand strict international control to enforce this measure.
> We believe that any government which first uses atomic weapons against any other country whatsoever will be committing a crime against humanity. . . .
> We call on all men and women of good will thruout the world to sign this appeal.

Many quite innocent persons discovered only afterward that the price of a concern for peace was their permanent branding as Com-

[37] U.S., Congress, House, Committee on Un-American Activities, *Review of the Scientific and Cultural Conference for World Peace*, 81st Cong., 1st Sess., 1949; U.S., Congress, House, Committee on Un-American Activities, *The Communist "Peace" Petition Campaign*, 81st Cong., 2nd Sess., 1950; U.S., Congress, House, Committee on Un-American Activities, *Report on the Communist "Peace" Offensive: A Campaign to Disarm and Defeat the United States*, 82nd Cong., 1st Sess., 1951; *Daily Worker*, June 11, 1950. The House Un-American Activities Committee included the Mid-Century Conference for Peace in its listing of "front" groups. However, the evidence does not appear sufficient to sustain this contention, although pro-Soviet elements may have had some part in the Conference. HUAC's "proof" is to list the sponsorship of such non-Communists as Carey McWilliams and I. F. Stone, who are then termed "the usual supporters of Communist fronts." Speakers at the Conference placed the blame for the Cold War on both the United States and the Soviet Union. U.S., House Committee on Un-American Activities, *Report on the Communist "Peace" Offensive*, pp. 51–61.

munists or traitors. "Sometime ago I signed a petition against the use of the atomic bomb," remarked a correspondent of Norman Thomas. "Since then I have been accused of siding with the Communists, which is far, far from my thoughts. When I signed the petition I noted that many of my friends . . . had already signed. And I am against such bombing." [38]

Pacifist organizations exhibited extreme caution when dealing with Communists, and consequently shunned all participation in Soviet-sponsored peace initiatives. "Communist-inspired 'peace' campaigns are not genuine," observed a F.O.R. pronouncement, and lead "to building up the Communist Party rather than pacifism or peace." It suggested that "the best way to test any 'peace' project or joint effort which is proposed is to discover whether its promoters" clearly stated "that it is opposed to militarism and war preparations *both* in Russia and in the United States, that it is critical of the foreign policy of both countries, and opposed to all forms of totalitarianism, including the Communist." Pacifists considered Soviet peace campaigns insincere. John Swomley remarked that "there is no evidence . . . to lead us to believe that Russia is providing any leader-

[38] U.S., House Committee on Un-American Activities, *Report on the Communist "Peace" Offensive,* p. 33; S. H. to Norman Thomas, August 30, 1950, Thomas MSS, Box 60. Thomas replied: "I am very sorry that you and a few folk like you signed the so-called Stockholm Peace Petition. It is a communist document and it is very unrealistic." Norman Thomas to S. H., August 31, 1950, Thomas MSS, Box 60. Within five months, the Stockholm petition had secured 273,470,566 signers around the world including Lazaro Cardenas, Thomas Mann, George Bernard Shaw, Henri Matisse, and Pablo Picasso. *New York Times,* August 13, 1950. Some of the Soviet-inspired "peace" efforts embarrassed Moscow, when participants proved to be more than the expected puppets. O. John Rogge of the United States, for example, the head of an American "peace" delegation, was invited to address the Presidium of the Supreme Soviet. The first American ever to do so, Rogge surprised everyone concerned by criticizing both the Russians and the Americans for blaming the other for all the problems of the Cold War, and by suggesting compromise positions on matters of political controversy. *Izvestia* was forced to criticize him the next day. At the World Peace Congress in 1950, Rogge charged that Communists resorted to violence in Korea and Tibet, and then repudiated the Stockholm pledge; consequently, he lost his post in the organization. The United States was spared the same embarrassment by the refusal of the American government to admit a "peace" delegation into the country. Senator Kenneth Wherry maintained that its admission "would simply add to our difficulties in stamping out revolutionary communism among our own people." U.S., House Committee on Un-American Activities, *Report on the Communist "Peace" Offensive,* pp. 26–27, 37–38.

ship for world peace. Her actions are similar to those of other power states. The Communist 'Peace Offensive' operates in the interests of one group of power states." [39]

Occasionally, peace activists went out of their way to disrupt the awesome unanimity of pro-Soviet propaganda efforts. Shortly before the March, 1949, Cultural and Scientific Conference for World Peace, a group of pacifists and non-pacifists of liberal to radical vintage decided, in Dwight Macdonald's words, "to expose the Conference for the CP front it was." After some preliminary meetings, the first one in Macdonald's apartment, they organized Americans for Intellectual Freedom, which held overflow countermeetings, featuring addresses by everyone from A. J. Muste to Arthur Schlesinger, Jr. Moreover, pacifists Robert Lowell and Macdonald and non-pacifists Mary McCarthy and George S. Counts, attending one of the Conference's sessions as surprise delegates, nearly broke up the meeting with questions addressed to Soviet representatives on intellectual freedom, civil disobedience, and conscientious objection in the Soviet Union. The Stalinist rout was complete when novelist Norman Mailer, one of the Conference's hand-picked speakers, and thus considered "safe," finished off the session with an attack upon the Soviet Union and the United States as "moving toward state capitalism" and "war." [40]

Nevertheless, despite a clear and unequivocal position on participation in Communist "fronts," the peace groups found the issue a divisive one, fraught with bitterness and suspicion. One long-time F.O.R. member resigned from the organization in 1950, "wearied" by " 'reformed Communists' lecturing liberal Christians and condescendingly regarding them as 'naive kids.' " *Fellowship* reported in

[39] Fellowship of Reconciliation, "Peace Fronts Today" (May, 1951), FOR MSS, Box 4; John M. Swomley, Jr., to Professor F. Siegmund Schultze, December 3, 1953, FOR MSS, Box 4; Bussey and Tims, *Women's International League for Peace and Freedom*, p. 196; Altbach, "The American Peace Movement," pp. 48–49; "Notes by A. J. Muste to Draft Statement on The Peace Movement and United Fronts" (June 27, 1950), FOR MSS, Box 3.

[40] Dwight Macdonald, "The Waldorf Conference," *Politics*, VI (Winter, 1949), special insert, 32A–32D. Mailer later said that he told the audience "only socialism could save the world, and America was not close to that, and Russia was not close, and people should not believe in countries and patriotism anyway, and peace conferences like this gave the idea that one could, and so were wrong." Lasch, *The New Radicalism*, p. 342.

the same year that four members threatened to resign because of the organization's "unreconciling" attitude, while another three protested against its "soft" attitude toward Communists and Russia. Other organizations experienced the same splintering effect. One pacifist told the W.R.L. that its "articles and behavior" made him "feel that there is a tinge of Communism" connected with its work for peace; that same year another remarked: "Don't wholly agree with your bitter anti-Communist stand." In 1950 several prominent members of the W.R.L.'s executive committee resigned because it had voted to send an observer to the Communist-dominated World Peace Council. The Communist "peace offensive" not only embarrassed the American peace movement, but caused it serious damage.[41]

By late 1950 the postwar peace movement was clearly well along in the process of disintegration. Typical of the movement's declining fortunes was the sensational but short-lived World Citizens movement. In late 1948 a former United States air force pilot, Garry Davis, flew to Paris, rushed to the temporary U.N. headquarters at the Palais Chaillot, and dramatically renounced his citizenship, proclaiming himself a "citizen of the world." Camping at the U.N. headquarters, Davis interrupted an Assembly session to present his plea until seized by United Nations guards. But Robert Sarrazac, a former lieutenant-colonel in the *maquis*, finished his speech: "We, the people, long for the peace which only a world order can give. The sovereign states which you represent here are dividing us and bringing us to the abyss of war." He called on the astonished delegates to cease their national disputes and "raise a flag around which all men can gather, the flag of sovereignty of one government for the world." Inspired by Davis' sensational activities, 250,000 people from many nations registered as World Citizens, while approximately 400 cities and towns throughout France, Belgium, Denmark, Germany, and India proclaimed themselves "mundialized," or world territory. In the United States, where reaction was relatively restrained, pacifists

---

[41] A. B. to A. J. Muste, June 6, 1950, FOR MSS, Box 3; "Surfeit," *Fellowship*, XVI (December, 1950), 3; P.J.M. to War Resisters League, January, 1948, WRL MSS, Box 18; G. M. to War Resisters League, December 7, 1948, WRL MSS, Box 18; Abraham Kaufman to Sidney Aberman, November 10, 1950, WRL MSS, Box 2; Frieda Lazarus to Sidney Aberman, January 8, 1951, WRL MSS, Box 2.

picketed the French embassy, celebrated the news of Davis' conversion to pacifism, and declared the Glen Gardner cooperative community "mundialized." Then, suddenly, the bubble burst. In September, 1950, Davis applied for reinstatement of his United States citizenship, explaining that he had made a mistake.[42]

The established world government movement followed a similar course, somewhat less disastrous, perhaps, but no less discouraging. During 1948 and 1949, U.W.F. continued to grow larger, although correspondingly more conservative, until its membership stood at almost 50,000. In October, 1949, hearings began before the House Foreign Affairs Committee on a resolution, sponsored by 115 Representatives and 21 Senators, "to seek development of the United Nations into a world federation." Favorable testimony at the hearings was provided by Alan Cranston, Cord Meyer, Jr., Thomas K. Finletter, and Harrison Brown of the U.W.F. and by forty-five members of the House of Representatives. In February, 1950, hearings resumed in the Senate on six Congressional resolutions, ranging from proposals for Atlantic Union to a "maximalist" world federation plan, submitted by the University of Chicago Committee to Frame a World Constitution. Administration spokesmen, however, notably the Deputy Undersecretary of State, Dean Rusk, exhibited indiscriminate opposition to all the resolutions, and consequently the Senate committee recommended that no action be taken. U.W.F. leaders remained hopeful of future Congressional action, but the tide was already running against them.[43]

[42] New York Times, September 13, 1948; "I Am a Citizen of the World," United States Peace Material Miscellaneous, 1950-1954; Garry Davis, Over to Pacifism; "Full Text of Statement of Religious and Peace Leaders Protesting Garry Davis Prosecution by French Government" (October 3, 1949), Allen MSS, Section C4, Box 8; Peacemaker, I (January 13, 1950), 1-2; "Executive Committee Meeting, October 6, 1949," WRL MSS, Box 2; Peacemaker, I (November 2, 1949), 1; Peacemaker, II (July 26, 1950), 1; New York Times, July 7, 1950; "Geneva, 1950," Common Cause, IV (March, 1951), 432-40; "Garry Davis Changes His Mind," Fellowship, XVI (November, 1950), 27; Peacemaker, V (August 3, 1953), 1, 3. The "Charter of Mundialization for All Townships and Towns of the World" proclaimed that "without denying any of our duties and rights towards our country and our nation, we declare ourselves symbolically 'world territory' linked to the world community." The Charter invited "every town and township of the world to join this Charter of solidarity." Common Cause, IV (September, 1950), 105.

[43] "Council Notes," World Government News, VII (July, 1949), 7; "UWF's Birthday Marks Half a Decade of Progress," 6-7; "American Congress and World Federation," Common Cause, IV (August, 1950), 5-33.

In early 1950 the world government movement began to crumble. Opposition sprang up in the twenty-three state legislatures which had previously passed resolutions favoring world federation. Bills rescinding prior legislation were passed in California, Rhode Island, Georgia, and Louisiana; by late 1951, sixteen states had repealed their resolutions supporting world government. At the fourth annual U.W.F. convention in October, "universalists" narrowly beat back a challenge from forces arguing that Russia be excluded from any federation; by the fifth convention, U.W.F. had lost its student wing over policy differences. Friendly publicity for world government sharply declined. "During the last six months there has been a marked decrease of intelligent discussion of the topic," complained an April, 1951, editorial in *Common Cause*. "Today journals of general interest just do not discuss the issue." Within a few months, *Common Cause* itself suspended publication for financial reasons, followed shortly thereafter by *World Government News*. G. A. Borgese noted gloomily: "Ideas too have their Valley Forges." [44]

What precipitated the collapse? According to one proponent of world government, "a climax was reached last June 25, when the North Koreans crossed the Thirty-Eighth Parallel." Like other elements of the peace movement, world federalists fluctuated in an inverse relationship to the Cold War; with its heightening, their strength began to ebb disastrously, particularly among their more superficial converts. The editor of *Common Cause* reported a new "political and intellectual climate which has been learning to . . . ignore the daydream of one world and clings to the 'facts of life.'" And the "chief fact of life," he added, "is that the worlds are two" and "cannot join in peace." In the context of a world at war, the prospect of peacefully composing international differences seemed at best utopian, at worst treasonable. "Patriotic" organizations spurred their members to action. In opposing world government, a D.A.R. official assured the faithful, "you are saving the United States

---

[44] "UWF's Birthday Marks Half a Decade of Progress," pp. 6–7; "Thought Needed," *Common Cause*, IV (April, 1951), 501; Frances B. Lucas, "World Government Status, September, 1951," reprint from *Daughters of the American Revolution Magazine*, SCAP MSS, Box 16; Elizabeth Mann Borgese, "1950: World Movement at the Divide," *Common Cause*, IV (December, 1950), 225–27; "Taking Bearings," *Common Cause*, IV (April, 1951), 449–50; "This Critical Hour," *Common Cause*, IV (June, 1951), 613.

from Communist Domination and Dictation." Thus, despite their efforts to adhere to "safe" positions, world federalists fared no better than their allies. "The world government movement will disintegrate as the world war movement accelerates," predicted Milton Mayer in May, 1950. "The end is in sight. . . . War will come faster than world government." [45]

The atomic scientists' movement reached its nadir in 1950. The Emergency Committee of Atomic Scientists, inactive since January 1, 1949, ceased functioning entirely by the end of 1950. Policy differences within the Committee had grown increasingly sharp. "Near the end of our days we could not really agree among ourselves as to the next step to take," recalled Harrison Brown. Einstein sadly remarked: "How can we presume to rescue the American people from their uncertainties if we cannot agree among ourselves?" Einstein and Szilard wanted to give the balance of the Committee's funds to the A.F.S.C. rather than to the *Bulletin of the Atomic Scientists,* which Einstein considered to have degenerated into "no more than a publication of neutral information," but the money eventually went to the *Bulletin.* "The break between the two camps appears all but complete," Eugene Rabinowitch wrote grimly in January, 1951. "Scientists—whose profession requires a recognition of facts, however unpleasant—cannot but admit the fact that their campaign has failed." [46]

After 1948 the steam went out of radical pacifism. The death of Gandhi in 1948 and the demise of *Politics* in 1949 were symbolic of the waning of much of the wartime radicalism and direct action. To some degree this resulted from the dissolution of wartime ties and of

[45] E. M. Borgese, "1950: World Movement at the Divide," p. 225; G. A. Borgese, "Common Cause," *Common Cause,* IV (June, 1951), 562; Margaret H. Worrell to Douglas MacArthur, January 27, 1951, SCAP MSS, Box 24; Frances B. Lucas, "World Government Status, September, 1951," reprint from *Daughters of the American Revolution Magazine* (September, 1951), SCAP MSS, Box 16; Mayer, *What Can a Man Do?* p. 107. A professor of political science at Northwestern University suggested that "the most realistic method" of attaining world government would involve "reform of the United Nations," which could "be accomplished only after the expulsion of Soviet Russia." Kenneth Colegrove to Douglas MacArthur, September 21, 1951, SCAP MSS, Box 15.

[46] Nathan and Norden, *Einstein on Peace,* pp. 504–505, 557–58; Pauling, *No More War!* pp. 220–21; Rabinowitch, "Five Years After," p. 4.

government-enforced groupings with other C.O.'s, and from the re-assimilation of pacifists into the non-pacifist community. "Pacifists are drawn chiefly from the ranks of comfortable, respectable people," Roy Kepler commented in 1949, "and they share with the non-pacifists the inclination to retire into their private lives." He noted, for example, that "the teaching profession is highly infiltrated by pacifist teachers," but that "many of them are doing nothing or very little directly about their pacifist viewpoints. By and large, they are . . . more interested in their particular field of study, their family, their record collections, their comfortable homes, their correct and genteel friends than they are in challenging people to think anew on the great issues of war and peace." [47]

Kepler, who had just completed an organizing trip around the country, brought back grim news for Peacemakers. "There are practically no Peacemakers' groups functioning outside of the Ohio area," he reported in that organization's journal, and "there are relatively few activities being carried on by individuals which are specifically re-lated to Peacemakers' activities." On his field trip he met people in different parts of the nation who told him they were Peacemakers. "Then they would ask me what Peacemakers was doing, or what it was going to do." Each explained that "they were too busy with personal affairs to do anything outside of their more-or-less usual pattern." He concluded that while the 1948 conscription issue had "brought a keen sense of urgency, and a flurry of activity," interest and participation had now slackened markedly. "A mere handful

[47] Roy Kepler, "Report on Country-Wide Trip" (1949), WRL MSS, Box 11. A psychological study of a Quaker work camp during this period encountered a similar phenomenon. Pacifism among the participants was heightened during the period of group isolation in the camp, but in the subsequent period of the return to their communities many of the participants began to assert community norms. Henry W. Riecken, The Volunteer Work Camp: A Psychological Evaluation, p. 123. One member of Peacemakers sadly informed Kepler that he intended to register for the draft, although as a C.O. "During the summer I decided to get married to a girl. . . . She is neither an ardent practicing pacifist nor socialist," he explained. Life "would be very hard" for her "if I were in jail either just before or after marriage. Needless to say, the middle-class society from which we come would exert unpleasant pressure on her." Thus, "just before she returned to Radcliffe I promised her I would register. . . . I have come to the conclusion that one has to continue to live as normal and balanced a life as possible in this war torn world." P. D. to Roy Kepler, October 12, 1948, WRL MSS, Box 15.

respond to take part in street meetings; almost no efforts are made to bring small groups together in cells." [48]

Even traditional pacifists were in trouble. Under the chill of the Cold War, the membership of the F.O.R. and the W.R.L. continued to dwindle, and their influence in the non-pacifist community to decrease. "This year the FOR tried to work up a conference on Militarism in Education," note the F.O.R. minutes in 1949, "but faculty members were too busy." A postcard from a Minneapolis contact, asked to set up a pacifist meeting in that city, replied: "Student FOR is defunct. Univ. of Minn. League for Dem. Socialism is defunct and there isn't much else with which I have any contact. Sorry." After a field trip across the country for the W.R.L. in 1950, Igal Roodenko reported: "I've begun to feel that at this point, simply to get people to know that the word pacifism exists is no mean accomplishment." A pall of gloom and pessimism shrouded the remaining adherents. Roy Kepler described "a kind of creeping paralysis of defeatism and despair among pacifists which leads to inaction in other than little fellowship groups of mutual commiseration and fear." [49]

In this manner, the promising stirrings in the postwar peace movement collapsed under the pressure of the Cold War. By 1950 few could see any cause for optimism. Supreme Court Justice William O. Douglas noted "the prevalence of the belief that full-scale war is inevitable. Many men of good will have lost hope for any solution short of war." The nation's peace forces grew bitter and discouraged. "The men who possess the real power in this country have no intention of ending the cold war," Einstein told A. J. Muste. Nor was there much chance of securing a change in policy, he acknowledged, for the public apparently agreed with government leaders. The postwar élan had run its course. Only despair remained. [50]

[48] *Peacemaker,* I (August 9, 1949), 4.

[49] "Minutes of Meeting of National Council, May 19-21, 1949," FOR MSS, Box 3; J. W. to War Resisters League, October 30, 1949, WRL MSS, Box 11; Igal Roodenko to War Resisters League, May 18, 1950, WRL MSS, Box 11; Roy Kepler, "Report on Country-Wide Trip" (1949), WRL MSS, Box 11. Kepler concluded that there was "no pacifist movement in the U.S." *Ibid.*

[50] William O. Douglas, "An Obligation to History," *Common Cause,* IV (January, 1951), 281; Nathan and Norden, *Einstein on Peace,* pp. 519-20.

CHAPTER VIII

Midcentury Nadir,
1950–1956

Precisely in a day when the individual appears to be utterly helpless, to "have no choice," when the aim of the "system" is to convince him that he is helpless as an individual and that the only way to meet regimentation is by regimentation, there is absolutely no hope save in going back to the beginning. The human being . . . must assert his humanity . . . again. . . . He must understand that this . . . is the one *real* thing in the face of the . . . mechanized institutions of our age.

A. J. MUSTE, 1952 [1]

Reduced to insignificant proportions by the Cold War, the peace movement had only begun its time of troubles. As the very forces it sought to restrain grew stronger and bolder, they subjected the peace movement to a withering attack that left it barely clinging to existence. In a strange half-life, the remnants of the historic movement continued their struggle against war, formulating radical alternatives to American military policies and serving as prophets in the Cold War wilderness. Yet rarely had the prospect seemed so bleak and their witness so hopeless.

The loyalty-security mania of the early Fifties has attracted considerable attention among scholars, who have concentrated upon sociological or psychological explanations of its development. But they have often failed to stress the obvious: that McCarthyism was the domestic counterpart of American foreign policy. Indeed the unique genius of the junior Senator from Wisconsin lay in tying his relatively insignificant concern with a few individuals who may once have had some connection to the American Communist Party to the great drama of world conflict. After describing "a conspiracy on a

[1] A. J. Muste, "Of Holy Disobedience," p. 18.

scale so immense as to dwarf any previous such venture in the history of man," McCarthy asked: "What is the objective of the conspiracy?" He answered grandly: "To diminish the United States in world affairs, to weaken us militarily, to confuse our spirit with talk of surrender." To what end, he asked, pressing his Cold War advantage. "To the end that we shall be contained and frustrated and finally fall victim to Soviet intrigue from within and Russian military might from without." [2]

Few Americans concerned with "subversion" doubted that unity was essential to the Anti-Communist Crusade. Polling public opinion in 1950, 1952, and 1954, Samuel Lubell was struck by the support which voters frustrated by the Korean War gave to McCarthy. "Why don't we clean up these Commies at home with our boys dying in Korea?" they demanded. Police Commissioner Eugene ("Bull") Connor of Birmingham, Alabama, vowed to "put the exterminator" to local "Reds." The opening prayer of the United States Senate in February, 1952, led by the Reverend Billy Graham, contained a two-pronged reference to "barbarians beating at our gates from without and moral termites from within." Operating on a similar theory, the government of the United States maintained six "detention camps" under the authority of the McCarran Internal Security Act. The *New York Times* observed that "in the climate of a national emergency hundreds, perhaps thousands, could be sequestered in security camps who were not actual, or even potential spies or saboteurs." [3]

[2] Joseph R. McCarthy, *America's Retreat from Victory*, pp. 168, 171–72. Of course, once in motion, fear of the Red Menace was an easy peg on which to hang any cause. The Bohn Aluminum and Brass Corporation took out a full-page, color advertisement in 1951, proclaiming: "CHEAP MONEY . . . that's what the Reds would like to see in America." It explained that "Moscow meddlers in positions of influence are promoting cheap money for America today," and concluded: "*Let's throw them out!*" Social psychologist Gordon Allport observed that "Russia came to serve as a satisfactory scapegoat—a distant menace capable of explaining many of our frustrations. 'Communists' became the symbolic cause of evil at home. Is my employment jeopardized? Blame the communists. Am I inconvenienced by inflation? Blame the communistic labor leaders. Are the colleges advocating dangerous internationalism? Oust the communist professors." "Cheap Money," *Collier's*, CXXVIII (October 27, 1951), 115; Gordon Allport, "The Role of Expectancy," *Tensions that Cause Wars*, ed. Hadley Cantril, pp. 62–63.

[3] Samuel Lubell, *Revolt of the Moderates*, p. 268; *Charlotte Observer* (N.C.), July 10, 1950, clipping in MacArthur MSS, Box 11; U.S., *Congressional*

Despite the fact that it was itself suspect in the eyes of the professed patriots, the peace movement threw its energies into the defense of civil liberties. It denounced the Smith Act and the McCarran Act and called for their repeal, while vigorously supporting efforts to abolish the House Committee on Un-American Activities and the Attorney General's "list." The F.O.R. assailed the demand for "repeated professions of loyalty to the State," the tendency to "make conformity to a political line rather than professional competence . . . the sole or chief test for employment," and the test of a man's "recanting" of past associations by a willingness to "inform." These practices seemed redolent of "totalitarian regimes" to the pacifist organization. The W.R.L. called the Smith Act "an outstanding example of the encroachments . . . upon fundamental freedoms" for regarding as criminal "mere language in the absence of any criminal acts." In a letter to the *New York Times*, Albert Einstein urged intellectuals to adopt "the revolutionary way of non-cooperation" with government "loyalty" investigations: "Every intellectual who is called before one of the committees ought to refuse to testify." [4]

Moreover, unlike some elements of the liberal community who deplored McCarthyism largely for its attacks upon non-Communists, the peace movement fought for the civil liberties of bona fide Communists. Pacifists and small groups of liberals and independent radicals signed and circulated amnesty petitions for American Communist Party leaders imprisoned under the Smith Act, and criticized government attempts to "outlaw" the Communist Party. Disliking

---

Record, 82nd Cong., 2nd Sess., 1952, XCVIII, Part 1, 739; *New York Times*, December 27, 1955. This is not to maintain that everyone in favor of American foreign policy approved of McCarthy, or to assert that McCarthy really cared about Communism, but merely to point out that the Cold War context offered him an opportunity to exploit the "Communist" issue in a manner denied to previous American demagogues.

4 Personal interview with A. J. Muste, June 2, 1966; "Report on Civil Liberties" (December 1, 1950), FOR MSS, Box 3; "National Board Resolutions Re: Civil Liberties," WILPF MSS, Box 4; W.I.L.P.F., "Internal Security" (1956), WILPF MSS, Box 32; "The F.O.R. and Civil Liberties, 1953" (May, 1953), FOR MSS, Box 4; "Statement on Civil Rights Adopted by the National Executive Committee of the War Resisters League" (October 30, 1949), WRL MSS, Box 2; *Catholic Worker*, October, 1950; *New York Times*, June 12, 1953; "National Board Resolutions Re: Internal Security Act," WILPF MSS, Box 4; Norman Thomas, *The Test of Freedom*.

Communism, they nevertheless contended that "real" Communists as well as "suspected" Communists were entitled to their liberties. It was not surprising that when the Communist Party agreed to admit a non-Communist "observer" group to its convention in February, 1957, to witness its procedures, the outside delegation consisted of members of the A.F.S.C., the Catholic Worker, the W.R.L., the F.O.R., and the American Civil Liberties Union.[5]

Pacifists conceded that the issue of domestic Communism was complex. "We recognize that in dealing with totalitarian Communism, we are not simply dealing with a political party," acknowledged the F.O.R. "Communism is, for example, the ideology or faith of an expansionist power-state, the Soviet Union, and of allied nations. We do not question that there is a sense in which Communist activities in this country constitute elements in the program of an international conspiracy." Yet it seemed "superficial and politically unwise to lump all Communist activities together as if they were equal and inseparable parts of a conspiracy engineered from abroad," the F.O.R. added. In the United States and around the world Communism "in certain phases represents a response to needs felt by certain sections of the population and engages in forms of propaganda and protest which are legitimate according to the tradition of democratic countries." The pacifist group found it "important to distinguish between such activities . . . and espionage, sabotage, and treason." But finally, the defense of the civil liberties of Communists rested upon more than political sophistication. "Those with whom we differ, whether at home or abroad, as well as our national

5 Curti, *The Growth of American Thought*, p. 761; Fred Rodell, "What Should We Do about the Commies?" *Progressive*, XII (January, 1948), 15; "The FOR and the Communists," *Fellowship*, XIV (September, 1948), 11; "Statement by Executive Committee, F.O.R., on Trial of Communist Party Leaders, November, 1949," FOR MSS, Box 3; *Catholic Worker*, November, 1949; *Peacemaker*, II (July 26, 1950), 1; "Outlawing the Communist Party" (May, 1954), FOR MSS, Box 4; "A Petition to the President of the United States on Amnesty for Smith Act Victims and Postponement of Trials" (December 20, 1955), FOR MSS, Box 28; "Statement on Amnesty for Smith Act Victims Adopted by the National Council of F.O.R., December, 1955," FOR MSS, Box 4; press release of letter sent to President Eisenhower, September 23, 1958, Muste MSS, Box 1. On pacifist attendance at the Party convention, see: Alfred Hassler, "Sharp Turn to the Center," *Fellowship*, XXIII (March, 1957), 23–26; Roy Finch, "The Communist Convention," *Liberation*, II (March, 1957), 4–6.

or class 'enemies,' are still without any exception human beings . . . and not categories," declared a pacifist pronouncement. As such, they held an equal claim to justice and human dignity.[6]

The loyalty investigations churned up an atmosphere of fear and suspicion extremely inhospitable to peace action. "In the United States," wrote Lewis Mumford, "reason is cowed by governmental purges" and "criticism and dissent . . . are identified as treason." Monogram Studios abandoned plans for a feature-length film on the life of Hiawatha, the Onondoga Indian chief immortalized by Long-fellow, because of its fear that Hiawatha's peace efforts among the Five Nations might serve the cause of Communist propaganda. *Time* magazine remarked: "The academic motto for 1953 is fast becoming: Don't say, don't write, don't go." [7]

Liberals and radicals soon felt the pinch. One Socialist Party supporter, working to collect the requisite signatures to place the Party's name on the ballot, told Norman Thomas: "It gets to be a harder and harder job . . . as people get more and more scared to sign anything for fear of being thought subversive." In response to a fund appeal, the Socialist-oriented Workers Defense League received a rash of replies exemplifying the popular fear; one contributor simply signed "A Coward," a second remarked that "my husband and I are afraid to sign our names to this," while fifteen others provided no signature whatsoever. Even the liberal supporters of American Cold War policy were not exempt from the suspicion that they participated in a Communist plot. When James Wechsler, liberal editor of the *New York Post*, testified before Senator Mc-Carthy's subcommittee, he presented a voluminous quantity of evidence attesting to his bitter relations with the Communist Party

---

[6] "The F.O.R. and Civil Liberties, 1953" (May, 1953), FOR MSS, Box 4. Pacifists drew an interesting parallel between Communist and non-Communist Americans. "Like millions of their non-Communist fellows," Communists "have fallen prey to the temptation to hate the sinner as well as the sin, and to believe that it is possible to achieve good ends by evil means. Just as most Americans believe that by building H-bombs and guided missiles they are also building peace, so do Communists believe that by denying freedom and suppressing dissent they are constructing a free and democratic society." Hassler, "Sharp Turn to the Center," p. 26.

[7] Lewis Mumford, *In the Name of Sanity*, p. 7; "A Red Is a Red Is a Red," *Common Cause*, IV (December, 1950), 280; "Red," *Fellowship*, XVI (November, 1950), 1; N. M. Thomas, *The Test of Freedom*, p. 135.

since he had abandoned it in the Thirties. None of this, however, swayed the Senator. "I am convinced that you have done exactly what you would do . . . if you wanted to have a phony break and then use that phony break to the advantage of the Communist Party," McCarthy concluded disarmingly. "I feel that you have not broken with communist ideals. I feel that you are serving them very, very actively." [8]

Self-styled loyalty experts frequently organized attacks upon pacifists. In a pamphlet entitled "How Red is the Federal Council of Churches?" the American Council of Christian Laymen listed the F.O.R. as a "radical-pacifist group using Christian terms to spread Communist propaganda," and the W.R.L. as the co-sponsor of "numerous Communist-controlled movements." Actor Robert Montgomery charged on his radio and television program in 1951 that members of the Philadelphia Peace Caravan, sponsored by the F.O.R., were stooges of the Communist Party and that the F.O.R. itself was Communist. An excerpt from the files of the House Committee on Un-American Activities called the F.O.R. "allegedly a strictly pacifist organization" which maintained "that class war is necessary." Insinuations could be as devastating as direct accusations of subversion. In November, 1954, Herbert Philbrick's column, "The Red Underground," carried in the *New York Herald Tribune* and sixteen other newspapers, announced that "highly trained and skilled underground Communist party agents" would infiltrate a F.O.R. anniversary dinner scheduled in Boston. The organization had "many" members who were "loyal and sincere," Philbrick added in a dubious compliment, but now stood in danger of serving as a "transmission belt" for Communist propaganda. Pacifist heroes, tried posthumously, fared poorly. When E. B. White wrote a satire for the *New Yorker*, maintaining that if McCarthy knew of Thoreau he would damn him as a security risk, William F. Buckley, Jr., came back with the claim that "Thoreau *was*." [9]

[8] Rosamond Clark to Norman Thomas, August 28, 1952, Thomas MSS, Box 63; Thomas, *The Test of Freedom*, pp. 159–60; Fleischman, *Norman Thomas,* pp. 270–71; Wechsler, *The Age of Suspicion,* p. 286.
[9] "Red," *Fellowship,* XVI (June, 1950), 2; "Minutes—F.O.R. Executive Committee, April 26, 1951," FOR MSS, Box 4; "Minutes—National Council Meeting, May 30–31, 1951," FOR MSS, Box 4; *Washington Post,* April 5, 1953;

The inflammatory accusations of the Anti-Communist Crusade often led to action against the pacifist heretics. A F.O.R. member was removed from her job as city librarian of Bartlesville, Oklahoma, a post she had held for 35 years. A local Citizens Committee, composed of members of the American Legion, the D.A.R., and the United Daughters of the Confederacy, had complained of her to the city commissioners, who thereupon questioned the pacifist librarian on "subversive" literature in the library (the *Nation*, the *New Republic*, and *Soviet Russia Today*), about her race relations activities (she had organized a local CORE group), and as to whether or not she was a Communist (she was not). An hour after the interview, the city manager telephoned to announce that her employment had been terminated "forthwith." In New York two Legionnaires attacked a pacifist distributing leaflets during a Loyalty Day parade. Goaded on by bystanders, they knocked him to the pavement and commenced beating him, yelling "dirty Communist" from time to time until the police arrived. In Baltimore three members of the Society of Friends and of the F.O.R. lost their jobs when they refused to sign a loyalty oath required of all state and municipal employees by Maryland's Ober Law. A F.O.R. member lost his teaching position at a New Jersey college for failure to sign that state's loyalty oath.[10]

The tactics of persecution took their toll of pacifist strength. "The mass hysteria . . . has now reached a climax that is making our work difficult and presenting us with new problems," noted the

---

"Smear," *Fellowship*, XXI (January, 1955), 1–2; William F. Buckley, Jr., and L. Brent Bozell, *McCarthy and His Enemies: The Record and Its Meaning*, p. 309n.

[10] "Loses Job for Race Activities," *Fellowship*, XVI (November, 1950), 28; *Peacemaker*, II (June 1, 1950), 1; "Three to Lose Jobs over Loyalty Oath," *Fellowship*, XVI (May, 1950), 22. Pacifists who cooperated in any way with Communists now encountered great difficulties. Willard Uphaus, for example, a Christian pacifist, was active from 1949 to 1953 in an assortment of peace campaigns involving Communists. Although he knew of their presence, he did not let this fact dissuade him from efforts in which he believed. As a result, he was dismissed from his post in the Religion and Labor Foundation after pressure from the C.I.O., cited by the House Committee on Un-American Activities, and eventually prosecuted and convicted by the State of New Hampshire for refusing to produce the names of those persons attending his World Fellowship camp. In 1960 he began a one-year prison term. Willard Uphaus, *Commitment*.

W.I.L.P.F.'s administrative secretary. W.R.L. members distributing leaflets in Times Square found people afraid to accept their mimeographed circulars; sometimes they waited twenty minutes before a passerby took one. Pacifist ministers told A. J. Muste that they could not talk about peace to their congregations because they would be labeled as Communists. *Fellowship* observed in late 1950: "Anti-Communist feeling and hysteria make it far more difficult to get a hearing for the pacifist position now than at any time during World War II." Membership in pacifist organizations melted away. The W.R.L. dwindled to a tiny hard core, while the F.O.R. lost 3000 members—about one quarter of its total. "Is Peace a bad word?" asked a F.O.R. pronouncement. "Because the Communists misuse the word, are Americans going to agree that they prefer war?" [11]

Quasi-pacifist organizations such as CORE experienced serious difficulties in the early Fifties because of the "subversive" onus attached to social action. One local Woolworth's manager, for example, questioned on his employment practices, fired back: "Do you have anything on you to show that you are 100% American, and not on the list of the Justice Department?" A typical incident occurred during July, 1951, when nine CORE members held a sit-in at a Whelan's drugstore counter in Washington, D.C. Met with belligerent refusal of service and a horde of children chanting "Communist" for several hours, the demonstrators turned wearily to leave only to be followed by the juvenile gang. According to a CORE account, the latter "were voluble with their charges of 'Communist' and 'Go Back to Russia!' Although we tried to reason with them, they were too excited to listen, and followed down the street throwing stones, firecrackers, and miniature torpedoes." In such an atmosphere, CORE led only a tenuous existence. [12]

11 Mildred Scott Olmstead, "Report of the Administrative Secretary" (November, 1950), WILPF MSS, Box 13; personal interview with James Peck, April 21, 1966; "Minutes of National Council Meeting, Dec. 1–2, 1950," FOR MSS, Box 3; "Action on Korea Draws Few Protests," *Fellowship*, XVI (September, 1950), 19; "Membership Statistics" (1954), FOR MSS, Box 4; "Is Peace a Bad Word?" (1950), FOR MSS, Box 28.

12 "Interview with Mr. Smith, Manager of Woolworth's 5 & 10¢ Store" (July 10, 1954), CORE MSS; "Summer Interracial Workshop Bulletin" (July 31, 1951), CORE MSS. In 1953–1954, CORE's entire income totaled $7000, donated by a few hundred contributors. The F.O.R. minutes for 1951 note that George Houser, still employed on a full-time basis by the religious pacifist

Public fears of atomic spies and espionage made the atomic scientists a focal point of public concern. In the early Fifties the hapless scientists were subjected to constant political pressures, epitomized by the Oppenheimer hearings of 1954, which labeled the prominent physicist a "security risk" and denied him reinstatement to his post in the Atomic Energy Commission. The proceedings in the Oppenheimer case enraged the scientific community. Dr. Vannevar Bush told the loyalty panel: "No board should ever sit on a question in this country of whether a man [served] his country or not because he expressed strong opinions. If you want to try that case, you can try me." Others fled from government service rather than commit themselves to the new security regulations. Postmaster General Arthur Summerfield boasted proudly of Republican "progress in rooting out the eggheads." In late 1954 Albert Einstein remarked: "If I would be a young man again and I had to decide how to make my living, I would not try to become a scientist or scholar or teacher. I would rather choose to be a plumber or a peddler in the hope to find that modest degree of independence still available under present circumstances." [13]

The advocates of world government, or, as Senator McCarthy often referred to them, the "one-worlders," provided a favorite target for professional patriots. "World Government Means Communism" read a headline in the Bridgeport (Conn.) *Telegram* during late 1952. Others, more charitable, propounded slight variations on this theme. Representative Lawrence H. Smith of Wisconsin told a meeting of the Veterans of Foreign Wars that world government

---

organization, worked "in his spare time" as the executive secretary of CORE. Billie C. Ames to CORE contributors, September 7, 1954, CORE MSS; "Minutes of F.O.R. Executive Committee Meeting, January 12, 1951," FOR MSS, Box 4.

[13] Grodzins and Rabinowitch, *The Atomic Age*, p. 393; Alsop, *We Accuse!* p. 38; Marquis Childs, *Eisenhower: Captive Hero*, p. 183; Albert Einstein, Letter to the Editor, *Reporter*, XI (November 18, 1954), 8. One scientific employee was summoned to answer the following charge: "A confidential informant, stated to be of established reliability, who is acquainted with and who has associated with many known and admitted Communists, is reported to have advised as of May, 1948 that the informant was present when the employee was engaged in conversation with other individuals at which time the employee advocated the Communist Party line, *such as favoring peace and civil liberties* when these subjects were being advocated by the Communist Party." Gellhorn, *Security, Loyalty, and Science*, pp. 152–53, emphasis added.

was "just as dangerous as the communism we are fighting." *USA Confidential,* which defined the United World Federalists as a "crack-pot organization" and "the most dangerous of the international groups," maintained that it did "the spade work to turn the U.S. into a state in a united world that will be dominated on a popular vote basis by Russia." A representative on the United States commission of UNESCO remarked sardonically: "I have found recently that to be an advocate of peace or of world government is almost equivalent to advocating the overthrow of the United States Government by force." [14]

Local and federal government agencies often acted upon this conclusion. In February, 1953, *Newsweek* reported that "loyalty investigators are now asking would-be government employees if they ever were members of the United World Federalists." The question, claimed the magazine, was "designed largely to satisfy congressional suspicions of any group's plugging projects in which Communist nations participate." During that same year the State Department directed United States overseas information centers to remove Clarence Streit's *Union Now* from their shelves. A rider introduced in 1952 by Senator Pat McCarran of Nevada had barred funds to agencies which promoted "one-world government." In May, 1953, when the Maryland state branch of U.W.F. held a public meeting in Baltimore, a special state agent, working with two plainclothes detectives of the city police department, took down the license plate numbers of the guests' cars and the names of the people in the audience. The investigation occurred under the jurisdiction of the state's Subversive Activities Act, adopted in 1949, which authorized the maintenance of a secret file on seditious persons and acts.[15]

Individuals prominently identified with the cause of world government could not help but find it a liability. The appointment of Raymond Gram Swing as a commentator for the Voice of America

---

[14] Curti, *The Growth of American Thought,* p. 760; "Opposition Renews Attacks on Scattered Fronts," *The Federalist,* I (January, 1952), 6–7; "Lait and Mortimer Attack UWF," *The Federalist,* II (May, 1952), 8; *New York Times,* April 9, 1950.

[15] "U.S. Department of Justice Denies Asking 'Would-Be' Employees about UWF," *The Federalist,* II (March, 1953), 4; "Book Burning," *The Federalist,* III (October, 1953), 8; "Maryland Revisited," *The Federalist,* III (June, 1953), 3; Buckley and Bozell, *McCarthy and His Enemies,* pp. 313–14.

unleashed newspaper blasts against his patriotism and an investigation by Senator McCarthy's subcommittee; the right-wing periodical *Counter Attack* alleged that he "often followed an appeasement line." During the 1952 primary campaigns Senator Estes Kefauver, an advocate of Atlantic Union, faced repeated charges of conspiring to "surrender our sovereignty to foreign countries without firing a shot." In March, 1953, at the performance of a play in Hagerstown, Maryland, sponsored by a local chapter of U.W.F., four American Legion posts picketed and distributed mimeographed statements of the alleged "facts" about Norman Cousins, Rex Stout, and Oscar Hammerstein II, as culled from the files of the House Committee on Un-American Activities.[16]

While the world federalist leadership fought back against the loyalty-security zealots, often winning token victories of public apologies or retractions, the anti-Communist hysteria devastated the rank and file of the already declining movement. It was all very well for Norman Cousins to fly down from his offices at the *Saturday Review* in New York to confront a rural Maryland mob, but far harder for townspeople to combat their own community's daily fear and suspicion. Grenville Clark wrote bravely in 1952: "We have endured irresponsible and false attacks. . . . Some indeed have left our ranks, so that we stand now with smaller numbers than in our first flush of enthusiasm and over-optimism. But . . . we are more experienced, more compact and more mature in our thinking." [17]

Ironically, the loyalty hunt tore through the American peace movement at a time when it had already largely ceased to pose any effective opposition to the American military. In the Fifties the United World Federalists adopted increasingly conservative policy

[16] Swing, *"Good Evening!"* pp. 264, 276–81; "Opponents Hit Kefauver," *The Federalist*, II (June, 1952), 6; "The Myth that Threatened One American Town," *The Federalist*, III (April, 1953), 8–10; Buckley and Bozell, *McCarthy and His Enemies*, p. 313. At the end of the play the American Legion adjutant for the State of Maryland climbed onto the stage and charged that Cousins had been cited by the House Committee on Un-American Activities for speaking at the Scientific and Cultural Conference for World Peace. Cousins later explained that he had indeed been "cited" in the HUAC report, but for speaking at the Conference at the request of the State Department and for needing a police escort to leave the hall. "The Myth that Threatened One American Town," pp. 8–10.

[17] Grenville Clark, "A Winning Cause," *The Federalist*, II (Summer, 1952), 3.

positions until they became virtually indistinguishable from those of the American government. Norman Cousins, U.W.F. vice-president, told a radio audience in 1952 that "America represents the hope of men everywhere." Moreover, as the Cold War settled into a seemingly permanent pattern of East-West hostility, world government appeared chimerical. "Realists" turned their attention to less grandiose projects. "Seven years ago, when world law was mentioned, people said it was too soon," complained Cousins in late 1952. "Now, when it is mentioned, they say it is too late." [18]

Socialists and others on the democratic Left reluctantly backed American defense policies with only minor reservations well into the 1950's. Responding to a plea by A. J. Muste for America to take a "unilateral initiative" in disarmament, Norman Thomas replied: "Repeatedly men have been forced to use clumsy and self-defeating tools in their struggles for a larger measure of freedom and justice. I desperately want to avoid war," he wrote, "but for America to avoid war simply by surrender to communism would in no way avoid the ultimate violence" of "Stalin's imperialist communism." Muste responded that Thomas and other radicals failed "to make a real effort to determine whether non-violent resistance would not be at least as effective and much less costly" than nuclear war. In addition, the pacifist leader remarked, "you now have to condone the use of more and more destructive and diabolical weapons," as well as "get involved in a situation where unwillingly you seem to . . . play the game of the reactionary interests in the United States and elsewhere." Thomas sadly answered: "The dilemma which you describe is very real." [19]

Like the more traditional pacifists, radical pacifists continued their activities in a greatly reduced form. Non-registration for the draft persisted as the favored approach to conscription for a few young

---

[18] "More Birthday Messages," *The Federalist*, I (March, 1952), 7; Norman Cousins, "The H-Bomb and World Federalism," *The Federalist*, II (January, 1953), 15. For the support of world federalism in the Fifties by conservative business elements, see the dozens of letters from Midwestern businessmen enclosed in: C. A. McElvain to Douglas MacArthur, July 5, 1951, SCAP MSS, Box 38.

[19] Fleischman, *Norman Thomas*, pp. 250-66; Norman Thomas to A. J. Muste, January 15, 1951, A. J. Muste to Norman Thomas, February 19, 1951, Norman Thomas to A. J. Muste, February 21, 1951, Thomas MSS, Box 62.

men of radical libertarian ideas. An issue of *Alternative*, the pacifist-anarchist periodical banned from the mails during the Korean War by the New York postmaster for "advocating or urging treason, insurrection or forcible resistance to . . . [the] law of the United States," told the reader to "become an open non violent resister"; "REFUSE TO BE DRAFTED!" its editors proclaimed. Abandoning the policy it had pursued during World War II, the A.F.S.C. declined to serve as an "approved" employer of C.O.'s in the early Fifties. On the other hand, despite the official shift in Quaker policy, most pacifists continued to accept alternative service.[20]

Throughout these years the Catholic Worker organization served as the center of a unique brand of anarchist pacifism. Robert Ludlow, whom Dorothy Day called the "theorist of our pacifism," contended that rather than submit to "government by *representation*," the "*whole* people composing a community should take care of what governing is to be done." Sometimes outsiders found this combination of anarchism and pacifism confusing. Ammon Hennacy, recalling his questioning by a police captain, commented afterward: "He thought that anarchists were bomb-throwers and killers. I told him the biggest bomb-thrower was the government." Although devoting the bulk of their time, as always, to the maintenance of their Houses of Hospitality for the poor, Catholic Workers remained militant bearers of the peace testimony. "If the history of the world has taught us anything," wrote the young editor of the *Catholic Worker*, Michael Harrington, "it is that . . . war itself cannot be justified." [21]

In the repressive climate of the Fifties some pacifists perceived a special virtue in the "resistance" ethos. "I am paying 50 per cent of my 1952 income tax and sending the balance to people who will buy something fit for human consumption with it," announced Milton Mayer. "Like every other horror-stricken American," he noted, "I

20 *The Non-Cooperator and the Draft*, p. 10; news release on *Alternative* (November 15, 1950), Allen MSS, Section C4, Box 8; *Alternative*, III (September–October, 1950), Allen MSS, Section C4, Box 8; George Loft to Norman Thomas, September 30, 1952, Thomas MSS, Box 63; Muste, "Of Holy Disobedience," p. 4.

21 Day, *The Long Loneliness*, pp. 259–63; Hennacy, *Autobiography of a Catholic Anarchist*, p. 202; Michael Harrington, "The Catholic Church Rethinks War," *Fellowship*, XX (June, 1954), 10.

keep asking myself, 'What can a man do? What weight does a man have . . . that he isn't using to save his country's soul and his own?'" A. J. Muste found resistance "a necessary and indispensable measure of spiritual self-preservation, in a day when the impulse to conform, to acquiesce, to go along, is the instrument which is used to subject men to totalitarian rule and involve them in permanent war."[22]

Peacemakers, the leading radical pacifist group, sharply declined in the early 1950's. Ironically, many of its troubles resulted from the principled behavior of its members, who carried their militant anarchism to the logical extreme of complete disorganization. The Ohio branch, especially, while particularly active and devoted to radical pacifism, set a tone of permissiveness and total libertarianism that eventually doomed the organization to paralysis. At annual conferences speakers for every conceivable fad wasted much of the group's meeting time, while, according to A. J. Muste, "practically anything anybody sent in was printed" in its journal. The organization's helpless drift dismayed many of its supporters; one letter in the *Peacemaker* stated: "Peacemakers . . . suffer from lack of direction . . . ending up with no direction at all. . . . The most dedicated members feel a terrible need for DISCIPLINE." After several years of this type of aimlessness, leading activists such as Muste and Bayard Rustin dropped out of the organization, assisted in their departure by the accessibility of the militant War Resisters League, which had been in the hands of radical pacifists after late 1948. Peacemakers continued its activities but never regained the impetus of its first years.[23]

For the remnants of the peace movement, the choices on election day seemed impossible. A pacifist report on political action in 1952 asked "whether U.S. foreign policy is not essentially bi-partisan, the differences among major party candidates purely technical, each such candidate really a 'war' candidate, so that the vote is a Tweedle-

[22] Mayer, *What Can a Man Do?* pp. 80–81; Muste, "Of Holy Disobedience," p. 15.

[23] A. J. Muste to Art Springer, April 15, 1959, Muste MSS, Box 8; A. J. Muste to Margaret McCulloch, January 16, 1961, Muste MSS, Box 8; personal interview with Dave Dellinger, May 16, 1966; *Peacemaker*, V (June 22, 1953), 4; Olson, "Peace and the American Community," Presentation No. 3, pp. 6–7.

dee or Tweedle-dum." As "the military viewpoint" appeared "very weighty, if not dominant, in *both* parties," the position paper urged the pacifist not to "stultify himself by voting for either." The Socialist Party, virtually nonexistent as a political force, excited little interest. "It is questionable, apart from questions of terminology and general 'ultimate aims,' whether there is a decisive difference between Norman Thomas' position on war and peace and Truman-Eisenhower, or Kefauver, Paul Douglas, etc." observed the pacifist report. "The actual number and the percentage of pacifists who . . . look hopefully toward the Socialist Party . . . has markedly declined." Independent political action appeared hopeless. The F.O.R. contended that "because the nation is involved in a power struggle to which most of the people of the United States are committed . . . a small minority . . . will not be effective." Consequently, while most Americans concerned with ending the Korean War probably voted for Eisenhower, those involved in long-term peace action probably sat out the election.[24]

Anarchist and non-violent revolutionary emphases within the peace movement reinforced this conclusion. Addressing a pacifist conference at a Catholic Worker farm in 1952, Michael Harrington pleaded for support of the Socialist candidate. Ammon Hennacy reported: "He was practically alone among us anarchists. . . . Dorothy [Day] and I and others had gone through that parliamentary stage long ago." Many, like Peacemakers, saw direct action as a more promising route to social change than electoral politics. "The way to vote for peace," argued a Peacemakers pamphlet, "is to act and live peace," rather than simply mark a ballot. It suggested: standing up "for the right of anybody to have his say"; opposing "racial or religious discrimination in your neighborhood"; refusing "to be drafted for suicidal atomic and biological war," to make war weapons, or to pay taxes for these weapons; and going "quietly to work to organize . . . economic life on a basis of cooperation and

---

24 "Report of Subcommittee on Pacifist Political Activity in Connection with the 1952 Elections" (March 3, 1952), FOR MSS, Box 4; "Minutes—F.O.R. Executive Committee, April 26, 1951," FOR MSS, Box 4. For the swing to Eisenhower among many Americans anxious to end the Korean War, see: Louis Harris, *Is There a Republican Majority? Political Trends, 1952–1956*, pp. 22–26, 111–12; Lubell, *Revolt of the Moderates*, pp. 40–43; Coffin, *The Passion of the Hawks*, p. 21.

mutual aid." [25] Such were the politics of midcentury pacifism—and of despair.

From 1950 to 1956, then, the peace movement consisted of little more than a small band of isolated pacifists. "Americans . . . had few organizations to help them act to keep the nation's foreign policy from courting war," remarked an ad hoc Chicago committee. Even the remaining faithful were disheartened by the course of events. "For three hundred years we have professed a way of life which does away with the occasion for war," wrote Clarence Pickett of the A.F.S.C. "Have we been mistaken in believing that a world without war is possible?" Pacifism was "marking time," A. J. Muste told the readers of *Fellowship*. "The movement . . . is in a stalemate." [26]

Yet while the Cold War had relegated pacifism as a social movement to insignificance, it had not broken its intellectual vitality. In the dark days of the early 1950's the best of the pacifist thinkers subjected America's role in the international power struggle to a critical reexamination and, finding it wanting, sought to develop a viable political alternative. The result was an incisive critique of American foreign policy and a revolutionary call to non-violent action.

Pacifist foreign policy analyses in depth began with Quaker attempts to deal realistically and objectively with the Cold War rift that divided the world. *The United States and the Soviet Union*, written in 1949 by an A.F.S.C. working party, proposed a series of diplomatic moves to ease tensions between East and West, on the theory that "attention should be directed to . . . coexistence rather than to the victory of either over the other." Encouraged by the interest its first policy analysis engendered in intellectual circles, the A.F.S.C. published a second report in 1951, entitled *Steps to Peace*.

[25] Hennacy, *Autobiography of a Catholic Anarchist*, p. 274; Peacemakers, "Vote for Peace—How?" (1952), United States Peace Material, Miscellaneous, 1950–1954.

[26] Homer A. Jack, "Action for Peace," *Progressive*, XV (February, 1951), 23; Pickett, *For More than Bread*, p. 388; A. J. Muste, "What Is the FOR?" *Fellowship*, XXIII (January, 1957), 10. Commenting on this period several years later, the *Christian Century* recalled that "it became customary to deal with pacifism only by way of nostalgia." "Men of Peace Return," *Christian Century*, LXXVII (May 18, 1960), 597.

The study group complimented the State Department on a number of policy moves—its support of U.N.R.R.A. and the Marshall Plan, its "repudiation of Chiang Kai-shek, its pressure on the French in Indo-China and on the Dutch in Indonesia, its efforts for land reform in Japan, and its application of Point Four Aid." Nevertheless, the Quaker analysis condemned the fact that "the Truman doctrine of containment and its assumption that military force is the only language understood by the Communist high command has virtually dominated American foreign relations." It based this criticism on politics rather than pacifism. "Our insecurity stems from the rapid expansion of Russian influence, but we should recognize that a major reason for this expansion is the economic appeal of Communism," declared the study group. "A foreign policy aimed chiefly at impressing a handful of men in the Kremlin and subordinating the problems of a billion Asians and half a billion Europeans is a policy which is doomed to failure." As an alternative, the A.F.S.C. called for an end to the arms race, transformation of the U.N. into an effective world organization, and a worldwide struggle against poverty.[27]

Like the Quakers, other pacifists were sensitive to America's failure to develop an appeal sufficiently revolutionary to compete with that of Communism. "The Kremlin is turning too many Americans into Tories," complained Harry Emerson Fosdick. "In one area of the world after another," Americans appeared "as the champions of standpattism against a ringing gospel of social change; whereas the fact is that if we are to beat the communists, we must prove ourselves their betters as pioneers of a juster social order." Pacifist Cecil Hinshaw contended that "the really dangerous advantage Communism has is its eager alliance everywhere with the forces of revolution against feudalism and intrenched wealth." Americans, on the other hand, were too often "defending the very forces and people we ought to be opposing," he added sadly.[28]

[27] American Friends Service Committee, *The United States and the Soviet Union: Some Quaker Proposals for Peace*, pp. 38–39; Pickett, *For More than Bread*, p. 406; American Friends Service Committee, *Steps to Peace: A Quaker View of U.S. Foreign Policy*, pp. 4–5, 9–15, 23–24, 31–64.

[28] Fosdick, *The Living of These Days*, pp. 310–11; Cecil E. Hinshaw, *Nonviolent Resistance: A Nation's Way to Peace*, p. 10. The F.O.R. asked the

The most sophisticated and widely read of the Quaker policy analyses, *Speak Truth to Power*, published in 1955, brought together the loose ends of pacifist thought in a pointed indictment of military power. Within America, noted Robert Pickus, a convert to Quakerism who initiated the study, there existed "considerable agreement" on the "positive requirements" for peace—fundamental attacks upon world poverty, an end to colonialism, the development of world organization, and disarmament. But "though widely discussed, paid almost universal homage by our leaders, and even occasionally embodied in Congressional resolutions, we do not *act* on these constructive policies," he maintained. Instead, economic assistance declined and became permeated with cynical political considerations, the arms race continued, the United Nations languished, unused by the major powers, and the United States supported undemocratic governments dedicated to the maintenance of the status quo. "Why? What is it that blocks our efforts?" Pickus asked.[29]

The Quaker study contended that the answer lay "in the nature and meaning of a Twentieth Century commitment to organized mass violence." The "real enemy," it suggested, "is not the Soviet Union but the false values by which men have lived in East and West alike," among them: "lust for power"; "the violation of human personality and infringements on its freedom and dignity"; "the spreading cult and practice of violence, and the poisonous doctrine that *our* ends justify any means." These were "not evils of which the Communists alone are guilty—they are a part of the main drift of our time." Far from uprooting this pervasive nihilism, the military power struggle exacerbated it and precluded more humane policies. If the United States truly wished to emerge as the champion of justice for the wretched of the earth, the study argued, it would have to throw off its commitment to organized violence. Until that day, "each man has the source of freedom within himself. He can

United States in 1953 to "face the question of whether its own material well-being can possibly rest on arms, or on any sort of monopoly of 'prosperity,' and must not rather be built on a world effort to meet equally the needs of all people regardless of nationality or race." "Statement by Executive Committee, Fellowship of Reconciliation, April 6, 1953," FOR MSS, Box 4.

[29] American Friends Service Committee, *Speak Truth to Power: A Quaker Search for an Alternative to Violence;* Robert Pickus, "Speak Truth to Power," *Progressive,* XIX (October, 1955), 6.

say 'No' whenever he sees himself compromised," concluded the Quaker pacifist. "*Speak Truth to Power* says this 'No' to the war machine and to the immoral claims of power wherever they exist as the essential moral and political act of our time. It calls on all men to say 'Yes' to courageous non-violence, which alone can overcome injustice, persecution, and tyranny." [30]

Cut loose politically from the foreign policies of both the United States and the Soviet Union, American pacifists sought to formulate a political position of their own; in the early Fifties, many began to talk of a "Third Camp." The Third Camp, explained A. J. Muste, entailed neither a third military power bloc nor the "neutralism" practiced by many of the Afro-Asian nations. Rather, it stood for a radical pacifist movement of international dimensions which would work throughout the world in support of the destruction of militarism, the overthrow of colonialism, the elimination of "racial and national discrimination," the abolition of poverty, the eradication of the "New Colonialism" of the United States and Russia, the emancipation of Russians and Americans from "the regimes which . . . exploit them and harness them in the service of global atomic war," and the "liberation of the human person" from those economic, political, and technological forces which "deprive him of his essential dignity and the possibility of self-realization." Third Camp adherents hoped to rally support among pacifists and independent radicals in the West, and especially within the underdeveloped nations, whose leaders often expressed their approval of pacifism and non-violence.[31]

The Third Camp movement, however, never reached very far beyond its intellectual genesis, although as a theoretical construct it proved popular for several years thereafter in radical circles. In October, 1953, a Peacemakers conference drew up a Third Camp proposal, while in November, 1954, a larger meeting, the Third Camp Conference, was held in New York under pacifist and Socialist auspices. Unlike Peacemakers, which stressed non-violence as the

---

[30] Pickus, "Speak Truth to Power," pp. 7–8.

[31] A. J. Muste, *The Camp of Liberation*, pp. 1, 3, 9–11; A. J. Muste, Lecture No. 5 (April 28, 1954), Muste MSS, 1st Series, Box 3. Something of the pacifist attachment to the struggles of the underdeveloped world is reflected in: Sidney Lens, *A World in Revolution*.

central element in the Third Camp position, many Socialists, accepting all other points at issue, disagreed with the pacifist emphasis. As a result, the Third Camp position lost some of its intellectual clarity and became, in *Fellowship's* words, "that common patch of ground on which both pacifists and socialists can stand as they oppose capitalism, Stalinism, totalitarianism, McCarthyism, and the cold war." Perhaps more significant in the collapse of the Third Camp was the failure of the underdeveloped and neutral nations to play the role assigned to them. "We thought," wrote one pacifist, that "the new nations . . . would naturally be free from the faults of the older and more corrupt nations." As this assumption gradually proved incorrect, most Third Camp adherents lost faith in the possibilities of this particular revolutionary alternative.[32]

Ironically, as pacifists turned to theoretical formulations to spur a lagging social movement, a dynamic social movement, led by a young Negro minister, embraced pacifism. In 1950 Martin Luther King, Jr., a twenty-one-year-old student at Crozer Theological Seminary, attended a campus lecture given by A. J. Muste. "I was deeply moved by Mr. Muste's talk," he recalled, "but far from convinced of the practicability of his position." Yet later that same year, a sermon by Mordecai Johnson, the president of Howard University, reinforced King's interest in *satyagraha*. The young seminarian found the message of the address "so profound and electrifying" that he immediately bought a half-dozen books on Gandhi's life and works. "As I read I became deeply fascinated by his campaigns of nonviolent resistance," he noted. "I came to feel that this was the only morally and practically sound method open to oppressed people in their struggle for freedom." However, King admitted, he had "a merely intellectual understanding and appreciation of the position,

32 "Peacemaker Declaration on a 'Third Camp,'" *Peacemaker*, V (October 4, 1953); " 'Third Camp' Concept Still in the Making," *Fellowship*, XX (February, 1954), 24; Olson, "Peace and the American Community," Presentation No. 3, pp. 8–9 and No. 6, p. 2; A. J. Muste to Charles Walker, November 4, 1960, Muste MSS, Box 10. As for the American government, it took a rather dim view of the "Third Camp." When 1000 copies of A. J. Muste's *Camp of Liberation* were mailed in November, 1954, to the A.F.S.C. office in Cambridge, Massachusetts, they were secretly seized and burned by the United States Post Office, which later officially admitted the action. The postal authorities classified the pamphlets as "non-mailable" propaganda. "Muste Pamphlet Burned in Boston," *Fellowship*, XXI (June, 1955), 28.

with no firm determination to organize it in a socially effective situation" when he arrived to assume his first church post in Montgomery.[33]

The Montgomery boycott began on December 1, 1955, when Mrs. Rosa Parks sat down in the third row of a crowded bus. Two stops later several white passengers boarded the bus, and the driver told Mrs. Parks and the other Negroes present to move to the crowded rear of the bus to enable the whites to sit down. Although the other Negroes retired to the back of the bus, Mrs. Parks, tired from her day's work as a seamstress and of her forty years of humiliating submission to Alabama's racial segregation, refused to move. Her arrest set the black community ablaze; the next day and every day thereafter for a year, the city's 50,000 Negroes boycotted the Montgomery buses. An old lady summed up their attitude with her remark: "It used to be that my body rode, but my soul walked; now my body may be tired, but my soul is free." White leadership in the struggle was provided by the Montgomery County Citizens Council, each member of which pledged to "defeat the NAACP, Integration, Mongrelism, Socialism, Communist ideologies, F.E.P.C., and One World Government." Black leadership centered in the Montgomery Improvement Association and its young director, Martin Luther King, Jr.[34]

"The experience in Montgomery did more to clarify my thinking on the question of nonviolence than all of the books that I had read," King remarked. "As the days unfolded I became more and more convinced of the power of nonviolence." Rather early in the struggle, King perceived that the movement was not so much a boycott as "an act of massive noncooperation," and consequently dropped the word "boycott" from his speeches. He told the readers of *Fellowship* that "this is a movement of passive resistance and the great instrument is the instrument of love." Even the rank and file caught the mood. During the trial of their ninety leaders, Negroes in atten-

[33] Martin Luther King, Jr., "My Pilgrimage to Nonviolence," *Fellowship*, XXIV (September 1, 1958), 6–7; King, "Pilgrimage to Nonviolence," *Christian Century*, LXXVII (April 13, 1960), 440.

[34] Homer A. Jack, "Christ and Gandhi in Montgomery," *Progressive*, XX (May, 1956), 25–27. The story of the bus boycott is described in detail in: Martin Luther King, Jr., *Stride Toward Freedom*.

dance wore cloth crosses with the words "Father, Forgive Them," while lapel buttons proclaimed "Victory Without Violence." "We see that the real tension is not between the Negro citizens and the white citizens of Montgomery, but it is a conflict between justice and injustice," King stated at the height of the protest. "If there is a victory . . . the victory will not be merely for the Negro citizens and a defeat for the white citizens, but . . . a victory for justice and a defeat of injustice." The press did not err when it announced that Gandhi had come to Montgomery.[35]

Montgomery represented the turning point for King. He later recalled that "living through the actual experience of the protest, nonviolence became more than a method . . . ; it became a commitment to a way of life." The knowledge that he had uncovered in the pacifism of direct action a force for shattering the nation's racial codes, led the young minister, together with Bayard Rustin and sixty other black leaders from ten Southern states, to form the Southern Christian Leadership Conference (S.C.L.C.) in January, 1957. Electing King its first president, S.C.L.C. called upon all Negroes "to assert their human dignity" by rejecting "further cooperation with evil." Moreover, going beyond the civil rights issue, King turned to what he called "a realistic pacifism," joining the F.O.R. He had come to the conclusion, he wrote later, that "the potential destructiveness of modern weapons of war totally rules out the possibility of war ever serving again as a negative good." King's analysis of the international situation, formerly under the sway of Niebuhr, now took on

[35] King, "Pilgrimage to Nonviolence," p. 440; King, *Stride Toward Freedom*, p. 51; Martin Luther King, Jr., "Walk for Freedom," *Fellowship*, XXII (May, 1956), 5–6; Jack, "Christ and Gandhi in Montgomery," pp. 25–26. Pacifists encouraged these developments. Bayard Rustin of the W.R.L. and Glenn Smiley, field secretary of the F.O.R., spent considerable time in Montgomery working with the Montgomery Improvement Association. Smiley sat next to King on the first integrated bus ride. "F.O.R. Executive Committee Minutes, January 8, 1957," FOR MSS, Box 4; Hentoff, *Peace Agitator*, p. 17; Brittain, *The Rebel Passion*, p. 105. It may be argued, of course, that the Negroes of Montgomery had a considerably less sophisticated understanding of non-violent resistance than King. Yet it seems doubtful that most participants in any mass movement ever attain more than a rudimentary comprehension of its intellectual framework. Surely it is curious to resist describing a Southern Negro as an adherent of non-violent resistance when at the same time accepting a Brittany fisherman as a bona fide Communist or an Indian peasant as a *satyagrahi*.

a pacifist tone. "War is not the answer," he told his congregation. "Communism will never be defeated by atomic bombs or nuclear weapons." Rather, "our greatest defense against Communism is to take offensive action in behalf of justice and righteousness. . . . We must . . . seek to remove . . . conditions of poverty, insecurity, injustice, and racial discrimination." [36]

Pacifists, astonished by their unexpected Montgomery gains of 1955, received further encouragement that same year from a resurgence of restiveness in the scientific community. The "thaw" in the Cold War occasioned by the Korean truce, Stalin's death, and the decline of McCarthyism revived interest in the international control of nuclear weapons among many scientists reluctantly committed to American military policies since 1948. For the first time since the heady, post-Hiroshima days, they commenced a series of calls for an end to war.[37]

The first break in their Cold War silence came with the Einstein-Russell appeal of July, 1955, signed by Percy W. Bridgman, Hermann J. Muller, Linus Pauling, and Albert Einstein of the United States, Cecil F. Powell, Joseph Rotblat, and Bertrand Russell of England, Frederic Joliot-Curie of France, Leopold Infeld of Poland, Hideki Yukawa of Japan, and Max Born of Germany. Lord Russell, at his press conference of July 9, declared that the signatories brought the statement before "all the powerful governments of the world in the earnest hope that they may agree to allow their citizens to survive." The text, drawn up by Einstein and Russell, began: "We are speaking on this occasion, not as members of this or that nation, continent or creed, but as human beings, members of the species man, whose continued existence is in doubt." Acknowledging that the East-West struggle might reasonably engage strong emotions,

36 King, "Pilgrimage to Nonviolence," p. 440; Lerone Bennett, Jr., What Manner of Man: A Biography of Martin Luther King, Jr., pp. 75-76, 82, 97-98; Nat Hentoff, "A Peaceful Army," Commonweal, LXXII (June 10, 1960), 276; King, "Pilgrimage to Nonviolence," p. 441; Martin Luther King, Jr., Strength to Love, p. 100. In early 1957 King was arguing on a sophisticated level for the use of "nonviolent resistance" to solve America's racial problem. See, for example: Martin Luther King, Jr., "Nonviolence and Racial Justice," Christian Century, LXXIV (February 6, 1957), 165-67.

37 Gilpin, American Scientists and Nuclear Weapons Policy, pp. 135-48; Grodzins and Rabinowitch, The Atomic Age, p. 537.

the signers wrote that "we want you, if you can, to set aside such feelings and consider yourselves only as members of a biological species which has had a remarkable history, and whose disappearance none of us can desire." Men "have to learn to think in a new way," the statement contended. "We have to learn to ask ourselves, not what steps can be taken to give military victory to whatever group we prefer," but "what steps can be taken to prevent a military contest of which the issue must be disastrous to all parties?" The appeal concluded on the same humanistic note with which it began: "Shall we . . . choose death, because we cannot forget our quarrels? We appeal, as human beings, to human beings: Remember your humanity and forget the rest." [38]

At the time of the statement's issuance, one of its authors, Albert Einstein, was already dead. In April, 1955, on his deathbed, Einstein laboriously committed to writing his final thoughts on the Cold War. "In essence, the conflict that exists today is no more than an old-style struggle for power, once again presented to mankind in semireligious trappings," he observed. "The difference is that, this time, the development of atomic power has imbued the struggle with a ghostly character; for both parties know and admit that, should the quarrel deteriorate into actual war, mankind is doomed." But despite this knowledge, the physicist charged, "statesmen in responsible positions on both sides continue to employ the well-known technique of seeking to intimidate and demoralize the opponent by marshalling superior military strength." They did not dare to pursue a course leading toward peace and "supranational security," he maintained, since "for a statesman to follow such a course would be tantamount to political suicide. Political passions, once they have been fanned into flame, exact their victims." At this point Einstein's hand faltered, and he wrote no more.[39]

Within a week of the Einstein-Russell appeal, a conference of fifty-two Nobel laureates at Mainau, Switzerland, issued its own statement. Calling on all nations to "renounce force as a final resort of policy," the scientists warned that "if they are not prepared to do this, they will cease to exist." The American signers of this proclama-

[38] New York Times, July 10, 1955; Pauling, No More War! pp. 158–59.
[39] Nathan and Norden, Einstein on Peace, pp. 640–41.

tion included Arthur H. Compton, Clinton J. Davisson, Edward A. Doisy, Joseph Erlanger, James Franck, P. S. Hench, E. C. Kendall, Fritz Lipman, H. J. Muller, William Murphy, Linus Pauling, W. M. Stanley, Max Theiler, Harold Urey, and G. H. Whipple.[40] Scientists had resumed the prophetic role involving the instruments of their own creation.

A final crack in the seemingly monolithic façade of Cold War America developed with the founding of *Liberation* in 1956 by a small group of radical pacifists. *Liberation* in large part represented the maturation of militant pacifism since its genesis in World War II, and consequently took up most of its concerns—utopianism, anarchism, non-violent revolution, civil rights, the Third Camp, and, of course, peace. It quickly became the organ and focal point of what some have called the "non-violent movement" and others have dubbed the "beat peace movement." A logical successor to Dwight Macdonald's *Politics,* it proved even more unusual, for *Liberation* began where *Politics* ended.[41]

The opening editorial in *Liberation,* published in March, 1956, deplored the "decline of independent radicalism and the gradual falling into silence of prophetic and rebellious voices." Despite fundamental shifts in technology and weaponry, "those who should furnish vision and direction are silent or echoing old ideas in which they scarcely believe themselves." What of liberalism and Marxism, the two traditional forces for social change? The editors found much in them to admire. Liberalism had emphasized "humaneness and tolerance" and the "liberties of the individual," while Marxism had broached the "fundamental demand for economic justice." And yet, in their eyes, time had shown both to be seriously flawed. Liberalism had never "come to grips with war, poverty, boredom, authoritarianism and other great evils of the modern world"; its failure to raise the "embarrassing questions" made it "often shallow, hypocritical

---

[40] Weinberg, *Instead of Violence,* pp. 101–102; Pauling, *No More War!* pp. 222–24.

[41] "Jottings," *Fellowship,* XXII (February, 1956), 24; W. R. Miller, "The Mightier Pen," p. 26; Dave Dellinger, Roy Finch, Charles Walker, and Bayard Rustin, "Monthly Magazine Prospectus" (1956), United States Peace Material, Miscellaneous, 1955–date; Olson, "Peace and the American Community," Presentation No. 10, pp. 1–2.

and dilettantish, all too often lacking in fundamental earnestness."
Marxism, on the other hand, had "underestimated the seriousness of
the growth of the State and its emergence as an instrument of war
and oppression"; moreover, as pacifists, the editors did not fail to
note that Marxism took the problem of means rather lightly.[42]

With liberalism and Marxism so hopelessly compromised, asked
the editors of *Liberation,* what remained relevant for a new radicalism? Their answer was as striking as it was vague. "We do not
conceive the problem of revolution or the building of a better society as one of accumulating power," they stated. "The national, sovereign, militarized and bureaucratic State and a bureaucratic collec-
tivist economy are themselves evils to be avoided or abolished."
Instead of seizing the State, radicals would seek "the transformation
of society by human decision and action." The editors declared their
rejection of "the faith in technology, industrialization and centraliza-
tion *per se,* characteristic of both the contemporary capitalist and
Communist regimes." Radical pacifist emphasis would be on "possibilities for decentralization, on direct participation of all workers or
citizens in determining the conditions of life and work, and on the
use of technology for human ends, rather than the subjection of man
to the demands of technology." Such, they predicted, would be "the
politics of the future." [43]

A poll of the readers of *Liberation* in 1959 provides some idea of
their social origins and political views. As usual, the prototype was a
middle class intellectual. Over two thirds of the readers sported a
college degree, while more than half of these had received one or
more graduate degrees. Concentrated most heavily in the professions, *Liberation* readers had "teacher" as their largest single occupational category. They clearly tended toward utopian and radical
views very different from those of the average American. Asked
which they preferred: "capitalism," "socialism," "mixed economy,"
"Communism," or "cooperative communities," about half chose "cooperative communities," with the remainder split primarily between
"socialism" and "mixed economy"; only about 2 per cent chose "capitalism" and 1 per cent "Communism." Most expressed no interest in

42 "Tract for the Times," *Liberation,* I (March, 1956), 3–5.
43 *Ibid.,* pp. 5–6.

political parties, although the favorite choice was "Socialist." Organizational affiliations, in numerical order, indicate a strong pacifist-radical-civil rights nexus: F.O.R., W.R.L., N.A.A.C.P., CORE, Friends, Committee for a Sane Nuclear Policy (SANE), Peacemakers, U.W.F., and the Socialist Party, with a heavy write-in vote for the A.C.L.U.; periodicals read do the same: *Fellowship, Catholic Worker, Progressive, Peace News, Reporter, Nation, Peacemaker,* and *Dissent.* Finally, their social thought tended toward a high degree of tolerance and libertarianism. Readers condemned loyalty oaths and the spanking of children, while defending extramarital sexual relations and homosexuality. Interracial marriage drew only one opponent, and he added: "opposed to all marriage." [44]

Yet despite its best efforts at intellectual innovation and a sudden flurry of activity in 1955 and 1956, the tiny American peace movement was not able to reestablish itself as a social force between 1950 and 1956. All too often it seemed to be talking to itself; only in Montgomery did a social movement flare up for a moment around a pacifist ideal. Politicians continued to pledge their unswerving fealty to the Cold War against the Communist Menace, while the nation girded itself for thermonuclear war with relative apathy. Ravaged by McCarthyism and rejected by many of its closest allies, the barely surviving peace movement failed to stir a ripple in public complacency.

[44] Roy Finch, "The Liberation Poll," *Liberation,* IV (November, 1959), 14–16. Authoritarianism has generally been correlated with jingoism as has libertarianism with pacifism. See, for example: Charles D. Farris, "Selected Attitudes on Foreign Affairs as Correlates of Authoritarianism and Political Anomie," *Journal of Politics,* XXII (1960), 62.

CHAPTER IX

Breakthrough, 1957–1958

> To call an H-bomb 'clean'
> Makes sense and sound divergent,
> Unless it's meant to mean
> The Ultimate Detergent.
> PUNCH, 1957[1]

Beginning in 1957 the American peace movement underwent a revival. Many of the forces active in the immediate postwar period, which had fallen silent with the emergence of the Cold War, returned to the struggle against war, reinforced by recruits from the ranks of the liberals and the previously uncommitted. Although they eventually focused the brunt of their criticism upon thermonuclear weapons, the immediate initiator of the renaissance was the atmospheric testing of the hydrogen bomb.

After the United States government's series of H-bomb tests in the Pacific during 1954, scattering radioactive ash on twenty-three Japanese fishermen, a small group of Americans began to concern themselves with the health hazards of nuclear "fallout." A petition circulated by the F.O.R. urged the immediate cessation of future tests on the grounds that "no nation has the right for purposes of military experimentation to inflict this horror upon innocent and defenseless multitudes"; significantly, non-pacifists such as Lewis Mumford and Norman Thomas were among the signers. Attempting to allay public fear, the United States Civil Defense Administration published a pamphlet explaining that "fallout is nothing more than particles of matter in the air." And while it admitted that these particles were radioactive, it went on to affirm: "RADIOACTIVITY IS NOTHING NEW . . . THE WHOLE WORLD IS RADIOACTIVE." Such clumsy explanations,

[1] Quoted in: "Verse," *Fellowship*, XXIII (November, 1957), 2.

however, failed to calm troubled minds. The Democratic Presidential candidate of 1956, Adlai Stevenson, brought the controversy into the election campaign when he suggested halting nuclear weapons tests. While Stevenson found it a poor political issue in a nation committed to the maintenance of military strength at all costs, the testing question now began to take hold, especially in scientific circles.[2]

Scientific concern over nuclear fallout first made itself felt as a serious force in 1957. In April, Albert Schweitzer broadcast an eloquent appeal to fifty nations to stop the testing of nuclear weapons. "Laugh off this Schweitzer manifesto," the New York *Daily News* advised its readers; it contravenes "the assurances of most nuclear scientists that fall-out from test explosions . . . is not dangerous at all." Perusers of the New York "picture newspaper" received a surprise, then, with the release of a petition in June by Linus Pauling over the signatures of 11,000 scientists, almost 3000 of them Americans, terming it "imperative that immediate action be taken to effect an international agreement to stop the testing of all nuclear weapons." Conservative newspaper columnist and radio commentator Fulton Lewis, Jr. angrily demanded a Congressional investigation of Pauling and his petition, which eventually took place under the auspices of the Eastland committee, but the fallout issue could no longer be evaded.[3]

Startled by this unexpected challenge to their authority, government spokesmen fought back. In an issue of *Life* magazine in early 1958, Edward Teller and Albert Latter, an employee of the Rand Corporation, dismissed the arguments of the scientists' petition,

2 "Stop the H-Bomb Tests!" FOR MSS, Box 28; Eugene J. Rosi, "Mass and Attentive Opinion on Nuclear Weapons Tests and Fallout, 1954–1963," *Public Opinion Quarterly*, XXIX (Summer, 1965), 280–97; Federal Civil Defense Administration, *Facts about Fallout* (1955), SANE MSS, Series 5, Box 3.

3 Gilpin, *American Scientists and Nuclear Weapons Policy*, pp. 155–56; New York *Daily News*, April 25, 1957; Pauling, *No More War!* pp. 160–78; U.S., Congress, Senate, Internal Security Subcommittee of the Committee on the Judiciary, *Testimony of Dr. Linus Pauling*, Part I, 86th Cong., 2d Sess., June 21, 1960; *New York Times*, June 12, 1957. The Senate Internal Security Subcommittee did its best to portray Pauling as a Communist agent. See, for example: U.S., Congress, Senate, Internal Security Subcommittee of the Committee on the Judiciary, *Report on the Hearings of Dr. Linus Pauling*, 87th Cong., 1st Sess., 1961.

never quoted or described in detail, as "at best half truths," which "if acted upon . . . could bring disaster to the free world." Radiation levels from nuclear tests, they argued, "need not necessarily be harmful—indeed, may conceivably be helpful." That March, the Atomic Energy Commission announced that a test ban was not technically feasible, since a recent underground nuclear explosion could be detected at a maximum distance of only 250 miles; some time afterward, following protests by the scientific community, the A.E.C. raised the maximum distance from 250 to 2300 miles. The government position, as outlined by Chairman Lewis Strauss of the A.E.C., was that the chance to develop bigger and better bombs than the Russians outweighed the possible damage caused by the tests to human life. He explained to a correspondent: "We have the choice of a very small risk from testing or a risk of the catastrophe which might result from a surrender of our leadership in nuclear armament, which has been, we believe, the deterrent to aggression since 1945." [4]

The testing of nuclear weapons provided the issue around which the National Committee for a Sane Nuclear Policy eventually developed. In early 1957 a small group of pacifists meeting in New York had formed a temporary Committee to Stop H-Bomb Tests, chaired by Lawrence Scott, an A.F.S.C. executive. On April 30 Scott sent out a memorandum to its members suggesting that the Committee secure a broader base by taking in "both pacifists and non pacifists." Committee members persuaded Norman Cousins to dispatch a letter

[4] Edward Teller and Albert Latter, "The Compelling Need for Nuclear Tests," *Life*, XLIV (February 10, 1958), 64, 66; Gilpin, *American Scientists and Nuclear Weapons Policy*, p. 182; Lewis Strauss to Adelaide Baker, March 29, 1958, National Committee for a Sane Nuclear Policy Manuscripts, Swarthmore College Peace Collection (SANE MSS), Series 5, Box 2. One member of the Federation of American Scientists, after reading the Teller-Latter article, wrote to the head of the scientists' organization: "The degree of perversion and distortion of scientific verity reflected therein are almost unmatched in the annals of science and are incredibly subversive of scientific and professional integrity." He proposed that Teller and Latter be expelled from the Federation. L. L. to Paul M. Doty, March 25, 1958, SANE MSS, Series 4, Box 3. A pacifist was more pleased by the article: "This is good evidence that our efforts have finally 'smoked them out' and that in forcing them to make a reply in as important a mass media publication as *Life*, we have evidence of the effectiveness of our program." Bradford Lyttle to Trevor Thomas, February 6, 1958, SANE MSS, Series 5, Box 2.

to leading non-pacifists concerned with peace work, while Clarence Pickett secured the cooperation of a broad cross section of pacifist groups; their efforts culminated in a meeting of twenty-seven prominent Americans on June 21 at the Overseas Press Club in New York. The aging secretary emeritus of the A.F.S.C. rose to begin the five-hour meeting with the statement: "Something should be done to bring out the latent sensitivity of the American people to the poisoning effect of nuclear bombs on international relations and on humanity." Toward the end of the session, those present decided to form an organizing committee—the Provisional Committee to Stop Nuclear Tests. Psychologist Erich Fromm, however, provided the group with the name it eventually adopted. "The normal drive for survival has been put out of action by present propaganda," he declared. "We must try to bring the voice of sanity to the people." [5]

On November 15 the National Committee for a Sane Nuclear Policy launched its first advertisement in the *New York Times.* "We Are Facing A Danger Unlike Any Danger That Has Ever Existed," the headline read. "In our possession and in the possession of the Russians are more than enough nuclear explosives to put an end to the life of man on earth," it noted, but "our response to the challenge . . . seems out of joint. The slogans and arguments that belong to the world of competitive national sovereignties . . . no longer fit the world of today or tomorrow." Going beyond the "national interest," the statement proclaimed a strong humanist message. "The sovereignty of the human community comes before all others. . . . In that community, man has natural rights. He has the right to live and to grow, to breathe unpoisoned air, to work on uncontaminated soil. He has the right to his sacred nature." If governments violated these rights, the manifesto continued, "then it becomes necessary for people to restrain and tame the nations." The National Committee for a Sane Nuclear Policy called for the imme-

[5] Lawrence Scott, "Memo One—Shared Thinking" (April 30, 1957), SANE MSS, Series 4, Box 4; Lawrence Scott to those interested in the formation of a Committee to Stop H-Bomb Tests, May 13, 1957, SANE MSS, Series 4, Box 4; Norman Cousins to Friend, SANE MSS, Series 4, Box 4; "New York Committee Against Testing Nuclear Weapons," SANE MSS, Series 4, Box 1; *SANE World* (April 15, 1964), SANE MSS, Series 1, Box 1; "A Short History of SANE," SANE MSS, Series 1, Box 1.

diate suspension of nuclear testing and proposed that the "challenge of the age is to develop the concept of a higher loyalty—loyalty by man to the human community." [6]

An ad hoc venture intended by its founders to serve a temporary educational purpose, SANE was not designed to become a permanent membership organization; but the first advertisement, as an organizational report later acknowledged, "started a movement." Within 6 weeks of its appearance approximately 2500 letters, the vast majority of them enthusiastic, poured into the understaffed SANE office in New York. People in all parts of the nation voluntarily placed the full-page advertisement in 23 different newspapers and donated an additional $12,000 to the new organization. As the statement appeared across the country, thousands of people wrote in to ask how they could help or join the Committee. By the summer of 1958 SANE had about 130 chapters representing approximately 25,000 Americans. When delegates from the local groups met in Pawling, New York, to establish a national organization, national leaders still hesitated but found themselves carried along by the enthusiasm of the local chapters. As SANE's Washington lobbyist, Sanford Gottlieb, later observed, the response to the first advertisement "was evidence of a vacuum in the American peace movement." Pacifists alone could not muster the necessary strength, while "world federalists concentrated on very long-term objectives. The liberal organizations were either concerned with domestic issues or so wedded to a military deterrent posture that they failed to challenge the main drift of American foreign policy." SANE "gave anxious citizens from varied backgrounds a single, meaningful issue on which to act—the cessation of nuclear weapons testing." [7]

[6] New York Times, November 15, 1957. Signers of the first advertisement included: Roger Baldwin (A.C.L.U.), John C. Bennett, Harrison Brown, Norman Cousins, Paul Doty (chairman, Federation of American Scientists), Clark Eichelberger (director, A.A.U.N.), Harry Emerson Fosdick, Erich Fromm, Robert Gilmore (executive secretary, A.F.S.C., N. Y.), Oscar Hammerstein II, Donald Harrington, John Hersey, Homer Jack, Lewis Mumford, Robert Nathan (chairman, A.D.A.), James G. Patton, Clarence Pickett, Eleanor Roosevelt, Elmo Roper, James T. Shotwell (president emeritus, Carnegie Endowment), Norman Thomas, Paul Tillich, and Jerry Voorhis (executive director, Cooperative League of America).

[7] Clarence Pickett to Helen Beardsley, November 7, 1957, SANE MSS, Series 5, Box 2; SANE World (April 15, 1964), SANE MSS, Series 1, Box 1; personal interview with Norman Thomas, October 4, 1966; Arno G. Huth,

Yet Gottlieb seems only partially correct in his assumption that SANE served a new constituency, for while it activated many young people and liberals previously committed to the Cold War, it also drew upon the peace movement's more traditional sources of strength. As sociologist Nathan Glazer has observed, SANE "was actually based on a coalition of two major groupings, both of which had their origins in older issues: the proponents of world government on the one hand and the pacifists on the other." Prominent SANE spokesmen like Norman Cousins, Oscar Hammerstein II, and Walter Reuther had all been officers in U.W.F., while SANE's executive secretary, Donald Keys, had been on the U.W.F. staff. Although SANE received little cooperation from the world government organization because of the latter's desire to avoid "eyebrow raising" activities, both groups, as Keys noted, began "on the premise that the time had come when man's loyalty to man must be put first." Moderate and traditional pacifists comprised a considerable percentage of SANE leaders, including Clarence Pickett, who shared the chairmanship of the organization with Norman Cousins, and Robert Gilmore, the director of the Greater New York Council for a Sane Nuclear Policy, although as Homer Jack, later SANE's executive director, pointed out, SANE was "pragmatic, not absolutist." Other veteran peace activists such as Norman Thomas rounded out the new roster of "nuclear pacifists." [8]

"Response to the First Statement issued by the National Committee for a Sane Nuclear Policy, November 15 to December 31, 1957" (January, 1958), SANE MSS, Series 4, Box 4; Donald Keys to J. David Bowen, August 29, 1958, SANE MSS, Series 5, Box 2; Sanford Gottlieb, "National Committee for a SANE Nuclear Policy," New University Thought, II (Spring, 1962), 156.

[8] Nathan Glazer, "The Peace Movement in America—1961," Commentary, XXXI (April, 1961), 290–91; Donald Keys to Bertram F. Willcox, March 2, 1959, SANE MSS, Series 5, Box 23; Donald Keys, "SANE, UWF, and the Future," SANE MSS, Series 1, Box 1; Weinberg, Instead of Violence, p. 4. The response to the first statement also indicated a considerable disparity in SANE's appeal. About 80 per cent of the responses and contributions came from New York, New Jersey, Connecticut, California, Illinois, and Pennsylvania, while no responses were received from 11 states and only a few from 22 others. New York and San Francisco responded well to the advertisement; Manhattan alone contributed almost one quarter of the total funds raised. On the other hand, a full-page advertisement in the Wichita (Kansas) Beacon (circulation 100,000) elicited total contributions of $8. Buffalo, Indianapolis, Minneapolis, New Orleans, Dallas, and San Antonio did not respond at all. Clearly, SANE did not have much drawing power in the hinterlands. Arno G. Huth, "Response to the First Statement issued by the National Committee for

While some Americans rejoiced at SANE's appearance, others greeted it with more typical Cold War reactions. The Reverend Daniel A. Poling, in a sermon at the Marble Collegiate Church in New York, labeled a SANE "March to Washington" to oppose nuclear tests as "hardly a forward march for freedom." The "most insidious and far-reaching menace of atheist Communism," Poling explained, "is its world-wide peace drive which heads now via the road to Washington." The New York *Daily News* adopted a milder approach toward SANE's efforts. "Far be it from us," an editorial declared, to charge SANE's leaders "with consciously trying to do a job for the Kremlin. We merely think that as regards nuclear weapons tests they are as nutty as so many fruitcakes." *Time* magazine, however, implied more insidious intent. After comparing SANE to Britain's Campaign for Nuclear Disarmament (CND), which allegedly believed that "nuclear disarmament will *probably* bring Communist domination, but that domination is preferable to the *prospect* of nuclear war," *Time* concluded: "The folks who listened to the horror stories without listening to evidence on fallout, to say nothing of survival . . . , the religious-minded who doubted that the ends of liberty and peace justified the means of nuclear deterrence, were all stepping up the pressure as the crucial Eniwetok tests drew nigh." Indeed, "it seemed to matter not at all that this was what the sworn enemies of religion, liberty and peace itself were telling them to do." [9]

Like nuclear pacifism, radical pacifism revived with the onset of the testing issue. In June, 1957, a small group of pacifists organized an ad hoc committee, Non-Violent Action Against Nuclear Weapons, to bring *satyagraha* into play against the testing of nuclear

a Sane Nuclear Policy, November 15 to December 31, 1957" (January, 1958), SANE MSS, Series 4, Box 4.

[9] *New York Times*, May 26, 1958; "How Sane the SANE?" *Time*, LXXI (April 21, 1958), 13–14, emphasis added. In a letter addressed to "fellow travelers," one respondent asked: "When will you stupid people realize that the only way to stop testing of atomic weapons is to destroy Communism?" Another disliked the implications of a "higher loyalty to the human community." He asked: "Do you mean that we Americans should surrender our sovereignty to a horde of delegates from barbaric countries to outvote us and take away our possessions?" R. C. to National Committee for a Sane Nuclear Policy, n.d., SANE MSS, Series 5, Box 3; L. F. to National Committee for a Sane Nuclear Policy, November 22, 1957, SANE MSS, Series 5, Box 5.

weapons that summer. Lawrence Scott, who with Robert Pickus and Robert Gilmore had been urging a more dynamic kind of peace activity than that engaged in by the A.F.S.C., became the chairman of the group. On the anniversary of the bombing of Hiroshima, August 6, about 35 pacifists assembled outside the gate of an A.E.C. bomb project in Nevada; 11 deliberately crossed over into military territory and were arrested. This was but the first of a series of dramatic acts of civil disobedience committed under the auspices of the group, which, reorganized in the fall of 1958 as the radical action arm of the traditional pacifist organizations, became the Committee for Non-Violent Action (CNVA).[10]

Perhaps the most engaging and successful of CNVA's non-violent action projects involved the 1958 voyage of the *Golden Rule*, commanded by Captain Albert Bigelow. Bigelow, the former housing commissioner of the State of Massachusetts and a lieutenant commander in the United States navy, serving on three combat vessels during World War II, had been stunned by the Hiroshima bombing of 1945, when he realized, as he later wrote, that "morally war is impossible." Over the next few years this view grew on him, until in 1952 he resigned his commission in the naval reserve one month before he became eligible for a pension. Subsequently, two of the Hiroshima maidens, brought to the United States for plastic surgery, lived with his family, while Bigelow himself became a Quaker and a pacifist. As a member of CNVA, Bigelow recalled the feeling of futility and despair in pacifist circles during 1957. In comparison with the H-bomb, "horror no longer had any meaning. Before the fury of its blasts Coventry, Pearl Harbor, Dresden, Stalingrad, Buchenwald, Dachau, Rotterdam, Guernica, Hiroshima, Nagasaki, Budapest, Algiers, were but zephyrs." The American announcement in September, 1957, of the H-bomb tests scheduled for Eniwetok in the summer of 1958 threw pacifists into deeper gloom. "What can a man do?" asked the former naval captain. "Then . . . spontaneously, intuitively, from the depths of our beings, simultaneously the

10 Young, *Visible Witness*, p. 20; Albert Bigelow, *The Voyage of the Golden Rule: An Experiment with Truth*, p. 24; Olson, "Peace and the American Community," Presentation No. 3, p. 8; George Willoughby to A. J. Muste, October 1, 1959, Muste MSS, Box 15; "Westtown Consultation on Direct Action at Westtown School, September 17–18, 1958," Muste MSS, Box 15.

idea was born. The idea was an act. . . . An act that could not be bypassed, could not be brushed aside, could not be ignored," he recalled. "The idea was to sail a vessel of protest into the bomb-test area."[11]

The *Golden Rule's* crew of four Quaker pacifists made preparations to sail in early 1958. In January it dispatched a letter to President Eisenhower, detailing its plans and adding: "For years we have spoken and written of the suicidal military preparations of the Great Powers, but our voices have been lost in the massive effort of those responsible for preparing this country for war. We mean to speak now with the weight of our whole lives." Bigelow told the readers of *Liberation:* "I am going because, like all men, in my heart I know that all nuclear explosions are monstrous, evil, unworthy of human beings." Upon their arrival in Honolulu, after sailing across the Pacific, the crew was served with a temporary injunction by a federal court to prevent them from leaving for the testing area. After consideration of the legal difficulties, the four pacifists made their decision: "We would sail—come what may." When they proceeded to sail, however, the government stopped their craft, arrested them, and placed them on probation. Undaunted, they sailed again, were stopped again, arrested again, and given sixty-day jail sentences which they served during the remainder of the bomb test period.[12]

In this manner the voyage of the *Golden Rule* might have come to an inglorious end, had it not been for the unexpected arrival of a second ship in Honolulu, the *Phoenix*. The ship's crew consisted of Earle Reynolds, an anthropologist previously employed by the A.E.C. in Japan, his wife and children, and a resident of Hiroshima. The *Phoenix*, built near Hiroshima under Reynolds' direction, had begun its voyage in 1954, arriving in Honolulu at the time of the *Golden Rule* incident after circumnavigating the globe. Intrigued by the local furor, the Reynolds family attended the trial of the pacifists, investigated the facts about fallout, radiation hazards and such,

[11] Bigelow, *Voyage of the Golden Rule,* pp. 20, 22, 45–46; "Summary Information on a Voyage to Eniwetok," SANE MSS, Series 4, Box 4.

[12] Bigelow, *Voyage of the Golden Rule,* pp. 42–43, 115–248; Albert S. Bigelow, "Why I Am Sailing into the Pacific Bomb-Test Area," *Liberation,* II (February, 1958), 4–6; Norman Cousins, "The Men of the Golden Rule," *Saturday Review,* XLI (May 17, 1958), 24.

and discovered to their astonishment that they agreed completely
with the crew of the *Golden Rule*. In protest, they wrote to the
newspapers, the head of the A.E.C., and the President, only to
receive soothing mimeographed replies. "Gradually the conviction
grew," recalled Reynolds, "that we must do more than talk. We must
seriously consider carrying on the work that the men of the *Golden
Rule* had begun." Reynolds, normally a law-abiding citizen and not
a pacifist, contemplated civil disobedience with uneasiness, but the
issue could not be avoided: "We decided to sail." On July 1, 1958,
Reynolds announced by radio to coast guard patrols that the *Phoenix* had successfully entered the nuclear test-zone area. A short time
later, he was arrested and sentenced to a prison term. "The *Phoenix*,
in its trip," he told Albert Bigelow, "*was* the *Golden Rule*." [13]

In contrast to pacifist activities of the preceding decade, these
events caused an immediate furor. Picket lines sprang up around
federal buildings and A.E.C. offices across the nation with signs
proclaiming: "Stop the tests, not the *Golden Rule*." Reynolds, out on
bail, engaged in a speaking tour which included fifty-eight major
talks, twenty other meetings, twenty-one radio broadcasts, and eight
television appearances. "I didn't even try to count the number of
newspaper interviews," the bewildered anthropologist wrote. Irritated government officials hinted at a Communist plot. On one television program the chairman of the A.E.C. told viewers that the
voyage of the *Golden Rule* had been prompted by a "kernel of very
intelligent and deliberate propaganda," which "might run up a sig-
nal which warrants inquiry." Members of the peace movement, such
as the leaders of SANE, were jubilant at the dramatic impact both
voyages enjoyed, and kept in close contact with the participants.
Why did the CNVA journeys attract such attention? Obviously, they

[13] Earle Reynolds, "Forbidden Voyage," *Nation*, CLXXXVII (November 15,
1958), 358–60; Earle Reynolds, *The Forbidden Voyage*; Norman Cousins,
"Earle Reynolds and His Phoenix," *Saturday Review*, XLI (October 11, 1958),
26–27; Bigelow, *Voyage of the Golden Rule*, p. 258; Barbara Reynolds to
Donald Keys, August 5, 1959, SANE MSS, Series 5, Box 21. On December 29,
1960, Reynolds' conviction was reversed by the San Francisco Court of Appeals,
which unanimously ruled that the A.E.C. regulation banning ships on the high
seas was invalid. This decision also applied to the *Golden Rule* case, although
the men had already served their sentences. Reynolds, *Forbidden Voyage*,
p. 281.

made good newspaper copy, but beyond this, as Albert Bigelow has suggested, they appealed to Americans for their simple idealism at a time of governmental and popular cynicism. "These tiny ships," noted the retired naval officer, "said that here were men who cared enough to become involved . . . to risk everything." [14]

Although the lead clearly passed to SANE and CNVA in this period, traditional pacifist groups assisted in hammering away at the nuclear testing issue. The W.I.L.P.F. engaged in petitioning campaigns against the H-bomb tests, gathering thousands of signatures, while the F.O.R. organized conferences of scientists on radiation hazards and supported the work of both CNVA and SANE. Their membership increased only slightly, but their level of activity and enthusiasm soared. "There is a feeling of lift and hope," observed the F.O.R. in 1958. "The achievement of peace has become no simpler, but there are signs that the apathy is lifting, and that we are finding more and more allies in unexpected places." [15]

One of the unexpected places, the academic community, now harbored a budding peace research movement. Although diplomatic historians and political scientists had always accorded international relations a considerable degree of attention, peace research officially began in 1952 with the establishment of a tiny organization of psychologists called the Research Exchange on the Prevention of War. This group distributed an informal newsletter for exchange of information and to encourage research projects. The idea gained a much wider audience, however, when it grew into an interdisciplinary group of well-known social scientists, who began publication of the *Journal of Conflict Resolution* at the University of Michigan in 1957.

[14] Bigelow, *Voyage of the Golden Rule,* pp. 159, 163, 269; Reynolds, *The Forbidden Voyage,* p. 180; Altbach, "The American Peace Movement," p. 58; National Committee for a Sane Nuclear Policy, telegram to a list of political leaders, n.d., SANE MSS, Series 4, Box 4; Donald Keys to Barbara Reynolds, July, 1959, SANE MSS, Series 5, Box 21; Lawrence Scott to Norman Cousins, February 28, 1958, SANE MSS, Series 4, Box 4. A non-pacifist psychiatrist wrote to Lawrence Scott of CNVA: "I find very stirring the voyage to Eniwetok in which individuals are opposing the drift to disaster that threatens all of us. I feel that the crew of the Golden Rule are true Heroes." Elizabeth Cattell to Lawrence Scott, March 11, 1958, Muste MSS, Box 5.

[15] "Members Bring 10,000 Signatures in Appeal to the President to End Nuclear Weapons Tests As First Step in Disarmament Agreement" (July 25, 1957), WILPF MSS, Box 32; John Swomley, "Nuclear Weapons Tests" (1957), FOR MSS, Box 6; "The Only Realism" (1958), FOR MSS, Box 28a.

According to Kenneth Boulding, one of the founders of the peace research movement, it was "not 'pacifist' . . . though it undoubtedly includes some pacifists among its participants. . . . It is inspired, however, by a belief that stable peace is both possible and necessary." [16]

Peace research in the universities was paralleled in the scientific community. As a result of the Einstein-Russell appeal the first of a series of conferences of scientists from both Cold War blocs met at Pugwash, Nova Scotia, in July, 1957, to discuss the problems caused by nuclear weapons. Among American scientists at the Pugwash conferences motives were diverse, but most hoped to bridge the gap between East and West and to rebuild the international scientific community as a force for peace and understanding. Although meetings in later years confined themselves to rather undramatic technical problems, the first Pugwash gatherings evoked an atmosphere of danger and excitement because of the previously forbidden contact. A Soviet scientist jokingly told an American: "If this meeting had been held five years ago, Senator McCarthy would have accused you of being disloyal and you might have lost your job." The American assented but replied: "If it had been held four years ago, Stalin would have had you shot." [17]

As the peace movement reasserted itself the testing issue gave way to an emphasis upon the dangers of nuclear weapons themselves. For some time SANE's leaders had considered expanding that organization's scope. In June, 1958, pondering what would happen if the United States did ban nuclear tests, Norman Cousins had asserted that such an action would "not represent the be-all and end-all of world peace and nuclear sanity. A truly sane nuclear policy

16 Kenneth E. Boulding, "The Peace Research Movement in the U.S.," *Alternatives to War and Violence*, ed. Ted Dunn, pp. 40–51. A few of the works generally characterized as "peace research" are: Emile Benoit and Kenneth E. Boulding (eds.), *Disarmament and the Economy;* Kenneth E. Boulding, *Conflict and Defense;* Morton A. Kaplan, *System and Process in International Politics;* Anatol Rapoport, *Fights, Games and Debates;* T. C. Schelling, *The Strategy of Conflict.*

17 Pauling, *No More War!* pp. 159–60; *New York Times*, July 10, 1957; Grodzins and Rabinowitch, *The Atomic Age*, pp. 500, 537–38; U.S., Congress, Senate, Internal Security Subcommittee of the Committee on the Judiciary, *Testimony of Dr. Linus Pauling*, Part II, 86th Cong., 2d Sess., October 11, 1960, p. 490.

will not be achieved until nuclear weapons are brought completely under control." Consequently, when, in 1958, both the Soviet Union and the United States voluntarily suspended tests and talk of intercontinental ballistic missiles (ICBM's) began to crop up, SANE turned its attention to the threat of nuclear annihilation. In September a national conference in New York City resolved to broaden the aims of the new organization from a nuclear test ban to general disarmament. While contact with Britain's Campaign for Nuclear Disarmament seems to have been very limited, and, indeed, SANE predated the formation of that organization, SANE became in many ways its American equivalent.[18]

Like SANE, CNVA turned its attention in 1958 from testing to the destructive power of thermonuclear weapons. During August of that year pacifists sought to halt the construction of a missile base at Cheyenne, Wyoming. Leaflets handed to workers asked: "How do you feel about helping to build a base for weapons that can kill millions of people?" While "you may have been told missiles are not meant to be used, they *will* be used if the defense department thinks they should be." When local authorities refused the CNVA group permission to enter the base to distribute these leaflets asking workmen to cease work on the missile site, three pacifists sat down in the road in front of the construction trucks. Dragged away by guards, struck by a gravel truck, and arrested by the police, these pacifists, and others who arrived later to follow their example, had little effect on the project and made little impression on the nation. Nevertheless, they signaled the beginning of a period when the custodians of nuclear weapons installations would have to contend with the militant tactics of *satyagraha*.[19]

[18] Norman Cousins to Peter Charlton, June 18, 1958, SANE MSS, Series 4, Box 2; Glazer, "The Peace Movement in America," p. 290; *SANE World* (April 15, 1964), SANE MSS, Series 1, Box 1. For CND's history and relationship to SANE, see: Frank Earle Myers, "British Peace Politics: The Campaign for Nuclear Disarmament and the Committee of 100, 1957–1962" (unpublished Ph.D. dissertation); L. John Collins to Donald Keys, November 19, 1958, SANE MSS, Series 5, Box 3; David Boulton (ed.), *Voices from the Crowd: Against the H-Bomb*, p. 11.

[19] "Six Reasons Why We Ask You to Stop Work on Missile Site Construction," Muste MSS, Box 2; "Non-violent Action against the Cheyenne, Wyoming Missile Base, Report #2," Muste MSS, Box 2; Lawrence Scott to George Willoughby, A. J. Muste, Bayard Rustin, and Robert Pickus, Au-

Non-violent actionists, often urged to "tell it to the Russians," did just that in 1958 during a trip to the Soviet Union. After describing pacifist activities in connection with American bomb tests and missile sites, CNVA members told Russian citizens that "in the name of humanity, we shall continue in every possible way, and at whatever cost, to appeal to our Government to stop the production and testing of nuclear weapons unilaterally and unconditionally." Then, in a challenge to Russians, they added: "In the name of humanity we hope that the Soviet peoples and Government will move a step further than they have and declare that they will not produce or test nuclear weapons regardless of what others might do." According to pacifist accounts, the Russians did not like this sort of talk any more than the Americans.[20]

The growth of "nuclear pacifism" beyond the fallout issue indicates that while some Americans may have concerned themselves solely with the problem of avoiding a dosage of radiation, many others were reexamining the nature of war in light of the development of thermonuclear weapons. This revival of a "survivalist" ethic, moribund since the immediate postwar period, occurred, appropriately enough, when the capacity to annihilate became mutual. Despite the sudden flutter at the obliteration of Hiroshima and the dire prophecies of the scientists, the American people never truly appreciated the possibility of their wholesale slaughter until the Soviet

gust 28, 1958, Muste MSS, Box 2; "Statement by Kenneth and Ellanor Calkins," Muste MSS, Box 2; "Cheyenne Anti-Missile Base Non-Violent Action Project," Muste MSS, Box 2. Strangely, neither sectors of the radical pacifist leadership nor local residents were particularly pleased by the *satyagraha* involved. Some pacifists argued that, unlike sailing a boat through the Pacific, obstructing traffic was an unnatural act, designed to hinder rather than appeal to the conscience of the onlookers through self-sacrifice. Others, such as A. J. Muste and Bradford Lyttle, defended the sit-down in front of the trucks. Considering the fact that they were being made a thermonuclear target by the installation of the base, local residents reacted with great hostility to the demonstrators. According to a newspaper account, one woman told a pacifist at the base: "If you were my daughter, do you know what I'd do? I'd kill you." Victor Paschkis to A. J. Muste, July 3, 1959, Muste MSS, Box 7; Bradford Lyttle to Lyle Tatum, October 17, 1958, Muste MSS, Box 2; A. J. Muste to Victor Paschkis, July 22, 1959, Muste MSS, Box 7; *Denver Post,* August 29, 1958, clipping in Muste MSS, Box 2.

[20] "An Appeal to the Soviet Peoples and Government" (May, 1958), Muste MSS, Box 15; Olson, "Peace and the American Community," Presentation No. 5, p. 5.

Union detonated a series of hydrogen bombs and demonstrated its advanced technology in the field of missiles and rocketry during the middle and late Fifties. Although the Soviet breakthrough in thermonuclear weaponry spurred an acceleration of the American "defense effort," it also cut the other way. Prominent political and military leaders now began to talk about the impossibility of victory in a war that rendered survival unlikely. "There are no alternatives to peace," declared President Eisenhower. Polls in 1946 had found two out of three Americans opposed to a joint Russian-British-American agreement to abolish armaments and military training; in July, 1958, 70 per cent of the nation favored a multilateral treaty on nuclear disarmament. Linus Pauling caught the mood when he declared in 1958: "It is the development of great nuclear weapons that requires that war be given up, for all time. The forces that can destroy the world must not be used." [21]

Beyond the justifiably frightened reaction of many Americans to the politics of mutual annihilation, however, lay a deeper level of disenchantment. *Liberation* rather aptly assessed it as "a sense of frustration and discouragement with the arms race, and with American foreign policy. There is a feeling that something is missing in it, that there is no *hope* in it." After a diet of more than a decade of *Realpolitik*, some Americans began to back away from the glorification of "toughmindedness" which the Cold War had hitherto encouraged. "These test explosions are for 'security,'" wrote E. B. White in the *New Yorker*, "but it would appear from some of the evidence at hand that we are now in the business of buying security for ourselves with the lives and bodies of unborn children and if that should prove to be the case, then I think this is the ugliest bargain I ever heard of. . . . I am ashamed to be part of this race of shrewd traders and selfish security hunters." In a widely read article written shortly thereafter, George Kennan, the architect of America's "containment" policy, indicated his own reappraisal of war. "If we must

[21] Evan Luard, *Peace and Opinion*, pp. 22–24; Curti, *The Growth of American Thought*, p. 766; Chase, *American Credos*, p. 70; Pauling, *No More War!* p. vii. A poll by the American Institute of Public Opinion in May, 1958, found a majority of respondents believing that 70 per cent of the American population would die in a thermonuclear attack. Dr. George Gallup reported that Americans were "in great awe of the death-dealing potential of the hydrogen bomb." Chase, *American Credos*, p. 46.

defend our homes," Kennan wrote, "let us defend them as well as we can in the direct sense, but let us have no part in making millions of women and children and noncombatants hostages for the behavior of their own governments." If this means "defeat," he added in a remarkable statement, "I can only reply: I am skeptical of the meaning of 'victory' and 'defeat' in their relation to modern war between great countries. . . . In any case it seems to me that there are times when we have no choice but to follow the dictates of our conscience, to throw ourselves on God's mercy." By the late 1950's, the defense of the "national interest" had traveled a long way.[22]

Finally, of course, the Soviet "thaw" following Stalin's death gradually undermined the rationale of the Cold War. The accession to power of the comparatively genial Khrushchev-Bulganin team, especially, symbolized Russia's metamorphosis since the grim terror of the Stalinist dictatorship. "The extent of the Great Thaw has taken me by surprise," Dwight Macdonald noted in 1956. Asking whether the change was "seasonal" or "geological," he concluded that it was "geological and that something new has happened." The disengagement from Austria by the United States and the Soviet Union, coupled with the vacuous but pleasant Geneva Conference of 1955, augured a more relaxed relationship between the two superpowers than many had previously expected. However, too much, perhaps, can be made the "Spirit of Geneva"; while it portended significant changes, at the time neither politicians nor the public exhibited markedly different reactions to the Cold War.[23]

After 1957, then, the American peace movement began a slow and unsteady revival, triggered by the nuclear testing issue but moving beyond it to a reassessment of thermonuclear war. To some degree,

[22] "Is There a Pacifist Revival?" *Liberation*, III (May, 1958), 3; *Fellowship*, XXIV (January 1, 1958), 20; George F. Kennan, "Foreign Policy and the Christian Conscience," *Atlantic Monthly*, CCIII (May, 1959), 47–48. Among other things, Kennan asserted: "We must concede the possibility that there might be some areas of conflict involved in this cold war which a Divine Power could contemplate only with a sense of pity and disgust for both parties, and others in which He might even consider us to be wrong." He added: "I cannot help feeling that the weapon of indiscriminate mass destruction goes farther than anything the Christian ethic can properly accept." *Ibid.*, pp. 45, 47.

[23] Eric Goldman, *The Crucial Decade—and After: America, 1945–1960*, pp. 287–94; Macdonald, *Memoirs of a Revolutionist*, p. 314; John Lukacs, *A History of the Cold War*, pp. 113–20.

the new flurry of activity reflected the relaxation of international tensions which followed Stalin's death; nevertheless, it did not rely upon a vitally different view of the Soviet system. Rather, the renaissance in the peace movement drew upon attitudes and modes of action generated by World War II—nuclear pacifism and radical pacifism—which achieved significant expression only with the development of weaponry that represented mankind's final thrust toward annihilation.

CHAPTER X

The Peace Movement Reborn, 1959–1960

Political scientists and politicians . . . have conceived of the realm of politics or power as largely autonomous. . . . It followed that the moral imperative, the "normative principle" of love, operated only tangentially and superficially on political institutions and struggles.

Every problem became one of strategy rather than ethics. How much do you have to give away before you can be practically effective, until finally there isn't anything to give away any more. . . . In one realm this concept of power as autonomous leads to the nihilism of Hitlerism and Stalinism and in another realm to the nihilism of nuclear war and war preparations. . . .

Our *political* task is precisely, in Martin Buber's magnificent formulation, "to drive the plowshare of the normative principle into the hard soil of political reality."

A. J. MUSTE, 1960[1]

Gathering momentum after 1958, the two prongs of the peace movement, non-violent action and nuclear pacifism, reached a peak with the dramatic events of 1960. The growth and development of SANE, the widespread use of non-violent resistance in the quest for peace and for racial justice, and the emergence of a postwar generation committed to new and different values from many of their elders, signaled an end to the Cold War lockstep among sizable segments of the American population. While not in a position seriously to alter government policy, the peace movement by 1960 had been reestablished as a significant social movement.

After 1958 SANE grew rapidly in size and influence. During the

[1] A. J. Muste, "Pacifism Enters a New Phase," *Fellowship*, XXVI (July 1, 1960), 25.

Geneva talks on disarmament it gathered thousands of signatures on petitions urging a test ban, and later held large meetings in Carnegie Hall in New York, Severance Hall in Cleveland, Orchestra Hall in Chicago, Shrine Auditorium in Los Angeles, and elsewhere. Inaugurating peace demonstrations in 1959 patterned after Britain's Aldermaston march, SANE worked in support of Senate Resolution 96, endorsing efforts to secure a test ban treaty. In May, 1960, at the height of its influence and prestige, SANE sponsored an overflow rally in Madison Square Garden addressed by Walter Reuther, Eleanor Roosevelt, Governor G. Mennen Williams of Michigan, former Republican Presidential nominee Alf Landon, and Norman Thomas. "For a moment," observed Nathan Glazer, "it looked as though SANE might grow into a really powerful force in American politics." [2]

But the Madison Square Garden rally served instead as SANE's high-water mark, for almost immediately thereafter it was torn apart by the Communist issue. Within a week of the New York gathering, Senator Thomas J. Dodd of Connecticut took the Senate floor to call upon SANE "to purge their ranks ruthlessly" of Communists. He charged that "the unpublicized chief organizer of the Madison Square Garden rally was a veteran member of the Communist Party," and that "the Communists were responsible for a very substantial percentage of the overflow turnout." While admitting that SANE was "headed by a group of nationally prominent citizens about whose integrity and good faith there is no question," Dodd contended that "evidence" existed "of serious Communist infiltration at chapter level." Then he released the real bombshell in the form of a "personal tribute" to Norman Cousins. "Not only did Mr. Cousins act immediately to suspend" the organizer of the rally, stated the chairman of the Senate Internal Security Subcommittee, "but when he saw me in Washington he asked for the subcommittee's assistance in ridding the Committee for a Sane Nuclear Policy of whatever Communist infiltration does exist. He offered to open the books

2 SANE World (April 15, 1964), SANE MSS, Series 1, Box 1; Glazer, "The Peace Movement in America," p. 290. Telegrams of praise were read at the New York gathering from Senator Hubert Humphrey of Minnesota, Senator Jacob Javits of New York, and Adlai Stevenson. "The Other Summit Conferences," Nation, CXC (June 4, 1960), 482.

of the organization to the subcommittee and to cooperate with it in every way."[3]

The Dodd crusade threw SANE's leadership into a minor panic. Although few Communists belonged to SANE, a sizable group of people had joined the organization, particularly in New York, who reacted favorably to the policies of Communist nations or who thought them worthy of a special loyalty from "progressive" Americans. Alarmed by this influx, several members of SANE's national board had suggested the adoption of a resolution, similar to that of the A.C.L.U., welcoming only those members willing to use a single standard in judging Soviet or American foreign policy. With the onset of the Senate investigation, they hastened to comply with Senator Dodd's advice by purging the organization.[4]

However, SANE's leadership cooperated with the Connecticut Senator to only a limited degree. When informed by Dodd of the subcommittee's secret investigation of Henry Abrams, the Garden rally's organizer, Cousins called Abrams into his office and told the latter that he would defend him against the Senate subcommittee, but first wanted Abrams to tell him, man to man, if he was a Communist. Abrams, prominently active in the American Labor Party and the Wallace campaign, refused to do so, but declared himself not under the orders of any individual or organization; Cousins thereupon relieved Abrams of his post in SANE. Answering Senator Dodd's public statement, SANE issued a spirited reply: "As a matter of democratic principle and practice we resent the intrusion of a Congressional Committee into the affairs of an organization which during its entire life has acted only in accordance with its declared principles." Yet, on the other hand, the day after the release of the Senator's blast, SANE's board adopted a resolution welcoming into membership only those persons "whose support is not qualified by adherence to communist or other totalitarian doctrine." Shortly thereafter, it demanded that chapters in the suspect New York area apply for charters on terms that would preclude pro-Soviet ele-

[3] U.S., Congress, Senate, Internal Security Subcommittee of the Committee on the Judiciary, *Communist Infiltration in the Nuclear Test Ban Movement,* 86th Cong., 2d Sess., 1960, pp. 35–40; *New York Times,* May 26, 1960.

[4] Glazer, "The Peace Movement in America," pp. 292–93; *SANE World* (April 15, 1964), SANE MSS, Series 1, Box 1.

ments. In this manner, and in the firing of Abrams, it cooperated with the Senator, although by no means to the extent Dodd alleged. "SANE has turned over no names to Senator Dodd. It has received no names from Senator Dodd. We have made no commitments to Senator Dodd. No commitments have been made to us," declared Cousins.[5]

Senator Dodd's attack upon SANE cut drastically into its membership, not merely because the leadership deliberately drove some elements out, but because large numbers resigned in protest against what they considered "McCarthyite" tactics within the organization. In his letter of resignation from SANE's national board, Robert Gilmore argued that "SANE could have responded to Senator Dodd's attack with a ringing challenge to the cold war stratagem of discredit and divide, with a clear affirmation of the right of everyone to debate and dissent. . . . The fact that SANE turned down this opportunity is, to my mind, a great tragedy." Stewart Meacham, another A.F.S.C. member on the national board, told Norman Cousins: "We cannot afford to admit the Dodd Committee into our disciplinary procedures. . . . We dare not to allow ourselves to be bullied into giving it a place or a role which it has no right to demand." One month later, Meacham resigned in protest from the board, thereby following Gilmore and Linus Pauling. About half of the SANE chapters in the Greater New York Council, which in turn comprised about half the chapters in the nation, refused to take out new charters and were expelled from the organization. Although SANE survived as the largest and most influential peace group, it was a badly shaken one.[6]

[5] A. J. Muste, "The Crisis in SANE," Liberation, V (July–August, 1960), 10–11; Glazer, "The Peace Movement in America," pp. 292–93; SANE World (April 15, 1964), SANE MSS, Series 1, Box 1; Roy Finch, "The New Peace Movement—Part II," Dissent, X (Spring, 1963), 139; Norman Cousins, Letter to the Editors, Liberation, V (December, 1960), 3.

[6] Robert Gilmore to Board of Directors of SANE, June 27, 1960, SANE MSS, Series 5, Box 11; Stewart Meacham to Norman Cousins, September 14, 1960, and October 18, 1960, SANE MSS, Series 5, Box 11; Stewart Meacham to Erich Fromm, February 6, 1962, Muste MSS, Box 6; Edward Meyerding to Jerome Grossman, December 5, 1960, SANE MSS, Series 5, Box 17; "Resolution Adopted by Executive Committee of the Long Island Committee for a Sane Nuclear Policy at Westbury, Long Island, July 25, 1960," SANE MSS, Series 5, Box 19; Glazer, "The Peace Movement in America," pp. 292–93. A member wrote to SANE's national office: "How could you? Sane people must

Most radical pacifists, especially those clustered about *Liberation,* condemned what they, too, considered a capitulation to McCarthyism. According to A. J. Muste, Cousins "committed a grave . . . error in the way he dealt with Senator Dodd and his threat to expose SANE." Instead of firing Abrams and instituting "loyalty procedures," wrote Muste, SANE should have told Dodd to do his worst. Muste acknowledged the problem caused by pro-Soviet elements in a peace organization, but relied upon a "clear definition of aims as the basic means to sort out those who belong in an organization." Some radical pacifists, however, found the issue more complex. "The government has no right to inquire into the activities of private organizations like SANE," wrote Roy Finch, but "an organization must inquire into its own activities." Thus, while "Abrams' refusal to answer to the Dodd committee was correct," his "refusal to answer to Norman Cousins was *not* correct." Finch suggested that SANE apologize to Abrams for not defending his rights before the Dodd committee, deny the right of the Dodd committee to investigate private organizations, criticize Abrams for "playing the game of concealment with Cousins and his fellow-workers," and reiterate "the point that SANE is third camp" and therefore not the place for Communists. The difficulty SANE encountered in resolving this complex issue, coupled with a heightened sensitivity of radical pacifists to any renewal of the loyalty-security crusades of the early Fifties, left a residue of bitterness and distrust between the two groups that might not otherwise have prevailed.[7]

While the rapidly expanding Committee for a Sane Nuclear Policy suffered a serious, though not fatal, setback in this period, CNVA, in

---

also be strong people. Strong enough to resist McCarthyism even when its name is Dodd, Walter, J. Edgar Hoover or whatever." One reason for Cousins' cooperation with Dodd lay in the fact that he did not perceive the Senator from Connecticut as another McCarthy. Indeed, he noted in one of the peace movement's greater ironies, Dodd "was Connecticut State Chairman of UWF at the time I was national President." R. F. Burlingame to National Committee for a Sane Nuclear Policy, November 10, 1960, SANE MSS, Series 5, Box 11; Cousins, Letter to the Editors, *Liberation,* p. 3.

[7] Muste, "The Crisis in SANE," pp. 11, 13; A. J. Muste to Stewart Meacham, February 13, 1962, Muste MSS, Box 6; A. J. Muste to Norman Cousins, September 24, 1960, Muste MSS, Box 9; A. J. Muste, "SANE and the Abrams Case" (June 23, 1960), Muste MSS, Box 9; Roy Finch to A. J. Muste, June 11, 1960, Muste MSS, Box 9; Glazer, "The Peace Movement in America," pp. 292–93.

particular, and radical pacifism, in general, flourished. In 1959 CNVA sponsored Omaha Action, a campaign directed against the Mead ICBM base west of the city of Omaha. The CNVA announcement of the project declared: "At the Omaha ICBM base—and wherever nuclear war preparations go on—great suffering and nameless torture are being prepared for countless men, women and children in our own country and in other lands. We do not want to see our own people so afflicted. We do not believe that we have the right, under any pretext . . . so to afflict another people." At the missile base, pacifists held a day and night vigil for one week, holding signs proclaiming "END MISSILE RACE—LET MANKIND LIVE." Denied coverage by the mass media, denied meeting rooms in the town and speaking engagements in its churches, and refused permission to talk to the workers at the base, the pacifists decided upon direct action tactics. With a crowd of townspeople, Legionnaires, and television cameramen watching, the seventy-five year old A. J. Muste and two others painfully climbed over the fence and were arrested. Daily, thereafter, groups of pacifists entered the base until most found themselves in jail. Although the judges, perturbed by the sincerity of the demonstrators, gave them suspended sentences, a number of the pacifists violated their paroles to return again to the base, and served six months in the local prison.[8]

Omaha Action was followed in 1960 by Polaris Action, a Gandhian assault on submarines bearing nuclear-tipped missiles. Sta-

[8] "Call to Nonviolent Action against Nuclear Missiles at the Omaha, Nebraska, ICBM Base and throughout the United States" (1959), Muste MSS, Box 7; Young, *Visible Witness*, pp. 5–17; A. J. Muste to Henry Hitt Crame, August 4, 1959, Muste MSS, Box 7; James Waltner, "Pacifist Witness at Omaha," *Mennonite* (August 11, 1959), pp. 483–84; A. J. Muste to Margaret McCulloch, August 5, 1959, Muste MSS, Box 7; "Another Conscience Speaks at Omaha," *Christian Century*, LXXVI (July 29, 1959), 868–69. Once again, peace activists "told it to the Russians." A. J. Muste and Bradford Lyttle used the occasion to write to Alexandr Nesmeyanov, president of the Soviet Academy of Sciences: "Omaha Action is an example of a type of activity to which peace workers here offer resort, namely an appeal to our own government to take unilateral action, to stop making H-bombs or missiles, whether or not the Soviet Union does the same. We wish that in your country some of your peace workers would similarly demand unilateral action on the part of your government." Bradford Lyttle and A. J. Muste to Alexandr Nesmeyanov, April 1, 1960, Muste MSS, Box 14.

tioned in the town of New London, Connecticut, a pacifist delegation from CNVA and Peacemakers made plans to row across the Thames to Groton and board the submarines. The first few times the missile-carrying ships were unaccountably absent, but by late 1960 demonstrators managed to board the *George Washington*, the *Patrick Henry*, and the *Ethan Allen*. Pacifists regularly passed out leaflets to townspeople and to workers of the Electric Boat Company, manufacturers of the nuclear submarines. Unlike Omaha Action, Polaris Action, after several months of effort, began to show results. A number of townspeople expressed sympathy for the demonstrators, while a handful of workers volunteered to give up their jobs if CNVA would find them other employment. Publicity was extensive, particularly with the appearance of the pacifist sloop *Satyagraha* at ports along the New England coast. Perhaps most important, considerable numbers of students from Northeastern colleges participated, receiving their first taste of civil disobedience and liking it. Placed in solitary confinement at the New Haven State Prison for interfering with the launching of a Polaris submarine and later non-cooperation, Victor Richman, a Columbia College sophomore, told a reporter: "I realized I had gone the limit of the punishment they had given me. I knew I could not be threatened any longer by the authorities." [9]

Pacifists utilized direct action techniques, but not civil disobedience, in a silent vigil at Fort Detrick, Maryland, the United States research center for chemical, bacteriological, and radiological weapons, more popularly known as germ warfare. Beginning in July, 1959, at the initiative of the F.O.R., the vigil lasted for two years, with hundreds, perhaps thousands, of participants. Pacifists were curious to know, as the organizer of the project phrased it, "what might happen if we just kept on 'leaning' on the conscience of the community and the nation?" Consequently, demonstrators reported in every day a few minutes before 7:00 A.M., erected their sign—

[9] Barbara Deming, "The Peacemakers," *Nation*, CXCI (December 17, 1960), 471–75; "Who the Pacifists Are," *Newsweek*, LVI (December 5, 1960), 31–32; A. J. Muste to Max Fitch, September 27, 1960, Muste MSS, Box 14; A. J. Muste to Norman Whitney, July 27, 1960, Muste MSS, Box 1; *New York Post*, November 29, 1960.

"VIGIL AT FORT DETRICK: An Appeal to Stop Preparation for Germ Warfare"—and stood silently watching people enter and leave the army center until 5:00 P.M.[10]

Reaction to the demonstration was mixed. Military officers cautioned the army unit at the base about the "Communist outfit" scheduled to arrive, and provided special bayonet drill and other necessary training. During the first few days, troops were kept at a state of combat readiness. One woman told the demonstrators: "I'd support my country no matter what. I'd kill 10,000 enemies to save 10 American lives." On the other hand, a prominent doctor in the local community joined the vigil for a time, commenting: "You people make it hard for me to sleep at night." A number of outside groups made public statements of support. Local citizens found themselves torn over the issue. "I'm a church member and I believe in peace," one worker at the base told the pacifists. "But I make twice as much now as I ever did, and even if it's blood money it's paying for the house, it's sending my son through college and I give generously to good causes, especially my church." [11]

Pacifists, who had long ridiculed civil defense plans,[12] made this

[10] Charles C. Walker, "The Vigil and Appeal at Fort Detrick," *Fellowship*, XXVI (January, 1960), 12–16; Brittain, *The Rebel Passion*, p. 68; Dorothy Hutchinson, "What the Vigil Means to Me," WILPF MSS, Box 32. An interesting study of government efforts in the field of germ warfare is: Walter Schneir, "The Campaign to Make Chemical Warfare Respectable," *Reporter*, XXI (October 1, 1959), 24–28.

[11] Walker, "The Vigil and Appeal at Fort Detrick," pp. 12–16; "Appeal at Fort Detrick Newsletter" (March 22, 1960), Muste MSS, Box 4.

[12] In 1955 the F.O.R. circulated a list of civil defense definitions, such as:

"DOG-TAGS—Small metal identification tags. . . . If tag is not vaporized, will be used to identify unvaporized remains, if any, by survivors, if any and if interested.

"MASSIVE RETALIATION—The policy under which, if 'they' began the war, you could take satisfaction, in the instant of being vaporized or cooked, in the knowledge that 'our' planes and guided missiles are going to do the same things to 'them' in just a few minutes. If 'we' started the war, massive retaliation would be what was vaporizing or cooking you.

"SHELTER—A now-obsolete hole in the ground in which citizens of a target city were supposed to crouch for protection against air raids."

In 1956, in a parody of civil defense pamphlets, the F.O.R. declared: "If you should happen to survive the attack, be prepared to help. Above all, don't panic, and don't give up the fight. Everyone you know may be dead, your home and business blown to radioactive bits, food and water unavailable, and the whole area too contaminated to sustain life, but don't get discouraged. We shall fight on to victory for our way of life!" Fellowship of Reconciliation,

link in the nation's military structure the target for the largest of their direct action demonstrations. Beginning in 1955 a small contingent of Catholic Workers and radical pacifists such as Dave Dellinger, Bayard Rustin, and Jim Peck had stood in City Hall Park in New York during the annual air raid drill, refusing to take shelter. Every year thereafter, a dozen or more radical pacifists had appeared, committing civil disobedience and serving prison sentences for it. A. J. Muste expressed their attitude when he told the New York State Director of Civil Defense: "Civil defense, after all, is an integral part of the total preparation for nuclear war. We, on the other hand, are convinced that the only way to a secure defense is for people to refuse to participate in any way in the preparations for war." In response to an article in the *Village Voice* and a letter in the *New York Post*, several newcomers arrived to take part in the 1959 demonstration in addition to the usual contingent. When they suggested broadening the 1960 demonstration, the regulars, mostly CNVA activists, agreed and organized the Civil Defense Protest Committee to spread the word.[13]

On May 3, 1960, approximately 2000 students and adults throughout New York City resisted the yearly drill. Ten minutes before the sirens were scheduled to blow, about 500 persons assembled in City Hall Park, with many more arriving all the time. Among those present were writers Nat Hentoff, Dwight Macdonald, Norman Mailer, and Kay Boyle. When the sirens began, police attempted to move the crowd, but this failed to work. Chief Civil Defense Officer Hearn mounted a loudspeaker car and asked the demonstrators to leave the park, concluding: "Come on now, are we all Americans or aren't we?" When the crowd still did not budge, he lost his temper and announced: "You are all under arrest." In fact, the police arrested only 26 people, none of them leaders of the action. The

---

A Sane Man's Guide to Civil Defense: Being a Glossary of Terms Useful for the Citizen Hoping to Remain Unvaporized after the Bombs Drop; Fellowship of Reconciliation, *How to Hide from an H-Bomb.* See also: Fellowship of Reconciliation, *How Will You Look in a Concrete Pipe?*

[13] *Catholic Worker,* July–August, 1955; Day, *Loaves and Fishes,* pp. 160–61; "International Civil Defense Demonstration, June 15, 1955" (April 22, 1955), FOR MSS, Box 4; Hentoff, *Peace Agitator,* p. 7; Robert Stein and Carolyn Conners, "Civil Defense Protests in New York," *New University Thought,* I (Spring, 1961), 81–83.

protest reached into New York schools. At City College about 300 students refused to take shelter, thereby creating that institution's largest demonstration in 10 years. At Queens College 2 professors declined to dismiss their classes and 70 other students refused to take shelter, while at Brooklyn College 150 students withheld their cooperation with the drill. About 500 New York high school students protested in assorted ways; at the High School of Music and Art one student, threatened with expulsion, explained: "It was the only way we knew to let the kids know that hiding under a desk was not the way to avoid getting killed." The W.R.L. newsletter told joyfully of "the biggest civil disobedience peace action" in modern American history.[14]

Yet in fact, the size of the demonstration reflected the new popularity of direct action tactics only in part, for public confidence in the civil defense program was never noticeably high. In March, 1960, Governor Robert B. Meyner of New Jersey told a Democratic Party luncheon that "going underground is no answer." Not only did the survival of human beings seem doubtful, he stated, but "what kind of world would they come up to? What would they use for air? What would they use for food? . . . What would they use for people?" The New York Times concluded from a poll of New Yorkers that they believed "protection against a superbomb at this time is almost hopeless." A Queens accountant observed: "Survival with fallout . . . would be miserable. I'd rather be dead." A Manhattan bank teller informed reporters that he might "run under the bomb and get it over with quickly." For a sizable constituency outside of pacifist ranks, civil defense appeared worthless.[15] Moreover, although civil defense represented a chink in the armor of the "Garrison State," by 1960 a new element served to swell peace demonstrations: the revival of campus political activism.

For the first time in a generation, large numbers of college students began agitating for peace. In April, 1959, pacifist and Socialist

14 Stein and Conners, "Civil Defense Protests in New York," pp. 81–83; "Protest," New Yorker, XXXVI (May 14, 1960), 33–34; "The Next Civil-Defense Drill," Nation, CXC (May 14, 1960), 415; A. J. Muste to Henry Stroup, May 4, 1960, Muste MSS, Box 3; Committee for Non-Violent Action Bulletin (May 20, 1960); A. J. Muste to André Trocmé, May 4, 1960, Muste MSS, Box 10; Hentoff, Peace Agitator, pp. 4–5.
15 Melman, The Peace Race, pp. 35–36; New York Times, September 2, 1961.

students in the Midwest organized the Student Peace Union, (S.P.U.), which emerged by 1960 with 5000 members and 12,000 subscribers to its *Bulletin*. According to its statement of purpose, the members of S.P.U. believed that "war can no longer successfully be used to settle international disputes and that neither human freedom nor the human race itself can endure in a world committed to militarism." They announced their intention of acting "independently of the existing power blocs" and of seeking "new and creative means of achieving a free and peaceful society." Such groups as TOCSIN at Harvard and SLATE at Berkeley assisted in rallying the peace forces on the campus, as did the student division of SANE. In May, 1960, a peace petition initiated by S.P.U. gathered 10,000 signatures on college campuses within a month. At Berkeley 3000 students turned out for a series of speeches in behalf of peace. In December over 1000 students demonstrated for peace and disarmament at Harvard.[16]

Pacifist sentiments appear to have had a considerable influence among American college students. A study of 1200 students in 16 colleges and universities found that 6 per cent favored unilateral disarmament and an additional 17 per cent reported that war was against their moral principles. The authors of the study concluded that about one fourth—a minority, although a sizable one—"could be considered as pacifistic." On the other hand, 44 per cent believed pacifist demonstrations harmful to the best interests of the American people. Perhaps most revealing, however, was the fact that only 54 per cent thought pacifism "not a practical philosophy in the world today." The authors concluded correctly that although students generally rejected pacifism, they "take pacifism seriously as an alternative approach." In this respect, young people broke sharply with previous generations. "The observers have been wagging their heads for a long time over the 'apathy' of the 'silent generation' of college youth," declared a F.O.R. editorial in 1960. "But what of now? What has suddenly happened to this silent generation?"[17]

[16] Ken Calkins, "The Student Peace Union," *Fellowship*, XXVI (March 1, 1960), 5–7; "Student Peace Groups," *New University Thought*, I (Spring, 1961), 76–80; Altbach, "The American Peace Movement," p. 65.
[17] Snell Putney and Russell Middleton, "Some Factors Associated with Student Acceptance or Rejection of War," *American Sociological Review*,

What, indeed, had happened to the campus generation that surfaced in 1960 to render it different from those that preceded it and from contemporary American society? Perhaps the answer lies in the fact that it had known neither of the great political and psychological crises of modern America—the depression and World War II. While others remembered the hard, lean years of the depression, and took comfort in the wide circle of middle class prosperity, the post-depression generation often found affluence a mixed blessing, and certainly nothing to grow terribly excited about. Freed from the preoccupation with success that characterized so many of the college students of the Fifties, it began to think in broader terms, sometimes of social justice. Discussing student political ferment in 1960, David Riesman remarked: "It is not the most underprivileged who are most concerned about justice and about the future. . . . Those who worry least about having enough . . . frequently show the clearest sense of responsibility." Similarly, unlike considerable numbers of their elders, who tended to analyze foreign relations as a choice of "appeasement" or "strength" with consequences appropriately labeled "Red or Dead," students, especially at the better universities, began to view international politics as a power struggle whose varying shades of gray made one hesitate at war, particularly thermonuclear war. Without the fears of economic and military disaster that haunted the thinking of large segments of elder generations, many youthful Americans began to question what John Kenneth Galbraith called the "conventional wisdom." For many, the revolt in the South marked the end of an uncritical celebration of Americanism.[18]

In 1960 the South's smoldering racial situation caught flame. On February 1, four black freshmen from North Carolina Agricultural

XXVII (October, 1962), 658, 665; "Silent Generation," *Fellowship*, XXVI (May 1, 1960), 3.

[18] David Riesman and Michael Maccoby, "The American Crisis," *The Liberal Papers*, ed. James Roosevelt, p. 45. Although most observers agree that the "silent generation" gave way to a vocal one after 1960, there has been little scholarly probing of the reasons for this change, beyond a discussion of the specific issues involved in renewed agitation (viz., peace, civil rights, etc.). It would not only be interesting to see a comparison of the social values of college students in 1955 and in 1960, but a study in some depth of the factors behind the obvious value displacement.

and Technical College entered the Woolworth chain store in downtown Greensboro, and sat down deliberately at the "whites only" lunch counter. Refused service, they remained seated until the store closed, returning the next day with about seventy other students to repeat the performance. Within ten days, similar demonstrations were held in Durham, Raleigh, Winston-Salem, Elizabeth City, Fayetteville, Charlotte, and High Point, North Carolina. The movement spread rapidly to Virginia, in the towns of Hampton, Portsmouth, Norfolk, Suffolk, Petersburg, and Richmond. Sit-ins, as they came to be called, commenced in Rock Hill, South Carolina, on February 12, and swept on thereafter to Columbia, Orangeburg, Greenville, Sumter, Denmark, and Florence. That same day, demonstrations reached Florida, where Negro high school students demanded service at a variety store lunch counter in De Land; Tallahassee students immediately began a similar campaign. On February 20 sit-ins commenced in Chattanooga, Tennessee, and extended to Nashville. Montgomery, Alabama, saw the first student invasion on February 25. Within a year of the Greensboro sit-ins, over 50,000 people in 100 Southern communities had participated in direct action demonstrations, of whom more than 3600 were arrested.[19]

The movement had sprung up as a reaction to the obviously inferior position accorded the Negro in American life. "For about a week," recalled David Richmond, one of the initiators of the Greensboro action, "we four fellows sat around the A & T campus, talking about the integration movement." On the morning of February 1, McNeil Joseph proposed that they go down to the local Woolworth's in the afternoon to demand service at its lunch counter. That evening, frightened by a rumor that they would be prosecuted for their action, they went to visit Dr. George Simkins, a dentist and president of the local N.A.A.C.P. Simkins, known as the most militant Negro in Greensboro, had heard of a successful attempt by CORE to desegregate a Baltimore restaurant and had read one of the organization's pamphlets. Consequently, despite his N.A.A.C.P. position, he placed a long-distance call to the CORE national office

[19] *New York Times*, February 3, 9–14, 20–21, 23–24, 26–28, 1960; Theodore Leskes, *The Civil Rights Story: A Year's Review*, pp. 3–5; Louis E. Lomax, *The Negro Revolt*, p. 124; Howard Zinn, *SNCC: The New Abolitionists*, p. 16.

in New York. It proved to be a crucial decision. Within a few days CORE field workers were in Greensboro, channeling the excitement of the local movement into Gandhian action.[20] As the Negro revolt spread, pacifists long active in civil rights activities organized and molded the popular uprising against centuries of oppression into a disciplined and courageous program of non-violent resistance.

In fact, CORE and other pacifist ventures in the civil rights field had been expanding rapidly before the breakthrough of 1960. On October 25, 1958, and again on April 18, 1959, Bayard Rustin directed a Youth March for Integrated Schools in the nation's capital, drawing 8000 young people on the first and 25,000 on the second occasion. CORE, which languished in the mid-Fifties with a handful of chapters and an income of less than $10,000, mushroomed dramatically in the late Fifties. James Robinson, the organization's executive secretary, told a national convention: "The year ended May 31, 1959 was the year of greatest development in the whole history of the Congress. The number of affiliated local action groups doubled; national membership doubled. Income more than doubled." He termed CORE's success "phenomenal." Activity in the South, especially, began to show results. In Virginia, CORE worked closely with the Reverend Wyatt T. Walker in planning a "March on Richmond" to integrate the public schools, which drew 2000 people in the rain to the state capitol. "Nonviolence has become the weapon of the South today," a field secretary told the CORE national council. Although the white press largely ignored these events, civil rights leaders sensed a rising militancy. "The time has come for a broad, bold advance of the Southern campaign for equality," Martin Luther King, Jr., declared in late 1959. "We must train our youth and adult leaders in the techniques of social change through non-violent resistance. We must employ new methods of struggle, involving the masses of the people." Three months later, the sit-ins rent the fabric of the "Southern way of life." [21]

[20] Zinn, SNCC, p. 16; New York Times, February 15, 1960; Lomax, The Negro Revolt, pp. 122–23; Oppenheimer and Lakey, A Manual for Direct Action, pp. 10–11.

[21] Oppenheimer and Lakey, A Manual for Direct Action, pp. 9–10; James R. Robinson, "Report to CORE Members and Friends" (July 21, 1959), CORE MSS; James R. Robinson, "Executive Secretary's Report to the 1959 Conven-

When the sit-ins began, as Jim Peck noted, "CORE placed its entire resources behind the student movement." It dispatched its two field secretaries to work with the students in Greensboro and in other towns where the sit-ins followed, while it mobilized its chapters and affiliated groups in the South to engage in sit-ins. In the North CORE organized picketing of Woolworth's, distributing over two million leaflets asking people to assist the Southern movement by boycotting the dime store chain. At the height of the campaign, picket lines were thrown up around all of the stores in the Los Angeles and Boston areas, while eighty-six stores in the New York area were picketed simultaneously. In the South CORE held classes in non-violent resistance and organized demonstrations. At Orangeburg, South Carolina, CORE instructed students of two local colleges for several days, then sent them out on February 25 for a series of sit-ins that closed all the lunch counters in the downtown area and produced a mass march of one thousand students through the startled Southern community.[22]

Throughout the nation pacifists played key roles in the struggle. Martin Luther King, Jr., Bayard Rustin, James Farmer, and Ralph Abernathy directed hundreds of demonstrations. Typical of many of the new breed of civil rights activists with a Gandhian approach was the Reverend James Lawson, who served a year in jail as a C.O. during the Korean War before becoming Southern secretary of the F.O.R. A member of Martin Luther King's S.C.L.C., Lawson masterminded the Nashville sit-ins, an activity which earned him expulsion from the divinity school of Vanderbilt University. Other F.O.R. officers active in the sit-ins, besides King and Lawson, included Glenn Smiley and Charles Walker, both dispatched to the South for emergency work. Thanks to the efforts of such seasoned radical pacifists, the Southern Negro explosion attained a rare combination of gentleness and militancy. The Reverend Fred L. Shuttlesworth

---

tion, June 17–19, 1959," Muste MSS, Box 3; Gordon R. Carey, "Report of Field Secretary" (February 21–22, 1959), Muste MSS, Box 3; Bennett, *What Manner of Man*, p. 113.

[22] Peck, *Cracking the Color Line*, pp. 26–27; James R. Robinson, "Report to CORE Members and Friends (CORE Year, June 1, 1959, to May 31, 1960)," Muste MSS, Box 3; Gordon R. Carey, "Report to the 1960 Conference-Convention," Muste MSS, Box 3; Zinn, *SNCC*, pp. 23–24.

told a packed meeting in a Greensboro church to "go to jail with Jesus" and "remove the dead albatross of segregation that makes America stink in the eyes of the world." However wrong Southern whites were on other issues, they hit upon an element of truth when they blamed "outside agitators" for much in the new tone of Southern race relations.[23]

With the success of the Southern movement, civil rights organizations such as CORE ceased to serve as adjuncts of pacifist groups, but grew into powerful independent entities. By mid-1960 CORE's staff tripled, while the number of local CORE groups jumped to fifty, of which only five were three years old. In 1961 its budget stood at almost a quarter of a million dollars. In addition, a second and entirely new organization evolved from the sit-ins—the Student Non-Violent Coordinating Committee (S.N.C.C.). Fearing that the sit-ins would die out without effective coordination between student groups, officials of the S.C.L.C. financed a meeting at Shaw University in Raleigh, North Carolina, during April, 1960. Two hundred delegates attended the conference from fifty-eight Southern communities in twelve states. In the keynote address, Martin Luther King, Jr., urged "the creation of the beloved community" through development of a vigorous program of non-violent resistance. The delegates voted to form S.N.C.C., whose first statement of principles read appropriately: "We affirm the philosophy or religious ideal of nonviolence as the fundamental of our purpose. The presupposition of our faith and the manner of our action . . . seeks a social order of justice permeated by love." [24]

The Southern sit-ins gave an enormous boost to the idea of non-

[23] Brittain, *The Rebel Passion*, p. 104; Ralph Abernathy to A. J. Muste, June 14, 1960, Muste MSS, Box 18; Hentoff, "A Peaceful Army," p. 277; Zinn, *SNCC*, pp. 21–22; "South Sit-Ins Continue: F.O.R. Staff, Volunteers Active," *Fellowship*, XXVI (April 1, 1960), 1; *New York Times*, February 15, 1960. Some observers claimed that earlier activities by King and S.C.L.C. were "the catalysts for this year's action." Hentoff, "A Peaceful Army," pp. 276–77.

[24] Gordon R. Carey, "Report to the 1960 Conference-Convention," Muste MSS, Box 3; James Farmer to Contributors, April, 1961, CORE MSS; Zinn, *SNCC*, pp. 32–37; L. Bennett, *What Manner of Man*, pp. 113–14; Robert Brookins Gore, "Nonviolence," *The Angry Black South*, ed. Glenford E. Mitchell and William H. Peace III, p. 147. The depth of S.N.C.C.'s initial commitment to pacifism is open to some question. Although it accepted nonviolent resistance as a means, S.N.C.C.'s interests, as exemplified by those of most of the Raleigh delegates, seemed confined to the race issue. On this issue, see: Ted Dienstfrey, "Conference on the Sit-Ins," *Commentary*, XXIX (June, 1960), 526.

violent resistance, applied for the first time in the United States on a mass scale. "Behind the bars for Freedom!" exulted James Farmer. "Here we have an idea whose time has come." After years of largely unrequited efforts in the fields of civil rights and peace action, pacifists had secured an enormous victory, not only for racial equality, but for a new type of revolution, for justice without violence, for Peace and Freedom. "These are great events in the South," declared *Fellowship*, "as important for man's future, perhaps, as anything happening anywhere." [25]

In 1960, like the civil rights movement, nuclear pacifism left the campus and the meeting room to take to the streets in public demonstrations. During May of that year 3000 people joined a march in San Francisco to end the arms race, culminating in a public rally at Union Square, while in New York some 5000 peace activists took part in a late evening parade after the SANE Garden rally. In July pacifist groups in Los Angeles sponsored a "Walk for Disarmament," which drew some 2500 to 3000 persons. On August 7, despite the SANE collapse in New York, 3000 demonstrators arrived at the United Nations to call for "nuclear disarmament on the fifteenth anniversary of the atom bombing of Hiroshima." Signs proclaimed: "Polaris Missiles Defend Only the Dead." For those who had known the desperate days of the early Fifties, the movement looked healthy indeed. "The pacifist movement," declared A. J. Muste, "has entered a new phase." [26]

The militancy of nuclear pacifism by 1960 reflected the continuing erosion of popular faith in the "balance of terror" and its guarantor, thermonuclear weapons. Reinhold Niebuhr now wrote: "Ultimately . . . the arms race must lead to disaster. . . . That is why the old slogans of 'bargaining from strength' and 'arms to parley' and 'deterring attack by the prospect of massive retaliation' have become irrelevant. A fresh approach is needed, prompted by an awareness of the common danger." In an address delivered at the 1959 convention of

[25] James Farmer to Contributors, April, 1961, CORE MSS; "Sit-Ins," *Fellowship*, XXVI (May 1, 1960), 3. For a different and more skeptical view of nonviolence in the sit-ins, see: John Colin Buhner, "The Political Theory of Non-Violence" (unpublished Ph.D. dissertation), pp. 153–85.

[26] "The Other Summit Conferences," p. 482; Ross Flanagan, Memorandum on "Public Demonstrations and Peace" (July 8, 1960), Muste MSS, Box 1; Robert Vogel to A. J. Muste, July 18, 1960, Muste MSS, Box 10; *New York Herald Tribune*, August 7, 1960; Muste, "Pacifism Enters a New Phase," p. 25.

the American Historical Association, Professor C. Vann Woodward of Johns Hopkins University explained that "the underpinnings of logic" which "served historically to justify resort to war as the lesser of several evils have shifted or . . . quite disappeared. Victory has been deprived of its historical meaning." Non-pacifists increasingly found themselves driven to a pacifist conclusion by the prospect of worldwide thermonuclear destruction. "I am in agreement with so much of what you say that I have no adequate over-all answer," John C. Bennett of Union Theological Seminary told A. J. Muste. "For the first time I agree with you that, if the USA did take the initiative along your lines, this would probably be a better policy in terms of prudence as well as in terms of ethical sensitivity." [27]

Moreover, many persons who had believed the threat of Soviet expansion necessitated extensive military defense measures, now began a reassessment of the Russian regime. "I think the policy of 'containment' . . . was the only one possible at the time," a non-pacifist stated in late 1959. "But it's outliving its usefulness." Norman Thomas took a far less intransigent position toward the Soviet government. In *Prerequisites for Peace*, written in 1959, he maintained that "an evolutionary process has begun. The assertion that 'you can't trust Russia' too glibly denies possibilities of evolutionary change from which official communism cannot be exempt." If the Communist leaders might be cynical, they were surely not suicidal, he thought. "Neither Marx nor Lenin, nor even Stalin, could foresee what nuclear warfare could mean. Certainly it is far more reasonable to assume that the Russians, including their dictators, will share our common desire for living than to assume that their talk of coexistence is wholly fraudulent from beginning to end." [28]

27 Reinhold Niebuhr, in an Introduction to Harrison Brown and James Real, *Community of Fear*, p. 5; C. Vann Woodward, "The Age of Reinterpretation," *American Historical Review*, LXVI (October, 1960), 12; John C. Bennett to A. J. Muste, March 29, 1959, Muste MSS, Box 9. In 1960 the biennial convention of the Amalgamated Clothing Workers criticized the Eisenhower Administration for "inadequate and ill-conceived" policies in the quest for peace. It called for new efforts to ease world tensions based upon the recognition that the real struggle was "not for supremacy but for survival." An "unremitting war on inequity and injustice is the only war we want," the union convention added. *New York Times*, June 2, 1960.

28 Chad Walsh to A. J. Muste, November 18, 1959, Muste MSS, Box 2; Norman Thomas, *The Prerequisites for Peace*, p. 39.

And yet for all of its radical action and marches, picket lines and publicity, the peace movement had very little political influence. "A peace movement has . . . come into being in recent years," wrote Nathan Glazer, but "failed to grow beyond a certain limited point. . . . It has made no impact on policy." Although it served as an effective educator in areas which might not otherwise receive public discussion, few political leaders took it very seriously, except perhaps as an occasional irritant. The "tone" of the 1960 election campaign, noted David Riesman, indicated "the fringe position of the pacifist groups in American life." [29] Thus, in 1960, while the cause of peace once again attracted a significant social movement, the prospects for the abolition of war appeared, at best, problematical.

[29] Glazer, "The Peace Movement in America," p. 289; Riesman and Maccoby, "The American Crisis," p. 23. Ironically, the peace movement may have had a very great impact upon the election, although indirectly. In late 1960, as Martin Luther King, Jr., languished in a Georgia jail, campaign strategists for Senator John F. Kennedy worked to develop a position on the matter. Harris Wofford, the former world government prodigy and now the Kennedy adviser on minority affairs, suggested that the Democratic candidate call Mrs. King and offer his assistance. John Kennedy did so, while his brother Robert arranged bail for the imprisoned civil rights leader. Vice-President Nixon, on the other hand, rejected the requests of Atlanta Republicans for a statement. Two days later the Negro pacifist announced that he planned to vote for the Democratic nominee. In the last week of the campaign the Kennedy forces distributed two million copies of a four-page pamphlet playing upon this theme. Democratic Party electoral analysts later concluded that the single most important move by Kennedy in gaining a sizable percentage of the Negro vote —considerably larger than Stevenson had received in 1956—was his call to Mrs. King. On December 13 President Eisenhower remarked ruefully that a "couple of phone calls" won the Negro vote for the Democratic Party. As Kennedy carried several key industrial states, such as Illinois, with approximately one million Negroes in Chicago alone, by only a few thousand votes, this 1960 telephone call initiated by a world federalist to a pacifist may have had significant political ramifications. *New York Times*, October 27, 1960, November 27, 1960, and December 14, 1960; L. Bennett, *What Manner of Man*, pp. 118–19.

Epilogue

In the early 1960's the peace movement retained its place in the national spotlight. Nuclear disarmament demonstrations drew thousands of sign-carrying supporters, and peace organizations mushroomed in cities and towns across the country. One of the liveliest of these new groups, Women's Strike for Peace, developed out of an almost spontaneous protest by fifty thousand women, who flocked to the picket lines in hundreds of middle class suburban communities. Peace activists utilized vigils and fasts, trespassed on military property, petitioned uneasy government officials, and ran their own candidates in independent political campaigns. At the colleges and universities student speakers warned of thermonuclear catastrophe, while professors turned their intellectual talents to the creation of disarmament scenarios. The predominant theme of most peace activities was the survival of mankind; "End the Arms Race—Not the Human Race," ran a favorite slogan of Women's Strike for Peace.[1]

Government officials and men of power in American life, although aware of the dissident clamor, continued to place their faith in an expansion of the nation's military might. In 1962, in response to the requests of the new President, John F. Kennedy, the Defense Department budget rose to $50,000,000,000, nurturing armed forces of approximately 3,000,000 men and a nuclear arsenal of 30,000 megatons—1,500,000 times the explosive power of the bomb that

[1] Altbach, "The American Peace Movement," pp. 63–64; Midge Decter, "The Peace Ladies," *Harper's*, CCXXVI (March, 1963), 48–53; "The New Peace Movement," *Nation*, CXCIV (March 3, 1962), 185–86; *New York Times*, November 25, 1961; Barbara Deming, "New Mission to Moscow: San Francisco to Moscow Walk for Peace," *Nation*, CXCIII (December 23, 1961), 505–509; Weinberg, *Instead of Violence*, pp. 4–6. Two of the best-known disarmament programs produced in the academic community during this period were: Charles E. Osgood, *An Alternative to War or Surrender;* Melman, *The Peace Race.*

destroyed Hiroshima. The mass media answered the gloomy pacifist warnings with soothing and highly dubious assurances. On its cover *Life* told anxious readers that in the event of a nuclear attack "97 out of 100 people can be saved." The *Saturday Evening Post* declared in a headline that "radiation from test fallout might be slightly harmful to humans . . . or slightly beneficial." [2]

And yet despite the Kennedy Administration's reliance upon accelerating military preparations, it granted peace activists a number of small-scale victories. Well into the Eisenhower era only two or three lowly officials had handled the State Department's feeble efforts in the area of disarmament, but in 1961 Congress and the President collaborated to produce the relatively powerful, semiautonomous Arms Control and Disarmament Agency. Although disillusioned in later years by the agency's failure to chart a radically new approach to disarmament, many in the peace movement were initially optimistic. Their hopes were raised with the announcement of the American-Soviet accord on a nuclear test ban treaty in 1963. SANE and other peace groups worked feverishly to mobilize public opinion behind Senate ratification, greeting the treaty as the first step toward the defusing of the potentially explosive East-West confrontation. As President Kennedy began to adopt the rhetoric of the peace movement, talking of a "world safe for diversity" and of a "peace race," many peace activists believed that they had achieved a breakthrough at the highest levels of power.[3]

By 1963 peace movement meetings hummed with talk of a "Kennedy opening to the left," and the tide of protest action began to ebb. Many Americans, galvanized into action by the issue of atmospheric nuclear testing, sat back with a sigh of relief after the passage of the test treaty. The peace movement, particularly nuclear pacifists, grew more "respectable" and merged in many instances into the liberal wing of the Democratic Party. SANE, the

[2] Waskow, *The Worried Man's Guide to World Peace*, p. 16; *Life*, LI (September 15, 1961), cover; Edward Teller and Allen Brown, "The Fallout Scare," *Saturday Evening Post*, CCXXXV (February 10, 1962), 36.

[3] Walter Millis and James Real, *The Abolition of War*, pp. 88–89; *New York Times*, September 27, 1961; Waskow, *The Worried Man's Guide to World Peace*, p. 65. Kennedy's American University speech received a very favorable response from peace activists. The text of the address can be found in: *New York Times*, June 11, 1963.

largest, most powerful peace organization, increasingly substituted lobbying and "responsible criticism" for demonstrations, causing much of its grass roots vitality to dry up. Moreover, other areas of struggle, particularly the civil rights movement, absorbed the energies of many peace movement regulars and of a sizable proportion of the idealistic young. Racial and economic issues upstaged thermonuclear war, and Mississippi, at least temporarily, eclipsed the Pentagon as a source of American outrage. Thus, in spite of their apparent effectiveness—indeed, often because of it—peace groups declined in size and vigor; SANE, Women's Strike for Peace, and the Student Peace Union decayed, acquiring many of the characteristics of "mailing-list organizations." [4]

In fact, however, the peace movement had less cause for rejoicing than it believed. By focusing upon the issue of thermonuclear warfare, as it had done since 1957, it was peculiarly vulnerable to a shift in military strategy taking place during the 1960's. President Kennedy had swung away from the Eisenhower Administration's program of thermonuclear confrontation and threats of massive retaliation, but not, as many peace activists thought, as part of a campaign for disarmament. Rather, the President sought to lessen the likelihood of thermonuclear war and at the same time expand the nation's capacity to wage "conventional" conflicts. Secretary of Defense Robert McNamara would no longer rely very heavily upon the nation's thermonuclear arsenal but would utilize counterinsurgency forces followed, if necessary, by a large land army. According to the new rules of the war game, H-bombs were out, napalm was in.[5]

Disoriented by the gradual phasing-out of thermonuclear strategy, the peace movement awoke to the new challenge posed by "conven-

[4] Olson, "Peace and the American Community," p. 429; personal interview with A. J. Muste, June 2, 1966; Donald Keys, "SANE, UWF, and the Future," SANE MSS, Series 1, Box 1; Nat Hentoff, "By Common Dissent," *Commonweal*, LXXV (January 19, 1962), 433–35; "Marching through Georgia," *Nation*, CXCVIII (January 27, 1964), 82–83; Elizabeth Sutherland (ed.), *Letters from Mississippi*; Sally Belfrage, *Freedom Summer*; Zinn, *SNCC*.
[5] William W. Kaufmann, *The McNamara Strategy*. See, also, the relevant sections of: Theodore C. Sorensen, *Kennedy*; Arthur M. Schlesinger, Jr., *A Thousand Days: John F. Kennedy in the White House*; Roger Hilsman, *To Move a Nation: The Politics of Foreign Policy in the Administration of John F. Kennedy*.

tional" destruction after the Johnson Administration's escalation of the Vietnam War. American bombing of villages, slaughter of civilians, and "pacification" programs replaced the hydrogen bomb as the target of the movement's ire; activists argued that from the standpoint of a Vietnamese peasant it was not much better to be napalmed than vaporized. For pacifists, of course, this point had always been clear, but for nuclear pacifists, long concerned with radiation hazards and the survival of humanity, the sudden horror of "conventional" war was felt with a special poignancy. SANE and other prominent organizations shook off their "respectability" and joined the outraged pacifists on picket lines and in protests. Campaigns of resistance to the military sprang up, blocking troop trains, closing down draft boards, obstructing recruitment, storming the Pentagon, and refusing to serve in the armed forces. Massive peace parades involving hundreds of thousands swept through the streets of the nation's cities demanding an end to the Vietnam War.[6]

The size and vigor of the antiwar demonstrations, the largest in the nation's history, indicated that millions of Americans had been jarred out of their Cold War posture. Part of this peace constituency simply represented the returning legions from other areas of endeavor, particularly in civil rights, where they had been less visible. Many other Americans, however, were genuinely new recruits to the peace effort. Some appeared convinced that the nation's social problems were incapable of solution while war and its attendant priorities continued. Others, supporters of the Cold War in its initial phases, found that it no longer served any useful purpose, and thus thought the Vietnam War unnecessary. Still others, repelled by the devastation of a tiny peasant nation, considered the war immoral. Finally, and perhaps most significantly in terms of numbers and

[6] "Battle of Vietnam Day," Newsweek, LXVI (October 25, 1965), 98; "March for Peace," Christian Century, LXXXII (December 8, 1965), 1501; "They March, Doubting They Will Overcome," New Republic, CLIII (October 30, 1965), 9; "Poetry of the Read-In Campaign," Nation, CCII (May 30, 1966), 653–55; "War Comes to the Campus," Newsweek, LXVII (May 23, 1966), 29–30; "No News: SANE Peace Rally and the New York Times," Nation, CCIII (December 26, 1966), 692; Louis Menashe and Ronald Radosh (eds.), Teach-Ins: U.S.A.; "The American Resistance," Liberation, XII (November, 1967), entire issue; Norman Mailer, "The Battle of the Pentagon," Commentary, VL (April, 1968), 33–57.

vitality, the antiwar coalition drew the support of the student movement which had first emerged in 1960, and which had become, by the mid-Sixties, the "New Left." [7]

The New Left, as epitomized by Students for a Democratic Society (S.D.S.) and the Student Non-Violent Coordinating Committee, began with the sit-ins of 1960. To the liberal, middle class students involved in the "freedom struggle," the pattern of racial indignity in the South represented but a temporary aberration in American life—one that the nation, when apprised of it, would readily eliminate. The issues seemed simple and clear-cut: Mississippi was a horrible stain on the national honor, for it harbored widespread poverty, racism, and injustice, while America was the land of promise, equality, and affluence; was it not the leader of the "Free World"? But as these idealistic students sweated with the poor in the nation's slums, endured beatings and assaults by its police, bore the wrath of its government and university officials, and saw themselves denounced by many of their former liberal idols, their assumptions began to change; increasingly, Mississippi appeared as only the exposed tip of the American iceberg. Stepping out of their comfortable, middle class lives, the students viewed the United States for the first time through the eyes of the exploited and the oppressed. To many it was a jolting experience, for they found, as had generations of radicals before them, that the enemy was at home.[8]

The radical perspective of the New Left coincided with a new respect that some Americans accorded left-wing ideology. Always

[7] See, for example, the arguments against the war in: J. William Fulbright, *The Arrogance of Power;* Howard Zinn, *Vietnam: The Logic of Withdrawal;* Staughton Lynd and Tom Hayden, *The Other Side;* Marvin Gettleman (ed.), *Viet Nam: History, Documents, and Opinions on a Major World Crisis;* American Friends Service Committee, *Peace in Vietnam: A New Approach in Southeast Asia;* Richard Goodwin, *Triumph or Tragedy: Reflections on Viet Nam;* *Ramparts Vietnam Primer;* Robert Scheer, *How the United States Got Involved in Vietnam; Vietnam Hearings: Voices from the Grass Roots.*

[8] Although much has been written about the New Left in recent years, there is no definitive work. The following, however, are instructive: Jack Newfield, *A Prophetic Minority;* Hal Draper, *Berkeley: The New Student Revolt;* E. P. Thompson, "The New Left," *Voices from the Crowd: Against the H-Bomb,* ed. David Boulton, pp. 96–105; Mitchell Cohen and Dennis Hale (eds.), *The New Student Left;* Tom Hayden, "The Politics of 'The Movement,'" *The Radical Papers,* ed. Irving Howe, pp. 362–77; Zinn, *SNCC;* C. Wright Mills, "On the New Left," *Studies on the Left,* II (1961), 63–72; Paul Jacobs and Saul Landau (eds.), *The New Radicals.*

liberal to radical on social issues, the bulk of the peace movement had, nonetheless, traditionally eschewed a purely Marxian interpretation of foreign affairs. But when the American government moved to crush social revolution in the "underdeveloped world," a small number of Americans discovered a sinister pattern to events. "Vietnam and the Dominican Republic unmasked for us an obvious aggressive economic imperialism," noted a S.D.S. organizer. On the domestic level, too, the apparent refusal of the wealthy and powerful to accord the poor and oppressed some measure of justice convinced still others of the existence of a deep-knit system of exploitation. Some members of the peace movement now reassessed their position; did the world really need peace, they wondered, or did it need revolution? Formerly pacifist, S.N.C.C. rejected nonviolence and began to talk of "guerrilla war" and "liberation struggles," while S.D.S. canonized Che Guevara, the martyred revolutionary leader. The deaths of A. J. Muste and Martin Luther King, Jr., further served to reinforce a growing rejection of pacifism and the drift toward an ethos of revolution.[9]

Yet despite its internal strains, the peace movement in 1968 reached an unprecedented position of power. Outrage led to protest, protest to a mass movement, and a mass movement to considerable influence in the political life of the nation.[10] For the first time since World War II, large numbers of Americans appeared to consider the "sentimental" pacifists more honest and realistic than the "tough-minded" generals. The sensitivity of the peace movement to the realities and complexities of international affairs at last began to be matched by a corresponding rise in political strength.

[9] Richard Rothstein, "ERAP: Evolution of the Organizers," *Radical America*, II (March–April, 1968), 1; Tom Hayden, *Rebellion in Newark: Official Violence and Ghetto Response*, pp. 63–72; Lionel Abel, "Seven Heroes of the New Left," *New York Times Magazine* (May 5, 1968), pp. 30–31, 128–35; James Weinstein, "Studies on the Left: R.I.P." *Radical America*, I (November–December, 1967), 1–6; Stokely Carmichael and Charles V. Hamilton, *Black Power: The Politics of Liberation in America*; Eldridge Cleaver, "Requiem for Nonviolence," *Ramparts*, VI (May, 1968), 48–49; *New York Times*, May 30, 1968. Much of the New Left's revolutionary zeal is apparent in 1967 and 1968 issues of *New Left Notes*, a S.D.S. journal, and the *Guardian*, formerly an organ of the more sedate Old Left.

[10] "The Power of Political Protest," *Progressive*, XXXII (May, 1968), 3–4; Andrew Kopkind, "The Thaw," *New York Review of Books*, X (April 25, 1968), 3–5.

Conclusion

In 1960 the peace movement commanded the loyalty of a sizable following in the United States for the first time since the halcyon days of the mid-Thirties. But there much of the similarity ended, for by 1960 two fresh developments gave mankind's age-old struggle against war a new perspective—the creation of alternative forms of social conflict and the overarching disaster awaiting humanity should it fail to adopt them.

Non-violent resistance, although a topic of discussion in pacifist circles since the beginning of Gandhi's epic struggles, remained little more than an American pacifist daydream until World War II. At that time the youngest generation of pacifists adopted it as their means of combating injustices which they perceived in their society's racial codes, in the government treatment of conscientious objectors, and in the federal prisons. In the immediate postwar period many of the young radicals entertained high hopes for dramatic social change and non-violent revolution, but their plans came to nought as the nation iced over in the chill of the Cold War. Although they engaged in a number of diverse projects, their efforts bore little fruit until the late Fifties, when they began a series of assaults upon two of the nation's seamier aspects—its military implements for mass destruction and its intricate system of racial injustice. By 1960 non-violent resistance had moved out of the category of Indian esoterica into the forefront of the American struggle against war and oppression.

Like non-violent resistance, nuclear pacifism developed out of the events of World War II—particularly the destruction of Hiroshima —when the potential annihilation of the human race first became evident. Although the "One World or None" concept had its superficial and paradoxical aspects, it nonetheless encouraged many non-pacifists to join the tiny pacifist minority in seeking an end to war. The answer hit upon by most nuclear pacifists, world government, enjoyed a considerable vogue for a time, only to fall victim to the Cold War. Much of the survivalist ethos dissipated after 1950, both because world government appeared increasingly chimerical at the height of Cold War hostilities, and because of the depredations upon the ranks of the remaining stalwarts by the junior Senator from Wisconsin's "fight for America." Only when both sides in the international power struggle brought the prospect of mass destruction one step closer to reality through the creation of thermonuclear striking forces did the nuclear pacifists regain their impetus and élan. The movement now returned to the first thought of the millions who had witnessed the fateful events of August, 1945: "No More Hiroshimas!"

Thus, unlike the peace movement of the Thirties, which disintegrated when confronted with a tragedy of epic proportions, the new peace movement had begun to develop a political as well as a moral relevance. It sought to grapple in the political arena with two of the most perplexing problems of the twentieth century: how to secure a larger measure of justice without betraying humane values; and how to avoid the mass slaughter which advances in science and technology portended.

Yet although the peace movement evolved into something quite different than it had been in 1935, American "defense" policies, as well as those of other nations, continued unabated. In part this reflected the peculiar circumstances surrounding World War II and their alleged "lessons." Many Americans believed that the United States had "tried disarmament" but that it did not work, or that the fight against fascism was the prototype for all wars, while still others in positions of power and influence found comforting aspects in the "Military Keynesianism" that pulled the United States out of the depression and contributed to its prosperity in subsequent decades. Perhaps more significantly, however, the peace movement faced the difficulties that had frustrated it throughout its history: popular beliefs in national, racial, economic, or religious superiority; the power of the State; and the tradition of a resort to violence to achieve one's aims. While the position of the peace movement offered a challenge to both the short-term and the long-term problems which bedeviled it, that position remained one of a minority, without significant access to the levers of power in American life.

As David Riesman has noted, Americans offered two major criticisms of the peace movement.[1] The first, popular within "patriotic" organizations and the poorly educated strata of American society, held that the peace movement was on the enemy's side. This study does not bear out that contention; from the Thirties through to 1960 the peace movement did not sympathize with the social systems or acts of aggression against which the United States military effort was ostensibly directed. On the other hand, it did not conceive of Germans, Italians, Japanese, Russians, Koreans, or Chinese as the "enemy," but as people. Such an attitude is subversive of war in the profoundest sense, and this goes far toward explaining the frequent popular identification of the peace movement with treason.

The subversive onus attached to peace action may also have developed from the curious relationship of pacifism to the political Left—a connection amply documented by this study. Superficially, there appears to be no reason why an opponent of militarism cannot be an economic conservative, a racist, and a foe of civil liberties. And yet this has rarely been the case; any analysis of peace activists finds them almost invariably on the libertarian Left. This coincidence of outlook suggests that pacifists and independent radicals probably share certain attitudes and personality traits: a basic humanitarianism, a crusading fervor, a rebellious anti-authoritarianism, and a sense of historical mission. Moreover, the fortunes of pacifism have been closely linked with those of radicalism. The peace movement has achieved its greatest popularity in the United States in times of liberal and leftist ferment and has suffered its strongest setbacks during periods of conservative and right-wing resurgence. The symbiotic relationship between the two movements belies the genteel, "passive" stereotype of pacifists. Indeed, they have served as a discomforting thorn in the side of middle class complacency.

A second and more serious criticism, often broached by intellectuals, is that the peace movement tended to be "all heart and no head"—well-meaning but naive. Leaving aside the illusions of the

[1] Riesman and Maccoby, "The American Crisis," p. 23.

warmakers, this charge still carries some degree of weight, particularly with respect to traditional pacifism. For example, although it understood the threat of fascism, perhaps better than most Americans, the peace movement reached a hopeless political impasse in the tragic context of the late Thirties. At times such as this, when it had no answer to the Nazi juggernaut but a moral faith, it bore some resemblance to the "sentimental" caricature with which Niebuhr tagged it. Nor is this completely surprising, for as a social cause based upon a moral ideal, the peace movement had an inherent weakness for mysticism and otherworldliness. Like other utopians and romantic radicals, pacifists could skillfully expose the pretensions of the established order and engage it in heroic combat without at the same time posing a relevant alternative.

And yet, between 1941 and 1960, the peace movement proved considerably more sophisticated than is commonly thought. Members of the peace movement were not less "realistic" than more bellicose Americans when they argued that: the bombing of non-combatants was a vicious practice of little military value; America's wartime ally, the Soviet Union, was a ruthless totalitarian state; the bombing of Hiroshima would initiate an atomic armaments race; America's postwar military moves were often provocative; Russia, whatever her flaws, was not attempting to conquer the world; the Korean War was of dubious benefit to the Koreans; America's support of right-wing, anti-Communist regimes exacerbated tendencies toward Communism; a military power struggle eroded domestic freedoms; domestic Communism posed a relatively insignificant problem; the military emphasis in American foreign policy precluded fundamental attacks upon poverty, colonialism, and injustice; nuclear fallout represented a health hazard; civil defense measures were relatively useless; and the nuclear arms race, if not halted, would lead to disaster. It appears that the American peace movement, while not flawless in its assessment of world events, often developed analyses of considerable political astuteness. Moreover, as the history of its two new action thrusts—non-violent resistance and nuclear pacifism—evidenced, it was indeed attempting, however clumsily, to deal with questions of power and its use.

But there is also a sense in which considerations of power harden and generate mechanistic qualities at which the mind boggles: when the cult of "all head and no heart" leads to the State Department employee checking the daily "body count," to the loyal Communist greeting the Nazi-Soviet Pact with the remark that "Hitler's a socialist too," to the conscientious German official finishing off another day of work at the Auschwitz crematoria. There is a point, beyond the power relationships of history, at which men ultimately take their stand. Like its predecessors, the mid-century peace movement took that stand. In a society grown accustomed to the mass extermination of human life, it led the assault on the forces of death.

Bibliography

MANUSCRIPT COLLECTIONS

Allen, Devere. Swarthmore College Peace Collection, Swarthmore, Pennsylvania.

Congress of Racial Equality. Swarthmore College Peace Collection, Swarthmore, Pennsylvania.

Fellowship of Reconciliation. Swarthmore College Peace Collection, Swarthmore, Pennsylvania.

Gregg, Richard B. Swarthmore College Peace Collection, Swarthmore, Pennsylvania.

MacArthur, Douglas. MacArthur Memorial, Norfolk, Virginia.

Muste, A. J. Columbia Oral History Collection, New York, New York.

———. Swarthmore College Peace Collection, Swarthmore, Pennsylvania.

National Committee for a Sane Nuclear Policy. Swarthmore College Peace Collection, Swarthmore, Pennsylvania.

Page, Kirby. Swarthmore College Peace Collection, Swarthmore, Pennsylvania.

Supreme Commander for the Allied Powers in Japan. MacArthur Memorial, Norfolk, Virginia.

Thomas, Norman M. Columbia Oral History Collection, New York, New York.

———. New York Public Library, New York, New York.

United States Peace Material, Miscellaneous. Swarthmore College Peace Collection, Swarthmore, Pennsylvania.

War Resisters League. Swarthmore College Peace Collection, Swarthmore, Pennsylvania.

Women's International League for Peace and Freedom. Swarthmore College Peace Collection, Swarthmore, Pennsylvania.

PUBLIC DOCUMENTS

Morgan v. *Virginia.* 328 U.S. 373. 1946.

U.S. Bureau of Prisons. *Federal Prisons, 1943–1948.*

U.S. Bureau of the Census. *Religious Bodies: 1936.* Vol. I. Washington, D.C.: U.S. Government Printing Office, 1941.

U.S. *Congressional Record.*

U.S. House of Representatives, Committee on Military Affairs. *Compulsory Military Training and Service: Hearings on H.R. 10132.* 76th Cong., 3d Sess., 1940.

——, Committee on Un-American Activities. *The Communist "Peace" Petition Campaign.* 81st Cong., 2d Sess., July, 1950.

——, ——. *Report on the Communist "Peace" Offensive: A Campaign to Disarm and Defeat the United States.* 82d Cong., 1st Sess., April 1, 1951.

——, ——. *Report on the Peace Now Movement.* 78th Cong., 2d Sess., 1944.

——, ——. *Review of the Scientific and Cultural Conference for World Peace.* 81st Cong., 1st Sess., April 19, 1949.

U.S. Selective Service System. *Conscientious Objection.* Special Monograph No. 11. 2 vols. Washington, D.C.: U.S. Government Printing Office, 1950.

——. *Selective Service and Victory: The 4th Report of the Director of Selective Service.* Washington, D.C.: U.S. Government Printing Office, 1948.

U.S. Senate, Internal Security Subcommittee of the Committee on the Judiciary. *Communist Infiltration in the Nuclear Test Ban Movement.* 86th Cong., 2d Sess., 1960.

——, ——. *Report on the Hearings of Dr. Linus Pauling.* 87th Cong., 1st Sess., 1961.

——, ——. *Testimony of Dr. Linus Pauling.* Part I. 86th Cong., 2d Sess., June 21, 1960.

——, ——. *Testimony of Dr. Linus Pauling.* Part II. 86th Cong., 2d Sess., October 11, 1960.

——, Subcommittee of the Committee on Military Affairs. *Conscientious Objectors' Benefits.* 77th Cong., 2d Sess., August 19, 1942.

U.S. Strategic Bombing Survey. *The Effects of Atomic Bombs on Hiroshima and Nagasaki.* Washington, D.C.: U.S. Government Printing Office, 1946.

——. *Japan's Struggle to End the War.* Washington, D.C.: U.S. Government Printing Office, 1946.

BOOKS AND PAMPHLETS

Aaron, Daniel. *Writers on the Left: Episodes in American Literary Communism.* New York: Harcourt, Brace & World, Inc., 1961.

Abrams, Ray H. *Preachers Present Arms.* Philadelphia: Round Table Press, Inc., 1933.

Adler, Mortimer J. *How to Think about War and Peace.* New York: Simon and Schuster, 1944.

Adler, Selig. *The Isolationist Impulse: Its Twentieth Century Reaction.* New York: Collier Books, 1961.

Agar, Herbert. *The Price of Power: America Since 1945.* Chicago: University of Chicago Press, 1957.

—— et al. *The City of Man: A Declaration on World Democracy.* New York: Viking, 1940.

Allen, Devere. *The Fight for Peace.* New York: The Macmillan Company, 1930.

Alsop, Joseph, and Stuart Alsop. *We Accuse! The Story of the Miscarriage of American Justice in the Case of J. Robert Oppenheimer.* New York: Simon and Schuster, Inc., 1954.

American Civil Liberties Union. *The Bill of Rights in War: A Report on American Democratic Liberties in Wartime.* New York: American Civil Liberties Union, 1942.

——. *Conscience and the War: A Report on the Treatment of Conscientious Objectors in World War II.* New York: American Civil Liberties Union, 1943.

——. *Freedom in Wartime: A Report of the American Civil Liberties Union in the Second Year of War.* New York: American Civil Liberties Union, 1943.

——. *From War to Peace: American Liberties, 1945–46.* New York: American Civil Liberties Union, 1946.

——. *In Defense of Our Liberties: A Report of the American Civil Liberties Union in the Third Year of the War.* New York: American Civil Liberties Union, 1944.

——. *In the Shadow of Fear: American Liberties, 1948–49.* New York: American Civil Liberties Union, 1949.

——. *In Times of Challenge: U.S. Liberties, 1946–47.* New York: American Civil Liberties Union, 1947.

——. *Liberty on the Home Front: In the Fourth Year of War.* New York: American Civil Liberties Union, 1945.

——. *Liberty's National Emergency: The Story of Civil Liberty in the Crisis Year 1940–41.* New York: American Civil Liberties Union, 1941.

——. *Our Uncertain Liberties: U.S. Liberties, 1947–48.* New York: American Civil Liberties Union, 1948.

——. *Security and Freedom: The Great Challenge.* New York: American Civil Liberties Union, 1951.

American Friends Service Committee. *The Experience of the American Friends Service Committee in Civilian Public Service.* Philadelphia: American Friends Service Committee, 1945.

——. *An Introduction to Friends Civilian Public Service.* Philadelphia: American Friends Service Committee, 1945.

——. *Pacifist Living—Today and Tomorrow.* Wallingford, Pa.: Pendle Hill, 1941.

——. *Peace in Vietnam: A New Approach in Southeast Asia.* New York: Hill and Wang, 1966.

——. *Peacetime Conscription: A Problem for Americans.* Philadelphia: American Friends Service Committee, 1944.

——. *Projects and Incentives.* Philadelphia: American Friends Service Committee, 1946.

——. *Speak Truth to Power: A Quaker Search for an Alternative to Violence.* Philadelphia: American Friends Service Committee, 1955.

——. *Steps to Peace: A Quaker View of U.S. Foreign Policy.* Philadelphia: American Friends Service Committee, 1951.

——. *The United States and the Soviet Union: Some Quaker Proposals for Peace.* New Haven: Yale University Press, 1949.

Amrine, Michael. *The Great Decision: The Secret History of the Atomic Bomb.* New York: G. P. Putnam's Sons, 1959.

Anders, Gunther, and Claude Eatherly. *Burning Conscience.* New York: Monthly Review Press, 1962.

Bailey, Thomas A. *A Diplomatic History of the American People.* 7th ed. New York: Appleton-Century-Crofts, 1964.

——. *The Man in the Street: The Impact of American Public Opinion on Foreign Policy.* New York: The Macmillan Company, 1948.

Bain, Leslie Balogh. *Chaos or Peace.* New York: M. S. Mill Company, Inc., 1943.

Bainton, Roland H. *Christian Attitudes toward War and Peace.* New York: Abingdon Press, 1960.

Barnet, Richard. *Who Wants Disarmament?* Boston: Beacon Press, 1960.

Beaton, Grace M. *Four Years of War.* Enfield, Eng.: War Resisters International, 1943.

——. *Twenty Years' Work in the War Resisters International.* New York: War Resisters League, 1945.

Becker, Carl L. *How New Will the Better World Be?* New York: Alfred A. Knopf, 1944.

Belfrage, Sally. *Freedom Summer.* Greenwich, Conn.: Fawcett Publications, 1965.

Bennett, Lerone, Jr. *What Manner of Man: A Biography of Martin Luther King, Jr.* Chicago: Johnson Publishing Company, Inc., 1964.

Benoit, Emile, and Kenneth E. Boulding (eds.). *Disarmament and the Economy.* New York: Harper and Row, 1963.

Bidwell, Percy W. (ed.). *Our Foreign Policy in War and Peace: Some Regional Views.* New York: Council on Foreign Relations, 1942.

Bigelow, Albert. *The Voyage of the Golden Rule: An Experiment with Truth.* Garden City, N.Y.: Doubleday & Company, Inc., 1959.

Blackett, P. M. S. *Fear, War, and the Bomb: Military and Political Consequences of Atomic Energy.* New York: McGraw-Hill Book Company, Inc., 1949.

——. *Studies of War: Nuclear and Conventional.* New York: Hill and Wang, 1962.

Bondurant, Joan V. *Conquest of Violence: The Gandhian Philosophy of Conflict.* Princeton: Princeton University Press, 1958.

Borgese, G. A. *Common Cause.* New York: Duell, Sloan and Pearce, 1943.

Boulding, Kenneth E. *Conflict and Defense.* New York: Harper and Brothers, 1962.

——. *New Nations for Old.* Wallingford, Pa.: Pendle Hill, n.d.

Boulton, David (ed.). *Voices from the Crowd: Against the H-Bomb.* Philadelphia: Dufour Editions, 1964.

Bowman, Rufus D. *The Church of the Brethren and War, 1708–1941.* Elgin, Ill.: Brethren Publishing House, 1944.

——. *Seventy Times Seven.* Elgin, Ill: Brethren Publishing House, 1945.

Bradley, David. *No Place to Hide.* Boston: Little, Brown and Company, 1948.

Brewer, William C. *Permanent Peace.* Philadelphia: Dorrance and Company, 1940.

Brinton, Howard H. *Sources of the Quaker Peace Testimony.* Wallingford, Pa.: Pendle Hill Historical Studies, 1942.

Brittain, Vera. *The Rebel Passion: A Short History of Some Pioneer Peace-makers.* Nyack, N.Y.: Fellowship Publications, 1964.

Brodie, Bernard (ed.). *The Absolute Weapon: Atomic Power and World Order.* New York: Harcourt, Brace and Company, 1946.

Browder, Earl. *The Second Imperialist War.* New York: International Publishers, 1940.

——. *Victory—And After.* New York: International Publishers, 1942.

Brown, Harrison, and James Real. *Community of Fear.* Santa Barbara, Calif.: Center for the Study of Democratic Institutions, 1960.

Buckley, William F., Jr., and L. Brent Bozell. *McCarthy and His Enemies: The Record and Its Meaning.* Chicago: Henry Regnery Company, 1954.

Bussey, Gertrude, and Margaret Tims. *Women's International League for Peace and Freedom, 1915–1965: A Record of Fifty Years' Work.* London: George Allen & Unwin Ltd., 1965.

Butler, Nicholas Murray. *Toward a Federal World.* New York: Carnegie Endowment for International Peace, 1939.

Byrnes, James F. *All in One Lifetime.* New York: Harper & Brothers, Inc., 1958.

——. *Speaking Frankly.* New York: Harper & Brothers, Inc., 1947.

Camus, Albert. *Neither Victims Nor Executioners.* Translated by Dwight Macdonald. New York: Liberation, 1960.

Cannon, James P. *Notebook of an Agitator.* New York: Pioneer Publishers, 1958.

Cantine, Holley, and Dachine Rainer (eds.). *Prison Etiquette: The*

Convict's Compendium of Useful Information. Bearsville, N.Y.: Retort Press, 1950.

Cantril, Hadley (ed.). *Public Opinion, 1935–1946.* Prepared by Mildred Strunk. Princeton: Princeton University Press, 1951.

———. *Tensions that Cause Wars.* Urbana, Ill.: University of Illinois Press, 1950.

Carmichael, Stokely, and Charles V. Hamilton. *Black Power: The Politics of Liberation in America.* New York: Random House, 1968.

Carter, Paul A. *The Decline and Revival of the Social Gospel: Social and Political Liberalism in American Protestant Churches, 1920–1940.* Ithaca, N.Y.: Cornell University Press, 1956.

Chapin, Victor. *The Hill.* New York: Rinehart and Company, 1955.

Chase, Stuart. *American Credos.* New York: Harper & Brothers, 1962.

Childs, Marquis. *Eisenhower: Captive Hero.* New York: Harcourt, Brace and Company, 1958.

Clark, Grenville, and Louis B. Sohn. *World Peace through World Law.* Cambridge, Mass.: Harvard University Press, 1958.

Coffin, Tristram. *The Passion of the Hawks: Militarism in Modern America.* New York: The Macmillan Company, 1964.

Cohen, Bernard C. *The Influence of Non-Governmental Groups on Foreign Policy-Making.* Princeton: World Peace Foundation, 1959.

Cohen, Mitchell, and Dennis Hale (eds.). *The New Student Left.* Boston: Beacon Press, 1966.

Cole, Wayne S. *America First: The Battle against Intervention, 1940–1941.* Madison: University of Wisconsin Press, 1953.

Compton, Arthur Holly. *Atomic Quest.* New York: Oxford University Press, 1956.

Corbett, Percy E. *Post-War Worlds.* New York: Farrar and Rinehart, 1942.

Cornell, Julien. *Conscience and the State: Legal and Administrative Problems of Conscientious Objectors, 1943–1944.* New York: John Day Company, 1944.

———. *The Conscientious Objector and the Law.* New York: John Day Company, 1943.

———. *New World Primer.* New York: New Directions, 1947.

Cousins, Norman. *Modern Man Is Obsolete.* New York: Viking Press, 1945.

———. *Who Speaks for Man?* New York: The Macmillan Company, 1953.

Culbertson, Ely. *Must We Fight Russia?* Philadelphia: John C. Winston Company, 1946.

———. *Total Peace: What Makes Wars and How to Organize Peace.* Garden City, N.Y.: Doubleday, Doran & Company, Inc., 1943.

Curti, Merle E. *The Growth of American Thought.* 3d ed. New York: Harper & Row, 1964.

——. *Peace or War: The American Struggle, 1636–1936.* New York: W. W. Norton & Company, 1936.

Davis, Elmer. *Two Minutes till Midnight.* Indianapolis: Bobbs-Merrill Company, Inc., 1955.

Davis, Garry. *Over to Pacifism.* London: Peace News Ltd., 1949.

Davis, Jerome. *Contemporary Social Movements.* New York: The Century Company, 1930.

Day, Dorothy. *Loaves and Fishes.* New York: Harper & Row, 1963.

——. *The Long Loneliness.* Garden City, N.Y.: Image Books, 1959.

Debs, Eugene Victor. *Walls and Bars.* Chicago: Socialist Party, 1927.

The Declaration of the Federation of the World. Raleigh, N.C.: Edwards & Broughton Company, 1942.

Detzer, Dorothy. *Appointment on the Hill.* New York: Henry Holt and Company, 1948.

Dewey, John. *Liberalism and Social Action.* New York: G. P. Putnam's Sons, 1935.

Divine, Robert A. *The Illusion of Neutrality.* Chicago: University of Chicago Press, 1962.

Doman, Nicholas. *The Coming Age of World Control.* New York: Harper & Brothers, 1942.

Draper, Hal. *Berkeley: The New Student Revolt.* New York: Grove Press, 1965.

Dulles, Foster Rhea. *America's Rise to World Power, 1898–1954.* New York: Harper & Brothers, 1955.

Eaton, Howard W. (ed.). *Federation: The Coming Structure of World Government.* Norman, Okla.: University of Oklahoma Press, 1944.

Eddy, Sherwood. *Eighty Adventurous Years: An Autobiography.* New York: Harper & Brothers, 1955.

Einstein, Albert. *The Fight against War,* ed. Alfred Lief. New York: John Day Company, 1933.

——. *Out of My Later Years.* New York: Philosophical Library, 1950.

Eisan, Leslie. *Pathways of Peace.* Elgin, Ill.: Brethren Publishing House, 1948.

Eliot, T. S. *The Rock.* New York: Harcourt, Brace and Company, 1934.

Emanuel, Cyprian. *The Morality of Conscientious Objection to War.* Washington, D.C.: Catholic Association for International Peace, 1941.

Federal Council of the Churches of Christ in America, Commission on the Relation of the Church to the War in the Light of the Christian Faith. *Atomic Warfare and the Christian Faith.* March, 1946.

——, Commission to Study the Bases of a Just and Durable Peace. *A Just and Durable Peace.* March, 1943.

——, ——. *A Righteous Faith for a Just and Durable Peace.* October, 1942.

Federal Union, Inc. *Let's Not Make the Same Mistake Twice.* New York: Federal Union, Inc., [1941].

Fellowship of Reconciliation. *As War Comes Nearer: A Statement by the Twenty-Fifth Annual National Conference of the Fellowship of Reconciliation, Chautauqua, New York, September 6–8, 1940.* New York: Fellowship of Reconciliation, 1940.

——. *How to Hide from an H-Bomb: A Brief Manual Designed to Inform the American Public of the Meaning and Purposes of "Operation Alert" and Similar Civil Defense Exercises.* New York: Fellowship of Reconciliation, 1956.

——. *How Will You Look in a Concrete Pipe?* New York: Fellowship Publications, 1955.

——. *The Meaning of Korea.* New York: Fellowship of Reconciliation, 1950.

——. *A Sane Man's Guide to Civil Defense: Being a Glossary of Terms Useful for the Citizen Hoping to Remain Unvaporized after the Bombs Drop.* New York: Fellowship of Reconciliation, 1955.

——. *What Is the Fellowship of Reconciliation?* New York: Fellowship of Reconciliation, 1941.

——. *Why America Should Not Adopt Conscription.* Philadelphia: American Friends Service Committee, 1940.

Fermi, Laura. *Atoms in the Family: My Life with Enrico Fermi.* Chicago: University of Chicago Press, 1954.

Filene, Peter G. *American Views of Soviet Russia, 1917–1965.* Homewood, Ill.: Dorsey Press, 1968.

Fleischman, Harry. *Norman Thomas: A Biography.* New York: W. W. Norton & Company, Inc., 1964.

Fosdick, Harry Emerson. *The Living of These Days: An Autobiography.* New York: Harper & Brothers, 1956.

Frazier, E. Franklin. *The Integration of the Negro into American Life.* Washington, D.C.: Women's International League for Peace and Freedom, 1945.

Freeman, Harrop A. *Coercion of States in International Organizations.* Philadelphia: Pacifist Research Bureau, 1944.

——, and Theodore Paullin. *Coercion of States: In Federal Unions.* Philadelphia: Pacifist Research Bureau, 1943.

Freeman, Ruth, aided by Robert and Etta Vogle. *Quakers and Peace.* Ithaca: Pacifist Research Bureau, 1947.

French, Paul Comly (ed.). *Common Sense Neutrality: Mobilizing for Peace.* New York: Hastings House, 1939.

——. *We Won't Murder.* New York: Hastings House, 1940.

Fulbright, J. William. *The Arrogance of Power.* New York: Random House, 1966.

Garfinkel, Herbert. *When Negroes March: The March on Washington*

Movement in the Organizational Politics for FEPC. Glencoe, Ill.: The Free Press, 1959.

Gellhorn, Walter. *Security, Loyalty, and Science.* Ithaca: Cornell University Press, 1950.

Gettleman, Marvin (ed.). *Viet Nam: History, Documents, and Opinions on a Major World Crisis.* Greenwich, Conn.: Fawcett Publications, 1965.

Gilpin, Robert. *American Scientists and Nuclear Weapons Policy.* Princeton: Princeton University Press, 1962.

Gingerich, Melvin. *Service for Peace.* Akron, Pa.: Mennonite Central Committee, 1949.

Glazer, Nathan. *The Social Basis of American Communism.* New York: Harcourt, Brace & World, Inc., 1961.

Goldman, Eric F. *The Crucial Decade—and After: America, 1945–1960.* New York: Vintage Books, 1961.

——. *Rendezvous with Destiny: A History of Modern American Reform.* 8th ed. revised. New York: Random House, 1962.

Goodwin, Richard. *Triumph or Tragedy: Reflections on Viet Nam.* New York: Random House, 1966.

Gregg, Richard B. *A Discipline for Non-Violence.* Wallingford, Pa.: Pendle Hill, 1941.

——. *Pacifist Program in Time of War, Threatened War, or Fascism.* Wallingford, Pa.: Pendle Hill, 1939.

——. *The Power of Non-Violence.* Philadelphia: J. B. Lippincott Company, 1934.

——. *Training for Peace: A Program for Peace Workers.* Philadelphia: J. B. Lippincott Company, 1937.

——. *The Value of Voluntary Simplicity.* Wallingford, Pa.: Pendle Hill, 1936.

Grodzins, Morton, and Eugene Rabinowitch (eds.). *The Atomic Age: Scientists in National and World Affairs.* New York: Basic Books, Inc., 1963.

Guetzkow, Harold S., and Paul H. Bowman. *Men and Hunger.* Elgin, Ill.: Brethren Publishing House, 1947.

Hagedorn, Hermann. *The Bomb that Fell on America.* Santa Barbara, Calif.: Pacific Coast Publishing Company, 1946.

Harris, Louis. *Is There a Republican Majority? Political Trends, 1952–1956.* New York: Harper & Brothers, 1954.

Hartmann, George W. *A Plea for Immediate Peace by Negotiation.* New York: War Resisters League, 1942.

Hassler, R. Alfred. *Conscripts of Conscience.* New York: Fellowship of Reconciliation, 1942.

——. *Diary of a Self-Made Convict.* Chicago: Henry Regnery Company, 1954.

Hayden, Tom. *Rebellion in Newark: Official Violence and Ghetto Response.* New York: Random House, 1967.

Hennacy, Ammon. *Autobiography of a Catholic Anarchist.* New York: Catholic Worker Press, 1954.

Hentoff, Nat. *Peace Agitator: The Story of A. J. Muste.* New York: The Macmillan Company, 1963.

Hershberger, Guy Franklin. *The Mennonite Church in the Second World War.* Scottdale, Pa.: Mennonite Publishing House, 1951.

——. *War, Peace, and Nonresistance.* Scottdale, Pa.: The Herald Press, 1944.

Herzog, Arthur. *The War-Peace Establishment.* New York: Harper & Row, 1965.

Hill, Reuben. *Families under Stress: Adjustment to the Crises of War Separation and Reunion.* New York: Harper & Brothers, 1949.

Hilsman, Roger. *To Move a Nation: The Politics of Foreign Policy in the Administration of John F. Kennedy.* Garden City, N.Y.: Doubleday & Company, 1967.

Hinshaw, Cecil E. *Nonviolent Resistance: A Nation's Way to Peace.* Wallingford, Pa.: Pendle Hill, 1956.

Holmes, John Haynes. *I Speak for Myself.* New York: Harper & Brothers, 1959.

——. *My Gandhi.* New York: Harper & Brothers, 1953.

——. *Out of Darkness.* New York: Harper & Brothers, 1942.

Horsch, John. *The Principle of Nonresistance as Held by the Mennonite Church.* Scottdale, Pa.: Mennonite Publishing House, 1927.

——. *War and the Christian Conscience.* Scottdale, Pa.: Mennonite Publishing House, 1930.

Houser, George M. *CORE: A Brief History.* New York: Congress of Racial Equality, 1949.

——. *Erasing the Color Line.* New York: Fellowship Publications, 1945.

——, and Bayard Rustin. *We Challenged Jim Crow! A Report on the Journey of Reconciliation, April 9–23, 1947.* New York: Fellowship of Reconciliation, 1947.

Howe, Irving, and Lewis Coser. *The American Communist Party: A Critical History, 1919–1957.* Boston: Beacon Press, 1957.

Hughan, Jessie Wallace. *If We Should Be Invaded.* New York: War Resisters League, 1939.

——. *New Leagues for Old: Blueprints or Foundations?* New York: Plowshare Press, 1947.

——. *Three Decades of War Resistance.* New York: War Resisters League, 1942.

Hugo, John J. *Weapons of the Spirit.* New York: Catholic Worker Press, 1943.

Huie, William Bradford. *The Hiroshima Pilot.* New York: G. P. Putnam's Sons, 1964.

Hutchins, Robert M. *The Atomic Bomb Versus Civilization.* Washington, D.C.: Human Events, 1945.

Hutchinson, Dorothy. *A Call to Peace Now: A Message to the Society of Friends.* Philadelphia: Peace Section, American Friends Service Committee, 1943.

Huxley, Aldous Leonard. *Ends and Means.* New York: Harper & Brothers, 1937.

Jacob, Philip E. *The Origins of Civilian Public Service.* Washington, D.C.: National Service Board for Religious Objectors, 1946.

Jacobs, Clyde E., and John F. Gallagher. *The Selective Service Act: A Case Study of the Governmental Process.* New York: Dodd, Mead & Company, 1967.

Jacobs, Paul, and Saul Landau (eds.). *The New Radicals.* New York: Random House, 1966.

Janeway, Eliot. *The Struggle for Survival: A Chronicle of Economic Mobilization in World War II.* New Haven: Yale University Press, 1951.

Jessup, Philip. *A Modern Law of Nations.* New York: The Macmillan Company, 1948.

Johnson, Walter. *The Battle against Isolation.* Chicago: University of Chicago Press, 1944.

Jungk, Robert. *Brighter than a Thousand Suns: A Personal History of the Atomic Scientists.* Translated by James Cleugh. New York: Harcourt, Brace and Company, 1958.

Kaplan, Morton A. *System and Process in International Politics.* New York: John Wiley and Sons, Inc., 1957.

Kaufmann, William W. *The McNamara Strategy.* New York: Harper & Row, 1964.

Kepler, Roy C. *Dynamic Peacemaking.* New York: War Resisters League, 1950.

King, Martin Luther, Jr. *Strength to Love.* New York: Harper & Row, 1963.

——. *Stride Toward Freedom.* New York: Harper & Brothers, 1958.

Lamont, Lansing. *Day of Trinity.* New York: Atheneum, 1965.

Lapp, Ralph E. *Atoms and People.* New York: Harper & Brothers, 1956.

——. *Kill and Overkill: The Strategy of Annihilation.* New York: Basic Books, Inc., 1962.

Lasch, Christopher. *The New Radicalism in America, 1889–1963: The Intellectual as a Social Type.* New York: Alfred A. Knopf, 1965.

Lash, Joseph P. *The Campus Strikes against War.* New York: Student League for Industrial Democracy, 1935.

Laurence, William L. *Men and Atoms: The Discovery, the Uses and the Future of Atomic Energy*. New York: Simon and Schuster, 1959.

Lens, Sidney. *A World in Revolution*. New York: Frederick A. Praeger, 1956.

Leskes, Theodore. *The Civil Rights Story: A Year's Review*. New York: American Jewish Congress, 1961.

Leuchtenburg, William E. *Franklin D. Roosevelt and the New Deal, 1932–1940*. New York: Harper & Row, 1963.

Libby, Frederick J. *The American Peace Movement*. Washington, D.C.: National Council for the Prevention of War, 1930.

——. *America's Foreign Policy*. Washington, D.C.: National Council for the Prevention of War, 1944.

Lilienthal, David E. *Change, Hope, and the Bomb*. Princeton: Princeton University Press, 1963.

Lindner, Robert M. *Stone Walls and Men*. New York: Odyssey Press, 1946.

Lippmann, Walter. *U.S. Foreign Policy: Shield of the Republic*. Boston: Little, Brown & Company, 1943.

Lipset, Seymour Martin. *Political Man: The Social Bases of Politics*. Garden City, N.Y.: Doubleday & Company, 1960.

Lloyd, Lola Maverick, and Rosika Schwimmer. *Chaos, War, or a New World Order?* 3d ed. revised. New York: Campaign for World Government, 1938.

Logan, Rayford W. (ed.). *What the Negro Wants*. Chapel Hill: University of North Carolina Press, 1944.

Lomax, Louis E. *The Negro Revolt*. New York: Harper & Brothers, 1962.

Long, Edward Leroy, Jr. *The Christian Response to the Atomic Crisis*. Philadelphia: Westminster Press, 1950.

Luard, Evan. *Peace and Opinion*. London: Oxford University Press, 1962.

Lubell, Samuel. *The Future of American Politics*. 2d ed. revised. Garden City, N.Y.: Doubleday Anchor Books, 1956.

——. *Revolt of the Moderates*. New York: Harper & Brothers, 1956.

Luce, Henry R. *The American Century*. New York: Farrar & Rinehart, Inc., 1941.

Lukacs, John. *A History of the Cold War*. Garden City, N.Y.: Doubleday & Company, Inc., 1962.

Lydgate, William A. *What America Thinks*. New York: Thomas Y. Crowell Company, 1944.

Lynd, Staughton, and Tom Hayden. *The Other Side*. New York: New American Library, 1966.

Macdonald, Dwight. *Memoirs of a Revolutionist: Essays in Political Criticism*. New York: Farrar, Straus and Cudahy, 1957.

Macgregor, George Hogarth. *The New Testament Basis of Pacifism.* Nyack, N.Y.: Fellowship Publications, 1954.

——. *The Relevance of an Impossible Ideal.* New York: Fellowship of Reconciliation, 1941.

MacIver, Robert M. *Towards an Abiding Peace.* New York: The Macmillan Company, 1943.

MacLeish, Archibald. *American Opinion and the War.* New York: The Macmillan Company, 1942.

Mallery, Otto Tod. *Economic Union and Durable Peace.* New York: Harper & Brothers, 1943.

Mangone, Gerard J. *The Idea and Practice of World Government.* New York: Columbia University Press, 1951.

Marshall, S. L. A. *Men against Fire.* New York: William Morrow and Company, 1947.

Mayer, Milton. *Conscience and the Commonwealth.* New York: Plowshare Press, 1944.

——. *What Can a Man Do?* Chicago: University of Chicago Press, 1964.

McCarthy, Joseph R. *America's Retreat from Victory.* New York: Devin-Adair Company, 1951.

Melman, Seymour. *The Peace Race.* New York: George Braziller, 1962.

Menashe, Louis, and Ronald Radosh (eds.). *Teach-Ins: U.S.A.* New York: Frederick A. Praeger, 1967.

Meyer, Cord, Jr. *Peace or Anarchy.* Boston: Little, Brown and Company, 1947.

Meyer, Donald B. *The Protestant Search for Political Realism, 1919–1941.* Berkeley: University of California Press, 1961.

Miller, Henry. *Remember to Remember.* Vol. II of *The Air-Conditioned Nightmare.* New York: New Directions, 1947.

Millis, Walter, and James Real. *The Abolition of War.* New York: The Macmillan Company, 1963.

Mitchell, Broadus. *Depression Decade: From New Era through New Deal, 1929–1941.* Vol. IX of *The Economic History of the United States.* New York: Holt, Rinehart and Winston, 1964.

Moellering, Ralph Luther. *Modern War and the American Churches.* New York: American Press, 1957.

Morgan, Arthur E. *Small Community Economics.* New York: Fellowship Publications, 1943.

Mumford, Lewis. *In the Name of Sanity.* New York: Harcourt, Brace and Company, 1954.

Muste, A. J. *The Camp of Liberation.* London: Peace News, 1954.

——. *Gandhi and the H-Bomb.* New York: Fellowship Publications, 1950.

——. *Korea: Spark to Set a World Afire?* New York: Fellowship of Reconciliation, 1950.

——. *Non-Violence in an Aggressive World.* New York: Harper & Brothers, 1940.

——. *Not by Might.* New York: Harper & Brothers, 1947.

——. *Wage Peace Now.* New York: Fellowship of Reconciliation, 1942.

——. *War Is the Enemy.* Wallingford, Pa.: Pendle Hill, 1942.

——. *What Would Pacifists Have Done about Hitler? A Discussion of War, Dictators, and Pacifism.* New York: Fellowship of Reconciliation, 1949.

——. *The World Task of Pacifism.* Wallingford, Pa.: Pendle Hill, 1941.

Naeve, Lowell, in collaboration with David Wieck. *A Field of Broken Stones.* Glen Gardner, N.J.: Libertarian Press, 1950.

Naeve, Virginia (ed.). *Friends of the Hibakusha.* Denver: Alan Swallow, 1964.

Nash, Vernon. *It Must Be Done Again: Thirteen American States Point the Way for the Nations Now.* New York: The Union Press, 1940.

Nathan, Otto, and Heinz Norden (eds.). *Einstein on Peace.* New York: Simon and Schuster, 1960.

National Service Board for Religious Objectors (ed.). *Congress Looks at the Conscientious Objector.* Washington, D.C.: National Service Board for Religious Objectors, 1943.

——. *The Conscientious Objector under the Selective Training and Service Act of 1940.* Washington, D.C.: National Service Board for Religious Objectors, 1942.

Nearing, Scott. *United World: The Road to International Peace.* Mays Landing, N.J.: Open Road Press, Inc., 1944.

Nelson, Donald M. *Arsenal of Democracy: The Story of American War Production.* New York: Harcourt, Brace and Company, 1946.

Newfang, Oscar. *The Road to World Peace: A Federation of Nations.* New York: G. P. Putnam's Sons, 1924.

——. *The United States of the World: A Comparison between the League of Nations and the United States of America.* New York: G. P. Putnam's Sons, 1930.

——. *World Federation.* New York: Barnes & Noble, 1939.

——. *World Government: A Suggested Formula for Use at the End of the War.* New York: Barnes & Noble, 1942.

Newfield, Jack. *A Prophetic Minority.* New York: New American Library, 1966.

Newman, James R., and Byron S. Miller. *The Control of Atomic Energy: A Study of Its Social, Economic, and Political Implications.* New York: McGraw-Hill, 1948.

Niebuhr, Reinhold. *Christianity and Power Politics.* New York: Charles Scribner's Sons, 1940.

——. *Moral Man and Immoral Society.* New York: Charles Scribner's Sons, 1941.

——. *Reflections on the End of an Era*. New York: Charles Scribner's Sons, 1934.

——. *Why the Christian Church Is Not Pacifist*. Toronto: The Macmillan Company, 1940.

The Non-Cooperator and the Draft. Philadelphia: Central Committee for Conscientious Objectors, 1963.

Olmstead, Frank. *They Asked for a Hard Job: CO's at Work in Mental Hospitals*. New York: Plowshare Press, 1943.

Oppenheimer, Martin, and George Lakey. *A Manual for Direct Action*. Chicago: Quadrangle Books, 1965.

Osgood, Charles E. *An Alternative to War or Surrender*. Urbana: University of Illinois Press, 1962.

Osgood, Robert E. *Ideals and Self-Interest in America's Foreign Relations*. 4th ed. Chicago: University of Chicago Press, 1964.

O'Toole, George Barry. *War and Conscription at the Bar of Christian Morals*. New York: Catholic Worker, 1941.

Pacifist Handbook: Questions and Answers Concerning the Pacifist in Wartime, Prepared as a Basis for Study and Discussion. Philadelphia: American Friends Service Committee *et al.*, 1939.

Page, Kirby. *How to Keep America Out of War*. Philadelphia: American Friends Service Committee *et al.*, 1939.

——. *Must We Go to War?* New York: Farrar & Rinehart, Inc., 1937.

——. *Now Is the Time to Prevent a Third World War*. La Habra, Calif.: By the author, 1946.

Pauling, Linus. *No More War!* New York: Dodd, Mead & Company, 1958.

Paullin, Theodore, *Comparative Peace Plans*. Philadelphia: Pacifist Research Bureau, 1943.

——. *Introduction to Non-Violence*. Philadelphia: Pacifist Research Bureau, 1944.

Peacemakers. *A Declaration to the American People*. Glen Gardner, N.J.: Libertarian Press, [1948?].

——. *Introducing Peacemakers*. Glen Gardner, N.J.: Libertarian Press, 1948.

Peaslee, Amos J. *United Nations Government*. New York: Justice House, 1945.

Peck, James. *Cracking the Color Line: Non-Violent Direct Action Methods of Eliminating Racial Discrimination*. New York: Congress of Racial Equality, 1962.

——. *Freedom Ride*. New York: Simon and Schuster, 1962.

——. *We Who Would Not Kill*. New York: Lyle Stuart, 1958.

Pei, Mario A. *The American Road to Peace: A Constitution for the World*. New York: S. F. Vanni, 1945.

Penick, James L., Jr., *et al. The Politics of American Science, 1939 to the Present.* Chicago: Rand McNally & Company, 1965.

Perkins Dexter. *The American Approach to Foreign Policy.* Cambridge: Harvard University Press, 1952.

Perry, Ralph Barton. *One World in the Making.* New York: Current Books, Inc., 1945.

Persons, E. L. *International Government for International Peace,* n.p.: By the author, 1942.

Peterson, H. C., and Gilbert C. Fite. *Opponents of War, 1917–1918.* Madison: University of Wisconsin Press, 1957.

Pickard, Bertram. *Peacemakers' Dilemma: Plea for a Modus Vivendi in the Peace Movement.* Wallingford, Pa: Pendle Hill, 1942.

Pickett, Clarence E. *For More than Bread.* Boston: Little, Brown and Company, 1953.

Ramparts Vietnam Primer. San Francisco: Ramparts Magazine, 1966.

Randall, John Herman, Jr. *Emily Greene Balch of New England: Citizen of the World.* n.p.: Women's International League for Peace and Freedom, 1946.

Randall, Mercedes M. *High Lights in W.I.L.P.F. History: From the Hague to Luxembourg, 1915–1946.* Philadelphia: Women's International League for Peace and Freedom, 1946.

——. *Improper Bostonian: Emily Greene Balch.* New York: Twayne Publishers, Inc., 1964.

——. *The Voice of Thy Brother's Blood: An Eleventh Hour Appeal to All Americans.* Washington, D.C.: Women's International League for Peace and Freedom, 1944.

Rapoport, Anatol. *Fights, Games and Debates.* Ann Arbor: University of Michigan Press, 1960.

Rauch, Basil. *Roosevelt: From Munich to Pearl Harbor.* New York: Creative Age Press, 1950.

Raven, Charles Earle. *The Theological Basis of Christian Pacifism.* Nyack, N.Y.: Fellowship Publications, 1951.

Reeves, George B. *Men against the State.* Washington, D.C.: Human Events, Inc., 1946.

Reves, Emery. *The Anatomy of Peace.* New York: Harper & Brothers, 1945.

——. *A Democratic Manifesto.* New York: Random House, 1942.

Reynolds, Earle. *The Forbidden Voyage.* New York: David McKay Company, Inc., 1961.

Richards, Edward C. M. *They Refuse to Be Criminals: Parole and the Conscientious Objector.* n.p.: Nur Mahal, 1946.

Rider, Fremont. *The Great Dilemma of World Organization.* New York: Reynal and Hitchcock, 1946.

Riecken, Henry W. *The Volunteer Work Camp: A Psychological Evaluation.* Cambridge, Mass.: Addison-Wesley Press, Inc., 1952.

Rogow, Abe. *A Plan for Immediate and Lasting Peace.* Bayonne, N.J.: By the author, 1943.

Roosevelt, Elliott (ed.). *F.D.R.: His Personal Letters, 1928-1945.* Vol. II. New York: Duell, Sloan and Pearce, 1950.

Rustin, Bayard. *"In Apprehension How Like a God!"* Philadelphia: The Young Friends Movement of the Philadelphia Yearly Meetings, 1948.

———. *Interracial Primer.* New York: Fellowship of Reconciliation, 1943.

Rutenber, Culbert G. *The Dagger and the Cross: An Examination of Christian Pacifism.* Nyack, N.Y.: Fellowship Publications, 1950.

Sargent, Porter. *War and Education.* Boston: By the author, 1943.

Scheer, Robert. *How the United States Got Involved in Vietnam.* Santa Barbara, Calif.: Center for the Study of Democratic Institutions, 1965.

Schelling, T. C. *The Strategy of Conflict.* Cambridge: Harvard University Press, 1960.

Schlesinger, Arthur M., Jr. *A Thousand Days: John F. Kennedy in the White House.* Boston: Houghton Mifflin, 1965.

Schmidt, Karl M. *Henry A. Wallace: Quixotic Crusade 1948.* Syracuse: Syracuse University Press, 1960.

Schwimmer, Rosika. *Union Now for Peace or War? The Danger in the Plan of Clarence Streit.* New York: By the author, 1939.

Seidler, Murray B. *Norman Thomas: Respectable Rebel.* Syracuse: Syracuse University Press, 1961.

Seldes, George. *Iron, Blood and Profits.* New York: Harper & Brothers, 1934.

Shannon, David A. *The Socialist Party of America: A History.* New York: The Macmillan Company, 1955.

Sheehan, Arthur. *Peter Maurin: Gay Believer.* Garden City, N.Y.: Hanover House, 1959.

Shridharani, Krishnalal. *War without Violence: A Study of Gandhi's Method and Its Accomplishments.* New York: Harcourt, Brace and Company, 1939.

Sibley, Mulford Q. *The Political Theories of Modern Pacifism.* Philadelphia: Pacifist Research Bureau, 1944.

———. *The Quiet Battle: Writings on the Theory and Practice of Non-Violent Resistance.* Garden City, N.Y.: Doubleday & Company, Inc., 1963.

———, and Philip E. Jacob. *Conscription of Conscience: The American State and the Conscientious Objector, 1940-1947.* Ithaca: Cornell University Press, 1952.

———, and Ada Wardlaw. *Conscientious Objectors in Prison, 1940-1945.* Philadelphia: Pacifist Research Bureau, 1945.

Sinclair, Upton. *A World to Win.* New York: Viking Press, 1946.

Smith, Alice Kimball. *A Peril and a Hope: The Scientists' Movement in America, 1945-47.* Chicago: University of Chicago Press, 1965.

Sorensen, Theodore C. *Kennedy.* New York: Harper & Row, 1965.

Speers, Wallace C. *Coorder Nations: A Proposal for World Coordination.* n.p.: By the author, 1943.

Spellman, Francis J. *The Road to Victory.* New York: Charles Scribner's Sons, 1942.

Steere, Douglas V. *The Soil of Peace.* Washington, D.C.: Public Affairs, 1946.

Stouffer, Samuel A., *et al. The American Soldier: Adjustment during Army Life.* Vol. I. Princeton: Princeton University Press, 1949.

——, *et al. The American Soldier: Combat and its Aftermath.* Vol. II. Princeton: Princeton University Press, 1949.

Straight, Michael. *Make This the Last War: The Future of the United Nations.* New York: Harcourt, Brace & Company, Inc., 1943.

Streit, Clarence K. *The Essence of Union Now.* New York: The Union Press, 1940.

——. *Federal Union of the Free.* Washington, D.C.: Federal Union, Inc., n.d.

——. *For Union Now.* Washington, D.C.: The Union Press, 1939.

——. *The Need for Union Now.* New York: The Union Press, 1940.

——. *Of Freedom and Union Now.* New York: Harper & Brothers, n.d.

——. *Union Now: The Proposal for the Inter-Democracy Federal Union.* New York: Harper & Brothers, 1940.

——. *Union Now with Britain.* New York: Harper & Brothers, 1941.

Sutherland, Elizabeth (ed.). *Letters from Mississippi.* New York: McGraw-Hill, 1965.

Swift, Charles R., III. *Prison Routine.* New York: War Resisters League, 1943.

Swing, Raymond Gram. *"Good Evening!" A Professional Memoir.* New York: Harcourt, Brace & World, Inc., 1964.

——. *In the Name of Sanity.* New York: Harper & Brothers, 1946.

Swomley, John M., Jr. *The Military Establishment.* Boston: Beacon Press, 1964.

Tate, Merze. *The United States and Armaments.* Cambridge: Harvard University Press, 1948.

Thomas, Evan W. *The Positive Faith of Pacifism.* New York: War Resisters League, 1942.

——. *The Way to Freedom.* New York: War Resisters League, 1943.

——. *Why We Oppose Military Conscription.* New York: War Resisters League, 1944.

Thomas, Norman M. *Appeal to the Nations.* New York: Henry Holt and Company, 1947.

——. *The Conscientious Objector in America.* New York: B. W. Huebsch, Inc., 1923.

——. *The Prerequisites for Peace.* New York: W. W. Norton & Company, 1959.

——. *Socialism on the Defensive.* New York: Harper & Brothers, 1938.

——. *A Socialist Looks at the United Nations.* Syracuse: Syracuse University Press, 1945.

——. *The Test of Freedom.* New York: W. W. Norton & Company, Inc., 1954.

——. *War: No Glory, No Profit, No Need.* New York: Frederick A. Stokes Company, 1935.

——. *What Is Our Destiny.* Garden City, N.Y.: Doubleday, Doran & Company, Inc., 1944.

——. *World Federation: What Are the Difficulties?* New York: Post War World Council, 1942.

——, and Bertram D. Wolfe. *Keep America Out of War.* New York: Frederick A Stokes Company, 1939.

United World Federalists. *Unity and Diversity.* New York: World Government House, [1947?].

Uphaus, Willard. *Commitment.* New York: McGraw-Hill, 1963.

Van Kirk, Walter. *Religion Renounces War.* Chicago: Willett, Clark and Company, 1934.

Vietnam Hearings: Voices from the Grass Roots. Waterloo, Wisc.: Artcraft Press, 1965.

Villard, Oswald Garrison. *Fighting Years: Memoirs of a Liberal Editor.* New York: Harcourt, Brace and Company, 1939.

——. *Our Military Chaos: The Truth about Defense.* New York: Alfred A. Knopf, 1939.

Voss, Carl Hermann. *Rabbi and Minister: The Friendship of Stephen S. Wise and John Haynes Holmes.* Cleveland: World Publishing Company, 1964.

Wallace, Henry A. *Toward World Peace.* New York: Reynal & Hitchcock, 1948.

Waller, Willard. *The Veteran Comes Back.* New York: Dryden Press, 1944.

Waskow, Arthur I. *The Worried Man's Guide to World Peace.* Garden City, N.Y.: Doubleday & Company, Inc., 1963.

Wechsler, James A. *The Age of Suspicion.* New York: Random House, 1953.

Weinberg, Arthur, and Lila Weinberg (eds.). *Instead of Violence.* New York: Grossman Publishers, Inc., 1963.

Wells, H. G. *Mind at the End of Its Tether.* New York: Didier, 1946.

West, Dan. *What Ought a Conscript Do.* Elgin, Ill.: Brethren Service Committee, 1940.

White, Elwyn Brooks. *The Wild Flag.* Boston: Houghton, Mifflin Company, 1946.

White, Walter. *A Man Called White.* New York: Viking Press, 1948.

White, William Allen. *The Autobiography of William Allen White.* New York: The Macmillan Company, 1946.

Whitney, Courtney. *MacArthur: His Rendezvous with History.* New York: Alfred A. Knopf, 1956.

Why They Cannot Go to War. Philadelphia: American Friends Service Committee and Women's International League for Peace and Freedom, 1940.

Why We Refused to Register. New York: Fellowship of Reconciliation et al., 1941.

Wilcox, Walter W. *The Farmer in the Second World War.* Ames, Iowa: The Iowa State College Press, 1947.

Willkie, Wendell L. *One World.* New York: Simon and Schuster, 1943

Wiltz, John E. *In Search of Peace: The Senate Munitions Inquiry, 1934–1936.* Baton Rouge, La.: Louisiana State University Press, 1963.

Wofford, Harris, Jr. *It's Up to Us, Federal World Government in Our Time.* New York: Harcourt, Brace and Company, 1946.

——. *World Federal Democracy: A Plan for Action.* Washington, D.C.: Federal Union, Inc., [1945?].

Women's International League for Peace and Freedom. *The W.I.L. in Wartime.* Washington: Women's International League for Peace and Freedom, 1943.

Wouk, Herman. *The Caine Mutiny.* New York: Doubleday & Company, Inc., 1951.

Wreszin, Michael. *Oswald Garrison Villard: Pacifist at War.* Bloomington, Ind.: Indiana University Press, 1965.

Wynner, Edith. *World Federal Government in Maximum Terms: Proposals for United Nations Charter Revision.* Afton, N.Y.: Fedonat Press, 1954.

——, and Georgia Lloyd. *Searchlight on Peace Plans: Choose Your Road to World Government.* 2d ed. revised. New York: E. P. Dutton and Company, Inc., 1949.

Yoder, Edward. *Compromise with War.* Akron, Pa.: Mennonite Central Committee, 1944.

Young, Wilmer J. *Visible Witness: A Testimony for Radical Peace Action.* Wallingford, Pa.: Pendle Hill, 1961.

Ziff, William B. *Two Worlds: A Realistic Approach to the Problems of Keeping the Peace.* New York: Harper & Brothers, 1946.

Zinn, Howard. *SNCC: The New Abolitionists.* Boston: Beacon Press, 1964.

——. *Vietnam: The Logic of Withdrawal.* Boston: Beacon Press, 1967.

ARTICLES AND PERIODICALS

Abel, Lionel. "Seven Heroes of the New Left," *New York Times Magazine* (May 5, 1968), pp. 30–31, 128–35.

Abrams, Ray H. "The Churches and the Clergy in World War II,"

Annals of the American Academy of Political and Social Science, CCLVI (March, 1948), 110–19.

"Action on Korea Draws Few Protests," *Fellowship,* XVI (September, 1950), 19.

Adler, Mortimer. "Five Hundred Years from Now or Five?" *Common Cause,* I (July, 1947), 9–10.

——. "World Government," *Commonweal,* XLII (August 31, 1945), 479.

Allen, Devere. "The Peace Movement Moves Left," *Annals of the American Academy of Political and Social Science,* CLXXV (September, 1934), 150–55.

Allport, Gordon. "The Role of Expectancy," *Tensions that Cause Wars,* ed. Hadley Cantril. Urbana, Ill.: University of Illinois Press, 1950.

"American Congress and World Federation," *Common Cause,* IV (August, 1950), 5–33.

"The American Resistance," *Liberation,* XII (November, 1967), entire issue.

"American Writers on Germany," *Common Sense,* XIII (June, 1944), 206–12.

Anderson, Nels, and Nathaniel H. Rogg. "Impact of the War on Labor and Industry," *American Journal of Sociology,* XLVIII (November, 1942), 361–68.

"Another Conscience Speaks at Omaha," *Christian Century,* LXXVI (July 29, 1959), 868–69.

"Area Bombing," *Commonweal,* XXXIX (March 17, 1944), 531–32.

Armstrong, O. K. "Grassroots Crusader," *Reader's Digest,* XLVIII (May, 1946), 45–49.

"Atomic Force, Its Meaning for Mankind," *University of Chicago Round Table,* No. 386 (August 12, 1945), pp. 1–12.

"The Atomic Scientists of Chicago," *Bulletin of the Atomic Scientists of Chicago,* I (December 10, 1945), 1.

Atwater, Elton. "Organizing American Public Opinion for Peace," *Public Opinion Quarterly,* I (April, 1937), 112–21.

Balch, Emily Greene, and Mercedes M. Randall. "Women's International League for Peace and Freedom." Appendix to Jane Addams. *Peace and Bread in Time of War.* 2d ed. New York: Kings Crown Press, 1945.

Baldwin, Hanson W. "When the Big Guns Speak," *Public Opinion and Foreign Policy,* ed. Lester Markel. New York: Harper & Brothers, 1949.

"Battle of Vietnam Day," *Newsweek,* LXVI (October 25, 1965), 98.

Bedau, Hugo A. "On Civil Disobedience," *Journal of Philosophy,* LVIII (October 12, 1961), 653–65.

Bell, Daniel. "The Background and Development of Marxian Socialism in the United States," *Socialism and American Life*, ed. Donald Drew Egbert and Stow Persons. Vol. I. Princeton: Princeton University Press, 1952.

——. Letter to the Editor, *Politics*, II (February, 1945), 62.

Benedict, Libby. Review of *Wars I Have Seen*, by Gertrude Stein, *New York Times Book Review* (May 20, 1945), p. 4.

Benedict, Ruth. "Primitive Freedom," *Atlantic Monthly*, CLXIX (June, 1942), 756–63.

Benedict, Stephen. "Breakers and Makers of Tradition," *Common Cause*, I (September, 1947), 107–108.

Bennett, Clif. "Resistance in Prison," *Prison Etiquette: The Convict's Compendium of Useful Information*, ed. Holley Cantine and Dachine Rainer. Bearsville, N.Y.: Retort Press, 1950.

Bethe, Hans. Review of *Brighter than a Thousand Suns*, by Robert Jungk, *Bulletin of the Atomic Scientists*, XIV (December, 1958), 428.

Bigelow, Albert S. "Why I Am Sailing into the Pacific Bomb-Test Area," *Liberation*, II (February, 1958), 4–6.

Billington, Ray Allen. "Origins of Middle Western Isolationism," *Political Science Quarterly*, LX (March, 1945), 44–64.

Blumer, Herbert. "Morale," *American Society in Wartime*, ed. William Fielding Ogburn. Chicago: University of Chicago Press, 1943.

Boeckel, Florence Brewer. "The Peace Movement in the U. S. A.," *Peace Year Book 1938*. London: National Peace Council, 1938.

Bohn, Herbert G. "We Tried Non-Violence," *Fellowship*, III (January, 1937), 7–8.

Bohr, Niels. "Science and Civilization," *One World or None: A Report to the Public on the Full Meaning of the Atomic Bomb*, ed. Dexter Masters and Catherine Way. New York: McGraw-Hill Book Company Inc., 1946.

Boisen, Anton T. "Conscientious Objectors: Their Morale in Church-Operated Service Units," *Psychiatry*, VII (May, 1944), 215–24.

Bolté, Charles G. "We're On Our Own," *Atlantic Monthly*, CLXXIX (May, 1947), 27–33.

"Book Burning," *The Federalist*, III (October, 1953), 8.

Bordwell, Percy. "A Constitution for the United Nations," *Iowa Law Review*, XXVIII (March, 1943), 387–421.

Borger, Catherine. "National Organizations and International Policy," *International Conciliation*, No. 409 (March, 1945), p. 223.

Borgese, Elizabeth Mann. "1950: World Movement at the Divide," *Common Cause*, IV (December, 1950), 225–32.

Borgese, G. A. "Common Cause," *Common Cause*, IV (June, 1951), 562–64.

——. "Of Atomic Fear and Two 'Utopias,'" *Common Cause*, I (September, 1947), 84–89.

———. "One World and Seven Problems," *Common Cause*, I (July, 1947), 3–5.

———. "Still It Is Korea," *Common Cause*, IV (October, 1950), 113–15.

Boulding, Kenneth E. "The Peace Research Movement in the U.S.," *Alternatives to War and Violence*, ed. Ted Dunn. London: James Clarke and Company, Ltd., 1963.

"Brief History of the Committee," *Common Cause*, I (July, 1947), 11–27.

"A Brief Review of Thirty-Five Years of Service toward Developing International Understanding," *International Conciliation*, No. 417 (January, 1946), pp. 17–39.

Brown, Earl. "American Negroes and the War," *Harper's*, CLXXXIV (April, 1942), 545–52.

Brown, Harrison. "The World Government Movement in the United States," *Bulletin of the Atomic Scientists*, III (June, 1947), 156–57, 166.

Buckler, Helen. "The CORE Way," *Survey Graphic*, XXXV (February, 1946), 50–51, 60.

Burgess, Ernest W. "The Effect of the War on the American Family," *American Journal of Sociology*, XLVIII (November, 1942), 343–52.

Bush, Merrill E. "World Organization or Atomic Destruction?" *School and Society*, LXIV (November 23, 1946), 353–55.

"Business-and-Government," *Fortune*, XIX (April, 1939), 66–67.

Cadbury, Henry J. "Peace and War," *The Quaker Approach to Contemporary Problems*, ed. John Kavanaugh. New York: G. P. Putnam's Sons, 1953.

Calhoun, Don. "Non-Violence and Revolution," *Politics*, III (January, 1946), 17–21.

———. "The Non-Violent Revolutionists," *Politics*, III (April, 1946), 118–19.

Calkins, Ken. "The Student Peace Union," *Fellowship*, XXVI (March 1, 1960), 5–7.

Cantril, Hadley. "Opinion Trends in World War II: Some Guides to Interpretation," *Public Opinion Quarterly*, XII (Spring, 1948), 30–44.

———, *et al.* "America Faces the War: Shifts in Opinion," *Public Opinion Quarterly*, IV (December, 1940), 651–56.

"Catholic Students Are against War," *Christian Century*, LVI (November 22, 1939), 1428.

Catholic Worker (New York). 1933–1960.

"Causes of the Peace Failure, 1919–1939," *International Conciliation*, CCCLXIII (October, 1940), 333–69.

"Cheap Money," *Collier's*, CXXVIII (October 27, 1951), 115.

Christian Century, LIII (October 14, 1936), 1374.

"The Church Pacifist," *Nation*, CXXXII (May 6, 1931), 494.

"The Churches and the War," *Time*, XXXVIII (December 22, 1941), 67–68.

Clark, Grenville. "A Winning Cause," *The Federalist*, II (Summer, 1952), 3.

Clark, Kenneth B. "Morale of Negroes on the Home Front: World Wars I and II," *Journal of Negro Education*, XII (Summer, 1943), 417–28.

Cleaver, Eldridge. "Requiem for Nonviolence," *Ramparts*, VI (May, 1968), 48–49.

Cogley, John. "A World without War," *The Moral Dilemma of Nuclear Weapons*, ed. William Clancy. New York: Church Peace Union, 1961.

Collier, John. "The Indian in a Wartime Nation," *Annals of the American Academy of Political and Social Science*, CCXXIII (September, 1942), 29–35.

Common Cause, IV (September, 1950), 105, 112.

Compton, Arthur H., and Farrington Daniels. "A Poll of Scientists at Chicago, July, 1945," *Bulletin of the Atomic Scientists*, IV (February, 1948), 44, 63.

Conant, James B. "Force and Freedom," *Atlantic Monthly*, CLXXXIII (January, 1949), 19–22.

Conscientious Objector (New York). 1939–1946.

Cook, Fred J. "Juggernaut: The Warfare State," *Nation*, CXCIII (October 28, 1961), 285.

"Council Notes," *World Government News*, VII (July, 1949), 7.

"Council of Federation of American Scientists Meets," *Bulletin of the Atomic Scientists*, I (May 1, 1946), 16.

Cousins, Norman. "Earle Reynolds and His Phoenix," *Saturday Review*, XLI (October 11, 1958), 26–27.

——. "The H-Bomb and World Federalism," *The Federalist*, II (January, 1953), 14–15.

——. Letter to the Editors, *Liberation*, V (December, 1960), 3.

——. "The Men of the Golden Rule," *Saturday Review*, XLI (May 17, 1958), 24.

——, and Thomas K. Finletter. "A Beginning for Sanity," *Bulletin of the Atomic Scientists*, II (July 1, 1946), 11–14.

"The C.P.S. Strikes," *Politics*, III (July, 1946), 177–80.

Cranston, Alan. "The Strengthening of the U.N. Charter," *Political Quarterly*, XVII (July–September, 1946), 187–200.

Crespi, Leo P. "Attitudes toward Conscientious Objectors and Some of Their Psychological Correlates," *Journal of Psychology*, XVIII (1944), 81–117.

——. "Public Opinion toward Conscientious Objectors," *Journal of Psychology*, XIX (1945), 209–310.

Curti, Merle E. "The Changing Pattern of Certain Humanitarian Organizations," *Annals of the American Academy of Political and Social Science*, CLXXIX (May, 1935), 59–67.

Dahlke, H. Otto. "Values and Group Behavior in Two Camps for Conscientious Objectors," *American Journal of Sociology*, LI (July, 1945), 22–33.

Daily News (New York). 1957.

Daily Worker (New York). 1941, 1950.

"D.A.R. Makes History at Chicago Meeting," *Life*, XII (May 18, 1942), 34–35.

Davidson, Bill. "Why Half Our Combat Soldiers Fail to Shoot," *Collier's*, CXXX (November 8, 1952), 16–18.

DeConde, Alexander. "On Twentieth-Century Isolationism," *Isolation and Security*, ed. Alexander DeConde. Durham, N.C.: Duke University Press, 1957.

Decter, Midge. "The Peace Ladies," *Harper's*, CXXVI (March, 1963), 48–53.

Deming, Barbara. "New Mission to Moscow: San Francisco to Moscow Walk for Peace," *Nation*, CXCIII (December 23, 1961), 505–509.

———. "The Peacemakers," *Nation*, CXCI (December 17, 1960), 471–75.

Detzer, Dorothy. "Dirge for Collective Security," *Fellowship*, IV (November, 1938), 6–7.

DeVoto, Bernard. "The Easy Chair," *Harper's* CLXXXVIII (March, 1944), 344–47.

Dewey, John. "Democratic Versus Coercive International Organization: The Realism of Jane Addams." Introduction to Jane Addams. *Peace and Bread in Time of War*. 2d ed. New York: Kings Crown Press, 1945.

Dienstfrey, Ted. "Conference on the Sit-Ins," *Commentary*, XXIX (June, 1960), 524–28.

"Dr. Holmes and Conscription," *Fellowship*, IX (February, 1943), 39.

Doggett, Caxton. "A Name for the Pacifist," *Christian Century*, LXI (October 11, 1944), 1163–65.

Douglas, William O. "An Obligation to History," *Common Cause*, IV (January, 1951), 281–84.

DuBridge, Lee A. "Science and National Policy," *Bulletin of the Atomic Scientists*, I (May 15, 1946), 12–14.

———. "What about the Bikini Tests?" *Bulletin of the Atomic Scientists*, I (May 15, 1946), 7, 16.

Duffield, Marcus. "Our Quarrelling Pacifists," *Harper's*, CLXVI (May, 1933), 688–96.

Eagleton, Clyde. "World Government Discussion in the United States," *London Quarterly of World Affairs*, XII (October, 1946), 251–58.

Editorial, *Life*, XIV (March 29, 1943), 20.

Einstein, Albert. "Atomic War or Peace," *Atlantic Monthly*, CLXXX (November, 1947), 29–32.

——. Letter to the Editor, *Reporter*, XI (November 18, 1954), 8.

——. " 'The Real Problem Is in the Hearts of Men,' " *New York Times Magazine* (June 23, 1946), pp. 7, 42–44.

——. "The Way Out," *One World or None: A Report to the Public on the Full Meaning of the Atomic Bomb*, ed. Dexter Masters and Katherine Way. New York: McGraw-Hill Book Company, Inc., 1946.

Ekirch, Arthur A., Jr. "C.P.S. and Slavery," *Pacifica Views*, II (August 25, 1944), 1, 4.

"Embattled Peacemaker," *World Government News*, VIII (August, 1950), 3–6.

"The Enemy," *Time*, XLII (July 5, 1943), 28–29.

"Expiation," *Time*, LI (February 23, 1948), 94–95.

"Facts about the Pacifica Foundation," *WBAI Folio*, VII (April 11–May 8, 1966), 31.

"Fallen Citadel," *Time*, XXXVIII (December 22, 1941), 33.

Farmer, James L., Jr. "The Race Logic of Pacifism," *Fellowship*, VIII (January, 1942), 24–25.

Farris, Charles D. "Selected Attitudes on Foreign Affairs as Correlates of Authoritarianism and Political Anomie," *Journal of Politics*, XXII (1960), 50–67.

Federal Council of the Churches of Christ in America, Commission on a Just and Durable Peace. "Christian Standards and Current International Developments," *International Conciliation*, No. 409 (March, 1945), pp. 142–49.

——. "The Churches and the Current International Situation," *International Conciliation*, No. 409 (March, 1945), pp. 150–66.

Federation of American (Atomic) Scientists. "Survival Is at Stake," *One World or None: A Report to the Public on the Full Meaning of the Atomic Bomb*, ed. Dexter Masters and Katherine Way. New York: McGraw-Hill Book Company, Inc., 1946.

Fellowship, XXIV (January 1, 1958), 20.

Fellowship, XXVI (February 1, 1960), 3.

Ferrell, Robert H. "The Peace Movement," *Isolation and Security*, ed. Alexander DeConde. Durham, N.C.: Duke University Press, 1957.

"Financial Report for 1941 to Members of the F.O.R.," *Fellowship*, VIII (January, 1942), 31.

Finch, Roy. "The Communist Convention," *Liberation*, II (March, 1957), 4–6.

——. "The Liberation Poll," *Liberation*, IV (November, 1959), 14–17.

——. "The New Peace Movement: Part I," *Dissent*, X (Winter, 1963), 86–95.

——. "The New Peace Movement: Part II," *Dissent*, X (Spring, 1963), 138–48.

Finletter, Thomas K. "An Editorial," *World Government News*, VI (May, 1948), insert.

——. "Timetable for World Government," *Atlantic Monthly*, CLXXI (March, 1946), 53–60.

"Firebirds' Flight," *Time*, XLV (March 19, 1945), 32.

Fischer, Louis. "Fascist Pacifism," *Nation*, CXLVII (October 29, 1938), 446–48.

"The FOR and the Communists," *Fellowship*, XIV (September, 1948), 11.

"The Fortune Survey," *Fortune*, XXIV (August, 1941), 75–78.

——, ——, XXXII (December, 1945), 303–10.

——, ——, XXXV (March, 1947), 5–30.

Four Lights. 1941–1944.

Frazier, E. Franklin. "Ethnic and Minority Groups in Wartime, with Special Reference to the Negro," *American Journal of Sociology*, XLVIII (November, 1942), 369–77.

"Freedom," *Fellowship*, XVI (September, 1950), 1.

Freeman, Harrop, and Theodore Paullin. "Federalism and Force," *Fellowship*, IX (January, 1943), 5–6.

Fromm, Erich. "The Case for Unilateral Disarmament," *Daedalus*, LXXXIX (Autumn, 1960), 1015–28.

Fuller, Helen. "Peace Now," *New Republic*, CX (February 14, 1944), 203–204.

"The Future of the C.O. Camps," *Christian Century*, LX (September 22, 1943), 1063–65.

Gallico, Paul. "What We Talked About," *While You Were Gone: A Report on Wartime Life in the United States*, ed. Jack Goodman. New York: Simon and Schuster, 1946.

"Gallup and Fortune Polls," *Public Opinion Quarterly*, V (June, 1941), 313–34.

——, ——, V (Winter, 1941), 666–87.

——, ——, VI (Spring, 1942), 140–74.

——, ——, VII (Spring, 1943), 161–78.

Gallup, George H. "Americans Are Looking for Peace," *The Federalist*, I (January, 1952), 12–13.

"Garry Davis Changes His Mind," *Fellowship*, XVI (November, 1950), 27.

"Geneva, 1950," *Common Cause*, IV (March, 1951), 432–40.

"Germany 1945: Current Notes," *Politics*, II (June, 1945), 170–72.

"Germfask C.O.'s Say *Time* Missed Real Story," *Fellowship*, XI (April, 1945), 65.

Glazer, Nathan. "The Peace Movement in America—1961," *Commentary,* XXXI (April, 1961), 288–96.

Gore, Robert Brookins. "Nonviolence," *The Angry Black South,* ed. Glenford E. Mitchell and William H. Peace III. New York: Corinth Books, 1962.

Gory, Adrian E., and David C. McClelland. "Characteristics of Conscientious Objectors in World War II," *Journal of Consulting Psychology,* XI (September–October, 1947), 245–57.

Gottlieb, Sanford. "National Committee for a SANE Nuclear Policy," *New University Thought,* II (Spring, 1962), 155–57.

Gould, Stanley. "Advice to the Landlorn," *Fellowship,* XV (September, 1949), 8–10.

Gregg, Richard B. "How Can Hitler Be Stopped?" *Fellowship* V (October, 1939), 6.

"Grim Lesson," *World Government News,* VIII (September, 1950), 3–5.

Guerard, Albert. "The Meaning of Victory," *Common Cause* IV (November, 1950), 169–71.

——. "The World Comes of Age," *Nation,* CLXII (April 20, 1946), 457–59.

Gurian, Waldemar. "World Government," *Commonweal,* XLII (September 28, 1945), 573.

"H-Mystery Man: He Hurried the H-Bomb," *Newsweek,* XLIV (August 2, 1954), 23–26.

Hamilton, Wallace. "Jim Quake," *Pacifica Views,* III (June 15, 1945), 2.

——. "Robin Hood: Latest Model," *Pacifica Views,* III (January 18, 1946), 2.

Harrington, Donald. "Pacifists Should Vote Socialist," *Fellowship.* XIV (May, 1948), 9–12.

Harrington, Michael. "The Catholic Church Rethinks War," *Fellowship,* XX (June, 1954), 8–10.

Hassler, Alfred. "Cops in Korea," *Fellowship,* XVI (September, 1950), 4–8.

——. "Pact with Death," *Fellowship,* XV (May, 1949), 10–14.

——. "Sharp Turn to the Center," *Fellowship,* XXIII (March, 1957), 23–26.

Hayden, Tom. "The Politics of 'The Movement,'" *The Radical Papers,* ed. Irving Howe. Garden City, N.Y.: Doubleday & Company, 1966.

Hentoff, Nat. "By Common Dissent," *Commonweal,* LXXV (January 19, 1962), 433–35.

——. "A Peaceful Army," *Commonweal,* LXXII (June 10, 1960), 275–78.

Hersey, John. "Hiroshima," *New Yorker*, XXII (August 31, 1946), 15–68.

High, Stanley. "Church Unmilitant," *New Republic*, CVI (June 22, 1942), 850–52.

——. "Peace, Inc.," *Saturday Evening Post*, CCX (March 5, 1938), 8–9, 89–92, 94.

——. "What, Then, Should the Church Do?" *Christian Century*, LIX (September 23, 1942), 1146–48.

Higham, John. "On Acquiring a Public Opinion," *Public Opinion Quarterly*, VIII (Winter, 1944), 488–99.

Holloway, Vernon H. "A Review of American Religious Pacifism," *Religion in Life*, XIX (Summer, 1950), 367–79.

Holmes, John Haynes. "From My Standpoint," *Fellowship*, IX (January, 1943), 2.

Hopkins, George E. "Bombing and the American Conscience during World War II," *Historian*, XXVIII (May, 1966), 451–73.

Horlings, Albert. "Who Are the Appeasers?" *New Republic*, CIV (January 27, 1941), 110–12.

Houser, George M. "Bases of Pacifism," *Pacifica Views*, II (July 28, 1944), 1–2.

——. "We Say No to Jim Crow," *Fellowship*, XI (April, 1945), 61–63.

"How Sane the SANE?" *Time*, LXXI (April 21, 1958), 13–14.

Hughan, Jessie Wallace. Letter to the Editor, *Fellowship*, XX (February, 1954), 26.

"Hunger Strike at Lewisburg," *Pacifica Views*, II (October 27, 1944), 3.

Hutchins, Robert M. "Conscription—An Act of War," *Progressive*, XII (January, 1948), 9–10.

——. "1950," *Common Cause*, I (July, 1947), 1–2.

——. Review of *The Absolute Weapon: Atomic Power and World Order*, by Bernard Brodie (ed.), *New York Times Book Review* (June 9, 1946), pp. 6, 27.

"Is the Church Aloof?" *Christian Century*, LIX (October 14, 1942), 1246–49.

"Is There a Pacifist Revival?" *Liberation*, III (May, 1958), 3, 18.

Jack, Homer A. "Action for Peace," *Progressive*, XV (February, 1951), 23.

——. "Christ and Gandhi in Montgomery," *Progressive*, XX (May, 1956), 25–27.

Janowitz, Morris. "Black Legions on the March," *America in Crisis*, ed. Daniel Aaron. New York: Alfred A. Knopf, 1952.

Johnson, F. Ernest. "The Impact of the War on Religion in America," *American Journal of Sociology*, XLVIII (November, 1942), 353–60.

Jones, Edgar L. "One War Is Enough," *Atlantic Monthly*, CLXXVII (February, 1946), 48–53.

"Jottings," *Fellowship*, XXII (February, 1956), 24.

Kahler, Erich. "The Reality of Utopia," *American Scholar*, XV (Spring, 1946), 167–79.

Kahn, E. J., Jr. "A Soldier's Slant on Compulsory Training," *Saturday Evening Post*, CCXVII (May 19, 1945), 27, 94.

Kallen, H. M. "National Solidarity and the Jewish Minority," *Annals of the American Academy of Political and Social Science*, CCXXIII (September, 1942), 17–28.

Kelley, Ray R., and Paul E. Johnson. "Emotional Traits in Pacifists," *Journal of Social Psychology*, XXVIII (1948), 275–86.

Kennan, George F. "Foreign Policy and the Christian Conscience," *Atlantic Monthly*, CCIII (May, 1959), 44–49.

Kepler, Roy. "An Open Letter to CPS Men," *Politics*, II (June, 1945), 167–68.

King, Martin Luther, Jr. "My Pilgrimage to Nonviolence," *Fellowship*, XXIV (September 1, 1958), 4–9.

——. "Nonviolence and Racial Justice," *Christian Century*, LXXIV (February 6, 1957), 165–67.

——. "Pilgrimage to Nonviolence," *Christian Century*, LXXVII (April 13, 1960), 439–41.

——. "The Social Organization of Nonviolence," *Liberation*, IV (October, 1959), 5–6.

——. "Walk for Freedom," *Fellowship*, XXII (May, 1956), 5–7.

Kopkind, Andrew. "The Thaw," *New York Review of Books*, X (April 25, 1968), 3–5.

"Korea—The Continuing Tragedy," *Christian Century*, LXVIII (July 4, 1951), 790–91.

Kreinheder, Albert. "War in Education," *Pacifica Views*, I (July 23, 1943), 2–3.

"Lait and Mortimer Attack UWF," *The Federalist*, II (May, 1952), 8.

"The Last Word," *World Government News*, VI (December, 1948), 3–5.

Latourette, Kenneth. "Christianity and the Peace Movement," *The Church, the Gospel and War*, ed. Rufus M. Jones. New York: Harper & Brothers, 1948.

Laurence, William L. "The Bikini Tests and Public Opinion," *Bulletin of the Atomic Scientists*, II (September 1, 1946), 2, 17.

"Let's Keep America Strong in the Air!" *Time*, XLVI (July 23, 1945), 14–15.

Levcik, Jan. "Buchenwald before the War," *Politics*, II (June, 1945), 173–74.

Lewis, Edward R. "Are We Ready for a World State?" *Yale Review*, XXXV (Spring, 1946), 491–501.

Life, LI (September 15, 1961), cover.

Life, XIV (March 29, 1943).

Lippmann, Walter. "One World of Diversity: Tolerance and Power Equilibrium," *Vital Speeches*, XIII (December 15, 1946), 138–40.

"Loses Job for Race Activities," *Fellowship*, XVI (November, 1950), 28.

Luft, John and W. M. Wheeler. "Reaction to John Hersey's 'Hiroshima,'" *Journal of Social Psychology*, XXVIII (1948), 135–40.

Mabee, Carleton. "Evolution of Non-Violence," *Nation*, CXCIII (August 12, 1961), 78–81.

MacArthur, Douglas. "The Surrender of Right to Make War," *Vital Speeches*, XII (April 15, 1946), 389–91.

Macdonald, Dwight. "Atrocities of the Mind," *Politics*, II (August, 1945), 225–27.

——. "By Way of Rejoinder," *Politics*, I (July, 1944), 179–80.

——. Editorial, *Politics*, II (August, 1945), 225.

——. "Henry Wallace," *Politics*, IV (March–April, 1947) and (May–June, 1947), 33–44, 96–117.

——. "The Questionnaire: Preliminary," *Politics*, IV (May–June, 1947), 122–24.

——. "The Responsibility of Peoples," *Politics*, II (March, 1945), 82–93.

——, and James Peck. "Should Pacifists Vote for Henry Wallace?" *Fellowship*, XIV (March, 1948), 6–15.

——. "Small Talk," *Politics*, V (Winter, 1948), 56–57.

——. "Thomas for President?" *Politics*, I (October, 1944), 278–81.

——. "The Truth about U.N.," *Politics*, III (November, 1946), 338.

——. "The Waldorf Conference," *Politics*, VI (Winter, 1949), special insert, 32A–32D.

——. "Why Destroy Draft Cards?" *Politics*, IV (March–April, 1947), 54–55.

——. "Why I Am No Longer a Socialist," *Liberation*, III (May, 1958), 4–7.

——. "Why 'POLITICS'?" *Politics*, I (February, 1944), 6–8.

Maechtle, Lowell E., and Hans H. Gerth. "Conscientious Objectors as Mental Hospital Attendants," *Sociology and Social Research*, XXIX (September–October, 1944), 11–24.

Magnes, Judah L. "A Tragic Dilemma," *Christian Century*, LVII (March 27, 1940), 406–407.

Mailer, Norman. "The Battle of the Pentagon," *Commentary*, VL (April, 1968), 33–57.

"The Manoukian Case," *Pacifica Views*, I (September 10, 1943), 2.

"March for Peace," *Christian Century*, LXXXII (December 8, 1965), 1501.

"Marching through Georgia," *Nation*, CXCVIII (January 27, 1964), 82–83.

Marshall, C. B. "Organized Groups," *Public Opinion Quarterly*, IV (March, 1940), 151–61.

Marshall, Peter. "How Many Worlds Make One?" *Antioch Review*, XIV (December, 1954), 508–12.

"Maryland Revisited," *The Federalist*, III (June, 1953), 3.

Masland, John W. "The 'Peace' Groups Join Battle," *Public Opinion Quarterly*, IV (December, 1940), 664–73.

———. "Pressure Groups and American Foreign Policy," *Public Opinion Quarterly*, VI (Spring, 1942), 115–22.

———, *et al.* "Treatment of the Conscientious Objector under the Selective Service Act of 1940," *American Political Science Review*, XXXVI (August, 1942), 697–701.

Matthews, J. B. "Pacifists Prefer Thomas," *World Tomorrow*, XV (October 26, 1932), 402.

Mayer, Milton. "How to Win the War," *Politics*, I (March, 1944), 45–46.

———. "Vicarious Atonement," *Fellowship*, XIV (September, 1948), 14–16.

McWilliams, Carey. "What We Did about Racial Minorities," *While You Were Gone: A Report on Wartime Life in the United States*, ed. Jack Goodman. New York: Simon and Schuster, 1946.

Mead, Margaret. "The Women in the War," *While You Were Gone: A Report on Wartime Life in the United States*, ed. Jack Goodman. New York: Simon and Schuster, 1946.

Mecartney, John. Letter to the Editor, *Fellowship*, XIV (October, 1948), 38.

"Men of Peace Return," *Christian Century*, LXXVII (May 18, 1960), 597.

Meyer, Cord, Jr. "What Are the Chances?" *Atlantic Monthly*, CLXXVIII (July, 1946), 42–45.

Miller, William Robert. "The Mightier Pen: American Peace Journalism, 1815–1960," *Fellowship*, XXVI (May 1, 1960), 21–26.

Millis, Walter. "War As a Moral Problem," *The Moral Dilemma of Nuclear Weapons*, ed. William Clancy. New York: Church Peace Union, 1961.

Mills, C. Wright. "On the New Left," *Studies on the Left*, II (1961), 63–72.

Mills, Ruth Harper. "The Fascinated Readers," *Politics*, V (Winter, 1948), 59–63.

"Modified Pacifism," *Christian Century*, LXI (July 26, 1944), 870–72.

"More Birthday Messages," *The Federalist*, I (March, 1952), 7–8.

Morgenthau, Hans J. "The Pathology of Power," *American Perspective*, IV (Winter, 1950), 6–10.

Morris, Jane. "Anti-Federalists Win in Virginia," *The Federalist*, I (March, 1952), 6.

Mumford, Lewis. "Gentlemen: You Are Mad!" *Saturday Review of Literature*, XXIX (March 2, 1946), 5–6.

——. "Kindling for Global Gehenna," *Saturday Review of Literature*, XXXI (June 26, 1948), 7–8, 29–31.

Muste, A. J. "The Crisis in SANE," *Liberation*, V (July–August, 1960), 10–13.

——. "ERP—Promise, Menace or Dilemma," *Fellowship*, XIV (February, 1948), 8–10.

——. "A Footnote on International Police," *Fellowship*, VIII (August, 1942), 136.

——. "Forth—to War?" *American Scholar*, VII (Autumn, 1938), 387–402.

——. "Pacifism Enters a New Phase," *Fellowship*, XXVI (July 1, 1960), 21–25, 34.

——. "Sit Downs and Lie Downs," *Fellowship*, III (March, 1937), 5–6.

——. "The Trend—The Historical Imperative of Civilization," *Peace Is the Victory*, ed. Harrop A. Freeman. New York: Harper & Brothers, 1944.

——. "A Vote for Wallace Will Be—A Vote for the Communists," *Fellowship*, XIV (July, 1948), 5–9.

——. "What Is the FOR?" *Fellowship*, XXIII (January, 1957), 7–13.

"Muste Pamphlet Burned in Boston," *Fellowship*, XXI (June, 1955), 28–29.

"The Myth that Threatened One American Town," *The Federalist*, III (April, 1953), 8–10.

Naeve, Lowell. "A Field of Broken Stones," *Prison Etiquette: The Convict's Compendium of Useful Information*, ed. Holley Cantine and Dachine Rainer. Bearsville, N.Y.: Retort Press, 1950.

Nation, CXXXVI (May 24, 1933), 571.

"National Organizations of Scientists," *Bulletin of the Atomic Scientists of Chicago*, I (December 10, 1945), 2.

Nelson, Donald M. "What Industry Did," *While You Were Gone: A Report on Wartime Life in the United States*, ed. Jack Goodman. New York: Simon and Schuster, 1946.

Nelson, Lowry. "Farms and Farming Communities," *American Society in Wartime*, ed. William Fielding Ogburn. Chicago: University of Chicago Press, 1943.

Neuberger, Richard L. "What the Home Folks Say about Events Abroad," *Harper's*, CLXXIX (September, 1939), 407–12.

Nevins, Allan. "How We Felt about the War," *While You Were Gone: A Report on Wartime Life in the United States*, ed. Jack Goodman. New York: Simon and Schuster, 1946.

Newhall, Dave. "Principles and Power," *Pacifica Views,* II (March 23, 1945), 1, 3.

"The New Peace Movement," *Nation,* CXCIV (March 3, 1962), 185–86.

Newton, David R. "The Macedonia Community," *Politics,* V (Winter, 1948), 27–30.

New York Herald Tribune. 1941–1960.

New York Post. 1960.

"The *New York Sun* Retracts Inaccurate Statements about the Bulletin," *Bulletin of the Atomic Scientists,* IV (February, 1948), 63.

New York Times. 1933–1968.

"The Next Civil-Defense Drill," *Nation,* CXC (May 14, 1960), 415.

Niebuhr, Reinhold. "The Myth of World Government," *Nation,* CLXII (March 16, 1946), 312–14.

——. "The Use of Force," *Pacifism in the Modern World,* ed. Devere Allen. Garden City, N.Y.: Doubleday, Doran & Company, Inc., 1929.

——. "Why I Leave the F.O.R.," *Christian Century,* LI (January 3, 1934), 17–19.

"No News: SANE Peace Rally and the New York Times," *Nation,* CCIII (December 26, 1966), 692.

"Of Symbols and Emblems," *Common Cause,* IV (November, 1950), 223.

Oldham, G. Ashton. "A Message from the President of the World Alliance," *World Alliance News Letter,* XXI (September, 1945), 1.

"One Planet: America Ponders the Vision of a Federation of the World," *Newsweek,* XXVIII (October 14, 1946), 44–45.

Oppenheimer, J. Robert. "The New Weapon: The Turn of the Screw," *One World or None: A Report to the Public on the Full Meaning of the Atomic Bomb,* ed. Dexter Masters and Katherine Way. New York: McGraw-Hill Book Company, Inc., 1946.

"Opponents Hit Kefauver," *The Federalist,* II (June, 1952), 6.

"Opposition Renews Attacks on Scattered Fronts," *The Federalist,* I (January, 1952), 6–7.

"The Other Summit Conferences," *Nation,* CXC (June 4, 1960), 482.

Ottley, Roi. "Negro Morale," *New Republic,* CV (November 10, 1941), 613–15.

——. "A White Folks' War?" *Common Ground,* II (Spring, 1942), 28–31.

"Our Readers and the Election," *Liberation,* I (October, 1956), 15–17.

"Pacifist Cons Fight Jimcrow," *Pacifica Views,* III (July 27, 1945), 2.

"The Pacifist Conscience," *Christian Century,* LX (September 8, 1943), 1006–1008.

"The Pacifist Revolution," *Pacifica Views,* I (June 11, 1943), 1–2.

"Pacifists Prefer Prison," *Christian Century,* LXI (January 26, 1944), 100–101.

Page, Kirby. "20,870 Clergymen on War and Economic Injustice," *World Tomorrow,* XVII (May 10, 1934), 222–56.

Parsons. Wilfrid. "The Ethics of Atomic War," *Peace in the Atomic Age.* Washington, D.C.: Catholic Association for International Peace, 1947.

Paullin, Theodore. "I'll Pay My Taxes," *Fellowship,* XIV (January, 1948), 12–13.

——. "A New International Order—Functional or Constitutional," *Peace Is the Victory,* ed. Harrop A. Freeman. New York: Harper & Brothers, 1944.

——. Review of *The World Federation Plan,* by Ely Culbertson, *Fellowship,* IX (February, 1943), 38.

Peacemaker. 1948–1960.

Pearson, Norman Holmes. "The Nazi-Soviet Pact and the End of a Dream," *America in Crisis,* ed. Daniel Aaron. New York: Alfred A. Knopf, 1952.

Peck, George T. "Who Are the United World Federalists?" *Common Cause,* I (July, 1947), 28, 36.

Peck, James. "The Ship that Never Hit Port." *Prison Etiquette: The Convict's Compendium of Useful Information,* ed. Holley Cantine and Dachine Rainer. Bearsville, N.Y.: Retort Press, 1950.

——, and Dwight Macdonald. "Should Pacifists Vote for Henry Wallace?" *Fellowship,* XIV (March, 1948), 6–15.

Peffer, Nathaniel. "Politics Is Peace," *American Scholar,* XV (Spring, 1946), 160–66.

Pelcovits, N. A. "World Government Now?" *Harper's,* CXCIII (November, 1946), 396–403.

"Personalities and Projects," *Survey,* LXXXV (October, 1949), 552–53.

Pickett, Clarence E. "They Cry for Help!" *Peace Is the Victory,* ed. Harrop A. Freeman. New York: Harper & Brothers, 1944.

Pickus, Robert. "Speak Truth to Power," *Progressive,* XIX (October, 1955), 5–8.

"Poetry of the Read-In Campaign," *Nation,* CCII (May 30, 1966), 653–55.

"Politics as Usual?" *World Government News,* VI (August, 1948), 3–4.

Possony, Stefan T. "The Atomic Bomb," *Review of Politics,* VIII (April, 1946), 147–67.

Powell, Adam C., Jr. "Is This a 'White Man's War'?" *Common Sense,* XI (April, 1942), 111–13.

"The Power of Political Protest," *Progressive,* XXXII (May, 1968), 3–4.

Prattis, P. L. "The Morale of the Negro in the Armed Forces of the United States," *Journal of Negro Education,* XII (Summer, 1943), 355–63.

"Protest," *New Yorker,* XXXVI (May 14, 1960), 33–35.

"Public Opinion Polls," *Public Opinion Quarterly,* VII (Winter, 1943), 736–64.

Putney, Snell, and Russell Middleton. "Some Factors Associated with

Student Acceptance or Rejection of War," *American Sociological Review*, XXVII (October, 1962), 655–67.

"Quakers Affirm Peace Witness," *Christian Century*, LVII (July 17, 1940), 909–10.

Quarles, James. "E Pluribus Unum: 1946 Model," *World Affairs*, CIX (September, 1946), 181–85.

Rabi, I. I. "The Social Responsibility of the Scientist," *Integrity and Compromise: Problems of Public and Private Conscience*, ed. Robert MacIver. New York: Harper & Brothers, 1957.

Rabin, Albert I. "Rorschach Test Findings in a Group of Conscientious Objectors," *American Journal of Orthopsychiatry*, XV (1945), 514–19.

Rabinowitch, Eugene. "Five Years After," *Bulletin of the Atomic Scientists*, VII (January, 1951), 3–5, 12.

"Randolph Withdraws from Anti-Jimcrow League," *Fellowship*, XIV (October, 1948), 34.

Rankin, Jeannette. "Two Votes against War—1917, 1941," *Liberation*, III (March, 1958), 4–7.

"Red," *Fellowship*, XVI (June, 1950), 1–2.

——, ——, XVI (November, 1950), 1.

"A Red Is a Red Is a Red," *Common Cause*, IV (December, 1950), 280.

Redfield, Robert. "The Price of Peace," *Common Cause*, I (September, 1947), 81–82.

Reeves, George B. "It Happened Here," *Pacifica Views*, III (September 21, 1945), 1.

——. "Why They Went to Prison," *Pacifica Views*, I (April 7, 1944), 1, 4.

"Report of Chicago Conference on More Disciplined and Revolutionary Pacifism," *Fellowship*, XIV (May, 1948), 26.

"A Report to the Secretary of War," *Bulletin of the Atomic Scientists*, I (May 1, 1946), 2–4, 16.

Reves, Emery. "National Sovereignty—The Road to the Next War," *World Affairs*, CIX (June, 1946), 109–16.

——. "World Government Is the First Step," *Reader's Digest*, XLVIII (February, 1946), 109–17.

Reynolds, Earle. "Forbidden Voyage," *Nation*, CLXXXVII (November 15, 1958), 358–60, 368.

Ridenour, Louis. Review of "Hiroshima," by John Hersey, *Saturday Review of Literature*, XXIX (November 2, 1946), 16.

——. "The Scientist Fights for Peace," *Atlantic Monthly*, CLXXIX (May, 1947), 80–83.

Riesman, David. "Private People and Public Policy," *Shenandoah*, X (Autumn, 1958), 47–67.

——, and Michael Maccoby. "The American Crisis," *The Liberal Papers*, ed. James Roosevelt. Garden City, N.Y.: Doubleday & Company, Inc., 1962.

Roberts, Owen J. "Real World Parliament to Keep Peace," *Vital Speeches,* XII (May 1, 1946), 426–28.

Rodell, Fred. "What *Should* We Do about the Commies?" *Progressive,* XII (January, 1948), 15–16.

"Rodent Exterminators," *Time,* XLV (March 19, 1945), 32, 34.

Rosi, Eugene J. "Mass and Attentive Opinion on Nuclear Weapons Tests and Fallout, 1954–1963," *Public Opinion Quarterly,* XXIX (Summer, 1965), 280–97.

Rothstein, Richard. "ERAP: Evolution of the Organizers," *Radical America,* II (March–April, 1968), 1–18.

Rubin, Morris. "The Choice for President," *Progressive,* XII (September, 1948), 3–4.

Rustin, Bayard. "The Negro and Non-Violence," *Fellowship,* VIII (October, 1942), 166–67.

——. "Non-Violence vs. Jim Crow," *Fellowship,* VIII (July, 1942), 120.

" 'Safe Now in the Wide, Wide World': College Editors and Commencement," *Atlantic Monthly,* CLXVIII (August, 1941), 182–92.

Schneir, Walter. "The Campaign to Make Chemical Warfare Respectable," *Reporter,* XXI (October 1, 1959), 24–28.

Schoenfeld, Howard. "The Danbury Story," *Prison Etiquette: The Convict's Compendium of Useful Information,* ed. Holley Cantine and Dachine Rainer. Bearsville, N.Y.: Retort Press, 1950.

Schuman, Frederick L. "Toward the World State," *Scientific Monthly,* LIII (July, 1946), 5–19.

Schwarzenberger, Georg. "The Prospects for International Law," *Review of Politics,* VIII (April, 1946), 168–82.

"Science Dons a Uniform," *Bulletin of the Atomic Scientists,* II (November 1, 1946), 11.

"Scientists Comment on State Department Report," *Bulletin of the Atomic Scientists,* I (April 15, 1946), 12.

Seidman, Harold. "The Colleges Renounce War," *Nation,* CXXXVI (May 17, 1933), 554–55.

"Senate Hearings on Atomic Energy," *Bulletin of the Atomic Scientists of Chicago,* I (December 10, 1945), 3.

"Shall We Vote?" *Liberation,* I (October, 1956), 3–7.

"The Shame of American Writers," *Common Sense,* XIII (May, 1944), 187.

Shapiro, Karl. "New Guinea Letter," *New Republic,* CIX (July 12, 1943), 46.

"Signals Green?" *World Government News,* VI (February, 1948), 7–8.

"Silent Generation," *Fellowship,* XXVI (May 1, 1960), 3.

"Sit-Ins," *Fellowship*, XXVI (May 1, 1960), 3.

"Smear," *Fellowship*, XXI (January, 1955), 1–2.

Smith, Alice Kimball. "Behind the Decision to Use the Atomic Bomb: Chicago, 1944–45," *Bulletin of the Atomic Scientists*, XIV (October, 1958), 288–312.

"South Sit-Ins Continue: F.O.R. Staff, Volunteers Active," *Fellowship*, XXVI (April 1, 1960), 1.

Sprout, Harold H. "Pressure Groups and American Foreign Policies," *Annals of the American Academy of Political and Social Science*, CLXXIX (May, 1935), 114–23.

Stein, Robert, and Carolyn Conners. "Civil Defense Protests in New York," *New University Thought*, I (Spring, 1961), 81–83.

Stimson, Henry L. "The Decision to Use the Atomic Bomb," *Harper's* CXCIV (February, 1947), 97–107.

Straight, Michael. "A Non-Pacifist Answers," *Pacifica Views*, II (January 26, 1945), 1–3.

"Student Peace Groups," *New University Thought*, I (Spring, 1961), 75–80.

"A Student Strike against War," *Literary Digest*, CXIX (March 23, 1935), 17.

Suchman, Edward A., *et al.* "Attitudes toward the Korean War," *Public Opinion Quarterly*, XVII (Summer, 1953), 171–84.

Summers, Joseph Holmes. "Quakerism, Pacifism and Democracy," *Christian Century*, LX (September 22, 1943), 1068–1070.

"Surfeit," *Fellowship*, XVI (December, 1950), 1–3.

Szilard, Leo. "A Personal History of the Atomic Bomb," *University of Chicago Round Table*, No. 601 (September 25, 1949), pp. 14–16.

——. "The Physicist Invades Politics," *Saturday Review of Literature*, XXX (May 3, 1947), 7–8, 31–34.

"Taking Bearings," *Common Cause*, IV (April, 1951), 449–50.

Tate, Merze. "The War Aims of World War I and World War II and Their Relation to the Darker Peoples of the World," *Journal of Negro Education*, XII (Summer, 1943), 521–32.

Taylor, Senator Glen H. "Why a World Republic?" *Free World*, X (December, 1945), 26–31.

Teller, Edward. "Atomic Scientists Have Two Responsibilities," *Bulletin of the Atomic Scientists*, III (December, 1947), 356.

——, and Allen Brown. "The Fallout Scare," *Saturday Evening Post*, CCXXV (February 10, 1962), 36.

——, and Albert Latter. "The Compelling Need for Nuclear Tests," *Life*, XLIV (February 10, 1958), 64–66, 69–72.

"That Man Wallace," *Fellowship*, XIV (May, 1948), 27–28.

"They Call Him 'Bull,'" *Time*, XLVI (September 10, 1945), 23.

"They March, Doubting They Will Overcome," *New Republic*, CLIII (October 30, 1965), 9.

" 'Third Camp' Concept Still in the Making," *Fellowship*, XX (February, 1954), 24.

"This Critical Hour," *Common Cause*, IV (June, 1951), 613.

Thomas, Norman M. "Advances in the Quest for Peace," *Recent Gains in American Civilization*, ed. Kirby Page. New York: Harcourt, Brace and Company, 1928.

——. "Norman Thomas Replies," *Fellowship*, III (February, 1937), 13.

——. "Our War with Japan," *Commonweal*, XLII (April 20, 1945), 7–10.

Thompson, E. P. "The New Left," *Voices from the Crowd: Against the H-Bomb*, ed. David Boulton. Philadelphia: Dufour Editions, 1964.

"Thou Shalt Not Appease," *Nation*, CXCIII (September 9, 1961), 129.

"Thought Needed," *Common Cause*, IV (April, 1951), 501.

"Three to Lose Jobs over Loyalty Oath," *Fellowship*, XVI (May, 1950), 22.

Time, XLVI (July 23, 1945), cover.

"Tract for the Times," *Liberation*, I (March, 1956), 3–6.

Tucci, Niccolo. "Two Observations on World War III," *Politics*, II (July, 1945), 196.

"Uneasy Money," *World Government News*, VI (November, 1948), 7.

"Unnecessary Sectarianism," *Christian Century*, LIX (November 11, 1942), 1382–85.

Urey, Harold C. "How Does It All Add Up?" *One World or None: A Report to the Public on the Full Meaning of the Atomic Bomb*, ed. Dexter Masters and Katherine Way. New York: McGraw-Hill Book Company, Inc., 1946.

"U.S. Department of Justice Denies Asking 'Would-Be' Employees about UWF," *The Federalist*, II (March, 1953), 4.

"UWF'S Birthday Marks Half a Decade of Progress," *The Federalist*, I (February, 1952), 6–7.

"Verse," *Fellowship*, XXIII (November, 1957), 2.

"The Victory of Violence," *Pacifica Views*, III (August 31, 1945), 1, 4.

Villard, Oswald Garrison. "Issues and Men," *Nation*, CXLVII (July 2, 1938), 18.

Vinson, J. Chalmers. "Military Force and American Policy, 1919–1939," *Isolation and Security*, ed. Alexander DeConde. Durham, N.C.: Duke University Press, 1957.

"Virginia Senate Acts," *The Federalist*, I (February, 1952), 8.

Votaw, Albert. "Resistance in C.P.S.," *Politics*, III (September, 1946), 272–74.

Walker, Charles C. "The Vigil and Appeal at Fort Detrick," *Fellowship*, XXVI (January, 1960), 12–16.

"Walkout," *Pacifica Views*, III (August 31, 1945), 2.

Wallace, Henry A. "Letter to the President," *Bulletin of the Atomic Scientists*, II (October 1, 1946), 2–3.

———. "Whose Atomic Secret?" *New Republic*, CXVI (February 17, 1947), 26–27.

Waltner, James, "Pacifist Witness at Omaha," *Mennonite* (August 11, 1959), pp. 483–84.

"War Comes to the Campus," *Newsweek*, LXVII (May 23, 1966), 29–30.

War Resisters League, "National Council for the Prevention of War," *Peace Calendar and Appointment Book, 1965*. New York: War Resisters League, 1964.

" 'War without Violence,' " *Pacifica Views*, II (May 25, 1945), 1–2, 4.

Washington Post. 1941–1960.

Washington Star. 1948.

Weaver, Robert C. "With the Negro's Help," *Atlantic Monthly*, CLXIX (June, 1942), 696–707.

Wehrly, Herbert. "CPS Resistance," *Pacifica Views*, III (May 24, 1946), 1, 4.

Weil, Simone. "Reflections on War," *Politics*, II (February, 1945), 51–55.

Weinstein, James. "Studies on the Left: R.I.P.," *Radical America*, I (November–December, 1967), 1–6.

"What Do Pacifists Propose?" *Presbyterian Tribune*, LVI (August, 1941), 4.

"Where UWF Stands," *World Government News*, VI (March, 1948), 7–8.

"Which Road to Peace in 1948?" *Town Meeting: Bulletin of America's Town Meeting of the Air*, XIII (December 30, 1947), 3–24.

White, Walter. "What the Negro Thinks of the Army," *Annals of the American Academy of Political and Social Science*, CCXXIII (September, 1942), 67–71.

"Who the Pacifists Are," *Newsweek*, LVI (December 5, 1960), 31–32.

Wickware, Francis Sill. "What We Think about Foreign Affairs," *Harper's*, CLXXIX (September, 1939), 397–406.

Wiener, Norbert. "A Scientist Rebels," *Atlantic Monthly*, CLXXIX (January, 1947), 46.

Wilcher, Denny. "Conscientious Objectors in Prison," *Christian Century*, LXI (March 8, 1944), 302–304.

———. "Shall the C.P.S. Camps Continue?" *Christian Century*, LIX (December 16, 1942), 1556–59.

Willen, Paul. "Who 'Collaborated' with Russia?" *Antioch Review*, XIV (September, 1954), 259–83.

Woodward, C. Vann. "The Age of Reinterpretation," *American Historical Review*, LXVI (October, 1960), 1–19.

"World Opinion on World Government," *Common Cause*, I (September, 1947), 101–103.

Wright, Quincy. "Making the United Nations Work," *Review of Politics,* VIII (October, 1946), 528–32.

Zahn, Curtis. "Notes on My Life among the Dead Men in Denims," *Prison Etiquette: The Convict's Compendium of Useful Information,* ed. Holley Cantine and Dachine Rainer. Bearsville, N.Y.: Retort Press, 1950.

UNPUBLISHED MATERIAL

Altbach, Philip G. "The American Peace Movement, 1900–1962: A Critical Analysis." n.p., 1963. (Azographed.)

Bowers, Robert Edwin. "The American Peace Movement, 1933–1941." Unpublished Ph.D. dissertation, Department of History, University of Wisconsin, 1949.

Buhner, John Colin. "The Political Theory of Non-Violence." Unpublished Ph.D. dissertation, Department of Government, Indiana University, 1963.

Chatfield, Earl Charles, Jr. "Pacifism and American Life, 1914 to 1941." Unpublished Ph.D. dissertation, Department of History, Vanderbilt University, 1965.

Harrington, Mayne A. "Recent Thought on World Peace." Unpublished Ph.D. dissertation, Department of Political Science, Georgetown University, 1947.

Holloway, Vernon Howard. "American Pacifism between Two Wars, 1919–1941." Unpublished Ph.D. dissertation, Yale University, 1949.

Kuusisto, Allan A. "The Influence of the National Council for Prevention of War on United States Foreign Policy, 1935–1939." Unpublished Ph.D. dissertation, Department of History, Harvard University, 1950.

Lund, Doniver A. "The Peace Movement among the Major American Protestant Churches, 1919–1939." Unpublished Ph.D. dissertation, Department of History, University of Nebraska, 1955.

Muste, A. J. "Of Holy Disobedience." 4th ed. revised. Raymond, N.H.: Greenleaf Books, 1965. (Mimeographed.)

Myers, Frank Earle. "British Peace Politics: The Campaign for Nuclear Disarmament and the Committee of 100, 1957–1962." Unpublished Ph.D. dissertation, Department of Public Law and Government, Columbia University, 1962.

Olson, Theodore W. "The Movement of Non-Violent Direct Action for Unilateral Disarmament: What Is It and What Does It Mean for the Church?" Unpublished Ph.D. dissertation, Department of Religion, Drew Univeristy, 1962.

——. "Peace and the American Community: A Manual for Instructors in a Work and Study Program for Peace Internes." New York, 1963. (Mimeographed.)

Pacifica Library Associates. "Pacifica Studies on Conscientious Objection." Glendora, Calif., 1942. (Mimeographed.)

Peacemakers. "Handbook on Nonpayment of War Taxes." n.p., 1966. (Mimeographed.)

Schaffer, Ronald. "Jeannette Rankin, Progressive-Isolationist." Unpublished Ph.D. dissertation, Department of History, Princeton University, 1959.

Witte, William Darwin Swanson. "Quaker Pacifism in the United States, 1919–1942, with Special Reference to Its Relation to Isolationism and Internationalism." Unpublished Ph.D. dissertation, Columbia University, 1954.

Wynner, Edith. "Ely Culbertson's So-Called Plan for World Federation." New York, 1943. (Mimeographed.)

PERSONAL COMMUNICATIONS

Dellinger, David. Editor of Liberation. Personal interview, New York City. May 16, 1966.

DiGia, Ralph. Administrative secretary, War Resisters League. Personal interview, New York City. April 21, 1966.

Muste, A. J. Former executive secretary of the Fellowship of Reconciliation and chairman of the Committee for Non-Violent Action. Personal interview, New York City. June 2, 1966.

Peck, James. Publicity director, War Resisters League. Personal interview, New York City. April 21, 1966.

Randall, Mercedes M. Former editor of Four Lights and former chairman of the literature and education committees, Women's International League for Peace and Freedom. Personal interview, New York City. April 26, 1965.

Roszak, Theodore. Former editor of Peace News. Letter to the author. February 7, 1966.

Thomas, Norman M. Former Socialist Party Presidential candidate. Personal interview, New York City. October 4, 1966.

Index

Abernathy, Ralph, 271
Acheson-Lilienthal proposals, 168
Allen, Devere, 8, 14
Alvarez, Luis, 149
America First Committee, 24–25, 27–28, 36
American Civil Liberties Union, 73, 82n, 216
American Federation of Teachers, 10
American Friends Service Committee: action organization of American Quakers, 13; attitude toward League of Nations, 27; rejection of World War II, 45; criticism of, 58; supports alternative service program, 70; awarded Nobel Peace Prize, 151; opposes conscription, 163; observes Communist Party convention, 216; rejects cooperation with Selective Service, 225; calls for new foreign policy, 228–29
American League Against War and Fascism, 14, 20
American League for Peace and Democracy, 20
American Legion, 24, 99
American Peace Mobilization, 23–24
American Student Union, 14, 20
American Veterans Committee, 99, 162
American Youth Congress, 14
Americans for Democratic Action, 21, 193–94
Americans for Intellectual Freedom, 206
Americans United for World Government, 170
Arms Control and Disarmament Agency, 277

Ashland strikes, 89
Association of Catholic Conscientious Objectors, 53–54
Atlantic Union Committee, 199, 208
Atomic bomb: use at Hiroshima, 125; reaction of churches, 126–27; reaction of peace movement, 127–28; public opinion on, 128–29; guilt reaction, 130–31; initiates nuclear pacifism, 131–34; influences world government movement, 139–43; reaction of atomic scientists, 143–50; proposals for control, 147–48, 166, 168–69; change in public opinion on, 166–67; resistance to, 177–78; see also Atomic scientists
Atomic Energy Commission, 242, 249
Atomic scientists: initiate atomic bomb project, 143; efforts to prevent use of bomb, 143–46; reaction to use of bomb, 146; organizations, 147, 165–66; and civilian control of atomic energy, 147–48; guilt reaction, 148–49; conversion to the cause of peace, 149–50; difficulties of movement, 166–68; support Baruch Plan, 168–69; criticism of, 175–77; rejection of military employment, 177–78; pressures upon, 188–89; decline of movement, 189–90, 210; reaction to 1948 election, 194; reject development of H-bomb, 199–201; accused of disloyalty, 221

Balch, Emily Greene: considers World War II inevitable, 32n; supports war, 52–53; receives Nobel Peace

Balch, Emily Greene (*Continued*)
Prize, 151; wary of world government, 178–79
Baldwin, Hanson, 103, 178
Baldwin, Roger, 7
Baruch Plan, 168–69
Becker, Carl, 110–11
Bell, Bernard Iddings, 126
Bell, Daniel, 194
Benedict, Ruth, 114
Bennett, James V., 87, 91
Bennett, John C., 234
Berlin crisis, 187–88
Bethe, Hans, 165, 176, 190, 200
Bigelow, Albert, 247–48, 250
Bikini bomb tests, 166–67
Bishop, Corbett, 77, 85, 89–90
Boeckel, Florence Brewer, 27
Borgese, G. A., 172–73, 209
Boulding, Kenneth, 251
Bowles, Chester, 172
Brethren, Society of the: traditional pacifism, 13; pacifism during World War II, 45; support alternative service program, 83n; *see also* Historic Peace Churches
Brinkley, David, 107
Brittain, Vera, 59
Brown, Harrison, 173, 208, 210
Bush, Vannevar, 131, 221
Businessmen, 2, 7–8
Buttrick, George A., 22, 53
Byrnes, James F., 130, 144

Campaign for World Government, 134, 172–3
Carman, Harry J., 7
Carnegie, Andrew, 1
Carnegie Endowment for International Peace, 9, 19, 52
Cary, C. Read, 61
Catholic Association for International Peace, 19
Catholics and war, 44, 59
Catholic Worker, 13, 53, 216, 225, 227, 265
Catt, Carrie Chapman, 5, 5n, 19

Central Conference of American Rabbis, 6
Chalmers, Allan Knight, 43
Chavez, Dennis, 170
Churches: reject war in the Thirties, 5, 6; accept World War II, 22, 37, 43–45; on atomic bomb, 125; *see also* Federal Council of Churches
Church Peace Union, 9, 20
Civil defense protests, 264n, 265–66
Civil Defense Protest Committee, 265
Civilian Public Service camps: intellectuals in, 49; creation of, 70–72; opposition to, 72–84
Civil Rights Act, N.J., 1949, 161
Civil rights and pacifists, 64; *see also* Fellowship of Reconciliation, Congress of Racial Equality, *and* Civil rights movement
Civil rights movement, 268–273, 278
Clark, Grenville: criticizes U.N. charter, 137; supports world government movement, 140–41, 171; notes effects of McCarthyism, 223
Clayton, William L., 199
Coffee, John, 75
Cogley, John, 121–22
Cold War, 164, 166, 182, 187–88, 189, 209, 212, 228, 235
Collett, John, 58
Committee Against Discrimination in Military Service and Training, 185
Committee for a People's World Constitutional Convention, 171
Committee for Non-Violent Action, 247–250; opposes nuclear missiles, 252–53, 261–62
Committee for Non-Violent Revolution, 154–56
Committee on the Cause and Cure of War, 19
Committee to Defend America by Aiding the Allies, 21–22
Committee to Stop H-Bomb Tests, 242
Communist Party: peace efforts in the Thirties, 8, 20, 23–24; relations with postwar peace movement, 187–89, 203–207, 229; supports Henry A.

Wallace, 190; civil liberties defended by pacifists, 215–16

Compton, Arthur H., 145–47, 190, 237

Compton, Karl T., 168

Conant, James B.: supports Cold War, 190; opposes H-bomb, 200

Congress of Racial Equality: formation of, 67–69; relation to F.O.R. 67–68, 160–61; postwar growth, 160; accused of Communism, 220; civil rights efforts from 1958 to 1960, 269–72

Connor, Eugene "Bull," 214

Conscientious objectors: denied employment, 38; number during World War II, 41; characteristics of, 48–49; in C.P.S. camps, 72–84; in prison, 84–94; return home, 152–53; concern with cooperatives, 158

Conscription, 122–23, 184–87

Cooperatives, 158–59

Counts, George S., 206

Cousins, Norman: reaction to atomic bomb, 133, 167; supports world government, 139, 171–72, 224; discusses Baruch Plan, 169; accused of Communist ties, 223; opposes nuclear weapons, 242–43, 245, 251–52; relations with Senator Dodd, 258, 260

Cowles, Gardner, Jr., 116

Cranston, Alan, 208

Culbertson, Ely, 136

Czechoslovakia coup, effect of, 183, 187

Danbury Prison: strikes, 87–89; picketing, 91–92

Daughters of the American Revolution, 115, 209–10

Davies, Joseph E., 116–18

Davis, Elmer, 104

Davis, Garry, 207

Day, Dorothy: founds Catholic Worker movement, 13; difficulties during World War II, 38–39; reacts to atomic bomb, 127–28; opposes political action, 227

Dellinger, Dave: activities during World War II, 56–57; advocates non-violent resistance, 93–94, 153–54, 163, 265

Denver Committee on Foreign Relations, 108

Detroit Committee on Foreign Relations, 35

Detzer, Dorothy: influence on Nye Committee, 11; criticizes Munich Pact, 18; forswears ties with America First, 29; discusses W.I.L.P.F.'s wartime role, 52–53, 56

DeVault, Don, 73

DeVoto, Bernard, 98, 114–15

Dewey, John, 118, 120

Dies Committee, 58

Dodd, Thomas J., 258–61

Douglas, Helen Gahagan, 131

Douglas, William O., 212

Draft evasion, 42n

DuBridge, Lee, 200

Dulles, John Foster, 126, 181

Eagleton, Clyde, 142

Eddy, Sherwood, 9, 16

Eichelberger, Clark, 22

Einstein, Albert: opposes war in Thirties, 4; rejects pacifism, 16; supports world government, 102, 140, 143; criticizes nuclear weapons, 146, 148, 165, 177n, 201; supports Henry A. Wallace, 174; rejects Marshall Plan, 185; analyzes collapse of peace efforts, 210, 212; condemns loyalty investigations, 215, 221; assesses Cold War, 236

Einstein-Russell Appeal, 235–36, 251

Eisenhower, Dwight D., 116, 254

Elliott, William A., 37

Emergency Committee of Atomic Scientists: formation of, 165–66; supports Baruch Plan, 169; collapse of, 210

Farmer, James: appeals for racial justice, 64; founds CORE, 66; leads

Farmer, James (*Continued*)
demonstrations, 271; lauds non-violent resistance, 273

Farmers, in peace movement in Thirties, 7

Fascism, effect on peace movement in Thirties, 15–18, 33

Federal Council of Churches: during World War II, 43; reaction to atomic bomb, 126–27; supports the United Nations, 138; urges amnesty for C.O.'s, 162; approves Korean War, 202

Federal Union, 135, 142

Federation of American Scientists, 165, 168

Federation of Atomic Scientists, 147–48

Fellowship of Reconciliation: activities in Thirties, 11, 32; supports Socialist candidate, 26; during World War II, 54–55, 57–58 61; civil rights efforts, 64–65, 67–68, 161; relations with radicals, 92–93, 152–53; attitude toward U.N., 138; postwar decline, 152; opposes Korean conflict, 203; relations with Communists, 205, 215–16; difficulties during Fifties, 212, 217–18; rejects political action in 1952, 227; opposes H-bomb tests, 248, 250; supports Fort Detrick vigil, 263; pleased by student activism, 267

Fermi, Enrico, 145, 200

Fermi, Laura, 149

Finch, Roy, 153, 261

Finletter, Thomas K., 169, 171, 208

Fosdick, Harry Emerson: pacifism in Thirties, 3, 12, 43; opposes Nazis, 17; rejects militant pacifism in wartime, 59; attacks saturation bombing 59; supports United Nations, 138; criticizes American conservatism, 229

Foster, William Z., 14

Foundation for World Government, 195*n*

Franck, James, 144

Franck Report, 143

Freeman, Harrop, 58

Friends Peace Committee, 30

Friends, Society of, 13–14, 45, 48, 59, 82; *see also* Historic Peace Churches *and* American Friends Service Committee

Fromm, Erich: supports Norman Thomas for President, 194; suggests name for SANE, 243

Gallico, Paul, 113

Gandhi, Mohandas: influence of, 31, 51, 63, 66; comments on atomic bomb, 132; effect of his death, 210

Gara, Larry, 187

Gilmore, Robert, 245, 260

Glazer, Nathan: discusses SANE, 245, 258; assesses importance of peace movement, 275

Golden Rule, 247–48

Gottlieb, Sanford, 244–45

Graham, Billy, 214

Graham, Frank, 170

Gregg, Richard, 31–32, 190

Griffin, James A., 140

Groves, Leslie R., 145

Hagedorn, Hermann, 128

Halsey, William F., 105

Hammerstein, Oscar II, 223, 245

Hapgood, Powers, 9

Harrington, Donald: defense of civil disobedience, 187*n*; support of Socialists in 1948, 197

Harrington, Michael: criticizes war, 225; supports Socialist candidate, 227

Hartmann, George W., 57

Hassler, Alfred: criticizes NATO, 199; analyzes Korean conflict, 203

Hauschka, Theodore, 178

Hays, Brooks, 172

H-bomb: reaction of scientists, 200–1; public reaction, 200–1; effect on peace movement, 240, 247

Hecht, Selig, 165

Hennacy, Ammon, 51, 225, 227

Hersey, John, 130

Hershey, Lewis B., 74
Higham, John, 100
Higinbotham, W. A., 176
Hinshaw, Cecil, 156, 229
Hirabayashi, Gordon, 61
Hiroshima bombing, *see* Atomic bomb
Historic Peace Churches: history of, 13–14; opposition to World War II, 44–45, 56; wartime programs, 60; role in Civilian Public Service, 70–71
Hogness, Thorfin, 144, 165
Holliday, W. T., 171
Holmes, John Haynes: support of Socialist Party, 9, 197; as a leader of the F.O.R., 11; attacks Nazis, 17; opposition to World War II, 19; support of League of Nations, 27; urges pacifists not resist actively World War II, 56, 83
Hoopes, Darlington, 9
House Committee on Un-American Activities, 215
Houser, George: calls for creation of non-violent resistance movement, 63, 92, 152; work in CORE, 66–68, 160; elected to W.R.L. council, 153; supports Socialist ticket in 1948, 197
Houston Committee on Foreign Relations, 36
Howe, Quincy, 107
Hughan, Jessie Wallace, 35; Socialist activities of, 8; founder of War Resisters League, 12; appeal to aid the Jews, 40–41
Hughes, Donald, 144
Hull, Hannah Clothier, 52
Humber, Robert Lee, 141, 171
Hutchins, Robert M.: reaction to atomic bomb, 125, 131, 167; calls for world government, 139, 141, 172; opposes conscription, 164
Huxley, Aldous, 31, 110

Isolationists, 26–27, 29, 36

Jack, Homer, 245

Japanese, American reaction to, 104–6, 129
Jews: pacifism in Thirties, 6; pacifist reaction to persecution of, 40–41; support of World War II, 44
Johnston, Olin, 170
Jones, E. Stanley, 55
Jones, Rufus, 45
Journal of Conflict Resolution, 250
Judd, Walter, 172

Kaufman, Abraham, 153
Keep America Out of War Congress, 14n, 51
Kefauver, Estes, 223
Kennan, George, 254–55
Kennedy, John F., 278
Kepler, Roy, 152–53, 211–12
King, Martin Luther, Jr.: development of non-violent resistance philosophy, 232–35; activities in Montgomery Improvement Association, 233–34; forms S.C.L.C., 234; joins the F.O.R., 234; calls for non-violent resistance, 270–71; addresses S.N.C.C. convention, 272; death of, 281
Kingsley, George, 77
Korean War, 201–3
Krug, J. A., 112

Labor movement, 8, 47–48
Laidler, Harry, 8
Lapp, Ralph, 149
Lash, Joseph, 20
Latter, Albert, 241
Laurence, William, 167
Lawrence, Ernest O., 145
Lawson, James, 271
League for Non-Violent Civil Disobedience Against Military Segregation, 186
League of Nations Association, 9, 19
Lerner, Max, 194
Lewisburg Penitentiary strikes, 88
Lewis, Fulton, Jr., 241
Libby, Frederick J., 5, 10, 26, 28
Liberation, 237–39, 254

Lilienthal, David, 167–68, 189
Lindbergh, Charles, 25, 28, 36
Lippmann, Walter, 101, 108
Literature: effect on peace movement in Twenties and Thirties, 1–2; anti-military novels, 98–99
Lloyd, Lola Maverick, 134
Loeb, James, 193
Lowell, Robert, 49n, 206
Luce, Henry, 107
Ludlow, Robert, 225
Lund, Robert L., 140

MacArthur, Douglas, 181
Macdonald, Dwight: discusses non-violent resistance, 62; creates *Politics*, 94–95; becomes a pacifist, 94–95; criticizes fear of appeasement, 102; reaction to atomic bomb, 128, 132; elected to W.R.L. council, 153; discusses cooperative communities, 159; attacks conscription, 163; criticizes Truman Doctrine, 183; assesses Marshall Plan, 184; abandons pacifism, 188; attacks "Stalinism," 196, 206; notes "Thaw," 255; resists civil defense, 265
MacLeish, Archibald, 36
Magnes, Judah, 16
Mailer, Norman, 98, 206, 265
Manasco, Carter, 38
Mann, Thomas, 140
March on Washington Movement, 64–66
Marshall Plan, 183–85
Maurer, Emil, 30n
Maurin, Peter, 13, 17
Mayer, Milton, 51, 156, 163, 175, 197, 210, 225–26
McCarran Internal Security Act, 214–15
McCarran, Pat, 222
McCarthyism, 214–24
McCarthy, Mary, 206
McCarthy, Joseph R., 213–14, 218
McKeon, Richard P., 172
McLaurin, Benjamin, 194
McLean, Franklin, 74

McMahon Act, 148
McNair, Lesley J., 104
Meacham, Stewart, 260
Mead, Margaret, 113
Mennonites, 13, 45, 60, 82; *see also* Historic Peace Churches
Meyer, Cord, Jr.: fears for U.N., 137; criticizes Baruch Plan, 169; president of U.W.F., 171; calls for an end to power rivalries, 174; Congressional testimony, 208
Meyner, Robert B., 266
Milgram, Morris, 47
Millis, Walter, 122
Mills, C. Wright, 194
Molotov-Ribbentrop Pact, 23
Montgomery boycott, 233
Montgomery County Citizens Council, 233
Montgomery Improvement Association, 233
Montgomery, Robert, 218
Morgenthau, Hans, 100
Morrison, Charles Clayton, 42
Morrison, Philip, 189
Muller, Hermann J., 235, 237
Mumford, Lewis, 167, 180, 217, 240
Munich Pact, 18
Murphy, Stanley, 86
Murray, James, 170
Murray, Philip, 140
Muste, A. J.: in the Twenties and Thirties, 12; attacks Munich Pact, 18; criticizes Communist peace efforts, 24; interest in non-violent resistance, 12, 31, 63, 226; analyzes labor's support of war, 48; reaction to Peace Now Movement, 57; reaction to People's Peace Now Committee, 57; calls for united humanity, 61; on race relations, 64; supports creation of C.P.S. camps, 71; criticized, 83; assesses postwar trends, 109; assails Russian favoritism, 119; reaction to atomic weapons, 133, 169; analyzes strength of peace effort, 152, 228, 273; connection with Peacemakers, 156, 226;

opposes conscription, 163–64; and atomic scientists, 175–76; discusses world government, 179–80; on need for renunciation of war, 181; assails Truman Doctrine, 183; on Marshall Plan, 184; reaction to 1948 election, 190–97; addresses Americans for Intellectual Freedom, 206; calls for disarmament initiatives, 224; Third Camp proposals, 231; criticizes "purge" in SANE, 261; efforts in CNVA, 262; opposes civil defense plans, 265; death of, 281
Muste, Constance, 197

Naeve, Lowell, 48, 86–88, 92
National Association for the Advancement of Colored People, 14, 46, 87, 186, 254
National Catholic Welfare Conference, 37
National Committee for a Sane Nuclear Policy: formation of, 242–45; first advertisement, 243–44; constituency, 245; criticism of, 246; expands scope, 251–52; rapid growth of, 257–58; Dodd investigation, 258–61; public demonstrations, 273; decline of, 277–78
National Council Against Conscription, 163
National Council for the Prevention of War: activities in Thirties, 10; support of neutrality, 19, 22; relations with isolationists, 28; decline, 32, 51–52
National Council of Jewish Women, 6
National Education Association, 10
National Federation of Temple Sisterhoods, 6
National Peace Conference, 9, 51
National Peace Week, 23–24
National Service Board for Religious Objectors, 71
NATO, 199
Negroes in World War II, 46–47
Nevins, Allan, 36, 100, 103, 111
New Left, 280

Newton, Ray, 14
Nickson, J. J., 144–45
Niebuhr, Reinhold: rejects war in Thirties, 7, 15; membership in Socialist Party, 9; breaks with pacifists, 15–16; view of world government, 139–40, 180; criticizes arms race, 273
Non-Violent Action Against Nuclear Weapons, 246–47
Non-Violent Direct Action Committee, 63
Nuclear pacifism, 126–50, 240–56, 278–79, 282–83
Nye Committee, 2, 11

Omaha Action, 262
O'Neil, James F., 162
Oppenheimer Case, 221
Oppenheimer, J. Robert: member of Interim Committee, 145; discusses atomic controls, 147; expresses guilt for use of bomb, 149; need for peace, 150; urges Soviet containment, 190; opposes development of H-bomb, 200
Oxford Oath, 7, 20, 98
Oxnam, G. Bromley, 126

Pacifica Foundation, 160
Page, Kirby, 9, 18–19, 26–27
Palmer, Albert W., 27
Parks, Rosa, 233
Patterson, Robert P., 199
Patton, George S., 98
Patton, James G., 170
Pauling, Linus: shock at Hiroshima bombing, 149; membership in Emergency Committee of Atomic Scientists, 166; supports atomic energy control, 189; signs Einstein-Russell Appeal, 235; calls for peace, 237; petitions to stop nuclear tests, 241; opposes use of nuclear weapons, 254; resigns from SANE, 260
Peacemakers, 156–57, 165, 211, 226–27, 231
Peace Now Movement, 57–58

Peale, Norman Vincent, 101
Pearl Harbor: effect on peace movement, 34, 36–37; effect on war sentiment, 34
Peck, Jim, 92, 153, 195–96, 265, 271
People's Peace Now Committee, 56–57
Pepper, Claude, 119, 170
Perkins, Dexter, 140
Petersburg Reformatory, 89
Philbrick, Herbert, 218
Pickett, Clarence, 70, 73, 195, 228, 243, 245
Pickus, Robert, 230
Plumley, Charles A., 129
Polaris Action, 262–63
Poling, Daniel A., 59, 246
Politics, 94–95, 196
Prisons and conscientious objectors, 84–92
Progressive, 51, 239
Progressive Citizens of America, 193
Provisional Committee to Stop Nuclear Tests, 243
Pugwash Conference, 251

Quakers, see Friends, Society of

Rabi, I. I., 190, 200
Rabinowitch, Eugene, 143–46, 165, 210
Radicals and the peace movement, 8, 94–95, 280–81, 284; see also Communist Party and Socialist Party
Ramsey, Paul, 43
Randolph, A. Philip, 64–65, 186
Rankin, Jeannette, 10, 35
Rauschenbush, Stephen, 11
Redfield, Robert, 173
Reeves, George, 153
Refugees, 17
Research Exchange on the Prevention of War, 250–51
Reuther, Walter, 245, 258
Reves, Emery, 136, 142
Rexroth, Kenneth, 62

Reynolds, Earle, 248–49
Richie, David S., 75
Rickenbacker, Eddie, 115
Riesman, David, 268, 275, 284
Roberts, Owen J., 139–40, 162, 199
Robinson, Dorothy Medders, 42, 52
Robinson, James, 270
Rogge, O. John, 202, 205n
Roosevelt, Franklin D., 1, 18, 20, 39, 70–71
Roper, Elmo, 199
Rovere, Richard, 194
Royal, Kenneth, 186
Rusk, Dean, 102–3, 208
Russell, Bertrand, 235–36
Russia, 115–20, 182–83, 253–55
Rustin, Bayard: becomes a pacifist, 24; works with M.O.W. Movement, 64–65; examines ties of civil rights to human rights, 69; criticism of pacifist leadership, 83; on W.R.L. executive committee, 153; participates in Freedom Ride, 161–62; opposes conscription, 163; criticizes atomic scientists, 175; fights army Jim Crow policies, 186; supports Socialist ticket in 1948, 197; leaves Peacemakers, 226; helps form S.C.L.C., 234; directs civil rights demonstrations, 270–71

SANE, see National Committee for a Sane Nuclear Policy
Sarrazac, Robert, 207
Satyagraha, 31–32, 64, 232
Sayre, John Nevin: leader of the F.O.R., 12; supports U.S. membership in World Court, 27; assesses condition of F.O.R., 54
Schweitzer, Albert, 241
Schwimmer, Rosika, 134, 136
Scott, Lawrence, 242, 247
Scudder, Vida, 9
Seaborg, Glenn, 144
Senior, Clarence, 8
Shapley, Harlow, 189, 194
Shuttlesworth, Fred L., 271–72
Sibley, Mulford, 93

Simkins, George, 269
Sinclair, Upton, 140
Sisson, Fred, 5
Sit-in movement, 268–73
SLATE, 267
Smiley, Glenn, 234n, 271
Smith Act, 215
Smith, Cyril, 148, 200
Smith, Jay Holmes, 63–64
Smith, Lawrence A., 221–22
Smith, Willis, 162
Socialist Party: peace orientation in Thirties, 8–9, 14n; aids Spanish Loyalists, 20; division over World War II, 21, 50; criticizes Soviet wartime policies, 118–19; supports creation of U.N., 138; 1948 election campaign, 190–91, 194, 197–98; backs Korean policy, 202; supports American defense policies in Fifties, 224; 1952 election campaign, 227
Sockman, Ralph W., 43
Southern Christian Leadership Conference, 234, 271–72
Spanish Civil War, 19–20
Speak Truth to Power, 230–31
Spellman, Francis J., 36, 99
Stanley, W. M., 237
Stassen, Harold, 142
Stein, Gertrude, 102
Stevenson, Adlai, 241, 258n
Stimson, Henry L., 144, 185
Stockholm Peace Pledge, 204–5
Stout, Rex, 104, 223
Straight, Michael, 121
Strategic Bombing Survey, 130
Strauss, Lewis, 242, 249
Streit, Clarence, 134–36, 141
Student Federalists, 170
Student Non-Violent Coordinating Committee, 272, 280
Student Peace Union, 266–67, 278
Students: support peace movement in Thirties, 6–7; in World War II, 100–1; a new campus generation, 266–68; form a New Left, 280
Students for a Democratic Society, 280

Summerfield, Arthur, 221
Swing, Raymond Gram: reacts to atomic bomb, 133–34; supports world government, 141, 171; fears Communist expansion, 187; denounced as "subversive," 222–23
Swomley, John, 101, 133, 164n, 205
Synagogue Council of America, 37
Szilard, Leo: helps to initiate atomic bomb project, 143; tries to prevent use of atomic bomb, 143–45; efforts for control of atomic energy, 147–48; member of Emergency Committee of Atomic Scientists, 165–66

Tax Refusal Committee, 157–58
Taylor, Glen, 142–43, 170, 194
Taylor, Lewis, 77, 86
Teller, Edward: opposition to military connection, 143; defends role of atomic scientist, 176–77; supports Soviet containment, 190; defends H-bomb project, 200; supports nuclear testing, 241–42
Third Camp movement, 231–32
Thomas, Elbert, 117
Thomas, Evan: discusses roots of war, 29–30; analyzes resistance to Nazis, 40; criticizes moderate pacifism, 56; attacks alternative service plan, 71, 78; respected by radical pacifists, 83; resigns from W.R.L., 188
Thomas, Norman: connections with the F.O.R., 9; urges admission of refugees, 17; criticizes Munich Pact, 18; supports Spanish Loyalists, 20; opposes American entry into World War II, 21; supports World Court, 27; relations with America First Committee, 27; supports World War II, 37; assesses Socialist Party position on World War II, 50; notes economic impact of World War II, 114n; criticizes Soviet wartime policies, 118; reaction to atomic bomb, 128, 167–68; favors world government, 137, 140; supports American

Thomas, Norman (*Continued*)
Cold War policy, 187, 190, 202, 224; attacks Progressive Party, 193; support in 1948 election campaign, 194, 197–98; opposes H-bomb tests, 240; activities in SANE, 245, 258; reevaluates Soviet foreign policy, 274
Thompson, Dorothy, 109, 194
Tobey, Charles, 170
TOCSIN, 267
Truman Doctrine, 183
Truman, Harry S.: reaction to atomic bomb, 125, 131; discusses possibility of world government, 142; 1948 election campaign, 194; calls for creation of NATO, 198
Trumbo, Dalton, 23

Union for Democratic Action, 21
United Nations, 137–38, 201, 203, 207
United States Civil Defense Administration, 240
United World Federalists: formation of, 171–72; constituency, 171–72; program, 173; view of the Cold War, 174; reaction to Marshall Plan, 185; supports Korean War, 201–2; Congressional efforts, 208; decline, 209; branded as subversive, 221–22; grows more conservative, 223–24; relationship to SANE, 245
Universal Military Training, 162–64
University of Chicago Committee to Frame a World Constitution, 172–73, 208
Urey, Harold: advocates world government, 140, 170; reaction to atomic bomb, 144, 149, 176; membership in Emergency Committee of Atomic Scientists, 165, 169; notes fear of "Communist" label, 188; supports Soviet containment, 190; signs peace appeal, 237

Vandenberg, Arthur, 36
Van Doren, Carl, 139, 171
Van Dusen, Henry P., 168

Van Kirk, Walter W., 43
Vietnam War, 279–80
Villard, Oswald Garrison, 17–18, 27–28
Voorhis, Jerry, 134, 140

Walker, Charles, 271
Walker, James J., 117
Wallace, Henry A.: criticizes Baruch Plan, 169; opposes Marshall Plan, 185; 1948 election campaign, 191–98; repudiates Progressive Party, 202; supports Korean War, 202
Wallgren, Mon, 75
Warburg, James P., 172, 199
Warren, Earl, 38
War Resisters League: formation of, 12; supports non-violent resistance, 31, 153; growth, 32, 54; reaction to the U.N., 138; postwar decline, 152, 212; difficulties over Communist issue, 207; attacks Smith Act, 215; accused of "Communist" connections, 218; opposes civil defense measures, 266
Weaver, Robert C., 46
Wechsler, James, 7, 193, 217
Weil, Simone, 95
Weisskopf, Victor, 166
Welles, Sumner, 117
Wells, H. G., 132
Wheeler, Burton K., 36
White, E. B., 139, 218, 254
White, Walter, 46
White, William Allen, 3, 22–23
Wiener, Norbert, 177
Wilcher, Denny, 77
Willkie, Wendell, 116, 136
Wilson, Edmund, 194
Wilson, E. Raymond, 138
Winchell, Walter, 116
Wise, Stephen, 3, 39
Wofford, Harris, Jr., 137, 275n
Wolfe, Bertram D., 194
Women and the peace movement, 4–5, 276
Women's International League for Peace and Freedom: formation of,